The Role of Government in Water Markets

Water is an increasingly scarce resource in developed regions throughout the world. Current methods to allocate it are not economically or environmentally efficient, but water markets offer one potential solution in the form of a regulatory response to water scarcity.

The debate on water markets is often polarized. Proponents of water markets portray them as systems where government is out of the picture, but some oppose markets because they believe water should not be commodified, but administered by public agencies. Casado Pérez argues that both sides of the debate are misguided, and that water markets require a deeper and more varied governmental intervention than markets for other goods. Drawing on economic theories of regulation based on market failure, she offers an explanation of the different roles government should play to ensure a functioning water market, and suggests that governments might have to take a leading role if a water market is to work properly.

To analyze what impact government roles actually have on water markets operation, Casado Pérez examines case studies of California and Spain to assess the success of their water markets. She explores in-depth why water markets have been more extensively institutionalized in California than in Spain in the ten years since they were introduced, and how the role of government in each study impacts water market operation.

This unique analysis of governmental role in water markets, alongside qualitative studies of California and Spain, offers valuable scholarship in this increasingly important topic and will be of interest to students, practitioners, and policymakers in water law.

Vanessa Casado Pérez is an associate professor at the Texas A&M School of Law and an affiliated scholar at the Bill Lane Center for the American West at Stanford University. Her research focuses on property law and management of natural resources, particularly water.

The Role of Government in Water Markets

Vanessa Casado Pérez

LONDON AND NEW YORK

First published 2017
by Routledge
2 Park Square, Milton Park, Abingdon, Oxon OX14 4RN

and by Routledge
711 Third Avenue, New York, NY 10017

Routledge is an imprint of the Taylor & Francis Group, an informa business

© 2017 Vanessa Casado-Pérez

British Library Cataloguing in Publication Data
A catalogue record for this book is available from the British Library

Library of Congress Cataloging in Publication Data
Names: Casado Pérez, Vanessa, author.
Title: The role of government in water markets / Vanessa Casado
Pérez.
Description: Abingdon, Oxon ; New York, NY : Routledge, 2017. |
Includes index. | Based on author's thesis (J.S.D.-New York
University, 2014) issued under title: Government and markets :
the case of water.
Identifiers: LCCN 2016029138| ISBN 9781138655744 (hardback) |
ISBN9781317222705 (adobe reader) | ISBN 9781317222699
(epub) | ISBN9781317222682 (mobipocket)
Subjects: LCSH: Water-supply—Law and legislation—California. |
Water-supply—Law and legislation—Spain.
Classification: LCC K3496 .C376 2017 | DDC 333.91/17—dc23
LC record available at https://protect-us.mimecast.com/s/
ZpWJBRu3k9WQux?domain=lccn.loc.gov https://lccn.loc.gov/
2016029138

ISBN: 978-1-138-65574-4 (hbk)
ISBN: 978-1-315-62233-0 (ebk)

Typeset in Galliard
by Florence Production Ltd, Stoodleigh, Devon, UK

Contents

Acknowledgements

Over the past few years, I have received support from far more great people than I could mention here. To all of you, thank you. Some specific acknowledgements are, however, in order.

This book is based on my dissertation. Thus, I want to acknowledge the support of my committee and the professors at the New York University School of Law who found the time to discuss different parts of this project. In particular, I want to thank Professors Wyman, Kornhauser, and Epstein. Professor Wyman has been the most committed adviser a doctoral student could wish for, despite the student not being the easiest to deal with. Professor Kornhauser generously read many of the chapters, and his apparently simple questions – which I always feared – improved this project. Professor Epstein has always been generous with his time and willing to go the extra mile to help his students, myself among them.

In addition, I want to thank all those public officials, private practitioners, and scholars who have spared some of their time to help me understand the murky intricacies of water law and water management in California and Spain.

I am obliged to the New York University JSD Program because, beyond the financial and administrative support, it put forward the framework and the environment for a vibrant community of junior scholars to thrive and bloom. There, I started to learn what it means to be an academic. Without the Program and my classmates, this research would never have flowed from my dissertation. I want to acknowledge Hillary Nye's help to improve the language of this non-native speaker.

I finished writing this book whilst completing my Teaching Fellowship at Stanford Law School, and I will be forever grateful for the opportunity of having discussions about this project with scholars of different disciplines. Stanford Law School, the Bill Lane Center for the American West, and Water in the West have provided the perfect forums. From my Stanford time, I want to specially thank Buzz H. Thompson, whom I will always look up to, for giving me the opportunity to serve as a Teaching Fellow, and Bruce Cain for his career guidance and well-meant teasing.

At a personal level, first, I want to express my most sincere gratitude to those who showed me how nice people can be, and who bore with me in the meandering dissertation writing process. Second, I am incredibly grateful to my friends who have inhabited or still inhabit the sub-basement of 22 Washington Square North where the JSD Program office was, because they believed in my scholarly capabilities, taught me important academic and personal lessons, nudged me when necessary, and, especially, delivered unrequested hugs when they were most needed. You and your families have become my family away from home. Third, I am thankful for the care and friendship of the European academics I met during the JSD years.

Fourth, I want to thank all my friends, who – understanding or not my academic and personal worries – have always taken care of me and made me feel special. The list is long, but I want to highlight four people who have been there for me through thick and thin: Carmen Fernández, who never fails to keep in touch even though we live in different continents; Dori Yoldi, who tried to keep me sane while in NY and whose wit is always a good medicine; Preeti Hehmeyer, who has shown a steady, yet unwarranted, faith in me; and Jacob H. Russell, who has been my pillar during my Stanford times.

Last, but not least, I am deeply indebted to Albert Azagra, who knows more about water regulation than he would have ever imagined, and who has proven to be my unbeatable supporter.

Palo Alto, 16 June 2016

Most frequently used acronyms

ACA   Catalan Water Agency
BOE   *Boletín Oficial del Estado* (Spanish Official Gazette)
CEQA   California Environmental Quality Act
CH   Confederación Hidrográfica
CVP   Central Valley Project
CVPIA   Central Valley Project Improvement Act
CWA   2001 Spanish Consolidated Water Act
DWR   Department of Water Resources (California)
IID   Imperial Irrigation District
L   Law (Spanish Acts)
MWD   Metropolitan Water District of Southern California
NHP   National Hydrologic Plan
RBA   River Basin Authority
RD   Real Decreto (Spanish Decree; that is, administrative regulations)
RDL   Real Decreto Ley (Spanish Decree with the force of an Act enacted by the executive power during emergencies)
RDLeg   Real Decreto Legislativo (Spanish Decree with the force of an Act enacted, following a legislative mandate, by the executive power to give coherence to certain regulations and their subsequent amendments)
RDPH   Reglamento Dominio Público Hidráulico (Regulations implementing Spanish Water Acts)
SWP   California State Water Project
SWRCB   California State Water Resources Control Board
USBR   United States Bureau of Reclamation
WA   1985 Spanish Water Act

1 Scarcity, droughts, and the gap to be filled by water markets

1.1 Introduction: a toolkit for governing scarcity

Water scarcity is a growing challenge across the world. Water scarcity is addressed by governments using different tools, and water markets are one such tool. This challenges a common misconception, namely that governments and markets provide mutually exclusive responses to governing scarcity.

Governments have frequently handled water scarcity by carrying out engineering works to transport water from wet to dry areas where either agriculture or big urban areas have been settled. However, nowadays, this may no longer be an option. Environmental impact, fiscal costs, and lack of distributable surplus water all weigh against building large-scale dams and canals in places such as California and Spain, the two jurisdictions this book focuses on. In this scenario of scarcity, governments become prone to experiment with other tools, and markets come into play.

Water markets try to redress the imbalances between water rights allocation and water needs. For historical reasons, the distribution of water favors the agricultural sector, a water-intense productive activity which was the core of the Western economies for centuries. However, with the urban population growing and the agricultural sector losing economic relevance, concerns are being voiced about water misuse and misallocation by the agricultural sector. In addition, actions by administrative agencies in charge of managing water systems in Western economies have not proven effective at managing the situation. Administrative agencies have failed to use their command and control powers to ensure that current uses are not wasteful, and are usually accused of being captured. Seen at their best, they can only be credited with enacting emergency measures when the plants get dry, the soil cracks and the headlines explode. Such measures are, however, hard to predict, thus creating legal uncertainty. Worse still, they may be creating a moral hazard effect, undermining the incentives of individual users to plan ahead for low availability periods.

Markets have been advocated as a workable answer to the current challenges in water management. They have even been adopted by governments to deal with a wide range of environmental issues, broadly understood. Markets are, indeed, useful tools to manage scarcity, but for water markets to succeed, governments need to participate actively in the market by satisfactorily fulfilling a number of roles. When it comes to water markets, the invisible hand needs help from the visible hand of government in order to prove effective.

The bulk of this book is devoted to analyzing what roles governments should fulfill in water markets and how different degrees of fulfillment of these roles have an impact on market performance, as shown by the cases of California and Spain. However, this cannot be done without first defining and explaining water scarcity, presenting the different tools that may be used in order to address water scarcity, including water markets, and describing how scholarship has failed to understand water markets as a tool for agencies. These are the aims of the remaining sections of Chapter 1.

1.2 Water scarcity, an all-too-common problem

Water scarcity is defined as the situation where demand exceeds the water resources exploitable under sustainable conditions.[1] Scarcity is a rising problem in regions throughout the world. Supply and demand are mismatched: there is not enough water to cover the demand. Demand is growing, while supply is constant or might be even shrinking due to climate change.[2] Some regions, such as the Mediterranean, suffer from periodical droughts and a dry climate, and these harsh conditions are likely to get worse due to climate change. For example, an increase in the spatial variability of precipitation[3] and drought[4] in the already affected areas is expected. A rise in temperature of between 2.5°F and 10°F (2°C and 3°C) is estimated to translate into water scarcity for

---

1   Communication from the Commission to the Council and the European Parliament addressing the challenge of water scarcity and droughts in the European Union, at 2, COM(2007) 414 final (18 July 2007). For a broader definition, see also FAO water, 'Hot issues: water scarcity,' http://www.fao.org/nr/water/issues/scarcity.html ('Imbalances between availability and demand, the degradation of groundwater and surface water quality, intersectoral competition, interregional and international conflicts, all contributes to water scarcity').

2   Cal. Dept. Water Resources, 'California Water Plan, Pre-final draft Update 2009 Highlights,' at 2 (2009), http://www.waterplan.water.ca.gov/docs/cwpu2009/1009prf/highlights_pre-final_draft_spread2-101609.pdf ('Climate change is reducing our snowpack storage and increasing floods').

3   S. Solomon *et al.* (eds), *Intergovernmental Panel on Climate Change Working Group II, Fourth Assessment Report*, at 849 (2007).

4   Drought is defined as the scenario where there is a 'temporary decrease in water availability due for instance to rainfall deficiency,' in Communication from the Commission to the Council and the European Parliament addressing the challenge of water scarcity and droughts in the European Union, above note 1, at 2. The Spanish Drought Monitoring Group definition emphasizes that drought is a very elusive context since drought conditions are highly contingent to time and place, see Observatorio Nacional de la Sequía (Spanish Drought Monitoring Group), '¿Qué es la sequía?' ('What is a drought?'), http://www.mma.es/portal/secciones/aguas_continent_zonas_asoc/ons/que_es_sequia/ (in Spanish).

between 1.1 and 3.2 billion people.[5] The expected effects include a decrease in the snowpack, which is a natural reservoir for hot seasons, or drier soil which requires more irrigation to support crops.[6] These forecasted future problems will increase the urgency of the need for solutions, for which some regions have been longing for quite a long time. However, manifold causes explain the current situation, not only natural low availability. Water struggles are not new.

Historically, populations used to develop on river banks since water is essential for human living. However, this pattern changed. Water was always needed, but populations started to expand to areas where water was not readily available but was made available. The American West offers a well-known example. The Imperial Valley was formerly the Colorado Desert. It was not until 1853 that William Blake, a geologist from Yale, identified its soil as fertile if irrigated.[7] Settlers did not let the opportunity to use it as agricultural landscape. In 1901, the California Development Company began doing some diversions from the then plentiful Colorado River, and the Valley flourished. By 1929, 424,145 acres were irrigated,[8] and much more water would continue to be transferred there. In 1928, the Boulder Canyon Act was passed, authorizing the construction of the All-American Canal, Imperial Valley's lifeline from the Colorado River.[9] In 1942, the first deliveries from these infrastructures started. Water supply was guaranteed for the Imperial Irrigation District (IID), established in 1911, and other cities supplied by the All-American Canal.

Demand for water is not only sometimes misplaced, but has increased steeply during the past century. Population growth is one of the drivers, but water demand has trebled[10] in the last century, while the population has only doubled.

5   S. Solomon *et al.*, above note 3, in Communication from the Commission to the Council and the European Parliament addressing the challenge of water scarcity and droughts in the European Union, above note 1, at 2. See also UN Dev. Program, *Human Development Report, Beyond scarcity: Power, poverty and the global water crisis*, at 136 (2006) (today, about 700 million people in 43 countries live below the water-stress threshold of 1,700 cubic meters per person – an admittedly arbitrary dividing line. By 2025 that figure will reach 3 billion).

6   Joseph W. Dellapenna, 'Global Climate Disruption and Water Law Reform,' 15 Widener L. Rev. 409, 411 (2010) (hereinafter, Dellapenna, 'Global Climate').

7   Susan Leal, Congressman Edward J. Markey, and Peter Rogers, *Running Out of Water: The Looming Crisis and Solutions to Conserve Our Most Precious Resource*, at 60 (2010).

8   IID, 'Water History Timeline,' see http://www.iid.com/Modules/ShowDocument.aspx?documentid=9.

9   IID, 'All American Canal,' http://www.iid.com/index.aspx?page=176.

10 Posting of Elizabeth Mygatt to Earth Policy Institute Eco-Economy Indicators Water Resources, 'World's Water Resources Face Mounting Pressure' (2006), http://www.earth-policy.org/index.php?/indicators/C57/. For similar data, see Leal *et al.*, above note 7, at 2 ('Between 1900 and 2000, the world's population grew three-fold, but our water use has increased sixfold').

Beyond population growth, the drivers are changes in dietary habits, changes in lifestyle, and new demands for water. Urban sprawl has not always been carefully planned: the more people who live in single-family houses with lawns, the more water is required to water the lawn, and to wash the car. As a consequence, nowadays, some cities are struggling for water because population and changes have concentrated there.

While cities keep growing, the majority of water is still allocated to the agricultural sector. The agricultural sector has been the main consumer of water in many regions of the world because of its central economic role in the past and the fact that water is one of the main production inputs for irrigated agriculture. Globally, its consumption is around 70 per cent of water used. This is a common pattern in the distribution of water across uses in several jurisdictions. In California, in 2005, 74 per cent of all fresh water withdrawals were for agriculture.[11] In Spain, agriculture consumes around 80 per cent of the total water.[12] The mismatch between this water use figure and the contribution of agriculture to the gross domestic product is often criticized[13] because there is not enough water to cover all demands, and cities and industries are often struggling.

Furthermore, not only has the balance between uses changed, but new uses compete for the resource. In particular, environmental protection awareness has increased over the years and those who defend environmental protection have advocated for instream water uses that ensure stream flows for fish and wildlife. While these changes took place, water allocation did not vary substantially, nor did water law in many jurisdictions; existing water regimes are still often crafted for an economy centered on the primary sector, and have not developed a solution for water scarcity.[14]

The next section explores the different mechanisms that can be used to solve the mismatch between supply and demand.

---

11 USGS, 'Estimated Use of Water in the United States in 2005,' http://pubs.usgs.gov/circ/1344/pdf/c1344.pdf.

12 For data on Spain, see I. Heinz, M. Pulido-Velazquez, J.R. Lund, and J. Andreu, 'Hydro-economic Modeling in River Basin Management: Implications and Applications for the European Water Framework Directive,' 21 Water Res. Mgmt 1103, 1116 (2007). For California, see Department of Water Resources, 'Agricultural Water Use,' http://www.water.ca.gov/wateruseefficiency/agricultural/.

13 Robert Glennon, 'Water Scarcity, Marketing, and Privatization,' 83 Tex. L. Rev 1873, 1888 (2005).

14 Stephen E. Draper, 'The Unintended Consequences of Tradable Property Rights to Water,' 20 Nat. Resources & Env't 49, 49 (2006) ('Yet in many jurisdictions, the policies, laws, and regulations that control water use and availability remain rooted in earlier times when water needs and water availability were different').

1.3 Potential solutions to water scarcity[15]

There is a portfolio of proposals on how to deal with the structural scarcity problems and how to prevent a drought crisis from being too harsh; these strategies should prevent the need to undertake emergency measures in the midst of a crisis. The distinction tends to be drawn between strategies affecting demand and strategies affecting supply. This book uses this distinction, but it starts by focusing on the distinction between centralized and decentralized measures. This distinction leads to the subsequent discussion on the purported opposition between government and market, which is analyzed next.

Centralized strategies in this book mean strategies where the bodies of government responsible for water management enact regulations mandating actions that will contribute to solving the problem, some of them requiring agency action and others guiding the behavior of individuals. By contrast, decentralized measures are those that enable private actors to decide, exploiting their economically rational behavior to contribute to the solution of water scarcity. Centralized strategies act either on supply or on demand. The general explanation is complemented by illustrations from the strategies discussed or adopted in the Barcelona area as a response to the structural water deficit it suffers, and the 2008 drought crisis.

1.3.1 Supply side strategies

Traditional responses to scarcity tended to be measures affecting supply. These measures have contributed to the current water crisis. They sent the message that water was endless. For decades, engineers were in charge of water management agencies. Water could be provided by long-distance transfers or storage in dams. Sustainability was not part of the discourse then. Projections of future urban growth and consequent pressure on water resources were not planned for with a long-term view: water needed was water provided. However, using infrastructure to transfer water over long distances, or storing it to smooth supply across the year, are no longer viable solutions. The damming fever has passed in many countries. In many places, such as Catalonia, there is no possibility of improving supply through this strategy because rivers are already dammed and their flow is not as abundant as it used to be; there is no surplus to be distributed, and interbasin transfers are not only ecologically, but also politically challenging. For example, a transfer from the Rhône River (France) to Barcelona has been perennially discussed because this plentiful river does not suffer the same climatological stressors as the Catalan ones, but never implemented.

---

15 The author has published a version of this section in Vanessa Casado Pérez, 'All Dried Out: How Responses to Drought Make Droughts Worse,' 51 Tulsa L. Rev. 731(2016).

Two mandated transfers were discussed to tackle the late 2000s Barcelona drought: one from the Segre River and another one from the Ebro River.[16] Neither was a mammoth project.[17] Instead, they were small connections aiming at offering temporary relief to Barcelona by bringing purportedly surplus water, avoiding the curtailment of household water uses. However, the region had a conflictive past regarding water transfers,[18] and public opposition to these projects was acute. While the Ebro project was in its early stages, given the immediacy of the crisis, water started to be shipped to Barcelona by boat from Tarragona (which had surplus groundwater), Marseille (France), and the Provence Canal (France). The ships were expected to carry around 1.66 hm^3 (1,345.78 acr-ft) per month, which would have covered around 6 per cent of the demand in the Barcelona metropolitan area, for the duration of the drought period. This was an incredibly expensive source, even though the Spanish central government granted a waiver of the harbor fees. Water shipped by boat during that period cost above €13/m^3 (€16,000/acr-ft),[19]

16 Arnau Urgell, 'Transvassament de la Conca Alta del Segre a l'àrea metropolitana de Barcelona' ('Transfer from the Segre River Basin to the Metropolitan Area'), Territori (31 December 2008), http://territori.scot.cat/cat/viewer.php?IDN=172. The harsh situation during the spring of 2008 compelled the Spanish government to pass a Real Decreto-Ley (Real Decreto-Ley 3/2008, of 21 April 2008), a type of act reserved for extraordinary situations. This Spanish Decree authorized the connection of Barcelona with Tarragona, a town in the south of Catalonia which receives water from the Ebro River. Once built, this connection would have allowed a water transfer from the agricultural part of the Ebro system to the Internal Basins. In addition to the transfer, this decree also authorized the use of the pipe for transporting water under water leasing contracts, a market mechanism.

17 For example, the Ebro River's Tarragona-Barcelona connection entailed a transfer pipe which was not a mammoth project. It was relatively cheap to install and did not have a huge environmental impact. It was designed to be installed in the median of the highway which unites Barcelona with Tarragona (AP-7). This transfer project would have only conveyed 40 hm^3/year and this water was part of the allocation from the Ebro that Tarragona was not consuming. The expected cost was €150 million and its installation was expected to be completed within two months. See 'De la Vega garantiza que el agua del Ebro llegará a tiempo a Barcelona' ('De la Vega ensures that the Ebro's water will arrive to Barcelona on time'), *El País*, 15 April 2008.

18 The concept of basin varies from jurisdiction to jurisdiction. According to Directive 2000/60/EC of the European Parliament and of the Council establishing a framework for the Community action in the field of water policy (OJ 327, 12.22.2000) (hereinafter, the European Water Framework Directive) and the Spanish legislation (Article 16 Real Decreto Legislativo 1/2001, de 20 de julio, por el que se aprueba el texto refundido de la Ley de Aguas (Consolidated Water Act) (BOE 176, 30.07.2001)) a basin will include a river which flows into the sea and all its tributaries. According to this definition, the Yellowstone could not be considered a Basin, instead it will be managed as part of the Missouri River, while in the United States they are managed separately.

19 The amount of water shipped per month was expected to be 1,660,000 m^3 and the expected monthly cost €22 million. See Generalitat de Catalunya, 'Arriba el primer vaixell amb aigua potable al port de Barcelona' ('The first ship with drinking water arrives at Barcelona's harbor'), http://aca-web.gencat.cat/aca/documents/ca/sequera/RP_130508_roda_premsa.pdf.

while the cost of water from the river supplying the city, the Ter river, was only €0.08/m³ (€98.68/acr-ft).[20]

These emergency measures show that engineering solutions are still part of the portfolio. First, water availability could be increased by improving existing infrastructure in order to reduce transportation losses. During the Barcelona water crisis, which is described in more detail below, one case caught the public attention. In Badalona, a town of more than 200,000 inhabitants neighboring Barcelona, there was a water pipe losing more than 25,000 l of potable water per hour which could fill more than three Olympic size swimming pools per month. The situation was ongoing for months, and even once discovered in February 2008, it could not be fixed immediately because the town could not use other water mains. To repair it, an alternative pipe had to be installed and it needed six months to be laid.[21] However, this was the tip of the iceberg. Catalan water systems are far from full efficiency, but even if not all losses can be eradicated, systems should be improved as much as possible. In Catalonia, there is room to improve: 15.5 per cent of the water entering the system is lost.[22]

Second, water reuse could be a source of water for certain uses, such as landscape irrigation or farming. However, users can be quite reluctant to accept this water even though water is *per se* a reused asset. Recycling sewage water is more common for uses other than urban household consumption, but there are also interesting examples of waste water reclaimed for human consumption in Singapore and in Orange County, California.[23]

Third, desalination of seawater is often claimed to be the great untapped resource, but desalination cannot provide immediate relief. In Barcelona, desalination plants were planned for some years after the 2008 crisis. In 2010, production capacity of desalination plants reached 80 hm³.[24] However, desalination not only presents huge environmental challenges – such as brine disposal or the problems stemming from the energy needed to run the process – but it is also too expensive during times of normal water availability, as the Barcelona case shows where the desalination plants remain underutilized.

At some point in the future, these new sources may fulfill a larger part of the water needs, but we cannot keep increasing water consumption *ad infinitum.*

---

20 Interview with Gabriel Borràs and Josep Miquel Diéguez, members of the Supply Management Board at Catalan Water Agency (ACA) (27 December 2010).

21 'Una tubería pierde 18,000 litros por hora' ('A pipe leaks 18,000 l per hour') (27 February 2008), http://www.publico.es/actualidad/53631/una-tuberia-pierde-18-000-litros-por-hora.

22 DIBA (Barcelona Province Government), 'Control de fuites' ('leakage control'), http://diba.es/web/mediambient/fuites.

23 Leal *et al.*, above note 7, at 19–47.

24 The capacity of the Tordera Desalination Plant was enlarged and the Llobregat Desalination plant was inaugurated in 2009. These are the amounts they can produce, but actual production is adjusted according to the availability of traditional sources of water. See ACA, 'Dessalinitzadores,' http://aca-web.gencat.cat/aca/appmanager/aca/aca?_nfpb=true&_pageLabel=P18400639 711246265279363.

Better management of the dwindling water resources seems to be a more promising solution.

1.3.2 Demand side strategies

The second group of centralized strategies act on the demand side, i.e. reducing the amount of water consumed by people, farmers, and industries. These strategies vary in terms of how prescriptive they are. Gains from urban water saving could be important, but either slow or highly unpopular. They will be slow if they have to work by influencing people through education. Campaigns take time to bear fruit, even if some exogenous events such as a drought may boost public awareness and responsibility. An example of this type of measure is the public educational campaigns about efficient water use in Catalonia.[25] But the drought episodes in the 2000s were what made the population aware of the water problems. Consequently, consumption in Barcelona was reduced to 110 l per person per day (29.06 gl/person/day).[26] However, this has not been enough to solve the problems, and further reductions cannot be expected given that 90 l per person per day (23.78 gl/person/day) is the threshold point that the World Health Organization has established as the limit below which some sanitary problems may appear. It must be highlighted, however, that the current average consumption level is quite an achievement. For example, in 2009, the consumption in New York City per inhabitant was around 476 l/person/day[27] (125.75 gl/person/day).

If the measures are not voluntary, they may have a high political price. A 2007 Catalan government Decree[28] established the maximum amount of water that could be taken from the river for irrigation purposes, thereby curtailing

---

25 Educational campaign by the Catalan government: 'Estalvi d'aigua' ('Save Water'), http://www.gencat.cat/web/multimedia/cat/estalviaigua/index.htm. See also campaigns put forward during the 2009 drought, at ACA, 'Awareness campaigns,' http://aca-web.gencat.cat/aca/sequera/ca/campanyes-sensibilitzacio.jsp.

26 During the drought, people consume even 10 per cent less, see Joaquim Lloveras Macià, 'Consideracions sobre l'enginyeria per a l'estalvi d'aigua al sector domestic a Catalunya,' Dept de Projectes, ETSEIB, http://upcommons.upc.edu/e-prints/bitstream/2117/7564/1/consideracions.pdf. In 1999, the consumption was 18 per cent higher, see Barcelona City Council, 'Barcelona reduces water consumption by 15 per cent in 12 years,' http://w110.bcn.cat/portal/site/MediAmbient/menuitem.7120b3cf16112e13e9c5e9c5a2ef8a0c/?vgnextoid=70c609e15e936310VgnVCM10000072fea8c0RCRD&vgnextfmt=formatDetall&lang=ca_ES.

27 New York City government, 'History of Drought and Water Consumption, data for 2009: 125.8 gallons,' http://www.nyc.gov/html/dep/html/drinking_water/droughthist.shtml.

28 Decret 84/2007, de 3 d'abril, d'adopció de mesures excepcionals i d'emergència en relació amb la utilització dels recursos hídrics (Decree adopting exceptional and emergency measures in relation to the use of water resources) (DOGC 4860, 4.12.2007).

farmers' rights which they held in the form of licences granted by the water agency. The amount of water available for crops decreased with the seriousness of the drought situation. Municipalities – which are the level of government responsible for urban water supply – were empowered by the Decree to adopt measures immediately to ensure efficient use of water. For example, they could regulate restrictively the irrigation of private gardens and lawns. Household curtailments were a threat, but they never materialized. Government avoided them at all costs, even shipping expensive water by boat. Some measures may be less visible than a curtailment, but they take time to bear fruit. This is the case with mandating water saving tools, such as low-flush toilets, in new building developments.

More savings could be obtained in the agricultural sector. Farmers might not be using water efficiently because they pay low prices for it. They do not have incentives to improve irrigation techniques and reduce their demand. A soft measure to reduce inefficient uses would be campaigns on irrigation modernization, as well as the provision of subsidies to farmers to install more efficient systems to use the already subsidized water. Among the mandatory measures, the review of current allocations stands out because it allows water agencies to curtail current use if it is not efficient or it is wasteful. In some administrative regimes, like the Spanish one, water agencies may have the power to review the volume granted to a particular user if the agencies think that the purpose stated in the permit could be fulfilled with less water. However, farmers are a strong lobby group and permits are rarely revised or not renewed. Little water is freed through these measures. In prior appropriation systems, it is required that the water is put to beneficial use, but such a provision has not been interpreted in an ambitious enough way to push for efficiency.[29]

Another strategy to tackle overconsumption, for both urban consumers and farmers, is to increase prices. Some authors consider this a decentralized strategy since the ultimate decision power rests with the private agents, which may decide to consume less, despite the initial decision to get rid of subsidies being a governmental one. Basic economics would suggest that scarce water should have become more expensive since more users are competing for it, but this has not been the case: water is subsidized almost everywhere.[30] Water bills reflect, at best, the cost of extracting, diverting, distributing, and, sometimes, cleaning water, and almost never factor in scarcity or environmental damage. Water price does not reflect the true cost. The disparity between the average water tariff – excluding wastewater tariffs – in Germany (US$3.33/m^3) and Spain (US$1.47/m^3) is still striking, showing that scarcity prices are not taken

29 For the evolution of beneficial use and waste in prior appropriation, see Joseph L. Sax, Barton H. Thompson, Jr., John D. Leshy, and Robert H. Abrams, *Legal Control of Water Resources*, 4th edn, at 154–159 (2006).
30 Terry L. Anderson and Pamela Snyder, *Water Markets. Priming the Invisible Pump*, at 7 (1997).

into account, even though significant advances have been made in this field. For example, the 2000 European Water Framework Directive imposes the full cost recovery principle, which takes into account water services and environmental costs,[31] so water prices should increase to comply with the Directive. In any case, increasing water prices is a highly costly political measure.

Increasing the price for urban households raises questions of human rights and affordability, but there is a margin in which it is reasonable to act, since water can be saved not from essential needs, but from superfluous uses (watering the lawn, washing the car, bathing instead of taking a shower, or filling pools). While normal goods cost less the more you buy, in order to discourage sumptuous uses of water while protecting basic needs, water could be made more expensive the more you consume. Tariffs could be tiered to target volumes above necessary uses, taking into account the number of members of a household. As for farmers, the measure could work, but it is not without political costs. Agricultural demand is price-elastic.[32] However, farmers and irrigation organizations are influential constituencies in the agencies making these decisions, and it is highly unlikely that administrators will dare to take such an unpopular measure. [33]

All these measures – financial incentives, mandatory review and price increases – free up water, but it is an open question what should be done with this water. It will not automatically be granted to the cities or left instream to benefit the environment, but it potentially could, or alternatively new permits over it could be granted.

1.3.3 Decentralized solution: markets

Markets are a decentralized strategy to give incentives to the agricultural sector to be efficient while avoiding the obstacles that mandatory measures face. Markets can shift water from farmers to cities no matter what the water management system is, as long as rights to use water are transferable through leases or sales. Across the board, we may think urban users value water more highly, but the comparison must be in marginal terms: the first drops to irrigate a crop may have a huge value. Putting it in a more general way, water will be transferred from low value to high value uses: water might be transferred between farmers with low value (cereals) and high value crops (fruit trees) or between cities if one of them has a water surplus and their networks are

---

31 Art. 9 of the European Water Framework Directive.
32 Anderson and Snyder, above note 30, at 10 (review of several studies regarding agricultural water demand response to increase in prices).
33 See Maten Thobani, 'Tradable Property Rights to Water. How to improve water use and resolve water conflicts,' 34 Public Policy for the Private Sector 1 (1995) ('Raising water charges to the long-run marginal cost would result in prices that would bankrupt many farmers – an option that is usually politically and socially unacceptable. A more realistic way to bring about efficient use is to allow water trading').

interconnected.[34] The amount of water available will be put to the best possible use, assuming that there is no noise in the market. It will be done on a voluntary basis, making use of valuable local information. The possibility of selling water to users with a higher valuation for it will give incentives to low-value users to be more efficient in their uses or to cease their use altogether. The possibility of buying or leasing water would allow urban developers, urban water management agencies or farmers with high value crops to plan for periods where more water is required or to undertake new projects. The market is a hybrid measure: it can potentially reduce farmers' demand and it can, thus, increase the water supply available for cities, satisfying their growing demand. Water reallocation from the agricultural sector is cheaper than other expensive options to increase water supply without reducing anyone's demand, such as desalination. This point can be illustrated referring back to the IID. The increase of the urban areas of Los Angeles and San Diego, in combination with the Supreme Court decisions regarding the Colorado River which required California to reduce its allotment to the agreed 4.4 MAF,[35] required new water resources. The IID reached agreements with San Diego, which needed water after the 1990s drought, to transfer water coming first from fallowing and later from water saved through improvements in the irrigation infrastructure. It is important to note that transferring the amount of water employed in the least efficient agricultural uses would not eradicate this sector, which is a fear often expressed. Another critique that the market may face is whether farmers should profit from their past inefficiency by making a profit selling water in the market. Beyond what is fair, it is important to realize that markets may offer a feasible solution to introduce flexibility in water allocation and respond to droughts.

The next section shows that water markets have been advocated as the solution to our water woes. They have been portrayed as the opposite of the administrative, centralized systems, which have been blamed for the current situation of scarcity. However, this book claims that successful water market tools are not at the other end of the spectrum from centralized systems, but rather, require government to play certain key roles. Chapter 2 defines the roles that government agencies need to play, and Chapters 3–6 empirically illustrate these conclusions with two case studies on water markets in California and Spain.

1.4 Water governance models

As the 2008 Barcelona drought illustrates, water management has always been a contentious issue; few other fields may better reflect the struggle for power

---

34 'El Ter recuperarà cabal a partir de juny gràcies a una nova canonada' ('Ter River will recover part of its flow thanks to a new pipe'), Diari de Girona (23 March 2011), http://www.diaridegirona.cat/comarques/2011/03/23/ter-recuperara-cabal-partir-juny-gracies-nova-canonada/474265.html.

35 For an evolution of the Colorado's 'Law of the River,' see Sax *et al.*, above note 29, at 799–835.

among politicians and interest groups. As with many other scarce resources, there has been a discussion of who should decide on the allocation and regulation of water. At the risk of simplification, this debate always pits government against private actors as decision-makers. The choice seems to be between government centralization and market decentralization.[36] This distinction between government and markets is usually also seen as parallel to property regimes: the highest degree of governmental control is expected in regimes of public ownership of water, while private parties are the decision-makers in private property regimes. In the latter, private actors should be less constrained by public regulations on how to manage their water rights and the protections against potential interventions should be higher. However, this distinction regarding the depth of governmental intervention depending on the property rights is blurred in water, given the natural characteristics and the inter-dependency of uses and users of this fugitive resource: water rights require governmental oversight. As seen in the empirical case studies, water markets have been implemented in jurisdictions where water is public property since the rights to use water have been allocated and they can be transferable despite the fact that they are not the strongest form of property rights.[37] In fact, as the previous section portrayed, water markets are a tool for administrative agencies to deal with droughts and, more generally, to allocate water. This chapter seeks to describe how water markets have been portrayed, underscoring the problems of those descriptions, in order to set the stage for a more complete and useful description of water markets and the roles of the administration.

Thus, this chapter aims to underline the theoretical differences between centralized administrative systems and markets as water management tools. After portraying these two models and the typology of water markets, the advantages of water markets are listed. Those, to an extent, map the critiques that administrative systems have received. This book puts forward that the theoretical distinction between centralized systems and water markets does not hold in practice since government is indispensable for water markets to achieve their goals.

---

36 J.W. Milliman, 'Water Law and Private Decision-Making: A Critique,' 2 J. L. & Econ. 41 (1959).

37 Administrative regimes are paired with public property, riparian systems with common property, and prior appropriation with private property, see Dellapenna, 'Global Climate,' above note 6. However, the distinction is not clear cut. For example, §102 of the Cal. Water Code declares public ownership over water resources but California presents a dual system of riparian and appropriative rights where the latter prevail (Article X of the Cal. Constitution). The management regime shapes the type of property, not the other way around, because there seems to be potential variations on how to manage this same resource; in other words, it is not the nature of the resource what dictates which type of property we assign.

1.5 Centralized administrative systems

Regimes vary a great deal, both in the forms of regulation and in terms of institutional organization, but this book defines a centralized or administrative regime in general terms in spite of the risk of oversimplification. A centralized water management system is best understood as one where there is a water management agency which gathers information, ascertains preferences, establishes priorities, allocates water, and makes rationing decisions during tough seasons. The administrative agency decides whether someone can use water, how much, in which uses and for how long. If someone wants to use water, that person or body must apply for a water permit to the agency that will grant it if certain requirements, more or less broadly defined, are met. It looks like a mechanical, technocratic decision, but there is usually leeway for discretion.[38]

In general, it is contested whether the administration has the ability to gather so much local information and decide what is most valuable. Agencies, for example, decide on a case-by-case basis whether to grant a permit to use water in perpetuity or for a certain number of years. Deciding on a rolling basis makes it difficult to abide by the standards set in the long-term planning documents usually prepared by those same agencies. When deciding whether or not to grant a permit, unless there are competing applications, the relative social value of a particular use is difficult to assess. And, in any event, a certain use may be less valuable than future uses, but water may be already locked in. To make things worse, agencies often make those decisions relying on incomplete data because few jurisdictions have a reliable recording system in place.

Once the permit has been granted, usually for an indefinite or quite a long period, the agency may impose subsequent restrictions on the permit holder.[39] Although the licences can be considered new property and be understood as property rights, they receive less protection than the conventional property embodied in the Blackacre, fee simple ideal. These revisions could occur if a user is misusing its water right, i.e. it is not using water efficiently, or if public interest would be better served if water was put to a different use. However, these are hardly ever popular avenues to take against members of powerful

---

38 §1255 of the Cal. Water Code.

39 In prior appropriation schemes, which are the closest to private property, beneficial use might be an open door to control, ensuring that water is not wasted, but it will require litigation. In administrative systems, the agency can assess whether someone is using more water than he or she actually needs and may impose certain efficiency constraints. For a categorization of the different water regimes according to types of property, see Dellapenna, 'Global Climate,' above note 6, at 432. For a general exposition, see ibid. at 420–445. See also Joseph W. Dellapenna, 'The Importance of Getting Names Right: The Myth of Markets for Water,' 25 Wm. & Mary Envt'l L. Pol'y 317, 336–340 (2000) (hereinafter, Dellapenna, 'Getting Names Right'). For the evolution of beneficial use and waste in prior appropriation, see Sax *et al.*, above note 29, at 154–159.

interest groups, such as the agricultural sector, even though it is often blamed for wasting water.

In these systems, the price of water is usually subsidized for all users, but particularly for farmers. Subsidized prices mean that incentives for efficient use are not fully realized, despite the fact that many jurisdictions experience water shortages. Water is cheap, so it is rational to use more of it instead of, for example, using expensive irrigation methods. Command and control powers to strip of their rights those who are not using them efficiently are hardly ever used, so water is locked up for decades if permits are temporary or in perpetuity if they are permanent.

An additional issue that characterizes administrative systems is how they deal with water crises. Administrative systems, particularly those that have embraced concepts such as Integrated Water Management, should plan ahead for coping with water shortages. Some jurisdictions have established mechanisms of rationing *ex-ante* via Drought Plans. If that is the case, in these jurisdictions the uncertainty of water users should decrease because these users can expect how much water they will be able to use depending on how much water is naturally available. However, many jurisdictions, even those that have rules regulating allocations in times of low availability, deal with droughts on a case-by-case basis, using emergency rules. Such a scenario may not be efficient because water users cannot plan ahead since they are subject to the discretion of the agency's decision as to who gets water, and the agency may not have enough information to allocate water to those who value it the most. Agencies will always make these decisions at a certain level of generality, not focusing on the marginal value for each user. Instead, these decisions might be guided by the relative social value of user types at best, or the political influence of interest groups at worst.

The water management system in the region of Catalonia, to which Barcelona belongs, follows precisely this administrative model. In Spain, water is public property and its management is controlled by administrative agencies. On a regular basis, the Water Agencies deciding on the allocation of water are the basin authorities (Confederaciones Hidrográficas) or the agencies set forth by regional government, depending on whether the basin is under the power of central or regional government. In Catalonia, there are two relevant ones: the Confederación Hidrográfica del Ebro and Agència Catalana de l'Aigua. These two agencies are in charge of long-term planning and, following a cumbersome administrative procedure, grant permits to use water once users have applied for them. The agencies may subsequently review the permits reducing the volume granted, but it is not common for them to do so because some user groups, such as farmers, are extremely powerful. The management of droughts using emergency rules is perfectly illustrated by the general response and the emergency decrees enacted by the Catalan and Spanish governments as a result of the 2007–08 drought period. For example, the Catalan government announced cutbacks in the agricultural sector without any mechanism for farmers to obtain water if they wished to. The provision establishing water banks in the Decrees was never implemented. Instead, mandated transfers seemed to be the default rule. The transfers between the Ebro or Segre and the Barcelona metropolitan area were framed by certain officials as potential transaction frameworks, but such an approach was not accepted. However, if a market had been established, water that would have been used anyway could have been transferred from low-value users, who would decrease their use, to cities, alleviating the effects of the drought and compensating the low-value users.

1.6 Water markets

1.6.1 Definition

Water markets have been implemented or at least discussed in several jurisdictions such as Australia,[40] Chile,[41] Canada,[42] New Zealand, South Africa, and some western US States.[43] Furthermore, the World Bank defended them wholeheartedly as the preferred policy for water management,[44] and has influenced the decision of countries such as Mexico to adopt them.[45] However, there is no clear definition of water markets.

A broad definition of markets tends to equate markets with every regulation based on economic incentives[46] which encompasses price increases and transactions. Market detractors adopt an even broader one: they conflate water markets with privatization because they were often part of the same reform

---

40 Henning Bjornlund and Jennifer M. McKay, 'Aspects of Water Markets for Developing Countries – Experiences from Australia, Chile and the US,' 7 J. Env't & Dev. Econ. 767 (2002); Henning Bjornlund, 'Farmer participation in markets for temporary and permanent water in southeastern Australia,' 63 Agric. Water Mgmt 57, 59 (2003).

41 Carl J. Bauer, 'Bringing Water Markets Down to Earth: The Political Economy of Water Rights in Chile, 1976–95,' 25 World Dev. 639, 642 (1997). For Chile, see Ereney Hadjigeorgalis, '*Comerciando con incertidumbre: los mercados de agua en la agricultura chilena*' ('Trading with uncertainty: water market in Chilean agriculture'), 41 Cuadernos de Economía 3 (2004) (Two types of Chilean water markets can be distinguished: the spot one and the long-term one. In both, farmers participate but with different roles. Annual crop farmers are the sellers in both while they are sometimes buyers of spot transactions. On the contrary, permanent crops – such as orchards – are the buyers in long-term transactions).

42 Lorraine A. Nicol and K.K. Klein, 'Water Market Characteristics: Results from a Survey of Southern Alberta Irrigators,' 31 Can. Water Res. J. 91 (2006).

43 Bjornlund, above note 40.

44 World Bank, 'Water market,' http://water.worldbank.org/related-topics/water-market.

45 Mark W. Rosegrant and Hans P. Binswanger, 'Markets in tradable water rights: Potential for efficiency gains in developing country water resource allocation,' 22 World Dev. 1613 (1994).

46 Glennon, above note 13, at 1886 ('Market-based transfers can take many forms, from sales to leases, from forbearance agreements to dry-year options, and from land fallowing to conservation measures that save water'). Cf. ibid. 'Each offers the prospect of a win-win result as the seller secures a price that she finds attractive and the buyer secures a water supply worth the negotiated price' which requires price negotiation as Dellapenna, 'Getting Names Right,' above note 39, at 322.

agenda towards a purportedly better water management system. The World Bank has long favored, as part of what is called the Washington consensus, water markets and privatization of water utilities, and, consequently, critics take these proposals as though they were the same.[47] In contrast, Dellapenna uses one of the narrowest definitions. For him, water markets are:

> [a] setting where water users will be able to negotiate over the price of water and seek out the least cost provider, providers will be able to seek out the user willing to pay the highest price, and both will otherwise engage in the sorts of activities that give rise to the expectation that markets are likely to generate the 'highest and best' or at least the most economically efficient use of water.[48]

According to this definition, environmental water accounts or water banks are not markets because government fixes the price in them and it is deeply involved. According to him, only exchanges between similarly situated private actors without the intervention of public agencies constitute markets.[49]

This project adopts a middle ground definition. Building on the idea that water markets incentivize an efficient allocation of water, shifting water from agricultural uses to urban[50] or environmental uses, this book considers a market

---

47 Dellpenna, 'Getting Names Right,' above note 39, at 322, even though he criticizes merging both concepts, he thinks that labeling something as a market gives a positive glow to it. For a critique of too free markets illustrated with the Chilean experience, Carl J. Bauer, *Against the Current: Privatization, Water Markets, and the State in Chile* (1998). Jane Maslow Cohen, 'Foreword to Symposium of Waterbanks, Piggybanks, and Bankruptcy: Changing Directions in Water Law,' 83 Tex. L. Rev. 1809, 1816 (2005).

48 Dellapenna, 'Getting Names Right,' above note 39, at 322.

49 Dellapenna, 'Getting Names Right,' above note 39, at 358–365 (analyzing why labeling the California water bank 'market' is a misnomer).

50 This goal, which is politically controversial, is not always explicitly acknowledged but it can be inferred from governmental actions. Regarding Australia, see Rowan Roberts, Nicole Mitchell, and Justin Douglas, 'Water and Australia's future economic growth,' at 63 (2006), http://www.treasury.gov.au/documents/1087/PDF/05_Water.pdf ('For sellers, the revenue from the sale of water can supplement farm income and provide capital for other on- or off-farm activities, injecting additional income into regional communities. At the same time, farms and businesses that can use water to generate high rates of economic return, but are currently limited by their inability to obtain more water, will benefit by being able to buy water to increase production. Well-designed water markets will allow buyers and sellers to trade either permanent entitlements or annual allocations depending upon their individual preferences and needs'). For Chile, see Hadjigeorgalis, above note 41, at 3. For a Spanish example, see Ministerio de Medio Ambiente (Secretaría General para el Territorio y la Biodiversidad, Dirección General del Agua) and Confederación Hidrográfica del Júcar, 'Plan Especial de Alerta y Eventual Sequía en la Cuenca del Júcar, Anexo' ('Annex to the Special Plan for alert and drought scenarios in the Jucar Basin'), at 91 (2007), http://www.mma.es/secciones/acm/aguas_continent_zonas_asoc/ons/planes_sequia_isas/pdf/JUCAR_cap.pdf (the Spanish Administration identifies irrigators as potential sellers and municipalities and utility companies as potential buyers). The actual trade occurred in the 1991 California water banks illustrates this point too: urban or

any mechanism, temporary or permanent, which allows users with different marginal values to transfer the right to use water. If there is a decision on the seller's and the buyer's side to enter into a mutually beneficial transaction where water is transferred,[51] even in the midst of political noise, and no matter whether or how the price is fixed, this book considers it to be a market transaction. This definition, as with the one seemingly adopted by Thompson[52] or Adler,[53] includes not only private water transactions, most probably reviewed by the administration, but also water banks and environmental water accounts, both mechanisms where the price is normally fixed by the agency running them, as this chapter describes below. This definition leaves out other tools sometimes labeled market incentives, such as price mechanisms that discourage heavy consumption. It also leaves outside the definition water exchanges engaged in for operational reasons, i.e. a situation where a water wholesaler shifts sources of water between clients to make the most out of water, if there is no real transaction involved.

There are a myriad of transactions which could fit the definition just presented. The different experiences might be classified according to different criteria: what actors are involved (private actors, institutions, etc.), which mechanism is used (private contract or some type of institutionalized scheme), the origin of the water transferred (surplus, conservation, fallowing or reuse), or destination of the water (urban users, agriculture or the environment). However, instead of using one of these classifications, the most common experiences are reviewed: water banks, environmental water accounts, and contracts between private parties. This book includes in water markets those transactions involving

industrial users purchased 79 per cent of the water, see Richard E. Howitt, 'Empirical Analysis of Water Market Institutions: The 1991 California Water Market,' 16 Res. & Energy Econ. 357, 360 (1994). See also Gabrielle Bouleau and Matt Kondolf, *Rivers of Diversity: Evolving Water Regulation in California and the European Union*, at 5, Working Papers California-EU Regulatory Cooperation Project Workshop, http://www.transatlantic.be/publications/bouleau_kondolf_final.pdf ('urban claims for water supply and leisure activities are increasing in both areas [California and the European Union], as agriculture weighs less in the overall production and payroll. In both regions, the growing urban water uses try to challenge senior farmers' water rights which activity is largely subsidized'). For a general statement of the western states water market's initial goal of encouraging water to flow from agriculture to cities, see Bonnie Colby, Mark McGinnis, and Ken Rait, 'Mitigating environmental externalities through voluntary and involuntary water reallocation: Nevada's Truckee-Carson River Basin,' 31 Nat. Resources J. 757, 757 (1991).

51 Purchase of district shares, instead of water directly, can be considered or not part of the water market. Kaiser does consider them as a water market, Ronald A. Kaiser, 'Texas Water Marketing in the Next Millennium: a Conceptual and Legal Analysis,' 27 Tex. Tech- L. Rev. 181, 200 (1996).

52 Barton H. Thompson, Jr., 'Water as a public commodity,' 95 Marq. L. Rev. 17, 42 (2011) (includes environmental water accounts).

53 Jonathan H. Adler, 'Water Marketing as an Adaptive Response to the Threat of Climate Change,' 31 Hamline L. Rev. 730, 740 (2008) (includes water banks).

groundwater where data is available and where groundwater has been adjudicated or is subject to a permit system.

There are also some transactions that do not fit the definition used in this book. Excluded from consideration are land transactions where the main purpose is transferring water tied to the land, and informal transactions. Both could occur without markets in place. Land transactions could happen even in jurisdictions where water rights are not tradable, but appurtenant to land. Transferring the land with water tied to it implies the transfer of the water. This is the case in riparian systems still in place in the east of the United States. Those land transactions imply so many transaction costs that they are not a viable way to ensure that water is put to the most efficient use. Informal exchanges are common between irrigators, both in Western economies and in the developing world. Informal trading is also excluded. Those informal transactions between neighboring farmers have not been sufficient to solve water scarcity problems. Where necessary, their interaction with formal water markets would try to be asserted. This book focuses, thus, on formal water transactions between water right holders. Water rights are usually held by, among others, urban water districts, irrigation organizations, farmers, or big industrial users. Individual households using water for domestic use are excluded from this analysis because they have a contract with a provider which supplies them water and bills for it. Their water cannot be resold, and is thus outside of the scope of this book. Along the same lines, this book does not deal with the privatization of urban water systems that is often conflated with markets as previously mentioned.

1.6.2 Typology

a. Private transactions

Once rights are transferable, private parties may decide to enter into contracts, most probably subject to a review procedure because a change in the place where water is used and/or diverted may have effects on other water users or the environment. These transactions normally involve selling or leasing the right to use water, typically diverting it from a river into a property or receiving it through infrastructure.

Glennon and Pearce argue that water rights transfer contracts have to be crafted for every specific situation, and their completion requires an ongoing relationship to cover all the uncertainties that cannot be predicted at the outset; hence, parties to a contract transferring water are agreeing on how to agree.[54]

---

54 Robert Glennon and Michael J. Pearce, 'Transferring Mainstream Colorado River Water Rights: The Arizona Experience,' 49 Ariz. L. Rev. 235, 245 (2007) ('To accomplish the goal, both buyer and seller must agree to cooperate over a long period of time, and work together to resolve issues that cannot always be foreseen at the initial contract stage. Thus, the contract

This suggests that transaction costs abound. A broker, which is a professional – public or private – specialized in matching buyers and sellers of water rights, could lower these contracting costs.

In addition to the sale or lease of current water rights, a market in futures has also been proposed. It would allow market agents to plan ahead and to mitigate their risk aversion. An option contract in water consists in an agreement to have the option to acquire or lease the right to use water of the other party.[55] The trigger could be an external, objective factor, such as the level of rainfall which signals a dry year, or just the willingness of the seller to exercise the option. There have been some examples of option contracts such as the one between a city in Utah and a farmer. The farmer received a payment at the beginning of the 25-year contract to provide the city the option to lease the farmer's entitlement during dry years. In the years the option was exercised, the farmer received another cash payment.[56]

b. Water banks

Many of the experiences under the label 'water markets' entail brokerage frameworks where a public agency plays an intermediary role. These are usually known as 'water banks,' but they can be named differently depending on the jurisdiction.[57] A water bank can be defined as:

> [A] mechanism designed to facilitate the transfer of water use entitlements from one location or use to another. A water bank functions like an intermediary, or broker, similar in some ways to a financial bank that acts as a broker or clearinghouse between savers and borrowers. In the case of water banks – and unlike some brokers – there is some kind of public sanction for its activities.[58]

must include a significant dose of goodwill and reasonableness terminology that can be read, at least at times, as nothing more than an agreement to agree. There are no forms for such contracts idling on law firm shelves: instead, each must be custom drafted to meet the needs of the particular transaction, which can heavily depend on the exact type of water right being transferred'). Similarly, Emerick and Lueck acknowledge the complexity in water transactions arising from the consideration of third party impacts which is not usually an important factor in the transactions of other goods and, thus, have received little attention from the economic organization scholarship. See Kyle Emerick and Dean Lueck, *Economic Organization and the Lease-Ownership Decision in Water*, at 12 (12 May 2010), unpublished working paper, http://papers.ssrn.com/sol3/papers.cfm?abstract_id=1605523.

55 Richard Howitt and Ellen Hanak, 'Incremental Water Market Development: The California Water Sector 1985–2004,' 30 Can. Water Resources J. 73, 80 (2005).

56 See Kaiser, above note 51, at 198.

57 In California, they are labeled water banks, but in Spain, the same idea, is encompassed by the water exchange centers (centros de intercambio de derechos).

58 Agriculture and Resource Economics, Oregon State University, Public Policy & Economics, 'Water FAQs,' http://arec.oregonstate.edu/jaeger/water/FAQ1.html.

In some of these water banks, prices are fixed by the administration. Sometimes, the administration buys the right and then resells it, repackaging it in quantities that a seller may want to buy. The administration tends to charge its buyers for the operational costs.[59] In other schemes, the role of the agency might be similar to a clearinghouse, just ensuring that information is available to all the parties and matching them.[60] In water banks, as a spot market, delivery is supposed to occur immediately.

Even though there are a lot of experiences, the paramount example of such a water market is the California 1991 Drought Water Bank.[61] It was managed by the California Department of Water Resources (DWR), which acquired title to the water sold to the bank, pooling it before reselling. It operated as a spot water market, even though there was a time lag between the time water was sold to the market and the time it was sold to the buyers. Chapter 4 includes more information about it. Other examples exist in Idaho,[62] Texas,[63] Kansas, Colorado, and Washington.[64]

In many jurisdictions, water banks are not permanent. The majority of them envisage transactions not as sales but as leases. The establishment requires a decision by the water agency. The formal procedure for setting up such structures may delay the response in a crisis situation. This is the case in Spain where basin agencies – the agencies responsible for water management – are allowed to set up water banks (centros de intercambio de derechos) in exceptional circumstances, such as overexploitation of aquifers or severe droughts.[65] Underlying the Spanish approach seems to be the idea that water is essential and that society does not want to commodify it unless there is no other option. Some jurisdictions could opt for the reverse system: when the situation is dire, public agencies take control managing the crisis according to the public interest and water transactions are not allowed. In any event, more permanent bank schemes, such as the one in the Murray Darling Basin in Australia,[66] could be more successful since they would be already set up when a crisis strikes and there is a need for relief via water transactions.

---

59 See sections 4.6.4 and 5.6.4 for the description of water bank frameworks in California and Spain, respectively.

60 The relevance of the information on water transactions is emphasized in Kaiser, above note 51, at 202.

61 See Howitt, above note 50, at 360.

62 Lawrence J. MacDonnell and Teresa A. Rice, 'Moving Agricultural Water to Cities: The Search for Smarter Approaches,' 14 Hastings W.-N.W. J. Env. L. & Pol'y 105, 142 (2008). § 42-1761 of 142 Idaho Code Ann. (2011).

63 Kaiser, above note 51, at 202.

64 See ibid. at 201.

65 See Art. 71 of the Consolidated Water Act (CWA) (BOE 2001, 176).

66 OECD, Implementing Domestic Tradeable Permits: Recent Developments and Future Challenges, at 264 (2002).

c. Environmental water accounts

Environmental water accounts are a useful mechanism to cover the demand for environmental water, which contributes to the scarcity problem because it competes with existing users. Governments are using environmental water accounts to lease or buy water rights from consumptive water users with environmental goals.[67] They are an alternative to prescriptive regulation, which would require curtailing private rights in completely allocated or even over-allocated streams. These environmental water accounts may not differ much from water banks in the way they work, except for the presence of a monopsonist who does not resell the water.

One important difference between water banks and environmental water accounts is that in the latter, water is left in the river. Instead, positive externalities affecting third parties are likely to occur because there will be more water flow which, for example, dilutes pollution or means that less power is required to pump water from the river. Even though an environmental water account is usually managed by an agency, which can be an already existing one or one newly created by the co-operation of the several agencies with interests at stake, they could also be trusted to a non-profit organization,[68] in a similar way that wetlands mitigation banks have been established. Even if an environmental water account is in place, transferable property rights may provide private parties who care for environmental protection with an additional mechanism to ensure instream flow. Instead of begging the responsible agency for its protection, those parties could buy existing consumptive rights.

The CALFED Bay-Delta environmental water account (CALFED EWA)[69] is one of the best-known examples. It was an initiative by a consortium of federal and state agencies managing the complexities of the Delta of the Sacramento and San Joaquin rivers. The CALFED EWA bought more than 1,000 million m^3 between 2001 and 2003 for the preservation of certain endangered fish species as required by the US Environmental Protection Agency. In the CALFED EWA, the project agencies (the United States Bureau of Reclamation and the DWR) were responsible for water acquisition and the fishery agencies (the US Fish and Wildlife Service and the California Department of Fish and Game) were responsible for the management of the CALFED EWA assets. The CALFED EWA was developed to lessen the conflicts between current water users and the protection of endangered species by ensuring that right holders would experience fewer restrictions on their rights. It is a good example of the successful collaboration of the 25 state and federal agencies which have power

---

67 Howitt and Hanak, above note 55, at 76.
68 Alf W. Brandt, 'An Environmental Water Account: The California Experience,' 5 U. Denv. Water L. Rev. 416, 443 (2002).
69 For an analysis of the CALFED experience, see Jody Freeman and Daniel A. Farber, 'Modular Environmental Regulation,' 54 Duke L. J. 795, 837–876 (2005).

over the Delta, which suggests that water markets are viable in the likely scenarios of concurrent responsibility of multiple agencies.

1.7 Critiques of administrative systems and advantages of water markets

Water trading has been advocated as a solution to the shortcomings of centralized water management regimes. A water market offers, at least theoretically, four advantages: first, it pools information cheaply, embodying it in the price; second, it enhances innovation; third, it allows risk management; and, fourth, it overcomes certain political obstacles. These advantages can also be read as deficiencies of administrative systems for water management. In administrative systems, the regulators purportedly lack information, prices are subsidized, incentives to innovate are usually channelled through subsidies, risk management by private parties is not possible, and agencies are captured by interest groups. Despite this opposition between markets and government, as Chapter 2 demonstrates, market advantages are not erased by proper governmental involvement in water markets. Instead, certain roles played by administrative agencies are necessary to achieve these advantages.

1.7.1 Markets as information aggregators: pricing water at its real value

The ideal administrative system regarding water resources will entail long-term, continuous planning, taking into account scientific evidence and social preferences, even though they are particularly difficult to measure. However, permits to use water are given on a case-by-case basis, which seems to make difficult the achievement of an overall efficient allocation. For example, a new application could be more socially beneficial than other uses which have already been granted a permit to use certain amount of water, but that new application cannot be approved because the stream is already fully appropriated by less valuable uses, the rights to which have been granted for a certain number of years. The efficiency of the system cannot be improved until the next renewal.

Furthermore, it might be difficult for the administration to fully assess the different value that water has in many different uses and to assess the level of rivalry between them from the application materials. Even if the parties provide the information, the administration will make a decision at a specific point in time and cannot update it as regularly as would be desirable. In many jurisdictions, regulators rank the different uses to determine which uses to curtail in times of shortage[70] or to prioritize among applications. Ranks might hide

---

70 Milliman, above note 36. For a current example, see §§350, 353, and 354 of the Cal. Water Code.

other values, like the central role we give to domestic supply or the will to protect the agricultural sector. Even if there is no political noise behind them, ranks are highly contestable because they are a mere proxy for the value of water for a specific use without taking into account the marginal value for each user. For example, agriculture is usually regarded as a low-value use and we expect markets to reallocate water from the fields to urban and suburban areas. However, the first drop of water used to irrigate a crop of potatoes might entail a higher value than the water used for washing a car with a hose.[71] Markets could account for that. In an ideal world, administrative allocation combined with tiered pricing could approximate the market solution, but actual water management deviates a lot from the ideal.

Markets convey information through prices which provide an objective measure of the subjective values,[72] making it unnecessary for the public regulator to gather and pool all the information which is usually in private hands and extremely contingent on time and place. Water is an input in almost all human activities, and users are in an advantaged position to know how much water they need, and how valuable and substitutable it is for them.[73]

Drawing on the same idea, markets are more dynamic than an administrative system of management as they should respond to changes in demand through time or to shortages in supply more rapidly.[74] In a market framework, water prices are expected to reflect the full opportunity cost of the resource at any time with few, if any, temporal lags.[75] This will encourage efficient consumption, which cannot be achieved with current subsidized prices. Low-value users will face the choice between using their water at a low price or transferring all or

---

71 Andrew P. Morriss, 'Real people, real resources, and real choices: the case for market valuation of water,' 38 Tex. Tech L. Rev. 973, 983 (2006) (offering a similar example arguing that residential users pay a flat rate for drinking water and for watering their lawn even though the value of the second activity is lower than watering a golf course that a lot of people would enjoy).

72 See Donald R. Leal and Terry L. Anderson, *Free Market Environmentalism*, at 17 (2001).

73 R. Quentin Grafton, Clay Landry, Gary D. Libecap, and Robert J. O'Brien, *Water Markets: Australia's Murray-Darling Basin and the US Southwest*, at 1, NBER Working Paper No. 15797, http://www.nber.org/papers/w15797.pdf?new_window=1 ('Australia's Murray-Darling Basin (MDB) and the US Southwest offer a "window to the future" on the growing problem of water scarcity and the potential for water rights and markets to provide information on current consumption patterns and alternative values, incentives for adjustments in use, and smoother reallocation across competing demands').

74 Draper, above note 14, at 50. See also Morriss, above note 71, at 988 ('Market prices respond to events quickly, sending market participants signals about the impact of events on the goods and services sold in markets. As discussed earlier, by monitoring market prices, including future prices, an individual is able to learn a considerable amount about the likely course of events even without studying the underlying information driving the changes in market prices').

75 Draper, above note 14, at 50 ('For supporters of the model, a system of marketable rights to water would allow water users to consider the full opportunity cost of water, including its value for alternative uses').

part of it and receiving a higher price, particularly during low availability seasons, paid by buyers which could be growing urban areas or thriving agricultural producers. It is not necessary to change water tariffs to achieve the goal of the water markets this book focuses on. Water markets are supposed to give incentives to the agricultural sector to profit from the fact that they receive water at a cheap price and can sell it at a higher one, instead of imposing regulations on their irrigation practices to save water or rough mandated reallocations which will involve high political costs.

Given the pricing of water that water markets generate, some critique water markets because they allow private users to profit from selling water. This critique spurs from two somewhat conflicting viewpoints. On the one hand, some critique the mercantilization of water because they consider this resource a public good. From an equity standpoint, this commodification may increase the price to end users which is particularly problematic for poor communities. Even if a subsidy is applied and rates regulated, they fear that a utility purchasing water from an irrigation district may pass on the higher price to its consumers. However, primary needs amount to around 1 per cent of consumption in the United States[76] and they could be subsidized, leaving the rest of the allocation to market mechanisms. On the other hand, markets allow those not using water efficiently and paying a subsidized price for it to profit from selling it to other users who value it more. However, true as this statement is, markets convey incentives for efficient use that captured or slow responding agencies cannot.

1.7.2 Markets as innovation spurs

Another stated advantage of markets is that they incentivize water savings and innovation. In administrative systems, users have fewer incentives to make the most of the subsidized water they have assigned, even though there are users who could do with less water if they used it more efficiently. The agricultural sector presents unrealized potential for water savings. In the European Union, if farmers adopted different cumulative measures – ranging from investment in improving irrigation infrastructure, reuse of treated sewage water or changes in irrigation practices or crops – they could reduce current withdrawals up to 43 per cent.[77] In an administrative system, the upgrading of the different irrigation methods tends to be achieved, if at all, by providing subsidies to farmers[78]

---

76 Glennon, above note 13, at 1896.

77 See Ecology Institute, *EU Water Saving Potential. Final Report (Part 1 – Report)*, at 6 (2007), http://ecologic.eu/download/projekte/900-949/917/917_water_saving_1.pdf.

78 This suggests that even without any investment, water could be freed if properly managed. In the same vein, the Spanish Ministries of Agriculture and of the Environment have carried out since 2006 an Irrigation Plan (RD 2006/287 (BOE 2006, 60)) to improve irrigation agriculture efficiency investing €2,344 million. One of the programme goals is to change the social perception of the irrigators from squanderers to efficient water managers and protectors of the environment.

because water rights revisions reducing water rights to the minimum amount of water necessary are unpopular. Those subsidy programmes have sometimes not achieved real water savings because public agencies have not accounted for the rebound effect that may occur if farmers install sprinkler or drip irrigation. Even though those two irrigation systems may increase crop productivity, certain scenarios may consume more water. Furthermore, even if those systems save water, a subsidy programme runs into the same critics as a water market because farmers would not face the financial consequences of their inefficiency.

Moreover, administrative systems encourage wasteful consumption in some cases because a common provision in those systems requires right holders to use their water rights or, otherwise, they will be forfeited. A right holder will, accordingly, use the full amount of his rights even if he needs less. Where water rights are transferable, such a provision discourages speculation.

Water markets allow water users to profit by selling their water surplus, provided the transaction does not harm third parties. Cultivators, motivated by a higher price of water, can either completely cut their consumption – e.g. when farmers let their fields lay fallow – or sell the surplus arising from a more efficient use of water. More efficient uses of water can result from improving the irrigation channels, shifting towards more efficient irrigation practices, depending on the type of crop,[79] or growing new products that require less water use. New methods of irrigation and improvements in existing techniques may also be expected, and even modified crop varieties.

Scarcity may make water so valuable that entrepreneurs may also find new sources of water supply, such as water produced with new desalination techniques. Today, these are more expensive than increases in efficiency in current uses, but future research may make them cheaper. However, the regulatory framework needs to enable, or at least not discourage, such innovation. For example, in some jurisdictions recycled water may be exempt from permit regulations, while in others it will be necessary to apply for a permit. In other jurisdictions, water quality regulations might be too strict, preventing the use of recycled water for domestic consumption.

1.7.3 Markets as uncertainty management tools

Markets can help to shield users from water uncertainty. Uncertainty in the water realm is two-fold: (a) endogenous to regulation; and (b) exogenous to regulation, such as uncertainty due to natural variability of precipitation. Examples of the former are standards such as 'reasonable use' or 'public interest,' the vagueness of which undermines a sharp definition of property

---

79 Grafton *et al.*, above note 73, at 19.

rights,[80] complicating market success[81] given the potential discretionary powers that agencies have.

Water exchanges offer an opportunity to manage the exogenous, natural uncertainty, i.e. the variability of water availability. This translates into uncertainty regarding endowment of the parties to a transaction.[82] If rules of allocation in times of shortage are more or less clear, users can shield themselves from the risk of not receiving enough water according to their calculations by buying or leasing water from those who are more likely to receive water and do with less, thus entrenching their supplies.[83] For instance, junior appropriators have a chance that they may not receive water during summer months. Consequently, they may prefer contracting over this risk by buying or leasing rights from senior appropriators, which do not face such a high risk. Option contracts with an objective trigger could also be used in this context.[84] However, as Chapter 2 describes, both types of uncertainties are interlaced, and water markets' performance will suffer if rules of allocation are discretionary or uncertain.

1.7.4 Markets as a shield from politically-driven decisions

The main critique of administrative systems for water management is that agencies are captured and serve special interests, be they communities[85] or a

---

80 Michael Warburton, 'Toward Greater Certainty in Water Rights? Public Interests Require Inherent "Uncertainty" to Support Constitutional Governance of Our State's Waters,' 36 McGeorge L Rev. 139, 142 (2005). Standardization of property rights is extremely difficult since even if a wide range of dimensions are included in the permit or implicit in a common law right, each right to a stream has certain particularities. Bjornlund and McKay mention the following: '1) Security of supply specified as the probability of receiving the volumetric entitlement (including whether a government has the authority to cancel water rights, (. . .); 2) Reliability of delivery, specified as the period from ordering to receiving the water; 3) The period during which the water can be used. 4) The constraints on trade, such as spatial constraints, limitations on trade between sectors in the economy, 5) Some indication of the expected quality of the water. 6) The duration of the water right, either indefinite or for a specified period of time,' see Bjornlund and McKay, above note 40, at 791.
81 Warburton, ibid. at 143.
82 Emerick and Lueck, above note 54, at 25.
83 Barton Thompson, Jr., 'Uncertainty in Water Markets,' 36 McGeorge L. Rev. 117, 131 (2005) ('While the Governor's Commission focused only on the relevance of uncertainty to water markets, water markets play a pivotal role in reducing the harm from uncertainty (. . .). Water markets reduce the harm from uncertainty in two principal ways. First, water markets can enable water users to respond more effectively to the events about which they are uncertain. (. . .) Second, water markets allow water users who face uncertainty to reallocate the uncertainty to individuals or entities that can better bear the risk of the uncertainty'). See also Grafton *et al.*, above note 73, at 5.
84 Howitt and Hanak, above note 55, at 80–81.
85 James L. Huffman, 'Institutional Constraints on Transboundary Marketing,' in Terry L. Anderson and Peter J. Hill (eds), *Water Marketing. The Next Generation*, at 32 (1997).

particular sector, such as farmers. In contrast, markets purportedly decentralize decisions without allowing factors other than willingness to pay and marginal value to intervene. Markets leave to government the decision of how much water is in the initial allocation and who receives it, but private parties will decide subsequent allocations.

If the decision in a market does not depend on the discretion of the public regulator, interest groups have less interest in investing in rent-seeking.[86] Although in a market, interest groups might need to solve their disputes in the marketplace where they simply compete on equal terms,[87] the capture of the regulator could be transmitted to the market. The initial allocation may favor a particular group, and that has important distributional impacts and may be a source of unnecessary transaction costs. These transaction costs could even prevent an efficient outcome. In addition, interest groups might influence market design itself. An amendment of the status quo regulation – the administrative system in place before the introduction of market tools in water regimes – will draw the attention and the pressure of the dominant lobbies which may seek rules that are biased in their favor.[88] One example that might illustrate how markets are not shielded from interest group influences comes from the water banks in Idaho. In these banks, the price has been kept low to prevent any profit, allegedly to preserve the special values that water embodies, and irrigators have priority to buy water. So, if demand exceeds supply, non-irrigators are ranked at the bottom.[89]

Similarly, the strength of the various interest groups in different jurisdictions might be the reason which explains the different solutions for environmental protection adopted in market scenarios. In some markets, there have been public purchases of water to ensure instream flows;[90] while in others, a percentage of the water exchanged by private parties has to be devoted to environmental

---

86 Anderson and Snyder, above note 30, at 21 (rent-seeking entails that as result of a regulation benefits could be captured by certain interests groups and costs would be borne by the general public, not by the decision maker). See Morriss, above note 71, at 993.

87 Grafton *et al.*, above note 73, at 14 (arguing that voluntary exchanges may soften conflict over competing parties since they can reach mutually-beneficial agreements avoiding 'the divisive, time consuming rancor that has characterized arbitrary judicial and administrative water reallocation').

88 Gary Libecap, *Contracting for Property Rights*, at 26 (1989).

89 Barton Thompson, Jr., 'Water Markets and the Problem of Shifting Paradigms,' in *Water Marketing. The Next Generation*, above note 85, at 8.

90 The environmental water account is part of the CALFED Bay-Delta Program. To protect endangered fish, it purchased water, financing these actions with federal or state funds. In 2003, the purchases amounted to 240.5 million m³. See Howitt and Hanak, above note 55, at 81 (describing how the environmental water account and other environmental purchases have made water markets in California more active).

protection.[91] In still others, the tool used is the command and control one of minimum flow regulations. Each of these schemes may be explained by the relative strength of interest groups in the jurisdiction. The evaluation of those different mechanisms would depend on the values held by the beholder. Non-governmental organizations (NGOs) or public agencies paying for environmental water will make either their members or taxpayers realize the cost of their preferences. NGOs may want to tap on government resources by pushing mandatory regulations instead of market ones where the protection will depend on the meagre budget of the NGO. NGOs embrace the idea that water is public property and benefits the public, so perhaps the public should pay. However, those who care about environmental protection may consider paying for instream flow.

The groups favoring market mechanisms or opposing them will vary from jurisdiction to jurisdiction.[92] Therefore, the claim about market neutrality over interest group struggles and politically-driven decisions needs to be based on empirical facts, because the rules of the game might be skewed; it is not advantage that can be taken for granted.

Markets have also been advocated as a way to work around traditional conflicts[93] between neighboring jurisdictions sharing a watercourse. Theoretically, the market isolates the decision from the political arena. However, markets have not been a commonplace way out of transboundary resource conflicts.[94] Resource protectionism is not uncommon among jurisdictions, and it normally circumscribes water markets to a single jurisdiction.[95] In fact, even within jurisdictions there are circumstances where smaller political units have a say in the sale of water outside their boundaries. These organizations' powers are sources of transaction costs and may undermine water markets if they complicate the transmission of incentives to end water users.

---

91 In the Murray Darling Basin water market (Australia), a security exchange rate of 0.9 has been established when water is sold from South Australia to New South Wales or Victoria. Thus, a sale of 1 l from South Australia would mean that the buyer in Victoria will receive 0.9 l, see Murray-Darling Basin Commission, 'The Pilot Interstate Water Trading Project,' http:// www2.mdbc.gov.au/nrm/water_issues/water_trade/pilot_interstate_water_trading_project/.

92 See discussion in section 4.4.3.

93 See generally Thobani, above note 33. See also Huffman, above note 85, at 32. See also Victor Brajer, Al Church, Ronald Cummings, and Phillip Ronald, 'The Strengths and Weaknesses of Water Markets as They Affect Water Scarcity and Sovereignty Interests in the West,' 29 Nat. Resources J. 489, 495–497 (1989). But see Eyal Benvenisti, *Sharing Transboundary Resources*, at 25–31 (2002) (obstacles to the implementation of an international water market in international common pool resources implying that a market will be heavily regulated if adopted due to the difficulties in definition of property rights in water and the high transaction costs involved).

94 For a complete analysis of water transboundary resources, see Benvenisti, ibid.

95 For example, Oregon requires legislative approval for water transfers out of the state: §§537.830 and 537.801-810 of the Or. Rev. Stat.

2 Market failures and governmental roles

2.1 Introduction

The First Theorem of Welfare Economics[1] predicts that a competitive market brings about a Pareto optimal outcome.[2] This theorem supports at first sight the case for water markets. Unfortunately, water is not a textbook commodity.[3]

1 Ronald C. Griffin, *Water Resource Economics: The Analysis of Scarcity, Policies, and Projects*, at 107–109 (2005). Hal Varian, *Intermediate Microeconomics*, at 577–585 (2006). Allan M. Feldman, 'Welfare economics,' in *The New Palgrave Dictionary of Economics* (2008), http://www.dictionaryofeconomics.com/article?id=pde2008_W000050&edition=current&q=welfare%20economics&topicid=&result_number=1. Bernard Salanié, *Microeconomics of Market Failures*, at 1–8 (2000), 'a competitive equilibrium is for the common good,' assuming 'that all individuals and firms are self-interested price takers, (t)hen a competitive equilibrium is Pareto optimal.' Underlying the theorem, there are several assumptions, even though there is no absolute consensus about them since some have been relaxed for the sake of generality, such as: (a) competition – which can be understood as requiring numerous buyers and sellers; (b) agents must always prefer more of the good than less; (c) agents do not care about another's consumption; and (d) there are not externalities; (e) nor public goods. If these assumptions are not met the Pareto efficient outcome might not be achieved and, thus, social welfare might not be maximized.

2 Feldman, ibid. ('A situation is said to be Pareto optimal if there is no feasible alternative that makes everyone better off').

3 NSW Irrigator's Council, 'Response to ACCC – Australian Competition and Consumer Commission – BulkWater Charge Rules Issues paper' (2008), http://www.accc.gov.au/system/files/Sub%20238%20NSW%20Irrigators%20Council.pdf ('impose economic theory on a sector that is clearly not a textbook good or service is designed to fail'). Water is a fugitive, reusable, stochastically supplied good, which jointly has properties of common and public goods, is subject to economies of scale in its provision, and is life supporting, non-replaceable commodity associated with production (energy, agriculture, etc), transportation and waste disposal, and non-market and environmental values. See John J. Pigram, 'The value of water in competing uses. Irrigation and the Environment,' in M. Kay, T. Franks, and L. Smith (eds), *Water: Economics, management and demand*, at 191 (1997); J. Morris, E.K. Weatherhead, J.A.L. Dunderdale, C. Green, and S. Tunstall, 'The feasibility of tradeable permits for water abstraction in England and Wales,' in *Water: Economics, management and demand*, ibid. at 329.

Some of its particularities, combined with certain social and institutional factors, result in an inherently imperfect market or the lack of any market.[4]

Formal water markets, unlike markets in other goods that may arise from the bottom up, are purposively created by governments in order to make the allocation of water flexible and mitigate the effects of scarcity by allowing the allocation of water use rights to those who value them most highly. Some informal markets between irrigators do arise in a bottom up fashion, but the focus in this piece of work is not on those informal markets, because these are not sufficient to solve the current water stress challenges. It is important to note that even formal water markets are not the main allocation mechanism where they exist.

The most extreme advocates of water markets, who mirror those who strenuously criticize any centralized system of water management, usually recognize that water markets require governments to define property rights in water and to enforce these rights and the transactions which rely on them.[5] However, government intervention does not, and cannot, stop here in water markets. Beyond this, government needs to fulfill several roles for a market to operate successfully; as it may need to do in other natural resource markets. Even less ideologically oriented legal scholarship has failed to account for those roles. This chapter, after reviewing the literature on water markets, identifies the roles that government needs to play in water markets, the gap this book is filling in the literature. The roles are identified using the market failure rationales and mentioning non-economic reasons where those may play a role justifying governmental roles.

2.2 The case for water markets, a literature review

Advocates of water markets view them as opposed to administrative systems, implying that government is no longer part of the picture in water markets. They seem to orient their arguments to those authors who reject the idea of markets altogether. Between these two sides of the normative discussion, there are authors who look at how current water policies implementing market mechanisms have played out and how to improve them, and those who analyze the prerequisites for water markets to be implemented in developing countries. However, not even those policy-oriented scholars have theorized the different roles that government needs to play in order for water markets to go forward.

---

4   Robert A. Pulver, 'Liability rules as a Solution to the Problem of Waste in Western Water Law,' 76 Calif. L. Rev. 671, 694–701 (1988) (transaction costs, risk of monopoly due to the locality factor, bargaining failure, public good dimensions, environmental loss, and politics are explanatory causes for inherent water market imperfection).

5   Victor Brajer, Al Church, Ronald Cummings, and Phillip Ronald, 'The Strengths and Weaknesses of Water Markets as They Affect Water Scarcity and Sovereignty Interests in the West,' 29 Nat. Resources J. 489, 495–497 (1989).

This book conceives water markets as tools for public agencies to deal with droughts and water scarcity by establishing the framework to allow individual users to transfer water to more efficient users.

In order to better understand this book's contribution, this chapter reviews the abovementioned scholarship on the topic. It describes first the normative debate. Then, it presents the policy-oriented literature and the literature analyzing the prerequisites for water markets, mostly in the developing world, while highlighting the under-theorization of the role of government in water markets, i.e. the gap that sections 2.3 to 2.7, building on the economic theories of regulation, aim to cover.

2.2.1 A normative debate

A great deal of the literature debating the merits of water markets often reflects preconceived ideological views. The word 'market' has a gloss of rightness for some and a stigma for others. Both advocates and detractors assume that there is an opposition between markets and government.

At one end of this normative debate, free-market environmentalists generally argue for market solutions to environmental problems not only in the case of water, but also for other resources. Books by Anderson and Hill,[6] Anderson and Leal,[7] and Anderson and Snyder[8] pin down the application of free-market environmentalist ideas to water. World Bank policy proposals for water markets can also be included in this first group.[9]

They present the market as an alternative to government.[10] As Krier points out, 'They [free-market environmentalists] hope to rely on the market more or less entirely and side-step the government just about altogether.'[11] In fact,

---

6   See James L. Huffman, 'Institutional Constraints on Transboundary Marketing,' in Terry L. Anderson and Peter J. Hill (eds), *Water Marketing. The Next Generation*, at 32 (1997).

7   Terry L. Anderson and Donald R. Leal, *Free Market Environmentalism* (2001).

8   Terry L. Anderson and Pamela Snyder, *Water Markets. Priming the Invisible Pump*, at 7 (1997). Other works in this trend might be cited, including Huffman, above note 6; James L. Huffman, 'Water marketing in western prior appropriation states: a model for the East,' 21 Ga. St. U. L. Rev. 429 (2004); James L. Huffman, 'Markets, Regulation, and Environmental Protection,' 55 Mont. L. Rev. 425 (1994); Andrew P. Morriss, 'Real People, real resources, and real choices: the case for market valuation of water,' 38 Tex. Tech L. Rev. 973, 983 (2006); Rodney T. Smith, *Trading water: An Economic and Legal Framework for Water Marketing* (Council of State Planning Agencies, 1988); Mateen Thobani, 'Tradable Property Rights to Water. How to improve water use and resolve water conflicts,' 34 Public Policy for the Private Sector 1 (1995).

9   Thobani, ibid.

10   For a free-market environmentalists' vision of government, see Anderson and Leal, above note 7, at 3, 71, 115, 124–125, and 129.

11   James Krier, 'Tragedy of the Commons Part Two,' 15 Harv. J. L. & Pub. Pol'y 327, 328 (1992). See also ibid. at 338, Krier arguing that Hardin in the celebrated *Science* article takes government for granted without analyzing how it is compelled to take action.

it may be more accurate to say that they envision a minimization of the governmental role,[12] and limit government intervention to the enforcement of private parties' agreements once property rights are defined. Given that government has a secondary role to play,[13] it is less susceptible to being captured.[14] Some authors in this 'free-market' group acknowledge the difficulties of introducing a water market, given the compositional characteristics of the resource,[15] but they do not go beyond this. The natural characteristics of the resource and the historical evolution of its management require governmental intervention to overcome the said difficulties. When they analyze the need to control potential effects on third parties arising from a transaction – which if not internalized will amount to a market failure – they distrust government to play such a role, given the risk of governmental failure which they base on examples picked from a pure administrative system of water management.[16] They assume that almost all questions in water management can be delegated to markets in one way or another. For example, for them, there is no question that instream flow protection is to be channelled through markets. In fact, they advocate for complete private provision, i.e. government should not be the right holder of instream flow rights. Further, they reject the community externalities, that is the effects on the economy and life of a region beyond the parties to a transaction, that water transactions might cause, arguing that the situation is

---

12   See Anderson and Leal, above note 7.

13   Mateen Thobani, 'Formal Water Markets: Why, When and How to Introduce Tradable Water Rights,' 12 The World Bank Res. Observer 161, 174 (1997) ('Public institutions must establish the legal and regulatory framework to register the rights, to operate parts of the system that users cannot, and to settle disputes that cannot be resolved by user associations'). Interestingly enough, this author, see ibid. at 176, resorts to the administrative apparatus of formal markets to protect aquifers against depletion that might arise from the incentives given by the market to pump as much water as possible.

14   For instance, water banks would be justified if they lower transaction costs – taking into account the administrative procedures they require – and, consequently, ensure a higher number of transactions. But attention must be paid to how they have actually unfolded in practice. Market frameworks organized by the public regulator are more susceptible to capture. D.M. DiSegni Eshel argues that private bargaining is less affected by the pressure of political interest groups than an auction, see Dafna M. DiSegni Eshel, *The Microstructure of Water Markets: Bargaining vs. Auctioning Approaches*, at 9, The Hebrew University, Selected Paper Workshop on Water and Agriculture (2002), http://departments.agri.huji. ac.il/economics/kenes-dafna.pdf. On the contrary, it might be argued that even when price is regulated, the decision is decentralized, ensuring some of the advantages of markets because parties decide whether or not enter into an agreement or participate in the auction, see Thomas C. Schelling, 'Price as Regulatory Instruments,' in Robert C. Ellickson *et al.* (eds), *Perspectives on Property Law*, at 536 (2002).

15   See A. Greif, 'Contracting, Enforcement, and efficiency: Economics beyond the Law,' in M. Bruno and B. Pleskovic (eds), 'Annual World Bank Conference on Development Economics,' at 191–217 (1996), cited in K.W. Easter, M.W. Rosegrant, and A. Dinar, *Markets for water, Potential and Performance*, at 6 (1998). See also Thobani, above note 13, at 172.

16   See in general Anderson and Snyder, above note 8.

no different from any other economic transaction with winners and losers.[17] Free-market environmentalists assume that government prefers a regulatory scheme to a market because the former allows government to expand its power.

At the other end, there are sceptics of environmental markets. Some in this group disagree with the idea of treating water, or any other natural resource, as a commodity, because water is essential for daily life.[18] Their positions seem to suggest that water regulation, as that of other environmental goods, might be one of the areas where our position as consumers – where willingness-to-pay is an acceptable measure of our preferences – conflicts with our role as citizens.[19] Water seems to have community ties;[20] it is special and we cannot treat it as a consumer good. Other scholars anchor their opposition on the existence of market failures, which, according to them, deem markets unfit for managing environmental goods. For example, Blumm challenges the idea of markets if there are collective goods, such as a pristine river, involved.[21]

The straightforward answer that a free-market environmentalist might give to these opponents is that clothing and food are essential and we do not exclude them from the marketplace,[22] and that preferences for environmental protection can be channelled through markets if those worried about the environment buy rights to protect instream flow. This book treats market failures as a justification for governmental intervention, suggesting that water markets can work if governmental agencies properly support them.

There is still another group which is not, as such, against the mechanisms labeled in this book as markets, but against their denomination as markets. In fact, they side with public management of watersheds, given the inherently public attributes of water and, thus, these mechanisms within an administrative framework, such as water banks, do not challenge their view even though they

---

17 Huffman, 'Water marketing,' above note 8, at 436.
18 For a review of the debate, see Norman W. Spaulding III, 'Commodification and Its Discontents: Environmentalism and the Promise of Market Incentives,' 16 Stan. Envt'l L.J. 293 (1997). For a general theory of inalienability, see Margaret Jane Radin, 'Market-Inalienability,' 100 Harv. L. Rev. 1849 (1987).
19 See generally Mark Sagoff, *The Economy of the Earth: Philosophy, Law, and the Environment* (Cambridge University Press, 2008) (advocating for a social compromise on these issues).
20 See Alessandra Goria and Nicola Lugaresi, 'The Evolution of the National Water Regime in Italy,' at 18 (2002), http://www.euwareness.nl/results/Italy-cs-kaft.pdf. Environmental protection has aspects of a public good. Public goods are supposed to be undersupplied. The counterargument is that for every public good, there is a group with intense interest that would lobby for it, as happens with national defense, see Maxwell Stearns and Todd Zywicki, *Public Choice Concepts and Applications in Law*, at 74 (2009) (national defense is always described as the perfect example of a public good, but it is not apparently underprovided because several arms companies will push for an increase in military budget).
21 Michael C. Blumm, 'The Fallacies of Free Market Environmentalism,' 15 Harv. J. L. & Pub. Pol'y 371, 375 (1992).
22 Anderson and Snyder, above note 8, at 26.

criticize the misname.[23] This book does not adopt their position. The assertion of which roles of government are necessary applies to those mechanisms to reallocate water efficiently, no matter how they are characterized.

2.2.2 Policy-oriented literature

As mentioned above, there is a great deal of policy-oriented scholarship dealing with the operation of water markets. This group of scholars does not challenge the case for water markets but focuses on addressing the potential failures or external effects of water markets, usually focusing on the existing experiences of water markets in western US States. Several water law scholars, such as Sax,[24] Thompson,[25] and Glennon,[26] may be fairly included in this group. To a large extent, the position of this group is driven by the fact that they see markets as the sole solution for serving new uses, given that water has been fully appropriated and new sources are not tenable. These authors have been concerned about some of the roles section 2.5 describes, such as third party or environmental externalities and other potential problems arising from the particularities of water resources. They also engage in an institutional analysis of the roles of the different layers of water administrations from the perspective of community protection.[27] Accordingly, they emphasize that water markets are far from being free markets,[28] since some governmental oversight is needed to address externalities.[29] However, they do not offer a full account of the roles that government needs to take on, as this book does.

Sax[30] contests the free-market paradigm focusing on the particularities of water transactions in comparison to the reallocation of a factory, or to interstate commerce of other commodities. Instead of supporting the removal of legal

---

23   Joseph W. Dellapenna, 'The Importance of Getting Names Right: The Myth of Markets for Water,' 25 Wm. & Mary Envt'l L. Pol'y 317 (2000).

24   Joseph L. Sax, 'Understanding Transfers: Community Rights and the Privatization of Water,' 14 Hastings W.-N.W. J. Envt'l L. & Pol'y 33 (2008).

25   Barton Thompson, Jr., '57 perspectives on water policy and markets,' 81 Cal. L. Rev. 671 (1993) (analyzing the California case for water markets and the interplay between government rules and traditional institutions which tend to be reluctant to transaction with external actors).

26   See Robert Glennon, 'Water Scarcity, Marketing, and Privatization,' 83 Tex L. Rev 1873 (2005) (advocating for a community perspective in water markets in order to channel the potential externalities); see also Robert Glennon, 'The Quest for More Water; Why Markets are Inevitable,' Perc Reports (September 2006), http://perc.org/articles/quest-more-water (hereinafter, Glennon, *The Quest*).

27   Thompson, above note 25, at 701 (analyzing the California case for water markets and the interplay between government rules and traditional institutions that intend to keep water within their jurisdictions).

28   Janet C. Neuman, 'Beneficial Use, Waste, and Forfeiture: the Inefficient Search for Efficiency in Western Water,' 28 Envt'l L. 919, 992 (1998).

29   Glennon, *The Quest*, above note 26.

30   Sax, above note 24, at 38–39.

obstacles to transactions (e.g. review procedures[31] or limits on alienability) unqualifiedly, as free-market environmentalists do, Sax proposes standardized measures to account for externalities in order to promote water exchanges by reducing transaction costs without exempting them from control. Glennon and Pearce,[32] despite denying the free-market paradigm by recognizing that 'a true market-based private sector transfer is a challenge,'[33] argue for removing legal obstacles to water transactions.[34] Glennon and Pearce, using an Arizona case study, criticize particularly the variety of veto points which imply discretionary powers and the tension between bureaucracies.[35] These authors recognize the need for certain regulatory measures or governmental roles, but they do not identify everything that public agencies are expected to do.

Within the policy-oriented scholarship, but closer to the analysis presented in this book, are those who analyze the pre-conditions for markets, mainly for their establishment, but in some cases also for their operation. However, the focus of these scholars is not the roles of government. For example, Neuman offers, based on the evolution of water markets in western US States, an enumeration of the preconditions for water markets without focusing on institutions. The factors she underscores are:

> [W]ater scarcity in the face of increasing demands for both consumptive and instream uses of water; urban-rural competition for water supplies, along with differential economic values for those water uses; environmental

---

31 The term 'anti-commons' was created by Michael Heller to describe those situations where the fragmentation of the bundle of rights is such that it leads to inefficient outcomes because action cannot be taken given the numerous rights to veto. Michael Heller, 'The Tragedy of the Anticommons: Property in the Transition from Marx to Markets,' 111 Harv. L. Rev. 621 (1998). In water markets, the review process has been described as an example of the tragedy of the anti-commons, Stephen N. Bretsen and Peter J. Hill, 'Water markets as a tragedy of the anticommons,' 33 Wm. & Mary Entl. L. & Pol'y Rev. 723 (2009). Others see these review procedures not as a tragedy but as a comedy of the anti-commons, Enrico Bertacchini, Jef de Mot, and Ben Depoorter, 'Never Two Without Three: Commons, Anticommons and Semicommons,' 5 R. of L. & Econ. 163 (2006). These authors analyze water as a semi-commons – the term was created by Smith to describe a regime where private and common property uses interact entailing that exclusion rules and governance rules cohabit making both more precise the definition of rights of use – and argue that semi-commons would suffer from over-exploitation unless these rights to veto were in place. For a general view on the concept of semi-commons, see Henry E. Smith, 'Semicommons Property Rights and Scattering in the Open Fields,' 29 J. Legal Stud. 131; and for its application to water, see Henry E. Smith, 'Governing Water: The Semicommons of Fluid Property Rights,' 50 Ariz. L. Rev. 445 (2008).

32 Robert Glennon and Michael J. Pearce, 'Transferring Mainstream Colorado River Water Rights: The Arizona Experience,' 49 Ariz. L. Rev. 235 (2007).

33 Ibid. at 244.

34 Ibid.

35 Ibid. at 256.

regulation affecting water use; pressure on both surface and groundwater sources; and interstate water disputes.[36]

Most other analyses tend to suggest that a strong legal and institutional system and a fabric of agents with strong social and economic capacities are needed. The goal behind these analyses is the transplant of water markets to developing countries. Thobani,[37] who can be classified as a strong advocate of water markets, lists the requirements for markets to work: scarcity, flexible infrastructure, social approval, and public and private institutional capability. Again, his analysis does not specify what institutional capability means in practice. This book operationalizes the concept.

Also looking at the implementation in developing countries, Bjornlund and McKay present the most comprehensive attempt to offer a list of the preconditions for water markets,[38] although it is also incomplete as far as the roles of government are concerned. Cherry-picking from the experiences in Chile, Australia, and California, Bjornlund and McKay present the conditions that developing countries should ensure in order to have workable water markets, emphasizing the need to keep in mind the particularities of each region where market institutions will be established. Their analysis starts from examples and they base their requirements on past experience. In contrast, the roles analyzed in section 2.5 stem from the economic theories of regulation to then be illuminated with real world examples. Their enumeration, which adopts more of an institutional approach, includes: informational system about market operations, infrastructure to free up the spatial movements of water, settled rules about instream use and environmental protection, regulation of unused water, a complete evaluation of the benefits and costs of markets given the *status quo*, protection mechanisms for third parties, regulation of market microstructure, and delineated property rights across several dimensions (e.g. security of the supply, period of use, constraints on trade or quality).[39] The authors recognize the role of government in infrastructure provision, given its fixed costs and in establishing the market, but they do not go further,[40] and, for example, they do not cover potential monopoly problems. Since their interest is the implantation of these mechanisms in developing countries, these authors do not really analyze whether the different degree and type of governmental involvement is somewhat different in jurisdictions with fully functioning institutions.

---

36   Neuman, above note 28, at 992.
37   Thobani, above note 13.
38   Henning Bjornlund and Jennifer M. McKay, 'Aspects of Water Markets for Developing Countries – Experiences from Australia, Chile and the US,' 7 J. Env't & Dev. Econ. 767 (2002).
39   Ibid. at 788–792.
40   Ibid. at 789.

Lastly, it is worth mentioning, from the economics literature in water markets, the work of Brewer *et al.* who have published empirical studies assessing the performance of water markets in the US States and beyond, both qualitatively[41] and quantitatively.[42] They have looked among other variables at the length of contracts, volume traded, number of contracts to compare the different US States. They also analyzed legal changes in California's water market legislation and set up a framework for comparative, qualitative analysis of water markets across the world,[43] which includes a checklist of features which are positive for water transactions. Some of the features, which in their case stem from experiences across the world, are similar to the roles analyzed in sections 2.3–2.7.

2.3 Governmental roles: market failures

According to neoclassical economics, market failures justify government intervention[44] in markets. There is no absolute consensus on what amounts to a market failure, but the most commonly mentioned reasons for intervening in markets based on a market failure are:[45] the existence of a natural monopoly;

---

41   R. Quentin Grafton, Clay Landry, Gary Libecap, Samuel McGlennon, and Bob O'Brien, 'An Integrated Assessment of Water Markets: A Cross-Country Comparison,' 5 Rev. of Envt'l Econ. & Pol'y 219 (2011).

42   Jedidiah Brewer, Robert Glennon, Alan Ker, and Gary Libecap, *Water Markets in the West: Prices, Trading, and Contractual Forms*, at 39 (2007), Nat'l Bureau of Econ. Research, Working Paper 130002, http://www.icer.it/docs/wp2007/ICERwp30-07.pdf. Jedidiah Brewer, Robert Glennon, Alan Ker, and Gary Libecap, 'Transferring Water in the American West: 1987–2005,' 40 Mich. J. L. Reform 1021 (2007). Jedidiah Brewer, Michael Fleishman, Robert Glennon, Alan Ker, and Gary Libecap, 'Law and the New Institutional Economics: Water Markets and Legal Change in California,' 1987–2005, 26 Wash. U. J. of L. & Pol'y 183, 208 (2008).

43   Grafton *et al.*, above note 41.

44   Deborah Satz, *Why Some Things Should Not Be for Sale: The Moral Limits of Markets*, at 32 (2010) (However, it is only a prima facie case for intervention, since governmental action might be flawed by failures too). Barry C. Field, *Environmental Economics. An introduction*, at 69 (1994) (when discussing the mismatch of social and market values once the environment is taken into account, the author asserts that 'it [a market failure] will often call for public intervention, either to override the markets directly or to rearrange things so that they will work more efficiently').

45   Despite this common basis, there is not a single enumeration of market failures. The enumeration offered compiles the four rationales enumerated by Cooter and Ullen (Robert Cooter and Thomas Ullen, *Law & Economics*, at 43–47 (5th edn, 2007)) and Glicksman and Levy (Robert L. Glicksman and Richard E. Levy, *Administrative Law: Agency Action in Legal Context*, at 15–19 (2010)), which identify four conditions that might impede perfect competition in a market (and consequently the desirable outcome of general equilibrium), thus requiring corrective public policies: monopoly and market power, externalities, public goods, and informational asymmetries. Levi-Faur (David Levi-Faur, 'Market failures,' http://poli.haifa.ac.il/~levi/failure.htm) includes – apart from public goods, information asymmetries, and externalities – natural monopoly – which might be embodied in distortions of

undersupply of public goods; imperfect information; and uncompensated externalities. Government intervention is also warranted to reduce transaction costs since they prevent otherwise beneficial transactions from going forward.[46] Information asymmetry is usually identified with George Akerlof's famous 'Market for lemons'[47] or adverse selection in the insurance market. Such problems have not been much of a concern in water markets. There, information is key, but mostly as it affects the smooth operation of markets via the reduction of transaction costs.

The economic rationales for government intervention in markets may coexist with non-economic reasons for government action such as redistribution or human rights. The coexistence of different rationales does not necessarily mean conflict. Economic and non-economic rationales for government intervention may interact in a number of interesting ways in relation to water, due to its special, social interest. Even though Breyer states that any non-economic argument can be channelled through market failure rationales,[48] certain actions undertaken by government in relation to water markets are not clearly aimed at efficiency. For example, compensation for the effects on the local communities in areas from which water is sold might be the only avenue for completing the transaction while overcoming social unrest and not paying a political price. Portraying this as a transaction cost or as a solution to a market failure seems too great a stretch, despite the fact that its cost might be exceeded by the benefits of the transaction.

Government intervention to address market failures might take different forms, from compulsory regulation to soft law, conveying appropriate incentives to private parties or public agencies participating in the market. By drawing on the experience of current water markets and other environmental and non-environmental markets, this book aims to ascertain the proper degree of intervention after identifying the different failures using economic theory of regulation. The type and degree of government intervention that is warranted by the four rationales (public goods, natural monopoly, externalities, and

competition from the previous list – transaction costs (which have been analyzed under imperfect contracts in a similar fashion as market failures by Cooter and Ullen (Cooter and Ullen, ibid. at 225)) or moral hazard. Lastly, it is worth mentioning the classification of market failures related to an environmental market – CO_2 – offered by Gert Tinggaard (Gert Tinggaard, *Public Choice and Environmental Regulation*, at 48–49 (1998)), which lists political interference and differentiated products, which can be understood as a governmental failure and as a public good, respectively.

46 Levi-Faur, ibid. includes it among market failures. Cf. Cooter and Ullen, ibid. at 225, who analyze it as imperfect contracts.

47 George A. Akerlof, 'The Market for "Lemons": Quality Uncertainty and the Market Mechanism,' 84 Q. J. Econ. 488 (1970).

48 Cf. Stephen Breyer, *Regulation and Its Reform*, at 7–8 (1982) ('Some might argue that there are numerous other justifications for regulatory programs. Through lengthy argument, it should be possible to persuade those who advance other justifications that "market defects" of the sort listed in Chapter One lie at the bottom of their claims').

transaction costs) considered in water markets is difficult to specify with precision, and some overlap exists between the roles for government justified by different failures in water markets.

Government intervention is not cost free, and most costs are borne by society at large.[49] Some governmental actions result in governmental failure, which refers to instances of, for example, inefficient governmental action or regulatory capture. The idea is that the cure – governmental action – must not be worse for social welfare than the disease – market failure. Government intervention is, thus, only justified if it is welfare enhancing, i.e. where it entails more benefits than costs. Ideally, not only should it be beneficial overall, but it should also be crafted in such a way as to minimize costs.[50] Hence, where appropriate, this book also analyzes the comparative advantage of public bodies versus private ones.

This chapter offers a systematic application of the economic rationales for government intervention into water markets to provide a full understanding of which roles are necessary. This systematic analysis is lacking in legal scholarship as the literature review has shown. In particular, it covers: the definition of property rights, which is a public good; the control for externalities; the regulation of natural monopoly infrastructure; and actions to reduce transaction costs. It is important to note that some of the roles are pre-requisites for markets to exist, others are necessary for markets' operation, and still others are crucial for making sure that water markets work well and achieve their goals. This chapter, by identifying the roles warranted for government in water markets, is instrumental in assessing whether different degrees of governmental involvement explain the relative success of California and Spain in using water markets.

2.4 Definition of property rights

2.4.1 Property rights as public goods

As with other markets, a water market requires enforceable and transferable property rights and the enforcement of contracts over these property rights. The definition of property rights is assumed to be a function of government: this definitional role is the uncontested role that all scholars accept. This seems to run afoul of Demsetzian accounts where property rights arise bottom up. In other words, private individuals spontaneously organize to create a property regime delimiting private entitlements to a resource because the value of the

---

49 Griffin, above note 1, at 111 ('Some or even all policy options may have transaction costs that exceed the value of correcting the externality').
50 Manuel Schiffler, 'Intersectoral water markets: a solution for the water crisis in arid areas?' in Kay *et al.*, above note 3, at 362 and 365 ('Government regulation can help in reducing transaction costs by establishing and enforcing a clear framework').

resource has increased and it makes sense to assume the costs of establishing and implementing the regime. Property rights require some type of collective action.[51]

Property rights,[52] as with any efficient legal system, are a public good[53] and this explains why they are supplied by government. Pure public goods are characterized by their non-excludability and by their non-rivalry in consumption.[54] Non-excludability means that those not paying for the good cannot be excluded from accessing or using the good. Non-rivalry means that the consumption by one does not impair consumption by another. Traditional examples of public goods are national defense or lighthouses.[55] It is important to note that neither excludability nor rivalry are binary concepts.

---

51   Carol M. Rose, 'Property as Storytelling: Perspectives from Game Theory, Narrative Theory, Feminist Theory,' 2 Yale J. of L. & Human. 37, 48, 51 (1990). Carol M. Rose, ' "Enough, and as Good" of What?' 81 Nw. U. L. Rev. 417, 438 (1987) ('But a property regime, even though it expands the collective pie, in some ways runs counter to the interest of each individual. In a sense, a regime of property is a gigantic communal agreement not to succumb to the "prisoners' dilemma" – the dilemma of a "game" in which we are collectively better off by cooperation, but individually better off by "defection." ' Rose defends though that despite government enforces property rights, there is a more diffuse enforcement in our everyday life).

52   Jay B. Keshan and Rajiv C. Shaw, 'Deconstructing Code,' 6 Yale J. L. & Tech. 277, 378–80 (2004) (listing property rights regimes and highways among the classic examples of public goods).

53   Rose, ' "Enough, and as Good" of What?,' above note 51, at 438, 'Thus, in some ways, it is the community of recognizers that gives content to "appropriation," and thus the community's recognition of something as "property" is an essential element of the property regime that is supposed to make us all better off. It is in this sense that property is a "public good," or perhaps more accurately a "common good," since the property regime "belongs" in common to the community that follows its precepts.' A clearer case for the public good nature is made in J. Mark Ramseyer, 'Water Law in Imperial Japan: Public Goods, Private Claims, and Legal Convergence,' 18 J. Legal Stud. 51, 52, and 75 (1989), 'a public order that enforces private agreements to respect resource claims is itself a public good. Critical as the public order is to economic growth, few people will have the incentive to create it.' See also Francisco Campos-Ortiz, Louis Putterman, T.K. Ahn, Loukas Balafoutas, Mongoljin Batsaikhan, and Matthias Sutter, *Security of Property as a Public Good: Institutions, Socio-Political Environment and Experimental Behavior in Five Countries*, Discussion Paper No. 6982, 2013, http://ftp.iza.org/dp6982.pdf.

54   Agnar Sandmo, 'Public Goods,' in *The New Palgrave Dictionary of Economics*, above note 1, http://www.dictionaryofeconomics.com/article?id=pde2008_P000245. It is interesting to note that public goods might be partially rival between themselves. For example, trade would benefit from the increase in water certainty that the storage of water could provide, but flood control, another public good, has competing requirements because it implies that storage capacity should not be fully used. See Griffin, above note 1, at 193.

55   Johan den Hertog, 'General theories of Regulation,' in Boudewijn Bouckaert and Gerrit De Gees (eds), *Encyclopedia of Law and Economics*, at 223 and 230 (2000), http://encyclo.findlaw.com/5000book.pdf. What constitutes a public good is not always clear cut. For example, it is not clear cut whether education needs to be publicly provided; it may depend on the person's ideological viewpoint, which will also dictate whether the individual's education or an educated population is the product that matters, because individual education benefits the individual and some may not think in terms of merit goods, while many may not contest that an educated population benefits the undefined public.

The uses of the system of property rights are not rival and exclusion is expensive. Once the regime is in place, all of the residents in the jurisdiction are covered by it, but of course those who actually hold a right or those who may eventually hold a right benefit in a more direct way. In water, I may apply for a right to use water and I may be granted it if I fulfill the requirements; but if I do not, I am excluded.

According to standard economic theory, private markets undersupply public goods due to the free-rider[56] and the sucker effects,[57] which are two sides of the same coin. A private user would prefer not to pay for a public good and to free ride on the provision of it by others who cannot prevent him from consuming it. Likewise, no one wants to contribute to the provision of public goods if the others will cheat and not pay for their use: no one wants to be the sucker. Since this is so, the public interest theory of regulation calls for government intervention in order to supply or subsidize private supply because otherwise the good will be under-provided.[58] The provision of public goods can also be considered a positive externality, given that they benefit agents who have not fully paid for them or who have paid less than their marginal benefit since the costs are apportioned among a larger group.

The analysis of water markets does not start from a state of nature, and the role of government is usually taken as given.[59] Water is no longer an open access resource: when water markets are introduced, government is already involved and water rights already exist, be they conventional property rights with a usufructuary nature or administrative licences, which can be considered a weaker form of property rights.[60] Part of the collective action problem is already solved because government is in place.

---

56 Joseph W. Dellapenna, 'The Market Alternative,' in J.W. Dellapena and J. Gupta (eds), *The Evolution of the Law and Politics of Water*, at 374 (2009) ('[. . .] efficient management of public goods is problematic: If one invests in developing or improving a public good, others who invest or pay nothing ("free riders") will benefit from the investment because they cannot be excluded. This seriously inhibits investment unless the community takes responsibility for ensuring that all (or nearly all) pay for the benefits they receive').

57 Daphna Lewinsohn-Zamir, 'The "conservation game": the possibility of voluntary cooperation in preserving buildings of cultural importance,' 20 Harv. J.L. & Pub. Pol'y 733, 749 (1997).

58 The analysis offered here adopts the normative public interest theory more than the positive public choice one. For an overview of the different theories of regulation, see den Hertog, above note 55, at 223–224. The relative strengths of the interest groups in different jurisdictions play out and determine the divergent outcomes in regulation and its implementation. Nonetheless, it is important to note that other theories of regulation, grounded on public choice analysis, suggest that public goods are provided, and even over-provided, because some powerful interest groups lobby for them. For an analysis, see Richard L. Hasen, 'Clipping Coupons for Democracy: An Egalitarian/Public Choice Defense of Campaign Finance Vouchers,' 84 Cal. L. Rev. 1, 16 (1996). For example, the armament industry lobbies for national defense: even if each of the citizens of a country consume the same amount – although a naval army may be consumed more by coastal zones – this industry sector benefits more from this service funded by the general treasury.

59 Ramseyer, above note 53, at 52.

60 Elinor Ostrom, 'Private and Common Property Rights,' in *Encyclopedia of Law and Economics*, above note 55, at 332.

The role of defining property rights in relation to water markets needs to be qualified. In the majority of cases, government must assume the status quo and can only feasibly make incremental changes. Government is the clear choice in almost all jurisdictions, particularly in those where water is constitutionally recognized as public property and, thus, government has a monopoly over its allocation.

Government's capability to establish and enforce property rights is based on the need not only to overcome collective action problems, but also on the economies of scale of the standardization and enforcement activity.[61] As Libecap shows, such a top-down approach is also problematic because interest groups may push for regulations which are not the most favorable for social welfare, and changes in the status quo might be very difficult if those who have an interest in maintaining it are still powerful. Another account on property theory is that property rights arise or become better defined with scarcity, i.e. when their value increases.[62] Combining Libecap's approach with scarcity, a certain coalition of interests might need to be in place for government to undertake the reform of pre-existing property rights and make rights tradable if they are not outright tradable. This is likely to happen when the value of the asset rises as a result of scarcity, but the stock of the resource is still exploitable. In any case, what prompts government to undertake the definition is beyond the scope of this chapter; however, scarcity and interest group politics, which are not fully independent, are the standard account. This explains how government intervention comes into being, but it does not affect the conclusion that it has to be government which defines the rights.

It is also important to note that the incremental changes mentioned can also happen at a lower level. Irrigation communities or other institutions serving a collectivity might be the right holders of a large quantity of water which is then apportioned to the members of the institution. Some of the irrigation communities allow for internal trading. The rules within this institution could be modified by the institution itself. If this is the case, we may expect that the institution may increase the tradability of the shares held by its members and ensure them that they will not suffer negative consequences if they decide to trade their water. The irrigation institution is acting as a centralized power, much like a governmental entity does.

After justifying this role, the rest of this chapter analyzes its content, i.e. the definition of property rights in water markets. Section 2.4.2 describes the variables to take into account in the definition of property rights. In particular,

---

61 Glicksman and Levy, above note 45, at 15–16, include in their market failures' list standardization of the product (here, the property right to use water) as a public good, while Tinggaard (above note 45, at 49) enumerates it as an independent rationale in his list based on the CO_2 permit market, where he does not include any reference to public goods. For enforcement, see Ramseyer, above note 53.

62 Harold Demsetz, 'Toward a Theory of Property Rights,' 57 Am. Econ. Rev. 347 (1967).

it looks at volume, security, and tradability. The latter analyzes two policy choices government has to make when implementing water markets: whether to define instream flow rights as a way to protect the environment, and who should be allowed to trade. The choices made in relation to water rights' definition, as set out below, have implications for other governmental roles, particularly the reduction of transaction costs.

2.4.2 Variables in the property rights definition

Water is a very complex resource, and the different uses it allows require a very contingent definition of property rights. A definition of property rights has to cope with the complex nature of water by defining the time and place where this fugitive resource can be used, how much can be used, and how. The inherent complexity will also inform section 2.5, which is concerned with externalities, since any change, such as modifying the place of use or type of use as a result of a transaction, can have myriad effects on the river and its users.

In the western US States, prior appropriation rights are defined across the following characteristics: source of supply, amount, location of the point of diversion, use, location of the place of use,[63] timing, and point of return flow.[64] Appropriative rights traditionally have a further characteristic: date of diversion, which would define their relative position when water runs low. These characteristics usually appear one way or another in all water rights, no matter the jurisdiction or whether it follows a prior appropriation system. Not all characteristics need to be defined at the outset for all property rights. For example, in some jurisdictions, some may be left to the discretion of an agency to decide according to the changing circumstances. This is the case where the apportionment in times of drought is not defined in the right itself but left to the decision of the responsible water agency. Also, other regulations may indirectly define water rights. For example, water quality is in a sense implied by the characteristics on the list since it will depend on, among other factors, the type of use. However, it is likely that other regulations targeting quality will affect the rights.

Bjornlund and McKay, analyzing the potential of water markets to be implemented in developing economies, suggest that to maximize the outcome of markets, the following characteristics should identify a property right: (a) 'Security of supply specified as the probability of receiving the volumetric entitlement' (including whether a government has the authority to cancel water rights); (b) 'Reliability of delivery, specified as the period from ordering

---

63 §1260 of the Cal. Water Code regulates the content of the application to appropriate a right. See also the template to apply at the SWRCB website, http://www.waterboards.ca.gov/waterrights/water_issues/programs/permits/.

64 For the regulation of changes in water rights in relation to short-term water transfers, see §1726.b.2 of the Cal. Water Code.

to receiving the water'; (c) 'The period during which the water can be used'; (d) 'The constraints on trade, such as spatial constraints, limitations on trade between sectors in the economy'; (e) 'Some indication of the expected quality of the water'; (f) 'The duration of the water right, either indefinite or for a specified period of time.'[65] Bjornlund and McKay do not suggest a particular content for each of them; they just suggest that the regulators should take them into account.

It is important to highlight at this point that in property law literature it is well established that the more defined property rights are, the more transactions will take place. It can also be said that the more defined property rights are, the fewer uncompensated externalities will exist, because the encroachment on other rights will be noticeable and accounted for. It must be noted, however, that including more variables in a property right may decrease the fungibility of that right to use water and make it less attractive for potential buyers. The more open-ended the definition of one of these characteristics is at the outset, the more will be defined down the road indirectly through the review of transactions or other administrative powers. These later definitions may involve the discretion of the administration and increase the uncertainty surrounding water rights. Different jurisdictions may strike different balances, but each should aim at reducing transaction costs for water markets to work properly.

There is one variable defined in any form of water right directly or indirectly which has an impact on water transactions: volume. It has an impact because the way it is defined may reduce the potential externalities. It is analyzed first. Volume is also related to the two variables: security and tradability. These variables are studied next. Security is related to how much power public agencies or courts have to modify the right held by the individual right holder and how unexpected that modification could be. Tradability refers to the easiness with which a right to use water can change hands. Both security and tradability are defined at the outset, by regulations and decisions affecting the right while it is in force, and by the review when the right is transferred.

a. Volume

Notwithstanding markets, the volume of a water right is defined in terms of total water allocated or units of water per unit of time. Paper rights sometimes defined the volume of a right in a quantity larger than the actual quantity used. Even when accurate, the volume is usually defined as the volume diverted and farmers, the main water users, divert more water than they consume. For

---

65   Bjornlund and McKay, above note 38, at 791. Michael Warburton, 'Toward Greater Certainty in Water Rights? Public Interests Require Inherent "Uncertainty" to Support Constitutional Governance of Our State's Waters,' 36 McGeorge L Rev. 139, 143 (2005) (describing the inherent variability in water that makes difficult to sharply define property rights). See ibid. at 142, for a claim that uncertainty is also useful to balance private rights and public interests.

example, when using flood irrigation, a farmer diverts a lot of water and part of it goes back to the river via return flow. The mismatch between diversion and consumption may complicate planning for water agencies. The result has been that many streams are over-allocated and downstream users have been using the return flows of upstream users. This interdependency translates in more likelihood of externalities if water rights are transferable. Defining the amount tradable for each right or the right itself according to the volume consumed, not the total volume granted in the right or the volume diverted, would reduce potential externalities.[66] This definition ensures that fewer external effects will arise than if the exchange covers the full right on paper because allowing someone to transfer a higher amount than he or she has been consuming would allow the buyer to consume all of it and, thus, there will be less water in the river for environmental users and for other users who had been relying on the return flow. In prior appropriation jurisdictions, return flow is used by downstream users. Thus, a substantial amount of all this water may enter the production function of several other users and should not be transferred by the user who used to generate the return flow.[67] In permit-based jurisdictions, it is likely that subsequent permits may have been granted for that returned water. In sum, it is probable that water not consumed is being used by other agents and if suddenly the full volume of the right as granted on paper is consumed as a result of a transaction, even if there are no other changes in point of diversion or type of use, other agents will be affected.

Transactions negatively affecting third parties or the environment are not allowed, so it is likely that on a case-by-case basis not more than the consumptive use will be allowed to be transferred. If those effects are pre-empted or reduced by defining rights according to consumptive use at the outset, there is no, or less, need to review the proposed transactions.[68] Hence, it should translate into a leaner review procedure. This also shows how the different roles are related. Some type of averaging on top of the definition of the transferrable right as amount consumed is advisable. Climatological variability affects both the flow of the river and demand since farmers will not withdraw as much water in wet years as in dry ones where rainfall drops. Averaging or calculating the amount consumed according to models which take into account the relevant variables will inevitably offer only an approximate value, but still, relying on them will decrease the burden for private parties and make transactions easier.

66 Mark Squillace, 'The Water Marketing Solution,' 42 ELR 10800, 10805 (2012).
67 Pulver, above note 4, at 698, describes the partial non-rivalness and partial non-excludability that water presents. This characterization might be a consequence of the system itself since water rights are usually defined as diverted quantity minus return flow, at least, in what water markets are concerned.
68 In Spain, to prevent the transfer of too much water, the amount of water that can be transferred is calculated according to the average of the last five years. Art. 69.1 of the Texto Refundido de la Ley de Aguas (Consolidated Water Act), RCL No. 1 (BOE 2001, 176); implemented by 345.1.a RD 849/1986.

The definition of volume in property rights can still promote transactions in another way: favoring the internalization of positive externalities. Positive externalities may also arise from a transaction but they are not generally a source of concern. Nevertheless, they can be market boosts. If there are three users in a river: C (upstream), B (intermediate), and A (downstream), and A buys water from C, B (the intermediate user) will see more water flowing in front of his property and may need less energy to divert water. However, those effects are minimal and it is not easy to account for them. Accounting for them will most probably increase transaction costs more than it would increase benefits. However, one positive externality that may occur, an increase in the amount of water available if A consumes less than C, could be easily internalized. In fact, California's imported water regulations solve this problem. When water is imported into a basin and it is added to the pre-existing flow, the importer might not use up all the water, thus increasing the return flow. This increase, once abandoned by the importer, can be used by other parties, but the importer can at any point in time discontinue the importation of water,[69] consume a greater quantity of it than he did previously,[70] or sell it. Even if such a reform is not central for market purposes, it could boost the market.[71]

Lastly, a dimension of volume which clearly affects security is whether and how the right is affected by low availability of water. This is described in the next section.

b. Security

Security, which could also be called certainty,[72] encapsulates the idea of the right holder being sure that his right is not going to be affected by arbitrary restrictions, and that, instead, regulations are going to be pretty foreseeable. Security has a clear impact on how willing individual users will be to trade their rights.

Security depends on how subject to discretionary administrative decisions, related to the market or not, water rights are. Issues that affect security are, thus, manifold. First, purportedly it depends on the nature of the right: administrative licences could be more subject to administrative powers than traditional common law property rights. Those powers where they are discretionary will

---

69   Scott Slater, *California Water Law and Policy*, at Ch § 1-2 2.08 (6) (2015).
70   Scott S. Slater, 'A Prescription for Fulfilling the Promise of a Robust Water Market,' 36 McGeorge L. Rev. 253, 263 (2005) (citing *Stevens v Oakdale Irrigation Dist.*, 90 P.2d 58, 60–62 (Cal. 1939)).
71   Charles J. Meyers and Richard A. Posner, *Toward an improved market in water resources*, at 27 (1971). Meyers and Posner in 1973 proposed something similar. Their proposal would have allowed a *de facto* use of the return flow without rights being acquired to it, and provided the buyer does not take any action regarding that return flow.
72   Legislative Analyst Office, The Role of Water Transfers in Meeting California's Water Needs, at 12 (1999).

increase uncertainty. These powers include, among others, the reduction of the water right if the user is misusing it or the forfeiture of the said right if the user no longer uses it.

Second, and relatedly, how environmental protection is provided also affects security: open-ended standards could make regulation unforeseeable and open the door to arbitrary considerations. Environmental protection is seen by some consumptive rights holders as a threat to their rights since government may encroach on their rights to ensure the environment gets its share. In some jurisdictions, such regulations may be considered takings and deserve compensation, but in others they may be considered a burden to be borne by the right holder.

Third, it matters for security how the effects of drought are shared among users: whether the apportionment is defined at the outset as with prior appropriation systems or whether it is left to the discretion of the agency in the midst of emergencies. Apportionment can be defined beforehand. This is the case in a pure prior appropriation system where water is allocated according to temporal priority. Another system would be one where rights are defined as a percentage of the flow[73] or even a system that ranks types of uses[74] based on social value and grants priority to those ranked higher. Those ranks can also be seen as a protection to those, such as farmers, that would feel more acutely the uncertainty of water supply.[75] The alternative to those foreseeable systems is deciding on the allocation once the drought is occurring.

The direct or indirect mechanisms have different impacts on water trading because a buyer might be reluctant to enter into a transaction if the delivery of the seller's water is not reliable and it is difficult to calculate the probability of its occurrence. For the purpose of water markets, rules that define shortage allocation at the outset are preferable, assuming government has not been erratic in its enforcement in the past. If rules are defined beforehand and consistently enforced, it does not matter if the assignment does not respond to a higher value of water because water markets could correct the allocation designed by these priority rules since in water markets the marginal value of each user would be equalized. However, it would be better to aim at a more efficient initial allocation where possible to reduce the need to enter into transactions because those invariably involve costs. However, security crumbles in the

---

73   Mateen Thobani, 'Tradable Property Rights to Water. How to improve water use and resolve water conflicts,' 34 Public Policy for the Private Sector 3 (1995).

74   This is the case in Spain. Art. 60 of the Texto Refundido de la Ley de Aguas (Consolidated Water Act), RCL No. 1 (BOE 2001, 176).

75   Barton H. Thompson, Jr., 'Uncertainty and Markets in Water Resources,' 36 McGeorge L. Rev. 117, 127 (2005).
     In Spain, the Water Act establishes a ranking of uses to inform the decision of granting an administrative permit to use water, see Art. 60.3 of the Texto Refundido de la Ley de Aguas (Consolidated Water Act), RCL No. 1 (BOE 2001, 176).

absence of those rules or emergency regulations superseding the normal rules of priority responding to a harsh drought.[76]

Lastly, agencies reviewing water transactions can also affect how secure or certain the right is. Users have feared that their water rights would be revised if they were to enter into water transactions because that could be taken as evidence that the seller did not need the water or has been misusing it. Regulation needs to ensure farmers that entering into a transaction will not be used as evidence to reduce or forfeit their right. However, even if they enter into transactions, the standards applied by the agencies to review transactions could be very open-ended and it could be difficult to predict beforehand whether or not a transaction will be approved. Open-ended standards of review will thwart the possibility of users to plan ahead or make them reluctant to enter into transactions. Consistent precedent might mitigate this concern.

c. Tradability

A market cannot exist if there is nothing to trade. There may be so little water that nobody wants to sell it because the marginal value for any user is very high. However, beyond the physical availability of water, for a market to exist legal water rights have to be tradable.

Schlager and Ostrom identify five 'rights' which can make up the bundle of any right holder: access, withdrawal, management, exclusion, and alienation.[77] The relevant one for participating in a water market is precisely the right to buy or lease the resource (alienation). However, not even alienation can be an absolute right, given how complex water naturally is and how the actions of one user impact others. This implies that some mechanism to compensate for external-ities or to stop transactions producing them must be in place. The level at which such a decision is made matters, since externalities taken into account are only those within the jurisdiction's territory. Section 2.5 on externalities shows how a review of externalities indirectly contributes to the definition of property rights.

Tradability of rights may be restricted preventing certain types of transactions from happening because those create many externalities. If that is the case, the allowed transaction should receive less scrutiny, i.e. the review should be less

---

76 This is the case in New Mexico where the seniority of alfalfa farmers was not respected in the recent drought. See Felicity Barringer, 'New Mexico Farmers Seek "Priority Call" as Drought Persists,' at A11, *New York Times*, 27 March 2013.

77 Elinor Ostrom and Edella Schlager, 'Property Rights Regimes and Natural Resources: A Conceptual Analysis,' 68 Land Economics 249 (1992) (they consider that the different rights can be seen as a cumulative scale moving from possessing the minimal through full ownership. They also argue that the different rights can be assigned to different individuals. In addition, for regimes of commons, management, exclusion, and alienation can be decisions taken at the collective level; so instead of granting the right to manage the resource, an individual has the right to participate in the collective decision on how to manage it).

demanding. For example, some jurisdictions may not allow non-consumptive users to trade with consumptive users since more water will be diverted from the stream and that is highly likely to produce negative externalities.

Geography may impact tradability. On the one hand, it may decrease it. It may decrease it because of the lack of infrastructure, but provided water is very valuable, private parties may invest in it. Another source of restrictions is regulatory: some transactions between certain areas may be prohibited or subject to a demanding approval process. This may also respond to the aim of preventing externalities. For example, downstream to upstream sales translate into less flow in part of the river so they may not be allowed because externalities would predictably be high. However, those regulatory restrictions based on geography may also respond to political motives. Among other effects, keeping the water in the region may ensure that there are no job losses. For example, in California, lower level administrative bodies have established restrictions in relation to groundwater exports.[78]

On the other hand, tradability may be increased because rights are meant to be more fungible within the region, most probably at the cost of ignoring certain *de minimis* externalities or a public agency making up for them. Schemes where rights are fungible are more active transfer areas. In some areas, there are federal or state projects where the right holder is the state and federal agency and the place of use for those rights is all or part of the territory covered by the project. The users have contract rights with the agency. Within these projects' jurisdictions, if a market is set up, the reliability of supply is backed by the governmental entity[79] and it may, therefore, ignore or minimize certain externalities.[80] This is the case of transfers within Northern Colorado Water Conservancy District (NCWCD), which receives water from the Colorado-Big Thompson Project (C-BT), a project of the United States Bureau of Reclamation (USBR). In NCWCD, shareholders have fungible entitlements and transaction costs are very low.[81]

d. Institutional v. individual agents

In revisiting property rights in water with a view to promoting water markets, there is an issue that governments must confront. This is a policy choice that

---

78   Ellen Hanak, *Who Should Be Allowed to Sell Water in California? Third-Party Issues and the Water Market*, at 25–33 (2003).

79   Brian E. Gray, 'A Primer on California Water Transfer Law,' 31 Ariz. L. Rev. 745, 779–780 (1994) (reviews transfers by contractors of irrigation districts being the institutional actors the ones holding the rights).

80   For analysis of markets within districts, see C. Carter Ruml, 'The Coase Theorem and Western U.S. Appropriative Water Rights,' 45 Nat. Resources J. 169, 187 (2005).

81   Charles W. Howe, 'Protecting Public Values in a Water Market Setting: Improving Water Markets to Increase Economic Efficiency and Equity,' 3 U. Denv. Water L. Rev. 357, 359 (2000).

will have profound implications for the market: whether to grandfather in current institutional water right holders or to grant the right to trade water entitlements to the individuals being supplied by those institutions.

Beyond the rights held by state or federal agencies, it is often the case that current right holders are usually institutions – irrigation districts, mutuals, or water utility companies[82] – not the individuals (farmers or domestic consumers). Individual farmers usually hold shares in the institution or contractual entitlements to receive a certain amount of water, but not water rights. In urban areas, the situation is similar: consumers are supplied by agencies or companies and pay for the amount they consume. A system where households buy and sell the amount of water they have contracted for is not feasible because transaction costs will abound. However, it is possible, and even advisable, under certain circumstances, to set up a market where farmers can participate even if initially they were not the right holders. Farmers could lease their share or contractual rights to neighboring farmers or to others outside their irrigation organization. Large industrial water users also could be expected to participate in a water market selling the amount of water they have contracted for with a utility or their self-supply.

Not only it is more feasible to imagine individual irrigators selling their excess deliveries than urban households doing the same, but individual irrigators' water entitlements are the ones expected to be brought to the market.[83] We expect a market to give the proper incentives to farmers, encouraging them to adopt efficient irrigation practices. Water markets are conceived as an alternative to mandated technological improvements in irrigation and to subsidy programmes that come out of taxpayer pockets to achieve this goal. Making individual entitlements that did not amount to a fully-fledged tradable water right should also increase the number of agents in the market, making it more competitive; but this is not a necessary measure to achieve a working market in all places.

Government will need to make individual assignments transferable in those jurisdictions where the institutional bodies providing irrigation water are not able to convey the proper incentives to the farmers. An alternative option is to modify some of the internal rules of these bodies. For example, in analyzing water markets in the western US States, institutional bodies where the board is elected by citizens of the area as a whole are supposed to be blocking market

---

82   In the western US States, in 1978, 56.1 per cent of the acreage irrigated were self-supplied or provided by unincorporated mutuals, 16 per cent by incorporated mutuals, and 24.8 per cent by irrigation districts (a type of political subdivision of state government), see Stephen N. Bretsen and Peter J. Hill, 'Irrigation Institutions in the American West,' 25 UCLA J. Envtl. L. & Pol'y 283, 292 (2006–2007).

83   Glennon, 'Water Scarcity,' above note 26, at 1888 ('Let's be clear about one thing: we are talking about transfers from rural farming areas to cities. Most of the water that will sustain the expected 15 million additional Californians is going to come from agriculture. It has to').

transfers while those elected by the farmers are not.[84] If that is the case, certain modifications of the organizational rules may have the same, or a similar, effect as allowing individuals to trade.[85] Voting rules are the first thing that need to be modified. The potential mandated amendment of the organizational rules would have to take into account disparities in acreage of the different right holders if that is a variable which has weight in voting. A farmer owning a big part of the acreage within the district may have incentives to block external transactions in order to buy the water himself at a cheaper price internally since he will not face external competition. An ancillary reform if individual users are not allowed to trade in the market would be to establish how financial gains from water transfers should be distributed. If part of the gains of a transaction are received by the organization or shared among the members, those may have fewer interests to block the transaction. In general, establishing that individual entitlements as tradable should cut across all the different institutions, while changing organizational rules would be more case-specific.

Even assuming that interests are not perfectly conveyed, other costs have to be accounted for when deciding whether or not individuals' rights should be transferable: there are substantial differences between the market structure where mainly institutions participate and the one where individual agents join. In the former, transactions are likely to be simpler because there would be fewer parties, which would likely be repeat players, well-acquainted with their interlocutors, and more capable of obtaining information. Additional concerns relate to how community externalities will be accounted for.[86] Farmers and districts operating in farming areas should be less inclined to consider the effects on the community if they only act in their self-interest, but there are claims of a sense of solidarity within the farming community.[87]

The opposite model, allowing individual farmers to trade – requiring the transformation of their shares in irrigation districts or their rights under delivery contracts into transferable entitlements – has a main advantage: it would give individual farmers the appropriate incentives and increase the number of agents in the market. But there are two disadvantages with this option: one concerns the financing of fixed costs of infrastructure and another concerns the

---

84 For an analysis of mutual's policies regarding transfers, see Thompson, above note 25, at 724–725. For an analysis of the institutional obstacles in water districts, see ibid. at 728–730. For a comparison of different institutions regarding how they deal with community impacts, see ibid. See also Charles W. Howe, Dennis R. Schurmeier, and W. Douglas Shaw, Jr., 'Innovative Approaches to Water Allocation: The Potential for Water Markets,' 22 Water Resources Res. 439, 443 (1986) (analysis of the trading in the C-BT).

85 Thompson, above note 25, at 731.

86 Thompson, above note 25, at 733–734.

87 Kyle Emerick and Dean Lueck, *Economic Organization and the Lease-Ownership Decision in Water*, at 13, 12 May 2010, Working Paper, http://papers.ssrn.com/sol3/papers.cfm? abstract_id=1605523. See ibid. at 25 for the empirical evidence that irrigation organizations will consider the third party impacts where negotiating the length of the contracts.

atomization of entitlements, i.e. rights to use and, thus, sell water will be smaller than in the status quo. Allowing individual farmers to trade their entitlements may reduce the number of water users in an area because they might be transferring the entitlements to external users. Thus, the fixed costs of building and operating the infrastructure in that area, which has important economies of scale, would be apportioned among a smaller number of payers. This is a similar concern to the one raised where wealthy households are installing solar panels and disconnecting from the grid. In water, this scenario is one of the justifications for regulations capping sales outside the region, which is very difficult to disentangle from protectionism or from community externalities avoidance as set out below. There are, however, other ways of ensuring that adequate funds remain to finance infrastructure provision while allowing individual farmers to trade water rights. In fact, the legal institution of subrogation of the buyer in the seller's duties should be enough. Australia offers a good example of how to transition from institutional to individual agents participating in the market. It allows farmers to trade their water entitlements by allowing farmers to convert their shares or delivery rights into transferable property rights. To solve the apportionment of costs, the company or association running the irrigation infrastructure is allowed to charge a termination fee[88] to those users that permanently trade their water after converting their shares or delivery entitlements into tradable water rights.[89] A similar idea was also proposed by Meyers and Posner in the 1970s for the water markets in the United States. Their proposal, building on traditional contractual obligations, subrogated the transferee to the duties of the transferor regarding the payment of construction costs of the conveyance facilities and also required the transferee to pay for the operation and maintenance costs if the number of remaining users was insufficient to cover those costs.[90] The latter might be a better solution because it does not require an *ex-ante* calculation of operating and managing costs.

Choosing an individual over an institutional market model may not only affect the number of participants in the market, but it also may affect transaction costs in the market. If small sellers participate in the market, the asymmetries between them and more sophisticated players, such as municipal water utilities, might be troublesome. First, small agents might not have access to the same amount of information. Second, and relatedly, transactions might require a higher number of parties. If a large buyer needs to contract with several small ones, transaction costs could become insurmountable.[91] Consider, for instance,

---

88 Vicky Waye and Christina Son, 'Regulating the Australian Water Market,' 22 J. Envt'l L. 431, 445 (2010).

89 Ibid. at 441.

90 Meyers and Posner, above note 71, at 22.

91 For transaction costs of transactions where small holders participate, see Sarah Hollinstead, 'Water is Not Liquid: Securitization, Transaction Costs, and California's Water Market,' 33 Colum. J. Envt'l L. 323, 347 (2008).

the cost of ensuring that each of these sellers will receive enough water in the dry season to cover their obligations. Sometimes, the institutional actor has the authority to restrict water rights during drought periods or decide annually on the allocation to each seller. Hence, dealing with the institution itself would decrease uncertainty. Under an individual market model, an umbrella institution would be advisable. Government might have to play in the water market a role similar to the one it started to play in the mortgage market with Freddie Mac and Fannie Mae: securitization.[92] The description of the market maker role elaborates on these questions.

2.4.3 Instream flow protection

Instream flow is necessary for a number of activities occurring in rivers and services provided by rivers. Water flow is a public good for certain uses, mainly non-consumptive ones.[93] Beyond navigation and recreation, there are certain functions of instream flow which benefit the undefined collectivity. Rivers provide ecosystem services and instream flow is indispensable to support wildlife.[94] These services depend on many of the attributes that also define water rights: quantity, quality, location, and timing.

Protecting instream flow entails protecting the quantity of water in rivers and streams and its quality. The quality of that water is regulated separately through federal and state water quality standards or cap-and-trade systems based on pollution allowances, which is not the focus here. It is important to note that markets can have a certain impact on quality since, on the one hand, it is dependent on the quantity of water available and, on the other hand, a transfer may imply a change of use which may change water's composition. A water right traditionally used to irrigate might be now be used by a cattle farmer, with obvious impacts on the return flow composition. This should be picked up by the externalities review. The focus of this section on property rights definition is on quantity.

There are two main ways government can provide for instream flow protection: regulation and property rights. This role might not be necessary in itself to have a water use rights market; what is necessary for the existence of an efficient water market is that externalities to the environment are internalized

---

92 Ibid. 352–366.
93 Multiple boats can navigate in a river, until it gets congested, demonstrating that rivalry is not a binary characteristic. Excluding some boats from navigating is possible but may be too costly unless there is a risk of congestion. In addition, navigation enhances commerce which is a relatively uncontested welfare-enhancing activity and, thus, a type of public good. Carol M. Rose, 'The Comedy of the Commons: Custom, Commerce, and Inherently Public Property,' 53 U. Chi. L. Rev. 711 (1986).
94 In general, see Kate A. Brauman, Gretchen C. Daily, T. Ka'eo Duarte, and Harold A. Mooney, 'The Nature and Value of Ecosystem Services: An Overview Highlighting Hydrologic Services,' 32 Annu. Rev. Environ. Resources 67 (2007).

because otherwise there is no guarantee that transactions are socially beneficial and the environment and the community at large will be footing the bill. However, how government tackles environmental protection of river ecosystems has an important impact on water markets.

Government can protect instream flow by imposing duties on private parties. Regulation can take the form of rules or standards, i.e. it can establish a minimum flow requirement, reducing directly the existing consumptive rights, or it can rely on some narrative standards triggered by different circumstances such as a review of water rights or an application to build new water infrastructure. This regulation based on standards creates the most uncertainty, heavily impacting the security dimension.[95] It might nonetheless be mitigated as precedent accumulates, and may translate down the road into curtailments.

In the context of market exchanges, to enforce instream flow requirements, agencies can ensure that the instream flow requirements would still be satisfied after the transactions when reviewing them.[96] If the government has not established instream flow requirements, it could still attempt to protect instream flow by reviewing market transactions on the basis of whether they accord with the public interest, as is currently done in certain jurisdictions, or some similar principles such as non-injury to the environment.[97]

---

95 The effect is similar to the controversy regarding the Delta smelt; cutbacks were placed in certain areas by a Federal court based on the Endangered Species Act. See Joel K. Bourne, Jr., 'California's pipe dream,' at 132 and 144, *National Geographic*, April 2010.

96 Imagine A sells 1 hm^3 of water – which is the amount he consumes according to the estimation tables mentioned – to his upstream neighbor, B. The instream flow in that area of the river has to be at least 10 hm^3/s. Hence, if before the transaction the water flowing between B and A was 11 hm^3/s, the agency in charge of the review should authorize it, without discretion involved. This scenario is much more certain than if the parties lacked guidelines and had to calculate the average consumptions across seasons themselves, adopt a precautionary measurement (the lowest amount consumed), and the agency could correct it.

97 §1255 of the Cal. Water Code, 'The board shall reject an application when in its judgment the proposed appropriation would not best conserve the public interest.' Even though they seem to point to the same idea, the policy of California suggests that public trust, public interest and protection of the environment are separate rationales, http://www.waterboards.ca.gov/waterrights/water_issues/ programs/instream_flows/docs/ab2121_0210/adopted 050410instreamflowpolicy.pdf. California's petition for long-term transfers have to include reference to the measures required by the California Department of Fish and Game regarding the mitigation of the transfer's effect, see http://www.waterboards.ca.gov/waterrights/publications_forms/ forms/docs/trans_long_petition.pdf (§1735 of the Cal. Water Code). §1243 of the Cal. Water Code establishes that 'in determining the amount of water available for appropriation for other beneficial uses, the board shall take into account, whenever it is in the public interest, the amounts of water required for recreation and the preservation and enhancement of fish and wildlife resources.' For an analysis of the evolution of 'beneficial use,' see Gary D. Libecap, 'Water Rights and Markets in the U.S. Semiarid West: Efficiency and Equity Issues,' in Daniel H. Cole and Elinor Ostrom, *Property in Land and Other Resources*, at 401–402 (2013). Regarding the markets in instream water markets and the possibility of private entities to participate in certain states, see Rob Harmon on instream water markets (webchat), Aguanomics (3 December 2009), http://www.aguanomics.com/2009/12/rob-harmon-on-in-stream-water-markets.html.

The establishment of instream flow may be contentious in over-allocated streams though because it may reduce current rights. At the moment of their establishment, they could create uncertainty but after those initial times, minimum instream flow requirements provides buyers and sellers with greater security because it reduces the discretion of the administration. By knowing *ex-ante* which limits they have to conform to, private agents can plan with more security and assess how their transaction fares in relation to those requirements.

Reduction of current rights due to these mandatory instream flow requirements can also motivate water market transactions by prompting right holders to make up for the lost supply through water transactions. In fact, this has been the proposal put forward by some scholars, and it has taken place in practice in California's Central Valley, despite the fact that curtailments did not envision that. Stern suggests that a good way to enhance a practically non-existent water market and to de-stress hydro resources might be an approach similar to cap-and-trade. Caps on extraction from water-stressed areas should be tighter – i.e. the quantity of water allowed to be extracted under current permits or rights should be lower – than in areas where water is more abundant. Caps, following the European Trading Regime for CO_2 which limits emissions for power plants and large industries, would be applied only to large water right holders. Tighter caps on extraction in water-stressed areas, which are similar to the abovementioned curtailments in rights, would prompt individuals dependent on water from these areas to search for suppliers from more abundant areas. Stern's proposal would serve environmental goals and allow for the restoration of watercourses while boosting competition in wholesale water markets.[98] Stern's idea is similar to the proposal from Waye and Son to enhance the Australian water market even though the latter does not target only large right holders. They suggest capping extraction by all water right holders to prompt them to consider water purchases to satisfy their demands if their rights do not entitle them to enough water after the capping.[99]

The second way to protect instream flow in a rule-like way is to sharply define non-consumptive property rights to the flow,[100] which will increase the types of rights that exist over water. Once the rights are defined and allocated – perhaps by allowing the purchase of rights from existing water right holders who put the water to consumptive uses and leaving the water in the stream[101]

---

98 Jon Stern, 'Introducing Competition into England and Wales water industry: Lessons from the UK and EU energy market liberalization,' 18 Utility Pol'y 120, 121–122 (2010).

99 Waye and Son, above note 88, at 437 ('It was also the scene for the second step necessary to facilitate water trading, the introduction of a cap upon further extraction of water. Once water users could no longer extract additional water from the Basin, they were required to purchase water from those with excess capacity to meet supply shortfalls').

100 Huffman, 'Markets,' above note 8, at 430–434.

101 K. William Easter and Gershon Feder, 'Water institutions, incentives and markets,' in D.D. Parker and Y. Tsur (eds), *Decentralization and Coordination of Water Resource Management*, at 133 and 135 (1997).

– market transactions would have to respect the property rights in instream flow just as they must respect other third party consumptive rights. Thus, it is easier to determine if a transaction between A and B affects the water instream assigned to C – which might be, for example, a municipality that holds rights over the instream water near the municipal riverside park – if C's rights to instream water are defined as a certain volume of water per unit of time, than if C's enjoyment of nature was just protected under the broad public interest standard in the review of a transaction. Both rules – mandatory instream flows and property right definition over instream flow – will achieve the same level of security.

The difference between establishing mandatory quantities of instream flow and property rights lies in whether an administrative agency or the market is eliciting the preferences. Government may base its decision about minimum instream flows on scientific data and revealed social preferences, which are incredibly difficult to measure for non-market goods, but also, according to the ferocious critiques of administrative management, on the interests of lobby groups which have captured them. Given the difficulties of measuring the societal value of public goods in the administrative process, the governmental decision may be pictured as arbitrary. Thus, protecting instream flow by buying water rights could be a better solution to avoid some instances of governmental failures and also eliminate the possibility of takings challenges. Private parties could obtain instream flow rights and contribute, thus, to environmental protection or government could buy those instream flow rights using taxpayer money and, thus, internalize the cost of its actions. One successful example of government protecting the environment by acquiring water rights is the Environmental Water Account experience in the San Francisco Bay Delta.[102] Government could also be the provider of these public goods, in the market and beyond, charging not the general treasury but the groups with more intense preferences over them if they are easy to identify,[103] such as fishermen. Also,

---

102   Richard Howitt and Ellen Hanak, 'Incremental Water Market Development: The California Water Sector 1985–2004,' 30 Can. Water Resources J. 73, 76 (2005) ('Environmental water accounted for nearly a quarter of all purchases between 1995 and 2001, and 35% of the total in 2001').

103   Ronald H. Coase, 'The Lighthouse in Economics,' 17 J. L&Econ. 357 (1974). Lighthouses are local public goods since they are not excludable and non-rival. Nonetheless the population that benefits from them is more targetable. Of course, all of society wants fewer maritime accidents, and the coastal municipalities even more so, but those who benefit most from it are the ship-owners. They could be targeted to fund the lighthouses. Direct use of the lighthouses is difficult to measure and monitor, but proxies could be found, such as a fee for harbors, which might ease the administration. Despite the fact that some ships might free-ride, such as the ones just crossing the waters of a country without tying up in any harbor of it, the ships that moor, knowing that several others will cooperate, will not argue against the fee imposed. Similarly a special tax on ships' ownership could be levied. Both could be centralized and used to fund publicly or privately run lighthouses all across the coast.

water market transactions could be the source of earmarked funds to ensure the protection of the water environment by buying rights.

An important question relating to the definition of property rights in instream flow is who should be the holders of these rights. In some US States, only public agencies can hold those rights, but private parties cannot. If only government will be entitled to buy water rights for these non-consumptive uses, the public choice critiques and problems regarding the measurement of social preferences would still apply, but less so because even though government will be paying with taxpayer money, it would internalize the cost more than imposing mandatory instream flows.[104] There would still be the possibility of government purchases favoring certain groups at the expense of all taxpayers if government is one of the potential right holders, even though the process should be more transparent than the regulatory one.

Free-market environmentalists, while regarding instream flow requirements as a taking, claim that like-minded people can channel their preferences through market transactions expressing their willingness to pay for such environmental goods if non-consumptive property rights are defined.[105] They do not fear under-provision, given the difference in preference intensity between those who care deeply about the environment and the general population. In their opinion, the decision to protect instream flow should be left to the market. Hence, right holders should only be private parties (environmental groups or fishing clubs).[106] The general population will benefit, provided that consumption is not rival. There have been experiences that may offer support for the free market environmentalist argument such as the Oregon Water Fund[107] or the BEF Water Restoration Certificate (WRC) commercialized by the Bonneville Environmental Foundation (BEF), which enables buyers to take responsibility for their

---

104   The amount to allocate in these programmes would be decided in the political process, and the nature of the political process plays a role here. In fact, there are some economic advantages in using the political arena instead of the marketplace even when purchases and not regulation are at stake. If the decision is taken by public authorities, those who favor the provision of a public good are less afraid of free-riders and of being suckers. If they vote for those candidates or parties advocating the provision of public goods and they win, the public good will be provided and all will have to chip in since part of the tax revenues will be allocated to fund it. If they do not win, their loss has been low. This point is made by Lewinsohn-Zamir when analyzing the different arenas where our sets of preferences, citizen or consumer preferences, are expressed, see Daphna Lewinsohn-Zamir, 'Consumer Preferences, Citizen Preferences, and the Provision of Public Goods,' 108 Yale L.J. 377, 395 (1998). The amount of funds might be directly assigned to restoration programmes (such as the accounts set in §79075-7 of the Cal. Water Code which allocates funds for different watershed protection programmes – which include protection of instream flow) or indirectly, i.e. through the funds assigned to the agency or agencies' budgets.

105   See in general David M. Gillilan and Thomas C. Brown, *Instream Flow Protection: Seeking A Balance in Western Water Use* (1997).

106   Anderson and Leal, above note 7, at 99.

107   Janet C. Neuman and Cheyenne Chapman, 'Wading Into the Water Market: The First Five Years of the Oregon Water Trust,' 14 J. Envt'l L. & Litig. 135 (1999).

water consumption – water footprint – by returning water to the environment. Buyers can obtain a certificate and BEF will ensure that water rights will be left in the stream for such a quantity.[108]

Conventional wisdom concerning public goods casts doubt on the free-market environmentalists' proposal: if only private parties are allowed to hold rights to instream flow, stream flow and related goods will be under-provided, which is what prompts the need to protect instream flow in the first place if there is a market. The main critique of this private rights proposal is that the free-riding effect may crowd out these initiatives, despite the difference in marginal benefit between those agents with intense preferences and the general public. In some other examples of public goods, government has acted to counteract the under-provision by establishing frameworks whereby the free-rider and sucker effects are mitigated,[109] as in certain urban policies.[110] One potential avenue to pursue would be to transform public goods into local club goods.[111] For example, a fishing association might want to pay for protection of instream flow by buying water rights in the market if only its members are allowed to fish in that part of the river. This is feasible where policing costs of potential free-riders are low.[112] The purchases of the association might benefit the public in general because more available water can result in better ecosystem services and, thus, cleaner water for all.

Even if measures to enhance co-operation are taken, private contributions to public goods may be insufficient[113] to fulfill aggregate social prefer-

---

108   Bonneville Environmental Foundation, 'Water Certificates,' http://www.b-e-f.org/our-solutions/water/water-restoration-certificates/why-wrcs/. For more successful examples, see Anderson and Leal, above note 7, at 99–101. For a comprehensive review of the experiences until 1998, see Clay J. Landry, *Saving Our Stream Through Water Markets: A Practical Guide* (2008) (in particular, at 8 he reports that 2,364,020 acr-ft had been acquired in the western US States from 1990 to 1997).

109   Lee Anne Fennell, 'Beyond Exit and Voice: User Participation in the Production of Local Public Goods,' 80 Texas L. Rev. 1 (2001) (discussing other public goods such as security).

110   For a general discussion on purpose of cultural buildings, see Daphna Lewinsohn-Zamir, 'The "conservation game": the possibility of voluntary cooperation in preserving buildings of cultural importance,' 20 Harv. J.L. & Pub. Pol'y 733, 783–784 (1997).

111   The idea behind a club good is that there is a like-minded group of people enjoying the use of a certain good that otherwise would be a public good. Some economists differentiate them from local public goods in that the boundaries are territorial and without appealing to the distinguishing characteristics of individuals. Suzanne Scotchmer, 'Clubs,' in *The New Palgrave Dictionary of Economics*, above note 1, http://www.dictionaryofeconomics.com/article?id=pde2008_C000178&edition=current&q=club %20goods&topicid=&result_number=1. A combination of club and local goods might be more useful for the management of water resources.

112   See Elinor Ostrom, *Governing the Commons*, at 20 (1992). See also ibid. at 58–100 for an analysis of several cases of long enduring experiences of commons' management experiences.

113   James J. Murphy, Ariel Dinar, Richard E. Howitt, Erin Mastrangelo, Stephen J. Rassenti, and Vernon L. Smith, 'Mechanisms for Addressing Third-Party Impacts Resulting from Voluntary Water Transfers,' in J. List (ed), *Using Experimental Methods in Environmental*

ences.[114] Government may want to subsidize these activities, given the benefits that accrue to society from this public good. Ideally, it would be necessary for government to balance private provision in order to fulfill the social demand.

To sum up, what is important is that instream flow will not be negatively affected by market transactions. It will be easier to identify the effects on the flow if the transaction respects mandatory instream flows or the defined rights over instream flow for which government is one of the potential right holders and which must be respected as any other right. Narrative standards applied in transactions review give room for discretion and, thus, uncertainty. This uncertainty could be reduced in the long run through precedent, and such standards may still be necessary because the various dimensions of environmental protection in aquatic habitats might not be boiled down to a single quantity (the instream flow required or achieved buying rights). In any case, minimum stream flow could be a good proxy and less onerous in terms of transaction costs. It may be better to err on the side of caution and impose higher quantities *ex-ante* than open the door to narrative standards during the review if those quantities can mitigate some of the quality concerns. In addition, by defining rights over instream flows, the matrix of transactions expands.

An anticipated effect of potential restrictions on water use rights, which can take the form of mandated instream flows or curtailments of use rights, is that right holders who need more water than what is granted to them after the regulation will resort to the market to make up for their shortfall. Similarly, if

---

    and Resource Economics, at 91 and 97 (2005) (the authors run an experiment to test whether third parties acting as buyers in a water market could be a way to address externalities on public goods. The results show free-riding effect and under-contribution).

114 Measuring the social valuation is a very complex enterprise and the results are always contentious. Market does not always offer a measure of how much recreational fishermen value certain level of instream water, but it is desirable to come up with an objective way to quantify them. However, non-market valuation methods either based on hedonic pricing, travel-cost – which could be used for example to analyze how much recreational fishermen are willing to travel to catch fish in a certain stream – or survey methods, such as contingent valuation, do not offer non-contestable results. However, the complexity of the enterprise might explain why this approach has not been taken and regulation remains the preferred option to provide public goods. However, regulation imposing duties to third parties, such as not to erode the soil of the river or not to pollute, should suffer from the same flaws since a cost-benefit analysis should be done. For an analysis of these valuations, see John B. Loomis, 'Use of non-market valuation studies in water resource management assessments,' 109 Water Resources Update 3 (1997), http://www.ucowr.siu.edu/updates/pdf/V109_A2.pdf. See also, Griffin, above note 1, at 297–304 (non-market valuation techniques are covered: contingent valuation, hedonic pricing, and travel costs. The author states that 'Of these three techniques, contingent valuation has the best capacity to produce the functional information needed to conduct policy or project analysis'). For non-market valuation of leisure activities, see in general, Daniel J. Phaneuf and V. Kerry Smith, 'Ch. 15: Recreation Demand Models,' in Karl-Goran Maler and Jeffrey Vincent (eds), *II Handbook of Environmental Economics*, at 671–761 (2013).

instream property rights are allowed, the market will receive a boost from those buying water for the environment. This latter option will increase the security of consumptive water use rights because protection will not mean reduction of their rights to the same extent, but public purchases alone may be insufficient to undo current environmental damage.

2.5 Enforcement of property rights or externalities

2.5.1 Definition

Externalities are the other side of the coin of property rights definition. Externalities are the effects on other right holders or the environment that the parties to a transaction do not internalize. They abound in water because 'there is something inherently integrative about rivers. Their uses are, and must be, shared. Upstream uses affect downstream uses. Private uses affect public uses. Human uses affect natural river functions.'[115] In a water stream, each use is interconnected with others. For example, a farmer withdrawing water from a stream and irrigating his field and returning part of the water to the flow affects the downstream users of the same watercourse, by not only reducing the amount of water flowing, but also sending more nutrients down the river or pollution from his runoff.

We may assume that public agencies granting rights in those jurisdictions with a permit system take into account these interactions in the initial allocation of rights. In jurisdictions with common law types of rights, such as pure prior appropriation ones, new uses must not affect others, and if this occurs, the senior water users may sue the newcomer and a type of equilibrium will be established. However, when a transaction occurs in any system, the order is distorted. Externalities abound.[116] Among other effects, a transaction may

---

115 Peter Rogers, Lawrence MacDonnell, and Peter Lydon, 'Political decision making: real decisions in real political contexts,' in Russell and Baumann (eds), *The Evolution of Water Resource Planning and Decision Making*, at 229 and 241 (2009). Accordingly, the same water can be a private, public, or toll good, and different rights to use, access, or transfer may interact. Lakes offer another example, Brett M. Frischmann, 'Environmental Infrastructure,' 35 Ecology L. Q 151, 153 (2008), '[Lakes] can be used for fishing, boating, swimming, and for other recreational activities. Further, lakes can be used as subject matter for artwork, for commerce, for transportation of goods, for waste processing, as a sink for pollution, or as a drinking water source, to name a few. These uses are in addition to the socially valuable role lakes play in supporting a complex ecosystem.' See also Smith, 'Governing water,' above note 31 (building the semi-common model in which public and private exclusionary rights cohabit in water because the nature of the resource has implications for the spectrum of governance).

116 Robert Pindyck and Daniel Rubinfeld, *Microeconomics* (8th edn, 2012). Externality is a well-defined economic concept referring to '[an] action by either a producer or a consumer which affects other producers or consumers, but it is not accounted for in the market price.' For another definition, '[a] type of market failure where there is interdependence among economic agents for which a market or corrective policy is not in place,' see Griffin, above note 1, at 378.

affect the amount of water and often the quality of water in a stream, which, in turn, has an impact in users of the same watercourse, fish and wildlife, and perhaps the community where water is sold or leased from.

In the transactions this book focuses on, that would mean that if a farmer A is selling water to a city upstream C, less water will be available in the stream where B, another farmer in-between C and A, pumps his water. B may either not receive enough water[117] or need to change the pump in order to be able to extract the same amount of water. In an ideal world, A and C will compensate B for this cost if those are lower than the overall benefit of the transaction, or if B does not have the right not to be injured, B may pay A and C to stop their transaction if it is cheaper than installing the new pump.[118] In these simplified examples, externalities are conceived as a missing Coasean market[119] and B could be included in the transaction. However, the world of blackboard economics[120] is far from the real world where transaction costs are the rule, not the exception. If instead of just one intermediate farmer B, there are several, the situation may become unmanageable.

Given that in the real world such Coasean negotiations including all the actors are hardly imaginable, it is assumed that the market regulations should provide for a type of mechanism to make sure that third parties, such as B, are not negatively affected by the water transaction or that they are properly compensated. While the definition of property rights determines who has a right upon which others cannot encroach, and may help reduce the probability of third party effects, externalities will still occur, and procedures to make sure they are internalized should be spelled out. If review mechanisms were not in place, it could not be asserted that water markets would bring about a more efficient state of affairs than the status quo, i.e. than the allocation before a transaction occurs, because the non-internalized costs could be greater than the private benefits that accrue to the parties to the transaction. These negative externalities could also affect the environment which does not have a clear right holder to file suits to ensure that damage does not occur, unless property rights over instream flow have been defined. Even where those rights have been

---

117 Imagine that A had a right to 15 acr-ft which he completely consumed. B's right is also 10 acr-ft. The flow including both rights was 21 acr-ft. B used to divert 10 acr-ft but only consume 6 acr-ft. If A transfers his right to C, B will not be able to divert as much as he used to and he cannot satisfy his need because only 6 acr-ft will be flowing and this is not enough despite the fact that he used to return 4 acr-ft to the river.

118 Ronald H. Coase, 'The Problem of Social Cost,' 3 J. L. & Econ. 1, 44 (1960).

119 Ibid. at 8. The Coase Theorem is supposed to be central for the understanding of externalities. According to it, in a world of zero transaction costs, the parties will achieve an efficient transaction internalizing the potential effects regardless of the initial allocation of property rights.

120 Coase refers to the theoretical economic approach that is far from how the economy actually operates, see Ronald H. Coase, *The firm, the market, and the law*, at 28–30 (1988).

defined, as a result of a transaction, there might be effects on water quality which, despite not impairing the use by other right holders, may affect the environment more generally. These review mechanisms could also check whether the mandatory instream flows are still fulfilled after the transaction takes place.

Two preliminary considerations before analyzing the review procedures regarding externalities in a water market should be noted. The first relates to the scope of analysis. The unit of analysis does not go beyond the market boundaries. Therefore, it is endogenous and might be dictated by the jurisdiction of the body setting the market or the existence of infrastructure. Only the effects within the boundaries of the market are considered.[121] For example, if there is a market in one of the states sharing a river, the effects on out-of-state users of the same river would not be taken into account assuming the transactions do not violate the compact signed by the states sharing the river. At first sight, the larger the market, the more externalities may arise if a transaction occurs between distant agents because of the high number of potential third parties affected.

Second, externalities are difficult to measure. Externalities are not limited to examples where the quantity of water available might not be enough; there are also less obvious effects. For example, a lower level of instream flow might imply higher power consumption for a downstream farmer because his pump needs to work harder. Some of these complex effects are almost impossible to measure.[122] Improvement in measurement technology can make some difficult-to-measure effects knowable, but other impacts will still remain intangible,[123] such as the decrease in food self-sufficiency due to lowered agriculture production as result of a transfer. In sum, some externalities might have to be ignored because the cost of measurement, if possible, is much higher than the damage they cause and because water transfers review may not be the forum within which to undertake such analysis.

The following sections consider the mechanisms used to address externalities arising from transactions, i.e. the mechanisms to ensure that the effects of transactions on third parties are taken into account. The final section covers the effect on communities, which is a contested form of externality.

---

121 Charles W. Howe, 'Water Resources Planning in a federation of states: Equity versus Efficiency,' 36 Nat. Resources J. 29, 31–34 (1996).

122 Another example might be how the change of canals as part of an in-farm conservation policy to sell the water saved might have the result that some wetlands dry up and therefore migrant birds have no place of abatement in the area.

123 Manuel Schiffler, 'Intersectoral water markets: a solution for the water crisis in arid areas?' in Kay *et al.*, above note 3, at 362 and 365 (discusses foregone indirect benefits from water transfers and lists among these: preservation of rural livelihoods, food self-sufficiency and prevention of desertification).

2.5.2 Different mechanisms to ensure that the effects on third parties or the environment resulting from a transaction are internalized

The design of a review mechanism requires a choice of which institution will be in charge – an administrative agency or the courts – and a choice between an *ex-ante* or *ex-post* procedure. The choices are obviously related, since courts generally work after damage has happened, except in injunctive procedures. Both choices might be heavily influenced by the pre-existing structure. For example, it would be costly to establish a system of water courts replicating Colorado's one in jurisdictions with a purely hierarchical administrative structure. These options have a clear impact on transaction costs and, ideally, the scheme which minimizes transaction and, where possible, transition costs, should be preferred. In fact, transaction costs also inform a more fundamental choice: whether a review procedure is necessary or whether to levy taxes to establish a fund where potentially harmed third parties can apply for compensation. This connects with the standards of review and the burden of proof in the review procedures since it can be more or less demanding to the parties to the transactions or to those who claim to be harmed.

Any review procedure will impose transaction costs. Transaction costs[124] arising from these review procedures are always negatively regarded as a waste of money. However, as Colby suggests, perhaps they should not be considered so negative, since in the absence of a perfect definition of property rights with the resulting complete internalization of third-party effects, transaction costs could be a useful tool to ensure that transactions which provide net benefits go forward. According to Colby, often there are no perfect mechanisms to compensate for these environmental externalities in western US States because standing might be controversial[125] and only transactions causing outrageous effects are barred. Thus, transaction costs arising from the review procedure might be a good substitute for the lack of perfect compensation. If a transferee's ideal benefit function should be benefits from the new water bought minus price and costs imposed on third parties and the environment, in the absence of a compensation mechanism but with a lengthy review procedure, the formula would substitute the external costs compensation by a mix of compensation to other right holders and the 'policy-induced transactions costs.' Colby argues

---

124 See section 2.7 for an analysis of governmental roles related to lowering transaction costs.

125 Cf. Brian E. Gray, Richard E. Howitt, Lawrence J. MacDonnell, Barton H. Thompson, Jr., and Henry J. Vaux, Jr., 'A Model Water Transfer Act for California,' 4 Hastings W.-Nw. J. Envt'l L. & Pol'y 3 (1996); reprinted in 14 Hastings W.-N.W. J. Env. L. & Pol'y 591, 607 (2008) (citations refer to the latter text) (§506 (a) it gives standing to the California Department of Fish and Game and to the counties from which water is transferred to claim compensation in the review procedure for transactions of conserved water). For the argument that public entities should have standing in environmental claims on behalf of their citizens, see Robert A. Weinstock, 'The Lorax State: Parens patriae and the provision of public goods,' 109 Columbia L. Rev. 798 (2009).

that these costs are not dollars burned, but a redistribution of dollars from the applicants to the agents intervening in the transaction review process (agencies, lawyers, or consultants).[126] However, these dollars are not devoted to compensating the effects; they do not provide funds to mitigate environmental damage. In fact, Colby's analysis tries to rationalize the procedures that happen to be in place, but these procedures have not been put in place with a view to imposing transaction costs as a substitution for real costs.

a. Courts v. administrative agencies

The responsibility for review, either *ex-ante* or *ex-post*, could be assigned either to an administrative agency or to a judicial court. *Ex-ante* administrative review seems to be the most common solution. Chile stands out as the example for the judicial model: after amendments to water regulations in the 1980s, disputes over water transfers have been handled by civil courts, *ex-post*.[127]

An agency responsible for water management has certain strengths compared to a judicial court, especially if the court is a non-specialized one.[128] Agencies have experience in water management and data on many dimensions of a transaction – such as location of the original right – which in water is particularly important, given the weight that contextual factors have in water management.

Empirical data comparing New Mexico, where the state engineer is in charge of the review, and Colorado, which has a system of water courts – which may override the specialization advantage stated for governmental agencies – confirms this thesis *a minori ad majus*. According to Colby *et al.*, who conducted a study in the 1980s, a procedure in Colorado, from the moment where the application is filed to the moment where the decision is reached, takes on average 29 months, while in New Mexico it takes 4.3 months.[129] Colby also measures the 'policy-induced transaction costs' which she defines as including attorney's fees, engineering and hydrologic studies, court costs, and fees paid to state agencies, and excluding the price and the costs of implementation once the transfer has been approved if they are not induced by state policies. She finds that these costs in Colorado averaged US$187, while in New Mexico, only US$54.[130]

---

126   Bonnie G. Colby, 'Transactions costs and efficiency in Western water allocation,' 50 American J. of Agricultural Econ. 1184 (1990).

127   See in general Monica Ríos Brehm and Jorge Quiroz, *The Market for Water Rights in Chile* (1995).

128   Colorado (http://www.courts.state.co.us/Courts/Water/Index.cfm) and Montana (http://courts.mt.gov/water/default.mcpx) have water courts to solve conflicts related to water rights.

129   Colby, above note 126, at 1188. The data mentioned is from the study Bonnie G. Colby *et al.*, *Water Transfers and Transactions Costs: Case Studies in Colorado, New Mexico, Utah and Nevada*, Dep. Agr. Econ. University of Arizona (1989).

130   Colby, above note 126, at 1188.

Although it has also been asserted that delays, attorney fees, and other costs are lower in an administrative procedure than in the judicial system, it is important to take into account that even though the individual cases might be cheaper to handle through an administrative procedure, they may take place more often than judicial procedures, since only cases which entail important amounts of damages are litigated. Hence, an administrative review procedure can be more costly in the aggregate. However, it seems a cost worth paying if externalities are expected to be great. This will be the case particularly for long-term transactions. Who bears the costs of the review system is also a relevant issue. A fee could be imposed to cover the agency's or court's expenses.[131]

b. Ex-ante v. ex-post control

Regarding the *ex-ante/ex-post* choice, there is a theoretical question which has to be considered: whether the protection of third parties' interests and society in general would not be better channelled through a liability rule, which allows compensation *ex-post*, than through a property rule that implies that, in absence of an *ex-ante* agreement, if the environment or third parties would be affected, the transaction is blocked.[132] Under an *ex-post* control where the burden of proof is on the injured, parties affected will only claim compensation for the effects of a transaction when the costs of doing so are lower than the harm suffered. Thus, small injuries will not be protested, dispersing social costs, unless some aggregation mechanism is in place.

A situation wherein there are small damages coupled with a quite large number of heterogeneous affected parties is a likely scenario in water transactions. Analogously to the argument about how nuisance torts fall short for dealing with environmental problems, in water transactions bargaining with the affected parties may not occur efficiently. Courts may not be the best forum, even though class actions could be established; the most common mechanism is a review procedure, usually an administrative one operating *ex-ante*.

c. The most common mechanism: agency ex-ante review with open-ended standards

The prototypical review scheme is as follows: the parties to the transaction file for approval with the competent agency and it reviews the documents filed by

---

131 This is the case in California where the SWRB imposes a fixed filing fee plus some additional fees tied to quantity for inter-basin transfers. To this, the US$850 fee for the California Department of Fish and Game has to be added. See State Water Resources Control Board, 'Petition for Temporary Transfer of Water/Water Rights,' http://www.waterrights.ca. gov/forms/pet-temp-chg.pdf.

132 For the theoretical framework, see Guido Calabresi and A. Douglas Melamed, 'Property Rules, Liability Rules and Inalienability: One View of the Cathedral,' 85 Harv. L. Rev. 1089 (1972).

the parties, which may include engineering and hydrological studies.[133] The burden of proof lies on the applicant.[134] The assumption behind this rule must be that those entering into a transaction are in the best informational position to prove that the transaction is not harmful to others or the environment. Or, alternatively, that they are the parties who should bear the evidentiary costs.

The agency decides whether or not the transaction should go forward. Sometimes a third party participates, but it is not necessary because it is assumed that the agency, the trustee of the public interest, will make sure that third party rights are not negatively affected. The agency can decide not to approve a transaction if it affects other users without their being part of the procedure. Participation may facilitate the collection of information, however, saving time and expenses to the agency.

Participation may not only include private parties, but also agencies that have responsibilities affected by water management decisions. In particular, responsibilities over the environment or wildlife are often shared between different agencies. In some jurisdictions, regulation establishes that agencies providing for them might have to report on the transaction without deciding on it. However, they may hold different conceptions about what the public interest demands given their expertise and focus. For example, in California, the State Department of Fish and Game called to participate in the review procedure may hold a different public interest conception than the State Water Agency conducting it or the federal US Fish and Wildlife Service if it also participates.[135] Given that these different agencies have been taken into consideration in water planning and in the regulation of instream flows where they exist, including them in the review procedure may create unnecessary transaction costs.

These review procedures bar any transaction negatively affecting a third party, the environment, and, sometimes, the local economy of the area of origin. In economics parlance, these review procedures seem to be formally embracing a Pareto criterion,[136] not a Kaldor-Hicks efficiency

133   Bonnie Colby, 'Irrigated Water, Market in Reallocating,' in B. Alton Stewart and T.A. Howell (eds), *Encyclopedia of Water Science*, at 447 (2003) (describing transactions costs from obtaining legal approval of a water transfer in the western US states).
134   Meyers and Posner, above note 71, at 33–34 (proposal to shift it after a preliminary proof has been established).
135   Rogers *et al.*, above note 115, at 248 ('All types of governance systems have a concern for a public interest – albeit for smaller publics (...). There are instead guardians of separate "national" interests that involve the manner in which water is used. The interests historically were promotion of commerce and economic development utilizing river resources. Today such interests are more fractionalized and are pursued by a mix of federal agencies'). The different agencies allowed to participate in one way or another in the transfer approval illustrates this point.
136   Louis Kaplow, 'Pareto principle and competing principles,' in *The New Palgrave Dictionary of Economics*, above note 1, http://www.dictionaryofeconomics.com/article?id=pde2008_P000315&edition=current&q=Pareto&topicid=&result_number=2.

criterion.[137] In other words, changes are not allowed if someone is worse off than he or she was before even if the gains of those who win with the change – the transaction – are larger than the losses of those who are harmed.

The Coase Theorem seems to be formally ignored when this review procedure is in place: transaction review documents do not seem to envision bargaining between the transacting parties and the third party claimants affected.[138] What may occur is bargaining between private parties before reaching the administrative review or in the course of it, but in its shadow. Administrative procedures could do a better job at offering a forum for negotiation or allowing mechanisms for compensation instead of just a binary decision: authorization or not.

The standard of review does not bar any effect on third parties or the environment. In practice, some external effects, minimal ones, are simply unaccounted for. For example, in these review procedures the slight increase in power consumption that a user might need in order to use his pump if there is less water, but still enough to fulfill his right while pumping with the same technology, would not be compensated. The cost of measurement and review of these effects outweighs substantially the slight damage. There has been, in fact, a proposal to minimize the costs arising from the cumbersome administrative review procedure related to *de minimis* externalities. It consists in adopting 'substantial injury' or 'no unreasonable effect' as a standard for review, instead of 'no injury.'[139] A standard similar to 'substantial injury' is sometimes applied regarding the effect on the environment: transfers unreasonably affecting fish, wildlife, or other beneficial instream uses are not authorized.[140] These open-ended 'substantial' or 'reasonableness' tests import

---

137 Robert N. Stavins, 'Environmental economics,' in *The New Palgrave Dictionary of Economics*, above note 1, http://www.dictionaryofeconomics.com/article?id=pde2008_E000096& edition=current&q=stavins&topicid=&result_number=2. Griffin, above note 1, at 38.

138 See for example California's SWRCB petition for change involving transfers form, http://www.waterboards.ca.gov/waterrights/publications_forms/forms/docs/pet_transfer. pdf.

139 Meyers and Posner, above note 71, at 33 (claiming that a preliminary hearing should be enough not to care about minimal injuries).

140 §§1725 and 1735 of the Cal. Water Code; Spanish Water Act 102: 'El Organismo de cuenca podrá no autorizar la cesión de derechos de uso del agua, mediante resolución motivada, dictada y notificada en el plazo señalado, si la misma afecta negativamente al régimen de explotación de los recursos en la cuenca, a los derechos de terceros, a los caudales medioambientales, al estado o conservación de los ecosistemas acuáticos o si incumple algunos de los requisitos señalados en la presente sección, sin que ello dé lugar a derecho a indemnización alguna por parte de los afectados.' ('The basin agency may not authorize the transfer of water use rights, by reasoned decision, issued and notified within the prescribed period, if it adversely affects the system of exploitation of resources in the basin, the rights of third parties, environmental flows, the state or preservation of aquatic ecosystems, or if it breaches any of the requirements identified in this section, without giving rise to right to compensation for those affected.')

discretion into the agency decision,[141] but might be necessary to ensure that water markets move forward and that impacts on the environment, particularly on water quality, are captured since quantification of instream flow or non-consumptive instream flow rights cannot account for all the effects on the ecosystem.

A similar rationale to the one overlooking very small effects might be behind the different degree of thoroughness of the review procedures for short-term and long-term transactions in some jurisdictions, such as California.[142] A more streamlined review exists for short-term leases which may suggest the implicit assumption that the externalities are smaller and that costs of inaccuracy arising from a less detailed review would be short-lived. Hence, the cost of the review is minimized in order to ensure that the transaction will not be delayed, which is indispensable for short-term transactions. However, imposing a more lenient standard may come at a cost: it may require imposing restrictions on who can trade with whom, higher requirements either to be a seller/buyer, or a more demanding burden of proof.

In the same line, and particularly for short-term transfers, a mere communication could be required. The applicants would need to report to the agency that they are planning to enter into a transaction and offer prima facie evidence that the transaction will not affect other users or the environment. In that case, the agency, by itself or prompted by a third party who files the protest once the communication is publicized, may or may not take further action concerning the transaction. If the agency remains silent, the transaction goes forward. The same value could be given to the inaction of the agency where an authorization is required. If after a certain period of time the agency has not reached a decision, the transaction would be considered approved.[143] This scheme might give incentives to the administrative agencies to conduct the review in due time, which could help overcome bureaucratic delay, a source of transaction costs for the parties.

d. Compensation funds and taxes

An alternative to *ex-ante* procedures of authorization is system institutionalizing compensation *ex-post*. The transaction would be communicated to the agency, and then either a tax would be levied[144] or some deposit required in order for

---

141 See in general Warburton, above note 65.

142 Compare the short- and long-term transfer petitions, the latter being more demanding, see http://www.waterboards.ca.gov/waterrights/water_issues/programs/water_transfers/.

143 This model, frequent in other administrative procedures, is the one adopted in §504.f of the Model Water Transfer Act for California in Gray *et al.*, above note 125, at 605.

144 For an analysis of taxes, see section 2.5.2.d.

the transaction to be able to move forward.[145] Government would adjudicate compensation claims *ex-post* if affected users apply for it. The administration could determine compensation ad hoc or using scales[146] and the compensatory award would be paid with the aggregated funds from transactions or with the deposit of the particular transaction. This scheme would lower the transaction costs because its operation might be less costly than private bargaining.

In these cases, the protection of third parties is framed as a liability rule scheme. The burden of initiating the procedure or proving the damage before an arbitrator would lie on the party claiming compensation.[147] In these cases, in practice the result would be equivalent to a 'substantial injury' standard because those suffering from small negative effects will not have incentives to spend their time and money asking for compensation. This more streamlined procedure might be particularly useful in short-term transfers. Under current administrative review schemes, the quick relief that might be needed in dry summers can be impaired by a lengthy and costly procedure of approval or authorization. In fact, the Model California Water Transfer Act[148] recommended an 'in-house' compensation claim mechanism for short-term transfers of conserved water. Third parties could claim compensation in front of an arbitrator. The amount of compensation in the California model is limited to the tax revenues arising from the particular transaction. A similar compensatory scheme could work in water banks where the difference between the price paid by the buyer and the amount received by the seller can be partially designed to ensure that there are funds for redress of the potential damages.

A tax on water transfers[149] could not only be the source of those compensatory funds, but also ensure revenues to protect the riparian environment more broadly. Given the impossibility of finely calculating the effects of a water

---

145 Gray *et al.*, above note 125, at 606 (§§505–506); the fund is set with the security deposits the person who files a transfer has to pay. The amount of the security deposit is calculated by a fee per acre foot of water (§505.a). Compensation is limited to that amount. The funds remained after paying the judgment, if any, entered by an independent arbitrator would be returned to the transferor (§505.l).

146 Cf. Hanak, above note 78, at 89 (this could be advisable for direct externalities to other right holders, but the author casts a doubt on a claim-based system for community externalities, since there is no experience with such procedures in comparison with unemployment benefits, and farm workers might be disadvantaged relative to other more well-organized parties such as fertilizer companies).

147 §506.b proposed in Gray *et al.*, above note 125, at 608.

148 Current regulation differentiates between short- and long-term transactions to establish different level thoroughness of the review procedure (cf. §§1725–1732 with §§1735–1737), but the California Model of Transfer Act differentiated between whether water transferred is conserved water or not since conserved water should imply lower level of external effects, Gray *et al.*, above note 125, at 597–609.

149 Megan Hennessy, 'Colorado River Water Rights: Property Rights in Transition,' 71 U. Chi. L. Rev. 1661, 1684 (2004).

transfer, a tax could not be perfectly formulated. A tax is imperfect[150] because it is not perfectly tailored to the effects of particular transaction. On the contrary, it is set in advance as an average of the potential damages. That means that excess revenues or excess losses should be passed on to other years. A sustained drought may imply a negative balance for some years, and that may call for public supplementation of these funds.[151] As with any imperfect tax, it introduces distortions that may imply some efficiency costs compared to other ways of addressing these impacts; but the policy-induced transaction costs described above are an even rougher measure which, in addition, does not provide traceable funds.

Taxes have been in place in order to protect the environment, but not necessarily in monetary terms. Taxes have taken the form of a share of the water quantity transferred. The Oregon Water Code[152] provides that 25 per cent of water transferred should be left in the stream. This levy is far from perfect since transactions affecting critical streams may have more dangerous effects than in others where water is abundant. The Murray Darling Basin (Australia) model is more attuned to the different level of externalities that may arise depending on the location: it adopts a presumption that transactions from upstream to downstream are less damaging than the other way around, and that water must be left in stream when a transaction from a downstream user to an upstream one is completed.[153] On top of this, government provides some extra water, a public good.

2.5.3 Externalities on communities: a contested concept and a political necessity

Effects on communities are much more contested than externalities affecting other right holders or the environment and, thus, they deserve separate treatment. Going from the theoretical definition of externality to the political level blurs what should count as an external effect and whether it should be compensated. When critics of water markets warn against the potential effects

---

150 An experimental study that replicated many features of the California water network by Murphy *et al.* using a computerized market with a uniform price but with differences introduced by conveyance costs showed that revenue tax is more efficient than a per unit one, see Murphy *et al.*, above note 113, at 101–103.

151 See ibid. at 108 for the equity implications of cross subsidies from wet to dry years as a result of tax imperfections.

152 § 537.455-500 of the Ore. Rev. Stat.

153 A security exchange rate of 0.9 has been established when water is sold from South Australia to New South Wales or Victoria (downstream to upstream transactions). Thus, a sale of 1m³ from South Australia would mean that the buyer in Victoria will receive 0.9m³. However, when the upstream states are the sellers, all the water is transferred. Murray-Darling Basin Commission, 'The Pilot Interstate Water Trading Project,' http://www.mdba.gov.au/ sites/ default/files/archived/mdbc-SW-reports/2221-fact_sheet-Pilot_interstate_water_trading_project.pdf.

on third parties due to water market transactions, they usually include the negative effects on rural communities where water originates:[154] unemployment, emigration, environmental effects from a decrease in agricultural production, or even damage to intangible community life. It is important to note that the claims about these negative effects focus not only on economic effects, but also incorporate natural resource protectionism. People have internalized a sense of common ownership of water resources, and their sense of the community owning them might be narrow and not encompass the region receiving the water. Communities where water originates claim compensation or want to outright block the transaction. Disputes over these effects are recurrent no matter whether there is an interbasin mandated transfer or market transactions. In market transfers, it seems that the sentimental value of the water or the community impoverishment could be factored into the price, but the community does not generally have a say, and an individual farmer or farm company selling water might not have communitarian preferences.[155]

Beyond the non-economic arguments just discussed, the economic effects on employment of assets and labor exist. However, economists refuse to take some of the latter externalities, which they name 'pecuniary,' into account because they see them as simple market interdependencies.[156] They equate those effects with changes in price concurrent with the reallocation which have equity implications, but not real economic ones.[157] For them, water is no different from any other resource, so it creates no challenges different from, for example, the reallocation of the main manufacturing factory from one village to another region. However, even among economists, some argue that water is slightly different as far as effects on third parties are concerned.[158] In contrast to other goods, when water is reallocated there are no off-settings; water goes, but no other jobs are created in the area.[159] According to this conception, the effects

---

154 For a critique of water market based on the negative impacts it might have in a community, see Glennon, above note 52, at 1889. Hanak, above note 78, at 81 ('the same studies also demonstrate that there can be significant localized negative effects on individual farm workers and businesses and on local public agencies such as school districts. Thus, there may be ethical grounds for devising mitigation programs, even when a transfer does not trigger the legal requirement to do so').

155 Thompson, above note 25. Cf. Emerick and Lueck, above note 87, at 25.

156 Salanié, above note 1, at 89.

157 Howe, above note 121.

158 Indirect effects in economics, which might be called secondary effects, are also understood with the effect that water has on the demand of other inputs or the production of outputs when analyzing the link between growth and water. In fact, the chain may include ripple effects on all the economy. Griffin, above note 1, at 166–170. See also William M. Hanemann, 'The economic conception of water,' in Peter P. Rogers and M. Ramón Llamas (eds), *Water Crisis: Myth or Reality?*, at 78 and 84–7 (2006).

159 Griffin, above note 1, at 230 ('[. . .] the removal of resources other than water creates economic opportunities within originating regions. These opportunities are sharply reduced for water that may only generate employment for a small number of intermediaries and, in few cases, temporary jobs in the construction for new conveyance facilities').

of a water transfer in the agricultural community in the form of unemployed resources, be it labor, land, or machinery, should be compensated, at least temporarily.

Murphy *et al.* acknowledge the controversies regarding the definition of pecuniary externalities and accept that it is politically necessary to take them into account, but conceive of compensation in such cases as transitional, i.e. funds allocated to mitigate these issues should be temporary in order to encourage efficient behavior.[160] A transitional remedy might train workers to shift to other business sectors in the area or take the form of general assistance measures directed to improving the economic tissue of the region.[161] This transitional remedy, given its temporary nature, only makes sense for long-term transactions since the effects on employment and inputs will not be permanent in short-term transactions. In addition, remedies seem to be required when there is a massive exodus of water, not if there is a single transaction. Hence, a threshold of how much water needs to be transferred out for the effects on communities to be substantial should be calculated.

The harder effects on communities occur where water sold comes not from a more efficient use of the resource, but from the idling of fields. Behind this difference is the idea that if water transferred comes from a more efficient use of water, it involves fewer consequences for other factors employed since production is not curtailed. In contrast, fallowing may entail unemployment for farm workers (direct effects), fewer business transactions for farm suppliers (indirect effects), and broader effects on the rural communities in general (spillover effects).[162] All of these combined may produce a 'multiplier effect.'[163] Nonetheless, the first lands to be fallowed can be expected to be the ones producing low value-added crops and, thus, these tend not to employ much of other inputs.[164] A review of studies regarding the effects of fallowing between 6 and 25 per cent of farmland in an area shows that such actions affect usually

---

160   Murphy *et al.*, above note 113 at 110.
161   Hanak, above note 78, at 88–94 (the author discusses the advantages of disadvantages of targeted versus general programmes. Targeted programmes will devote funds to compensate those who are more directly affected such as unemployed farm workers or farm suppliers. Regarding the first, a claims-based system regarding cash compensation could be envisioned but high administrative costs and the political economy of the affected group disfavor it. Other targeted programs include job search and training programmes for laid-off workers. 'General assistance might take the form of measures to improve the economic environment of the area, for example, infrastructure investments or reduced sales taxes, or might support specific projects of benefit to area residents').
162   Hanak, above note 78, at 112.
163   Hanak, above note 78, at 81–82 (reviewing several empirical studies on land fallowing arising from water transfers, other pilot or environmental programmes or regulations, and from simulations).
164   Hanak, above note 78, at 124 (presenting the mitigating role that the mere economics on land fallowing have on the potential effects on communities).

less than 1 per cent of the economic activity of the region.[165] Despite this evidence, the Model Water Transfer Act for California suggested taking these costs into consideration when approving the transaction if the water sold comes from the process of land fallowing.[166] Given the harsher effects of fallowing and the heated response we may expect from communities, it should be considered whether public agencies should take this into account either in the review procedure or by establishing some *ex-post* mechanism.

The nested nature of the water management administration has given an avenue for these sorts of community concerns to play a role. Lower administrative levels such as in the counties in US States[167] have exercised their power to prohibit the transfer of water originated from fallowing, even at the cost of preventing otherwise beneficial transactions.[168] Such extreme measures should not be allowed if a market is to function properly, since these reflect a parochial view of public interest. This resistance needs to be overcome in order for a water market to operate.

A cap on transactions outside a jurisdiction is another mechanism to address this type of externality. It can be interpreted as protection of community life, but a justification based on the environmental impact in the basin could also be offered. Victoria in Australia imposed a 4 per cent cap on trade beyond the irrigation district, i.e. on volume of water access entitlements that can be traded permanently out of an irrigation district.[169] As a result of the cap, fewer workers will lose their jobs or need to find a job in another sector. These caps are similar solutions to the ones for environmental reasons,[170] in part because neither the environment nor communities have clear right holders who can defend their interests given the organizational problems of atomized groups.

There are mechanisms which are not exactly caps, but which impose practical barriers to transferring water over a certain amount out of the jurisdiction. For example, California established that, if more than 20 per cent of the total water

---

165 Hanak, above note 78, at 81.

166 Gray *et al.*, above note 125, at 601–602 (§404 (f)).

167 Hanak, above note 78, at 25–68; appendix C (in chapters 3–5, Hanak sets out the current practices of countries. These are the basis for the empirical study of Appendix C where the variables that explain why a country adopts export restrictions are tested). Thompson, *Institutional perspectives*, above note 25, at 723–726; 728–730 (1993) (describing the institutional obstacles to inter-regional trade posed by Californian mutual and water districts).

168 Hanak, above note 78, at 73 (IID Policy had, as some other local agencies, a policy disallowing fallowing as a source for water transfers).

169 There is a cap exchange rate that is not fulfilled by the individuals but by the state with its own entitlements to further mitigate potential effects. Hence even if the buyer in Victoria will receive 0.9 m^3, 0.09 m^3 more will be left in the river (10 per cent of 0.9 is 0.09 m^3) by the State from its own endowment. Hence, the water that is actually left in the river is 0.19 m^3, more quantity than before in aggregate, even though the flow between upstream and downstream will be reduced. Waye and Son, above note 88, at 444. See ibid. for an account on the inefficiency arising from the cap.

170 Murphy *et al.*, above note 113, at 92.

supply of a region is transferred and the water is coming from fallowed fields, a public hearing is required.[171] This provision should provide a forum for negotiating the compensation of community externalities even if there is no obligation to compensate those. The same idea underlies the legislative approval requirement in Oregon for water transfers out of the state,[172] which obviously implies very high transaction costs and which seems politically guided more than technically guided.

In practice, despite public opposition, transfers have occurred and in some of them concerns about community externalities have been addressed through the funds mentioned. These institutionalized funds, as a result of an agreement, not of a tax, have been set up to compensate for these externalities.[173] This embodies the Kaldor-Hicks criterion, i.e. the transaction is socially beneficial even if some lose. However, the criterion does not require compensation.

In cases where there have been a provision of funds to compensate the effects on the local economy, there are always two contentious issues regarding the funds: how much should be allocated and who should administer them. Since there is no institutionalized policy and the few cases have crafted solutions ad hoc, there are no answers to these questions. Nonetheless, an example from Butte County (California) in 2001 is worth mentioning. There, a fund was set up through the establishment of a fee (5 per cent, which amounted to US$3.75 acr-ft) without designing a fine-tuned model to calculate the specific impacts given the cost of such a design. This could be the model for short-term or low quantity transactions.[174]

The ideal mechanism should allocate the responsibility not to a local agency, but to a regional or state level agency to avoid capture and blockage of transactions. Local agencies may resist transactions because of the cost imposed on their area not taking into account that the transaction is positive on a larger scale. Further, some threshold should be established to determine when externalities on communities would be significant enough. The mechanism must spread the burden of the fund among all those transferring water, and not only the transferor who hits the threshold. Where such a threshold is met, that is where substantial amounts of water have been transferred outside the local economy for quite a long period of time, a mechanism to compensate those cases where water transferred originates from fallowing needs to be established. A fund to provide for the adaptation of the local economy could be the best solution. It should target agricultural workers and agricultural suppliers, but not the right holders themselves since the encroachment on their rights would have already been taken into account.

171 §1745.05 of the Cal. Water Code.
172 §§537.830 and 537.801-810 of the ORS.
173 Howitt and Hanak, above note 102, at 78–79 (fallowing arrangement for the IID's transfer to San Diego).
174 Hanak, above note 78, at 72 and 96.

2.6 Infrastructure

For water to be bought and sold it is very important to have connections between users with different valuations of water,[175] as they may or may not be along the same river. Different marginal values may occur between two neighboring farmers, but they are also very likely to occur between two areas with different climatological characteristics – for example, the humid north and the arid south. Markets are expected to price water according to its real value and, thus, high cost suppliers will enter a market when the price rises due to scarcity; and these high cost suppliers will likely be those that are further away from the buyer.[176] While natural gas and electricity must be transported via human-built infrastructure, natural interconnections for transporting water exist, such as streams and rivers.[177] However, water physical mobility[178] may still require transportation infrastructure to complement natural streams. For the purposes of water markets as defined in this book, what matters is large scale infrastructure between low value users – e.g. farmers – or their water sources and high value users – e.g. urban suppliers, other farmers producing high value crops, or industries – not the urban grid. The management of water infrastructure poses challenges because large scale water infrastructure is a natural monopoly, as discussed below.

175 Terence R. Lee and Andrei S. Jouravlev, *Prices, Property and Markets in Water Allocation*, at 49 (1998) ('The efficiency of competitive markets depends on water being relatively mobile. Adequate infrastructure allows for broader access to water markets by water buyers and sellers, and hence promotes competition and helps ameliorate the problem of market power').

176 Stern, above note 98, at 122. The key question is whether there is enough interconnection to allow equalize marginal prices. It is logical to think that the more far away to regions are, the more their climate patterns will vary. Differences in marginal value of water can be expected to increase as distance increases.

177 Thobani, above note 13, at 172 (arguing that markets require more complex infrastructure than administrative systems. According to him, for a water market to succeed, infrastructure in place has to be flexible). Natural waterways connect a watershed which makes a market within this scope easier to implement, see Slater, above note 70, at 269–270 (the author acknowledges that most of the trading occurs intra-basin and conveyance is necessary for inter-basin transfers not connected by natural streams). It is convenient to briefly refer here to California's regulation of natural waterways. The duty of the commingler is regulated in §7075 of the Cal. Water Code, 'Water which has been appropriated may be turned into the channel of another stream, mingled with its water, and then reclaimed; but in reclaiming it the water already appropriated by another shall not be diminished.' Agents' use of natural waterways to transport water is subordinated to the 'no injury' rule. Regarding quantity, the duty of the commingler using the channel entails that it cannot impair others' rights. However, in time of shortage, the position of the commingler is much more uncertain than the autochthonous ones since the presumption goes against him: if there is not enough water, the first use to be curtailed would be his. For an analysis, see Slater, above note 70, at 268.

178 In this book, 'mobile' is used to mean 'physical movement.' Brajer *et al.* understand mobile in a different sense. For them, it has to do with the possible transaction costs making difficult the exchanges even though the water rights might be transferable. Brajer *et al.*, above note 5, at 496–497 (1989).

Historically, without having markets in mind, water infrastructure has been built to satisfy constituencies settled in areas where water was not readily available. There are multiple examples: the western US States and Barcelona's water provision illustrate such a situation. Infrastructure is mainly owned by public agencies. Existing infrastructure might not be enough to satisfy the needs of a water market, but if water is scarce enough, it may be justified to build new interconnections. The next section analyzes the claim that government needs to provide water infrastructure based on the idea that it is a type of public good. Later, the management of water infrastructure given its natural monopoly nature is analyzed.

2.6.1 Provision

Some authors have identified water infrastructure as a requirement for a water market and assumed that the infrastructure must be publicly provided.[179] This often builds on the misconception of water infrastructure as a public good.[180] However, water infrastructure is excludable and, thus, not a public good.

One argument put forward in favor of public provision of water infrastructure is that water is necessary for social and economic development,[181] which is a

---

179   Bjornlund and McKay, above note 38, at 791.
180   Cesari Dosi and K. William Easter, 'Market Failure and Role of Markets and Privatization in Alleviating Water Scarcity,' 26 Int'l J. Pub. Admin. 265, 270 (2003).
181   See Griffin, above note 1, at 166. Dosi and Easter, ibid. at 276 (stating that people believe that water projects encourage development), see Hanemann, above note 158, at 85–87 (the author suggests that there are multiple causal paths between water and growth: water might be necessary but not sufficient for development or perhaps it is neither necessary nor sufficient for growth). Nonetheless, it is in any case sufficient for development, and the amount necessary is not high. Relatedly, it has been argued that there is a basic human right to water or that water is conceived as a merit good, according to which every individual has right to a certain amount of water. Peter Gleik offers a calculation based on water needed to drink, cook, basic hygiene, and cleaning, see P.H. Gleick, 'Basic water requirements for human activities: Meeting basic needs,' 21 Water Int'l 83–92 (1996). The basic standards are around 20 l, but between 50 l and 100 l is what should be aimed at for every person, see European Water Initiative, 'Water and Sanitation as Human Rights,' http://www.euwi.net/files/FAQ_Right_to_water-sanitation_0.pdf. It can be also interpreted in public health terms, which is a public good. This argument would not have a direct application to water infrastructure, but to water supply. However, regarding the human right to water, some argue that what must be guaranteed is connection to the grid, not water itself, see Independent Expert on the issue of human rights obligations related to access to safe drinking water and sanitation, written contributions, Germany II 2 (2010), http://www2.ohchr.org/english/issues/water/iexpert/docs/written-contributions/GermanyII.pdf. In any case, connection to the grid is probably a necessary step to provide water. Ensuring just connection to the grid, not water itself, may have the benefit of encouraging rational consumption of water by charging a price for the water consumed. This argument applies better to the urban grid, but it may also justify water interconnections through large scale infrastructure since water needs to be brought to the cities or rural areas from the natural sources. Edward B. Barbier, *Natural Resources and Economic Development*, at 259 (2005) (the Falkenmark index, 1,000 m³ per

clear public good. In addition, while it may be worthwhile for private companies to undertake the construction of part of the water net, poor areas may not be served. Rose argues that we do not need to rely on market failure rationales to justify government intervention into this type of infrastructure, as it constitutes a special, inherently public, type of property in itself, different from common property because it is not in the service of a group, but of the public at large.[182] Water infrastructure could be considered a public good in this broader sense because it is part of the highways for commerce,[183] as rivers were, because it transports the product: water, to use.

These explanations show that infrastructure ensures public goods, but not that it is in itself a public good. It may partially explain why government may, not whether it should, provide water transportation and distribution. Furthermore, public provision may also solve a collective action problem if all the farmers in one area need to organize to fund a water transportation project. It is also said that governments may have greater capacity to finance large scale infrastructure than the private sector does,[184] but it seems more motivated by the will of government to satisfy the demands of certain groups.[185] Public choice problems explain some of the mammoth, not always sustainable, infrastructure built in the past.

Infrastructure itself is not a public good. Public goods are non-rival and non-excludable. These are not binary characteristics, as the example of water infrastructure shows. Water infrastructure is non-rival until it gets congested, which may happen in water mains. It seems less likely to happen during droughts – when transactions are expected – because less water is available, but it still might be problematic if there is a type of hub that all water has to go through, such as the San Francisco Bay Delta in California. As for excludability, in a river, policing who is diverting water might be difficult, but large scale human built infrastructure is excludable, as the problem of regulating a natural monopoly shows. The worries about potential exclusion of third parties arise

---

year, per person has been proposed as an approximate threshold below which a country could experience economic distress). This index captures the idea that until certain threshold, water is essential since it cannot be substituted by any other good, see Hanemann, above note 158, at 78.

182 Rose, above note 93, at 720.

183 Carol Rose often makes the analogy between canals and roads in her article Carol M. Rose, 'Big Roads, Big Rights: Varieties of Public Infrastructure and Their Impact on Environmental Resources,' 50 Ariz. L. Rev. 409, 416 (2008). See also Rose, above note 93, at 718 and 722 (analogy between roads and rivers and analysis of the concept of public property).

184 See Griffin, above note 1, at 341. Other justifications for public provision have been offered. This is the case of over-discounting, which has been listed as a market failure in relation to water, and is related to underinvestment in long-term projects. The social discount rate would be, all things considered, lower than the private one. Provided that a government is able to ascertain the discount rate, it should correct private perceptions through financial incentives, or it should build facilities itself. See Griffin, above note 1, at 113.

185 Thobani, above note 13, at 163 and 172.

precisely because pipes and canals are not public goods by themselves and owners might be interested in setting them up given the future monopoly rents they could extract if the natural monopolist is left unregulated.[186]

The natural monopoly structure has translated into public ownership and management of water infrastructure[187] as it did for electricity and gas in many jurisdictions prior to liberalization. In sum, what is crucial for water markets is the regulation of third party access. Even in publicly owned infrastructure, there is a risk of discrimination, particularly where owned by agencies which have a dual function, i.e. they manage infrastructure, but also supply water to their customers.[188] The duties imposed on the owners, be they public or private, of infrastructure, which is a natural monopoly, are analyzed next.

2.6.2 Management of water infrastructure: third party access

Natural monopoly arises 'where there are large fixed costs and small marginal costs'[189] in an industry. According to this traditional definition, economies of scale, i.e. decreasing average costs, are a sufficient condition for a monopoly. Water infrastructure presents the cost structure of a natural monopoly,[190] as many large infrastructures for network industries do. In fact, water is difficult and more expensive to transport than gas or power:[191] the costs of transporting

---

186   Cf. demand side theory of infrastructure which challenges the classification of infrastructure as public good or natural monopoly by analyzing it with a commons framework, see Brett M. Frischmann, 'An Economic Theory of Infrastructure and Commons Management,' 89 Minn. L. Rev. 917 (2005).

187   Thobani, above note 13, at 161 ('The allocation of water rights is typically the responsibility of the government, as is the construction, ownership, and operation of the infrastructure such as dams, reservoirs, and canals').

188   San Diego consider that the MWD was abusing its power by charging too high rates for wheeling water San Diego had bought from the IID, see 'Water agencies' feud ramps up, U.T. San Diego' (12 March 2012), http://www.utsandiego.com/news/2012/mar/12/sdcwa-vs-metropolitan-feud-escalates-as-rate/.

189   Varian, above note 1, at 435–437.

190   'A situation that occurs when one firm in an industry can serve the entire market at a lower cost than would be possible if the industry were composed of many smaller firms. Gas and water utilities are two classic examples of natural monopolies. These monopolies must not be left to operate freely; if they are, they can increase prices and profits by restricting their output. Governments prevent such a scenario by regulating utility monopolies or providing utility services themselves,' Tatyana Soubbotina, *Beyond Economic Growth. An Introduction to Sustainable Development*, 2nd edn, at 140 (2004). Water infrastructure is precisely the example used to illustrate natural monopoly in The Economist, 'Economics AZ,' http://www.economist.com/research/Economics/searchActionTerms.cfm?query=natural+monopoly.

191   Waye and Son, above note 88, at 38. For example, in California, the largest energy users are the water agencies responsible for conveying water from north to south. Moving water from north to south accounts for 19 per cent of its overall electricity consumption, 32 per cent of its natural gas demand, and 88 million gallons of diesel fuel per year. Susan Leal, Congressman Edward J. Markey, and Peter Rogers, *Running Out of Water: The Looming Crisis and Solutions to Conserve Our Most Precious Resource*, at 24 (2010).

it 100 km represent about 50 per cent of the wholesale cost of water, while the equivalent is 2.5 per cent for natural gas and 5 per cent for electricity.[192] This may explain why fewer network connections exist for water than for other commodities which present natural monopoly cost structure.[193] For example, the natural gas network is usually country-wide, while water networks are regional. An additional reason for the current breadth of the infrastructure is the existence of natural river connections. Nonetheless, infrastructure connections exist jurisdiction-wide in areas the size of California and Spain, which are the two jurisdictions the empirical part of this project analyzes.

A second, more nuanced definition of natural monopoly focuses on the subadditivity of the cost functions: a natural monopoly exists when a single firm can serve the market with lower costs than two firms.[194] Although large buyers – e.g. some industrial users – may build new connections to bypass any system or find alternatives to this supply,[195] the duplication of the network in water is inefficient and it is not likely to occur.[196] Hence, whether water infrastructure is a natural monopoly boils down to an empirical question about the possibility of having alternative means for transporting water from point A to point B. If alternative routes do not already exist, the cost-structure discourages duplication of water mains. For example, San Diego is usually supplied by the Metropolitan Water District (MWD). It wanted to buy water from the Imperial Irrigation District directly, but transport it through MWD infrastructure. Building an alternative route would have been extremely expensive and created onerous delays. It would have cost US$3.5 billion and taken 15 years.[197] Replication can be presumed unfeasible. In fact, economies of scale translate in having institutions like districts or irrigation communities building and operating infrastructure on behalf of a group of users. In theory, alternative transportation methods could be used to avoid a natural monopoly, but surface water does not have many available alternatives. Transportation by vessel, which was a strategy adopted in the Barcelona drought emergency,[198] is not an adequate substitute given the high costs.

---

192   Alexander Gee, 'Competition and the water sector,' 2 Antitrust 38, 39 (2004).
193   Stern, above note 98, at 124.
194   Salanié, above note 1, at 115.
195   Richard J. Pierce, Jr., 'The State of the Transition to Competitive Markets in Natural Gas and Electricity,' 15 Energy L. J. 323, 328 (1994) (large buyers may opt out and the cost might be shouldered by small consumers).
196   Gee, above note 192, at 39.
197   'San Diego Buying Water and Its Freedom,' *New York Times*, 6 August 1996.
198   Generalitat de Catalunya, 'Arriba el primer vaixell amb aigua potable al port de Barcelona' ('The first ship with drinking water arrives to Barcelona's harbor'), http://aca-web.gencat.cat/aca/documents/ca/sequera/RP_130508_roda_premsa.pdf. In California, during the recent drought, communities in the Central Valley run out of usable groundwater and had to truck water to their homes, http://www.thenation.com/article/californias-drought-so-bad-some-communities-are-trucking-their-water/.

The main problem of a natural monopoly may be described as follows: it is socially desirable to have just one firm supplying the market, but that firm can exploit its market power to the detriment of consumers. Monopolies sometimes lead to vertical integration, i.e. the firm that owns the infrastructure also provides the product. There have been three options put forward to deal with natural monopolies: public provision of the good or service; unregulated private natural monopoly; or private provision subject to public regulation.

Connecting with the previous section, natural monopoly has long been used to justify the public provision of natural gas, electricity, telecommunications, and water to avoid the abuse of monopoly power by private companies. Public provision has been a common solution in different parts of the world for different industries (electric power, railroad, and telephone),[199] but there is no guarantee that public agencies will serve the aggregated public interest when they are competing with other agencies or with other water providers. Imagine a regional water agency which owns wholesale water infrastructure and ships water to different cities. One city decides that it wants to diversify its water portfolio and buy water from a district outside the area of the regional agency. The regional agency may not want to face competition and may prevent the district from selling water to the city by not allowing the use of the pipes and canals.

The second option is an unregulated, private monopoly. This proposal has been put forward by libertarian economists, such as Milton Friedman.[200] These economists offer a public choice explanation for favoring an unregulated monopoly: although a monopolist might exploit its market power, other firms might enter the market because the high returns give incentives to potential new entrants to innovate. According to these, it is better to avoid the capture of the regulator by a single firm because a *de iure* monopoly will pose higher barriers to entry than a *de facto* one. Once new companies enter, the market will be competitive and the previous monopolist will not be able to extract more rents. However, it presupposes a change in technology, i.e. an alternative product with lower fixed costs. In other words, the argument works for industries where substitutes for the product are feasible or where technological changes are foreseeable that might enable new entrants to challenge the

---

199   OECD, Indicators of regulation in energy, transport and communications (ETCR) (in 1975, where data starts, gas industry was vertically integrated in all countries except on some where the market share of the dominant player was between 50 and 90 per cent – Spain, Switzerland, Germany, Australia, the United Kingdom, and Norway – and those with a competitive market – the United States, Canada, and Japan), http://www.oecd.org/document/32/0,3746,en_2649_34323_35791136_1_1_1_1,00.html.

200   Joseph D. Kearney and Thomas W. Merrill, 'The Great transformation of regulated industries law,' 98 Colum. L. Rev. 1323, 1400 (1998). See also Richard Posner, 'Natural Monopoly and Its Regulation,' 21 Stan. L. Rev. 548, 620 (1969).

incumbent.[201] An example is the telecommunications industry where wireless technology enabled competition. In the case of water, it is unlikely that a feasible, alternative way to transport water will be found.

The third option is regulation of a natural monopoly. Liberalization of network industries with natural monopoly characteristics entails that the segments that are actually natural monopolies should be regulated,[202] but the ones that are contestable – i.e. where competition is efficient – should be opened for competition.[203] (De)regulation of network industries[204] – telecommunications, gas, power – has been built around this idea of unbundling the different segments – production, transmission, and distribution[205] – of what was earlier thought to be a single, monolithic product, ensuring competition in all the segments except in infrastructure and to ensure competition, infrastructure use has to be open to all. In other words, all natural gas extractors or carriers should be able to ship their product through the infrastructure to deliver it to their wholesale or retail buyer even though these producers and extractors are not the owners of the infrastructure. The same is required for water markets to flourish: infrastructure should be open to third parties.

Mandating third party access alone does not solve all the problems. The owner may still charge a very high price to wheel water through the pipes and canals actually discouraging competition.[206] The rate needs to also be regulated.

---

201 It can be also an expression of the theory of contestable markets: markets where entrants will threaten the position of the incumbent do not need to be regulated because competition, see Robert D. Willig, 'Contestable markets,' in *The New Palgrave Dictionary of Economics*, above note 1, http://www.dictionaryofeconomics.com/article?id=pde1987_X000440. Kearney and Merrill, above, at 1399–1400.

202 For water, Morriss, above note 8, at 999–1000 ('[. . .] the existence of a natural monopoly in any particular aspect of a water system does not justify the creation of a state monopoly on the entire water system. Thus, for example, suppose that the capital costs of water mains are such that it is inefficient to provide multiple mains in a region. This fact does not justify creating a monopoly on water distribution, for there are a wide range of potential strategies to limit the natural monopoly to the specific area where it exists. Delivery can be unbundled from supply (as was successfully done with natural gas), or contracting can be used to provide incentives for appropriate performance by the operator of the natural monopoly aspect of the system').

203 Kearney and Merrill, above note 200, at 1407.

204 Harry First, 'Regulated Deregulation: The New York Experience in Electric. Utility Deregulation,' 33 Loy. U. Chi. L.J. 911 (2002) (First calls the liberalization of the electric industry regulated deregulation because it is in hands of the regulatory agencies. He uses it to deny the existence of full market competition).

205 Richard Geddes, 'Public Utilities,' in *Encyclopedia of Law and Economics*, above note 55, at 1163.

206 Paul L. Joskow and Roger G. Noll, 'The Bell doctrine: Application in Telecommunications, Electricity and Other Network Industries,' 51 Stan. L. Rev. 1249, 1252–1253 (1999) ('[. . .] even unregulated monopolists frequently are inefficient and can have the incentive and opportunity to engage in anticompetitive actions that benefit their vertical affiliates, and these undesirable effects are enhanced by the presence of regulation').

Once third party access is mandated, there are two ways to ensure it: bilateral bargaining with a regulated rate for the use of infrastructure or pooling under the auspices of a neutral entity. Under both models, the establishment of a government agency to regulate and oversee the water market could be advisable. For example, when competition was introduced in the water sector in England and Wales, a new independent agency was created to oversee the market called Ofwat.

California follows the first model. The California Water Code[207] does not fix the rate, but it defines fair compensation. However, the definition leaves room for abuse of market power by the infrastructure owner because some of the concepts to be included in the compensation are ambiguous. In fact, the California Model Water Transfer Act, a model put forward by academics aimed at enhancing water markets, went into much greater detail than the regulation in force on how to establish the availability of unused capacity.[208] The model adopted in California is far from ideal, but more specific rate regulation may be difficult because it implies the need for information about cost structure and demand which might be difficult to obtain for the regulator.

Even with regulated rates, this bilateral scheme can imply high transaction costs if the number of parties involved is large. In some jurisdictions, such as in California's intricate water system where state, federal, and local infrastructures coexist and the criteria for setting the rates are very broad,[209] water transfers might require cumbersome agreements between multiple parties. Hence, a market pool under the auspices of a neutral entity[210] could be more efficient. This is the option followed, for example, in some European electricity markets[211] and the New York Independent System Operator (NYISO) for electricity.[212] The difference between this and the first model is that there is a pool instead of bilateral bargaining, and those who want to ship water through the system have a single interlocutor and face set rates. Transactions costs are expected to be lower. Under this model, the most sophisticated market for

---

207   §§1810–1814 of the Cal. Water Code.

208   Gray *et al.*, above note 125, at 613 (§901a).

209   §1811c of the Cal. Water Code.

210   Slater, above note 70, at 285. Red Eléctrica is the manager of the electricity pool – which is the TSO (Transmission System Operator) – and the unique transporter of power in Spain.

211   The Independent System Operator is one of the options for structuring the deregulated electricity market in the EU. There is an entity managing the infrastructure and refunding the owners of it. Art. 13 of Directive 2009/72/EC of the European Parliament and of the Council of 13 July 2009 concerning common rules for the internal market in electricity (OJ 14.8.2009 L 211/55).

212   According to the FERC (Federal Energy Regulatory Commission), 'New York ISO (NYISO) (established 1999) operates the region's power grid and wholesale electric markets: energy market two-settlement (day ahead and real-time) spot market with locational marginal pricing, regional and locational capacity market, and financial transmission rights market,' http://www.ferc.gov/market-oversight/mkt-electric/new-york.asp.

water would be one where producers physically put water into the system and sell it to willing buyers who receive the water from the pool, although not necessarily the water introduced by the specific producer with which they contracted. The price of water would include the transportation charges. The entity in charge of infrastructure operation will charge non-discriminatory rates based on distance (point of entrance to point of exit pricing),[213] and repay the owners of the infrastructure responsible for its construction and maintenance.

This model ensures that infrastructure capacity will not be strategically used to discourage competitors because the entity managing it is external to other market segments. This model replicates the characteristics of some already existing water umbrella institutions such as the C-BT where the institutions manage the infrastructure. This Project is actually the area where most water trading occurs in the western US States, given how fungible the property rights are.[214] The USBR owns the rights to Colorado's water and manages the infrastructure. Farmers and cities obtain their water by entering into long-term contracts with the Bureau. Contractors can trade their entitlements and the USBR will deliver the water accordingly.[215] In addition to facilitating infrastructure use and payments, the NCWCD fulfills the role of a broker.[216]

As far as transactions are concerned, this umbrella entity could also be in charge of the review process. This pooling system of infrastructure replicates certain features of water banks. Along these lines, Hollinstead, in her proposal for a market pool system in California, advocates for a public entity regulating the market and managing the infrastructure as a pool. Her position seems grounded in the particularities of the Californian system where much of the infrastructure is part of federal and state projects, and in the overall securitization framework she puts forward. In her view, the state agency has to fulfill several functions to reduce transaction costs. Contrary to her position, from a general standpoint not focusing on markets, it has been argued that the regulator and the operator should be separate and that the operator could be private, in reference to the Delta Conveyance on the framework of the State Water Project

---

213 This is the way rates are determined in the European gas market, see WRC/Ecologic, 'Study on the Application of the Competition Rules to the Water Sector in the European Community,' at 49 (2002), http://ec.europa.eu/competition/publications/water_sector_report.pdf. In William Hogan's proposal of a pool-electricity market, the price of electricity is both location-specific and time-specific, taking into account congestion costs, William W. Hogan, *An Efficient Electricity Pool Market Model*, Working papers of the Harvard Electricity Policy Group, 1994.

214 Jedidiah R. Brewer, Robert Glennon, Alan Ker, and Gary D. Libecap, 'Water Markets in the West: Prices, Trading, and Contractual Flows,' 46 Econ. Inquiry 91, 96, 106 (2008).

215 Janis M. Carey and David Sunding, 'Emerging Markets in Water: A Comparative Institutional Analysis of the Central Valley and Colorado-Big Thompson Projects,' 41 Nat. Resources J. 283, 287–288 (2001).

216 Ibid.

in California.[217] This latter position implies that the public nature of an agency does not ensure that it will maximize the public interest; a public agency could serve particular interests. The specific market structure may depend on the context where water markets are implemented. As least, third party access to natural monopoly infrastructure should be guaranteed.

2.7 Market maker

Beyond the roles outlined above, which respond to traditional market failures, there is a group of roles that government should undertake to actually bring about water markets. This means that water markets require certain roles performed by government to take off, operate smoothly, and actually become entrenched. These roles, similar to roles played in other markets by government or private agents, consist of providing information to facilitate search, matching buyers and sellers, making rights fungible by, perhaps, acting as intermediary, and guaranteeing certain transactions. In short, these roles aim at reducing transaction costs.

Transaction costs can be defined as the 'costs of reaching and enforcing agreements.'[218] Transaction costs may prevent otherwise efficient exchanges from taking place. Three types of costs are distinguished: '(a) the costs of locating and attracting potential trading partners and of pre-sale inspection; (b) contracting and fulfillment costs; (c) policing and enforcement costs.'[219] Transaction costs abound in economic transactions outside the world of blackboard economics and, in fact, one of their sources is regulation. It is important to note that transaction costs, and thus the roles defined here, are contingent on, among other things, how the governmental roles analyzed in previous sections have been fulfilled. Not only they are related to other governmental roles, but the four market maker functions are intertwined and the capabilities to undertake one build upon the other. For example, playing the function of a broker is closely related to the more traditional governmental function of registering the rights, because public agencies have access to the information about the rights and the potential restrictions on them.

---

217 'The Delta Conveyance,' http://www.aguanomics.com/2009/12/delta-conveyance.html (advocating for a separation between the operator and the regulator). In addition, in William Hogan's proposal, an institution 'poolco' operates the market overseen by an administrative agency to counteract the monopoly power, see Hogan, above note 213.

218 Barry C. Field, *Environmental Economics. An introduction*, at 193 (1994). There are different traditions in the definition of transaction costs: monetary, relational, or institutional, see M. Klaes, 'History of transaction costs,' in *The New Palgrave Dictionary of Economics*, above note 1. Monetary are direct costs from engaging in transactions (brokerage, transport, etc). Relational costs can be defined as Field, ibid., does. This is the definition embraced by the new institutional economics. Institutional approach adopts a broader view and allows comparison between market and non-market forms of allocation.

219 Klaes, ibid.

Many, if not all, of the roles listed, such as the matching function, do not necessarily need to be performed by government. As other markets show, brokers could fulfill, for example, the role of matching buyers and sellers. Thus, governmental action would only be justified if it has a comparative advantage over the action of private parties. Governmental action should, ideally, not only improve the overall social benefit, i.e. reduce costs more than it imposes, but also it must entail lower costs than the same actions undertaken by private parties willing to undertake them. It is possible that government is in a better position to implement all these functions because of economies of scope not only across these functions, but also in relation to other roles it fulfills. For example, given that a water agency reviews water transactions, it may be more efficient for it also to be the broker. However, private brokers could reduce the public agencies' advantage by offering other accessorial services, such as environmental effects consultancy, related to the approval of the transaction.

2.7.1 Information and recording

According to basic microeconomic theory, '[b]uyers and sellers will only make exchanges that maximize their interests if they have good information.'[220] Markets are supposed to aggregate atomized private information[221] better than the regulator.[222] In fact, this is one of the advantages claimed for water markets by advocates who defend their adoption instead of existing administrative systems. However, in the case of water markets, the situation might not be ideal, and potential contracting parties might be unable to locate each other or, if they can locate a counterparty, they may not know whether the right they claim is reliable.

Market agents need to know whether their counterparties have an entitlement to water. In fact, even if property rights are well defined, trade will be impaired if the seller is unsure about the title of the buyer. This may happen where rights

---

220 Glicksman and Levy, above note 45, at 18. For an analysis of the role of information flows in financial markets, see Ronald J. Gilson and Reinier H. Kraakman, 'The Mechanisms of Market Efficiency,' 70 Va. L. Rev. 549 (1984).

221 See also R. Quentin Grafton, Clay Landry, Gary D. Libecap, and J.R. O'Brien, Water Markets: Australia's Murray-Darling Basin and the US Southwest, at 1, International Centre for Economic Research, Working Paper No. 15 (2009), http://www.icer.it/docs/wp2009/ICERwp15-09.pdf ('Australia's Murray-Darling Basin (MDB) and the US Southwest offer a "window to the future" on the growing problem of water scarcity and the potential for water rights and markets to provide information on current consumption patterns and alternative values, incentives for adjustments in use, and smoother reallocation across competing demands').

222 Cameron Hepburn, 'Environmental policy, government, and the market,' 26 Oxford Rev. of Econ. Pol'y 117, 121 (2010). However, when ranking the different degrees of governmental involvement, ranks second – just after free market – the provision of certain information by government (mainly about externalities).

have not been adjudicated or appropriative rights are not registered. Even though there would be contractual remedies if a transaction fell apart, a better way to ensure access to that information is through a Public Registry, similar to the Land Registry, which will reduce the transaction costs of impersonal trade.[223]

Public Registries have public good characteristics and, thus, collective action problems arise in relation to their establishment.[224] Since this is so, government is in a better position to establish them, ensuring their accuracy and reliability.[225] In addition, government is in many jurisdictions the one granting water rights, and thus it must have information about those that are not consuetudinary. The information is also useful for agencies deciding whether to grant new rights or undertaking water planning. If rights are inaccurately registered, administrative decisions not related to markets will not be sound and the market will not work as smoothly. This is actually the idea behind titling programmes for land in developing countries[226] and should perhaps be implemented in water to be able to quantify historical common law or non-adjudicated water groundwater rights. In addition, Public Registries usually have an implied function of guaranteeing the validity of what is recorded in them. If Registers are backed by government, parties rely on them for their transactions since they certify the right of the counterparty. This is an extra function which connects with the role of guarantor, analyzed below.

Second, information about past transactions and clearing prices is also relevant: it may allow the potential parties to forecast and plan their decisions accordingly.[227] Agencies are always involved in transactions since they approve them. Thus, information about these transactions would be easier to gather for these public agencies than for private parties because they would have to

---

223   For a comprehensive study on Land and Commercial Registries, see Benito Arruñada, *Institutional Foundations of Impersonal Exchange Theory and Policy of Contractual Registries* (2012).

224   Benito Arruñada, 'Institutional Support of the Firm: A Theory of Business Registries,' 2 J. Leg Analysis 525, 526 (2010).

225   Ibid.

226   Olivier DeSchutter and Katharina Pistor, 'Governing Access to Essential Resources, scope paper for Workshop on Governing Essential Resources,' at 6, Columbia University, June 2013 (on file with the author).

227   The relevance of such a function was praised by the officials of the Catalan Water Agency. Furthermore, there are examples from the beginning of the twentieth century in irrigation communities holding auctions in the Tibi Dam in Alicante, Spain, where one of the complementary activities of the organization was to post the prices paid in past transactions and the water available, Ostrom, above note 112, at 79 (where the irrigation institution provided that type of information). Brandon Winchester, 'An Institutional Framework for a Water Market in Elephant Butte Irrigation District,' 49 Nat. Res. J. 219, 242 (2009) (a bulletin board with information on prices and conditions of supply and demand is a policy recommendation).

rely on self-reported transactions, and gaps or inaccuracies may arise. In any case, once the information is made publicly available, private parties could process it and produce new, useful informational products.

2.7.2 Match-making

The role of match-making – i.e. coordinating a buyer with a seller – has been played by government in water banks[228] or clearinghouses, but it could also be played by private brokers. Government playing such a role should not impede private companies from emerging as water market intermediaries, especially in mature stages of the market,[229] as the Australian case shows.[230] Australian brokers were not extremely successful in the first steps of markets, for example, they did not warrant that their suppliers had enough water to cover the transaction requirements.[231]

Although technological change is not likely to revolutionize water distribution as wireless technology did with telecoms markets, because it is highly unlikely that will change the way water is delivered,[232] technology might

---

228 Water banks can be defined as '[A] mechanism designed to facilitate the transfer of water use entitlements from one location or use to another. A water bank functions like an intermediary, or broker, similar in some ways to a financial bank that acts as a broker or clearinghouse between savers and borrowers. In the case of water banks – and unlike some brokers – there is some kind of public sanction for its activities,' Agriculture and Resource Economics, Oregon State University, Public Policy & Economics, 'Water, FAQs,' http://arec. oregonstate.edu/jaeger/water/FAQ1.html. From a more general perspective, Hollinstead describes clearing houses where government will not take title over the water but will only match information, Hollinstead, above note 91, at 365 ('provides information on the price, quantity, and location of water available for sale without purchasing that water or arranging for delivery offers a final option').

229 Bonnie G. Colby, 'Reallocating Water: Evolving Markets, Values and Prices in the Western United States,' 92 J. Contemp. Water Res. & Educ. 27, 27 (1993). For example, see Water Right Exchange, a broker company in Utah, http://www.waterrightexchange.com/.

230 In Australia, there are several companies which act as water brokers. For example, Waterfind, http://www.waterfind.com.au/. Brokers imply that new payoff function, theirs, enters into the picture, reducing – holding all things constant – the gains from trade. Thus, these agents acting as filters between the buyer and the seller are only economically justified if they reduce other transaction costs. For example, in a market where private actors face asymmetric information the expertise of a broker can match successfully different high value parties and low value parties, allowing more tailored contracts.

231 Waye and Son, above note 88, at 456 (brokers' misconduct was not widespread but they lack knowledge and familiarity with the system).

232 Lidia Ceriani, Raffaele Doronzo, and Massimo Florio, *Privatization, Unbundling, and Liberalization of Network Industries: a discussion of the dominant policy paradigm in the EU*, Working Paper 2009–09, 2009), http://wp.demm.unimi.it/tl_files/wp/2009/DEMM-2009_009wp.pdf ('In the last twenty years the perception that new technologies could weaken the traditional case for natural monopoly has increased').

improve water market performance and reduce the need for a match-maker. Theoretical proposals such as smart markets for gas or water[233] or the experience of market hubs in natural gas[234] suggest that advances in metering and electronic markets will be extremely positive for a water market.[235] There will be new platforms for water markets.[236] Incipient examples were tested in California, such as the online clearinghouse system 'WaterLink' put forward by CALFED in 1996[237] or webpages that contain electronic bulletin boards or databases where buyers and sellers can list their needs.[238] An interesting, but interrupted, initiative for Texas' Rio Grande was 'Water2Water,'[239] which adapted the business-to-business e-commerce method to the water realm. Water2Water, part of the Enron corporation, was an electronic trading floor where buyers

---

233   See in general, James J. Murphy, Ariel Dinar, Richard E. Howitt, Steven J. Rassenti, and Vernon L. Smith, 'The Design of "Smart" Water Market Institutions Using Laboratory Experiments,' 17 Envt'l & Resource Econ. 375 (2000).

234   Elisabeth Pendley, 'Deregulation of the energy industry,' 31 Land & Water L. Rev. 27, 29, 33 and 35 (1996).

235   Kathryn Kretschmer-Weyland, *Building a Smart Grid for Water, U.S. Mayor Newspaper*, The United States Conference of Mayors, 7 June 2010, 'Customer-care web sites can present usage data and other information to consumers, helping them make better decisions on using water, while specialized meter-data-management software makes it easier for utilities to understand what is going on in their systems.' In relation to technology, it has been argued that provision of water may entail a double monopoly since the technology needed for water management is also a monopoly if protected by a patent, see Ephraïm Clark and Gérard Mondello, 'Dynamic uncertainty and the pricing of natural monopolies: the case of urban water management,' in R-U. Goetz and D. Berga (eds), *Frontiers in Water Resource Economics*, at 69, 72 (2006) ('[. . .] the current situation of the water sector can be characterized as a "double" monopoly. The first element related to the specificity of the hydrous network which can be shared only at the price of resource wastage (work, capital). It corresponds to the traditional definition of a natural monopoly. The second element related to the patent protected technological advances in water management that create temporary technological monopolies and reinforce the structure of the natural monopoly'). This technology also has a public good dimension related to research; it thus might require public provision or incentives under the form of patent protection, see in general, Adam B. Jaffe, Richard G. Newell, and Robert N. Stavins, *A Tale of Two Market Failures. Technology and Environmental Policy*, Resources for the future Discussion Paper 04-38 (1994).

236   Donald F. Santa Jr and Clifford S. Sikora, 'Open access and transition costs: will the electric industry transition track the natural gas industry restructuring?' 25 Energy L.J. 113, 156, 157 (2004) (recognizing the relevance of software to implement a Poolco model).

237   Hollinstead, above note 91, at 365 (online clearinghouse by CALFED). Erin Schiller and Elizabeth Fowler, 'Executive Summary,' in *Ending California's Water Crisis: A Market Solution to the Politics of Water*, at 27 (1999) ('WaterLink enables water users to buy and sell water from their home computers. They can post and read bids and asks, access weekly and seasonal statistics on average prices and trading volumes, negotiate deals, and record trades').

238   Clay Landry, 'The evolution of e-water markets,' at 1, Global Water Intelligence (November 2000), http://www.globalwaterintel.com/archive/1/11/market-insight/the-evolution-of-e-water-markets.html.

239   Ibid.

and sellers could transact deals directly through the web. It aimed to include the transaction review by the Water Master – the administrative agency in charge of it – within a unique system to streamline the procedure, but in the mock trading the offer to sell or buy still had to be filed both with the website and with the Water Master.[240] If the integration would have happened, this would not have been much different than a water bank where the broker is the agency approving the transaction. However, it never took off.

2.7.3 Fungibility

When agencies or brokers play these abovementioned roles of matching and brokering, there is an ancillary function they can assume which makes rights more fungible: repackaging rights to serve the interests of the buyers, i.e. they can pool together different rights, pooling the risk associated with them. This is one way to make rights fungible, but not the only one.

As discussed in section 2.4.2, defining the transferable amount of a water right according to past average consumption will decrease transaction costs by ensuring that certain externalities do not arise. A party may not know how much water it is able to transfer[241] because meters, if installed, only calculate diversion, not actual net consumption. The costs of an ad-hoc calculation may deter the participation of small parties and, in any case, increase transaction costs. The described transaction costs can be lowered by establishing a publicly sponsored model that calculates consumption according to certain variables. These variables would include: average rainfall in the last month, average rainfall accumulated, type of crop, type of soil – which may be approximated also by some type of generalization from geographical areas – and irrigation method, to be able to calculate the salvaged water if a farmer adopts a more efficient method. This would not be an exact calculation, but would reduce the costly uncertainty for the parties, easing the review procedure if in place. The review procedure would be easier because private parties will not need to incur high calculation costs and the likelihood of the agency rubber stamping a calculation done using its model is higher. The guidelines standardizing the calculation can be considered a public good.[242]

---

240 Ibid.
241 An alfalfa farmer, who knows the amount of water he has assigned and how much he values his crop, will accept any price over his valuation to sell the water and let the land fallow. However, he may not know how much water he is actually using because, although he diverts all the water he is entitled to, he returns part of it to the river via runoff, seepage, or return flow.
242 Compare Glicksman and Levy, above note 45, at 15–16, with Tinggaard, above note 45, at 49. Glicksman and Levy include here standardization of the product (here, the property right to use water) as a public good, while Tinggaard enumerates it as an independent rationale in his list based on the CO_2 permit market, where he does not include any reference to public goods.

In fact, Colorado has developed a model that enables farmers to calculate consumption for the Lower Arkansas River basin[243] where farmers are not allowed to increase the amount they consume. Other agencies could follow its example. Many water or water-related agencies are already halfway there because they have very useful information already gathered. For example, the US Geological Survey offers a set of guidelines for reporting on water consumption;[244] the New Mexico Office of the State Engineer publishes estimations on water use by categories every four years;[245] and, in Catalonia – one of Spain's regions – the Water Agency (Agència Catalana de l'Aigua) offers an interactive map during the irrigation season calculating water needs per crop in every county.[246]

Even if available, parties might decide not to use the guidelines and undergo certain environmental studies[247] to evaluate more carefully the effects of their proposed transaction if it involves large quantities and the benefits from a precise definition might outweigh measurement and transaction costs; this might especially be the case in large, long-term transactions.

2.7.4 Guaranty

Beyond public registries, government offers a guaranty of the transaction in those instances where water agencies play the role of the middleman in transactions by buying and reselling the water. If the agency buys and sells the water, taking ownership of it in the interim, the buyer's trust is boosted because it can rely on the back-up by government. This might be particularly important in the early stages of the market or where agents are not sophisticated or do not trust market mechanisms because they are unfamiliar with them. However, the higher trust on the reliability of a right sold by an agency is explained by several powers the agencies have cumulatively. Agencies have control over potential curtailments, management of the infrastructure, and information

---

243 In the matter of the proposed compact rules governing improvements to surface water irrigation systems in the Arkansas river basin in Colorado, Case No. 09CW110, Water Division 2, Col.

244 USGS, 'Guidelines to prepare the reports on water consumption,' http://pubs.usgs.gov/tm/2007/tm4e1/.

245 New Mexico Office of the State Engineer, 'Water Use by Categories, Technical Report,' at 52 (2005), http://www.ose.state.nm.us/PDF/Publications/Library/TechnicalReports/TechReport-052.pdf.

246 ACA, http://aca-web.gencat.cat/aca/aetr/index.html. The agency might be obtaining the information as a by-product of other regulations, hence, it has a comparative advantage, see den Hertog, above note 55, at 235.

247 Hanak, above note 78, at 60 (an Environmental Impact Review costs US$300,000 or more: it is, at least, ten times more expensive than a less demanding Environmental Assessment. These studies are required by counties' authorities to issue water export permits since such authorization triggers the mechanisms established in the California Environmental Quality Act).

about water availability. It is usually said that water agencies may weaken property rights because they hold some discretionary powers. Accordingly, if these agencies endorse transactions, they are less expected to encroach on property rights. If they sell water rights, they will make sure they can fulfill them. However, the backup function may occur even without actually taking possession of the water or the water right. It may occur in those water distribution systems where an agency controls water supply and its contractors exchange their allowances, since the institution can actually decide who gets the water when, and once they have the transaction sanctioned by the agency, private parties can rely more on the delivery of the water purchased. In addition, water users have feared that trading water would trigger tighter scrutiny and if public agencies endorse and channel the transactions, they further reinforce the idea that water rights will not be reviewed if a user enters into a transaction.

Chapter 3 sets the stage for the case studies and operationalizes the roles enumerated in this chapter in order to guide the inquiry into the performance of Californian and Spanish water agencies.

3 Roadmap to the case studies

3.1 Introduction

Building on the theoretical part of the project, which answers the question of what forms of governmental intervention are required to establish and maintain a functioning water market, the empirical analysis focuses on two jurisdictions, California and Spain, and aims to explain why water markets have been more active in California than in Spain. The underlying hypothesis is that the different performances of market mechanisms can be explained by the type of governmental roles undertaken by water agencies in these jurisdictions and the degree of their fulfillment, although it is obviously difficult to measure the intensity of governmental performance.

This empirical question is addressed using a comparative qualitative approach.[1] Qualitative studies may offer a detailed narrative, setting the stage for future quantitative empirical studies.[2]

As the research question suggests, there is a comparative component to this project. A separate case study for each jurisdiction, California and Spain, is undertaken, followed by a comparison of the two. Given the absence of perfect natural experiments, California and Spain compare well in light of their

---

1 At a more general level, a recent article by Grafton *et al.* establishes a qualitative framework for analyzing water market institutions. These authors offer a list of points to be analyzed when assessing water markets. R. Quentin Grafton, Gary Libecap, Samuel McGlennon, Clay Landry, and Bob O'Brien, 'An Integrated Assessment of Water Markets: A Cross-Country Comparison,' 5 Rev. of Envt'l Econ. & Pol'y 219 (2011).

2 In quantitative analyses on western US States, qualitative variables are factored in indirectly. See Jedidiah Brewer, Robert Glennon, Alan Ker, and Gary Libecap, *Water Markets in the West: Prices, Trading, and Contractual Forms*, 39, Nat'l Bureau of Econ. Research, Working Paper 130002 (2007). Jedidiah Brewer, Robert Glennon, Alan Ker, and Gary Libecap, 'Transferring Water in the American West: 1987–2005,' 40 Mich. J. L. Reform 1021, 1031–1035 (2007) (attempting to explain the difference between the trading activity of different states using their institutional differences). Jedidiah Brewer, Michael Fleishman, Robert Glennon, Alan Ker, and Gary Libecap, 'Law and the New Institutional Economics: Water Markets and Legal Change in California,' 1987–2005 26 Wash. U. J. of L. & Pol'y 183 (2008) (legal changes are included here as explanatory variables).

similarities. Both California and Spain are developed jurisdictions[3] and their water management regimes were sophisticated before the introduction of market mechanisms.[4] Hence, the analysis presented here sets aside the ongoing debate over the application of market mechanisms to developing countries where institutions may not be fully entrenched.[5]

This chapter starts by analyzing the appropriateness of this particular comparison between the two jurisdictions here studied. The similarities between California and Spain are described to preliminarily establish that the specific comparison between the two jurisdictions is sensible, despite the differences that might be encountered. Additionally, the timeframe for the study is explained. Then, the dependent variable, market success, is analyzed, offering different measures that cumulatively contribute to assessing it. Lastly, the explanatory variables are operationalized, setting the stage for the individual case studies. The case studies can be considered individually as illustrations of the roles that government has played and should play in water markets.

Following this roadmap, Chapters 4 and 5 offer the qualitative case studies of water markets in California and in Spain, respectively. The case studies start by providing an overview on how market mechanisms come into existence in the two jurisdictions and a description of the institutions responsible for water management in each. Then, there is an analysis of how governments in California and Spain have undertaken, if they have, the different roles identified.

---

3 Spain was tenth in terms of GDP in 2008. See 2008 World Bank Ranking of economies according to Gross Domestic Product, http://siteresources.worldbank.org/DATASTATISTICS/Resources/GDP.pdf. California, if it were a country, would be the eighth economy in the world in terms of GDP according to the data provided by the Regional statistics of the US Bureau of Economic Analysis, see US Bureau of Economic Analysis, 'GDP by state 2008,' http://www.bea.gov/regional/gsp/, in comparison with World Bank Ranking.

4 Henning Bjornlund, 'Farmer participation in markets for temporary and permanent water in southeastern Australia,' 63 Agric. Water Mgmt. 57, 59 (2003) (arguing that despite the pressure that some international lending agencies have exercised to favor market-based approaches in developed countries, formal markets have only been established in a few countries, 'due to the need for fairly sophisticated institutional arrangements necessary to administer and implement such markets'). For California, see Gabrielle Bouleau and Matt Knodolf, *Rivers of Diversity: Evolving Water Regulation in California and the European Union*, 6, Working Papers California-EU Regulatory Co-operation Project Workshop, http://www.transatlantic.be/publications/bouleau_kondolf_final.pdf. For a review of Spanish history in water management, see Erik Swyngedouw, 'Modernity and Hybridity: Nature, Regeneracionismo, and the Production of the Spanish Waterscape, 1890–1930,' 89 Annals of the Ass'n of Am. Geographers 443, 450 (1999) (describing the relevance of water politics in Spanish history). Another hint on the development of Spanish water regulation is the fact that basin organizations existed since the 1920s, long before they were mandatory in the European Union through the European Water Framework Directive).

5 For the analysis of the lessons that mature water markets can provide to developing countries' water regimes, see Henning Bjornlund and Jennifer M. McKay, 'Aspects of Water Markets for Developing Countries – Experiences from Australia, Chile and the US,' 7 J. Env't & Dev. Econ. 767 (2002).

Then, Chapter 6 compares concisely the findings to assess whether the difference in the dependent variable – the activity of water markets – is explained by the fact that in California, the jurisdiction with more water market activity, government better fulfills the roles identified in Chapter 2.

3.2 The master and the purported disciple: California and Spain

California is often cited abroad as a model to follow in environmental matters; water law has even been singled out,[6] and its water market is probably the most well-known example of market mechanisms applied to water.[7] Furthermore, California has been recognized as a good case to compare with Mediterranean jurisdictions. In his analysis of the 1991 California Bank, Howitt acknowledges the similarities between Mediterranean regions and the 'Golden State':

> Mediterranean water economies are characterized by the same problems and climate that face California, namely spatial and temporal inequalities of water. Throughout the Mediterranean region urban and environmental water demands continue to grow, while agricultural water users wish to retain the cheaper water that was developed earlier. Nowhere is this problem more acute than in the economy of the State of California, USA, which in terms of its water uses, climate and conflicts has close parallels to Mediterranean countries.[8]

Since Spain is an example of a Mediterranean jurisdiction, this quotation supports the meaningfulness of the comparison chosen here. In fact, drawing on similar characteristics, Arrojo and Naredo, two Spanish scholars, offered in their 1997 book a descriptive comparison of Californian and Spanish water policy,[9] but at that point, Spain had not yet introduced water markets.

In fact, the changes in Spanish water regulation that introduced water market mechanisms were purportedly inspired by California's experience, but the mechanisms adopted were not similar. California's example was discussed extensively in the Spanish Environmental Committee during the legislative debate of the 1999 amendment.[10] Regarding the main theme of this project,

---

6 See Bouleau and Knodolf, above note 4, at 6.

7 Richard W. Wahl, 'Market Transfers of Water in California,' 1 W.-N.W. 49, 49 (1994) ('Over the past decade no state has enacted as much legislation specifically directed at facilitating voluntary market transfers of water as has California').

8 Richard E. Howitt, 'Empirical Analysis of Water Market Institutions: The 1991 California Water Market,' 16 Resource and Energy Econ. 357, 358 (1994).

9 Pedro Arrojo and Jose Manuel Naredo, *La gestión del agua en España y California* (1997).

10 In the debate in the Commission, California is mentioned more than 20 times. See Comisión de Medio Ambiente, Session No. 38 (1999) (Diario de Sesiones del Congreso de los Diputados 1999, 723).

i.e. the role of government in water markets, an interesting quote from this debate by the environmental economist Pedro Arrojo might enlighten the research since it points out that California is a jurisdiction where governmental agencies play an important role:

> A market might be used to pursue environmental goals, but this does not mean that the market by itself takes into account environmental or social and territorial equity values. These are very important questions for the US Administration; consequently, it assigns to the market what is naturally of the market and to the Administration what usually belongs to it, which in California amounts nowadays to more than 95% [the percentage refers to the amount of water resources totally under the control of agencies and not allocated in a privately decentralized fashion].[11]

Mr Arrojo defended introducing some market mechanisms, but maintaining them within administrative control. This quote's purpose was to attack the so-called free market that was going to be established in Spain, by suggesting that in California, markets have a marginal role and that government has the main responsibilities in water allocation and management. It is interesting to note that the fear expressed has to do with potential externalities that may be imposed on the environment or on communities, and not internalized by markets. Ensuring such externalities are internalized is understood as the natural realm for government.

In the legislative debates, those in favor of water markets pointed generally to California as a successful example of markets,[12] while opponents' praise focused only on the 1991 temporary California Drought Water Bank[13] and did not mention the fact that in California there were transfers outside the framework of water banks.

Even though the references to California in the Spanish discussion suggest that the two jurisdictions are similar, offering some figures will help establishing more firmly that California and Spain are similar enough to allow a meaningful comparison: (a) geo-climatologic conditions which include suffering from drought and periodical scarcity crisis; (b) demographic characteristics and trends which increase pressure on water resources; and (c) agriculture as the

---

11 Ibid. at 20660.
12 *El Mercado del Agua queda bajo control, con un precio máximo de 60 pesetas por metro cúbico*, ABC, 5 May 1999 ('Hay experimentos de mercados de agua que han funcionado muy mal en el mundo, como en Chile, y otros que han dado juego, como en California'; 'There are water market experiences which have been a failure, like Chile, or worked well, like California').
13 'Tocino está dispuesta a modificar su reforma de la Ley de Aguas si con ello logra el apoyo del PSOE,' *El País*, 16 March 1999 ('Nosotros nos conformamos con que se hiciera en los términos aplicados en California': Narbona, the representative for environmental issues of the Socialist Party said that they would be satisfied if the reform would be similar to California's water market).

major water consumer even though it does not represent a big share of the jurisdiction's economy.

Large parts of California and Spain are areas of Mediterranean climate,[14] where water is in short natural supply. Drought episodes[15] are common, making the scarcity problem more pronounced. Not only do these regions face similar water availability challenges currently, but in these regions water stress is predicted to be a problem in the future.[16]

In both jurisdictions rainfall, and thus water availability, diverges in different parts of the territory. In gross terms, the rainfall concentrates in the north, while the south is drier, but is where agriculture or cities have bloomed. California's variability might be illustrated by contrasting the north coast area where the average annual temperature is 55°F (12°C) and the average rainfall is 41.22 inches with the Colorado River Basin area where the average temperature is 73.4°F (22°C) and the annual rainfall is 4.41 inches.[17] Similarly, in Spain, the average precipitation varies from 59.06 inches in the north west with an average temperature of 50.9°F (10.5°C) to 7.87 inches in the south east where the average temperature is around 66.2°F (19°C).[18] This is harsh

14 California has five types of climates: Mediterranean (shared with the Mediterranean regions, parts of Chile, South Africa and Australia), Desert, Cool Interior, Highland, and Steppes. Data from the California Department of Fish and Game, Eric Kauffman. 'Climate and Topography,' http://www.dfg.ca.gov/biogeodata/atlas/pdf/Clim_12b_web.pdf. The Spanish Meteorological Agency (Environment and Rural areas Department) also recognizes different types of climate in Spain: apart from the Mediterranean, there are Highland, Atlantic or Oceanic, and Sub-tropical (in the Canary Islands) climates.

15 Drought is defined as the scenario where there is a 'temporary decrease in water availability due for instance to rainfall deficiency' in Communication from the Commission to the Council and the European Parliament addressing the challenge of water scarcity and droughts in the European Union, at 2, COM(2007) 414 final (18 July 2007). For a broader definition, see also FAO water, 'Hot issues: water scarcity,' http://www.fao.org/nr/water/issues/scarcity. html ('Imbalances between availability and demand, the degradation of groundwater and surface water quality, intersectoral competition, interregional and international conflicts, all contribute to water scarcity'). The Spanish Drought Monitoring Group's definition emphasizes that drought is a very elusive context since drought conditions are highly contingent on time and place, see Spanish Drought Monitoring Group, http://www.magrama.gob.es/es/agua/ temas/observatorio-nacional-de-la-sequia/que-es-la-sequia/. Spain is clearly a water-stressed country since more than half of the years from 1880 to 2000 could be classified as dry or very dry years, see Observatorio Nacional de la Sequía (Drought Monitoring Group), 'Database,' http://www.mma.es/portal/secciones/aguas_continent_zonas_asoc/ons/sequia_espagna/. California Department of Water Resources, 'Drought in California,' http://www.water.ca.gov/ waterconditions/drought/docs/Drought2012.pdf.

16 See e.g. 'Mapping future water stress,' BBC (2 February 2009), http://news.bbc.co.uk/2/ hi/7821082.stm (drawing on expert findings, maps for predicted water stress in 2020, 2050, and 2070 are offered. According to them, areas in Spain and California will suffer extreme stress).

17 California Department of Water Resources, Data Exchange Center, 'Precipitation,' http://cdec.water.ca.gov/snow_rain.html.

18 Milagros Couchoud Gregori, Presentation 'Régimen de Precipitación en España,' INE (2003).

for the areas where water is scarce, but it represents an opportunity for trading because it may prompt water reallocation: water could be bought from where it is abundant – and thus its marginal value is lower – by users in the dry areas, assuming that transportation costs are not prohibitive.

On top of that, rainfall varies across the year, which implies that in some periods, scarcity will be more severe, since less water will be available. Data from a couple of California locations will be illustrative. In a meteorological station at the Los Angeles Civic Center, 0 inches of precipitation were collected in September 2009 while 4.94 inches were collected in January 2010.[19] At the same time points, in Mt Shasta City, in the north, 0.02 inches and 15.62 inches, respectively, were recorded.[20] In Spain, the average rainfall in Barcelona for January is 1.57 inches, while in Bilbao it is over 4.72 inches; and, in July, which is expected to be a less humid month, Barcelona's average rainfall is 0.79 inches, while Bilbao's is 2.36 inches.[21] Even though water storage has been helpful in both jurisdictions to even out water throughout the year, variability across the year and across years is a challenge in areas where water is already scarce.

There are areas with a structural scarcity problem which indicates that they cannot or almost cannot quench their thirst under normal conditions because their natural resources are not enough to cover their uses. The Barcelona area consumes more hydro resources (701,266.645 acr-ft) than it naturally receives (621,816.871 acr-ft). The imbalance must be satiated by water coming from other regions.[22] Another way to portray the mismatch is by focusing on where resources and consumptive use are located. For example, the south coast in California had in 2005 4.93 per cent of the resources, 53.46 per cent of the Californian population, and 7.28 per cent of the consumptive use.[23] It is well

19 California Department of Water Resources, Data Exchange Center, 'Station data,' http://cdec. water.ca.gov/selectQuery.html (Station Code LCC).

20 Ibid. (Station Code MSC).

21 'Precipitaciones anuales y mensuales en ciudades españolas y europeas y otros datos climáticos, Capitales de Província Españolas,' http://javiersevillano.es/PrecipitacionMediaAnual.htm# provincia.

22 'Departament d'Agricultura, Pla de regadius de Catalunya 2008–2020' ('Catalonia's Irrigation Plan 2008–2020'), http://gencat.cat/agricultura/regadius/pla_regadius_2008_2020_text_ refos_clau_e1_vr_07943.pdf. The Water White Book, a document developed in 2000 which offers an overview of the status of hydro resources in Spain, identifies that the Segura basin has a problem of structural scarcity and that smaller units in the south Andalucía, Jucar, and Ebro Basins also face structural scarcity. *Libro Blanco del Agua en España* (*White Book on Water in Spain*), at 602–605 (2000), http://hercules.cedex.es/Informes/Planificacion/2000-Libro_ Blanco_del_Agua_en_Espana/Cap5.pdf.

23 Enrique San Martín González, 'Un anàlisis Económico de los trasvases intercuencas: el trasvase Tajo-Segura' ('An economic analysis of interbasin transfers: the Tajo-Segura transfer'), Tesis Doctoral, Dept. Economía, UNED (2011), http://e-spacio.uned.es:8080/fedora/get/ tesisuned:CiencEcoEmp-Esanmartin/Documento.pdf.

established that southern California gets a lot of its water from imports from northern California.[24] As an example, Cucamonga Valley Water District, which supplies San Bernardino, imports 49 per cent of its water.[25] These imbalances show that there is room for markets to operate.

Furthermore, both jurisdictions have suffered periodic droughts, which draw attention to the water management problems of these two jurisdictions. California has suffered drought periods in 1977–79, 1987–92,[26] and 2007–09,[27] all leading to the proclamation of a state of emergency by the governor. The Spanish climate is similar to California's and drought periods are also quite common. Over a similar time frame, Spain suffered the following drought periods: 1978–84, 1992–96, and 2005–08.

The area, population, and population density of the two regions are also quite comparable as Table 3.1 shows. This is important because if they were not, difference in market activity could be influenced by the larger population or density. Population is actually one of the controlling variables that Brewer *et al.* take into account in their empirical study comparing US States water markets.[28] The fact that California and Spain have similar population figures and similar patterns of change allows ruling it out as an explanatory variable because it will act as a constant.

More important than overall population figures are their growth trends because population growth and urbanization tend to translate into more water needs and conflict over declining water resources, thus increasing the need for

Table 3.1 Population and extension

	California[a]	*Spain*[b]
Km²	403,934.58	505,370
Inhabitants	36,961,664	45,548,573
Density (inhab/km²)	91.504085	90.12915883

[a] US Census Bureau, 'Quick fact: California,' http://quickfacts.census.gov/qfd/states/06000.html (data from 2000 for territory and estimation for 2009 of population).

[b] CIA, 'World Factbook: Spain,' https://www.cia.gov/library/publications/the-world-factbook.

24 Hilda Blanco *et al.*, 'Water Supply Scarcity in Southern California: Assessing Water District Level Strategies, Executive Summary' (2012), http://sustainablecities.usc.edu/quicklinks/H%20Blanco%20WSSC%20Exec%20Summary% 2012%202012.pdf.
25 Ibid. at XIV.
26 'California's water: a crisis we can't ignore,' http://www.calwatercrisis.org/ pdf/ACWA.WS.RecordDrought%202007.pdf.
27 California Department of Water Resources, 'California's Drought of 2007–2009,' http://www.water.ca.gov/waterconditions/drought/docs/DroughtReport2010.pdf.
28 Brewer *et al.*, 'Law and the New Institutional,' above, note 2 at 208.

reallocation. California and Spain's populations have grown steadily[29] in the last 100 years. Their urban growth is noticeable. In Spain, the percentage of the population living in urban areas has increased significantly: while in 1950, 51.9 per cent of the population lived in urban areas, in 2005, 77.3 per cent lived in them.[30] In California, in 1950, 61.6 per cent of the population was urban, while this percentage in 2000 reached 80 per cent.[31] The difference in percentages can be explained because Los Angeles' metropolitan area is larger than the Spanish ones (Barcelona and Madrid), while San Diego and San Francisco are more comparable to cities in Spain. Nevertheless, the problem is exactly the same: growing cities located in not very humid areas struggling for water. Urban water consumption per inhabitant, however, differs considerably. In the San Francisco Bay area, where the lowest urban water use in California has been registered, it is 151 gl per capita per day,[32] while in Spain the average is 39.36 gl (2009).[33] This difference must be taken into account when reading the transaction figures. On the one hand, it can be said that water markets should be more active in California because there is more water consumption and therefore urban areas have a greater thirst to quench. However, on the other hand, it could be said that California has more room to reduce water consumption in urban areas instead of resorting to markets.

In California, as well as in Spain, agriculture is the main water consumer even though agriculture is a small, albeit important, contributor to gross domestic product (GDP).[34] In California, during the period of study, agriculture

29 Department of Finance, '2008 California Statistical Abstract,' at 11 (2009), http://www.dof.ca. gov/html/fs_data/stat-abs/documents/CaliforniaStatisticalAbstract2008.pdf. For Spain, 1900–2000, see Teresa Menacho, 'Demografía y crecimiento de la población española durante el siglo XX,' http://www.ced.uab.es/publicacions/PapersPDF/Text205.pdf. For 2000–2001, data available at the National Statistical Institute, http://www.ine.es.

30 Ibid. ('Percentage of Population Residing in Urban Areas by Major Area, Region and Country, 1950–2050,' http://esa.un.org/unpd/wup/CD-ROM/Urban-Rural-Population.htm. Urban population is people living in municipalities with 10,000 inhabitants or more).

31 US Census Bureau, 'Urban and Rural Population: 1900 to 1990' (1995), http://www.census. gov/population/censusdata/urpop0090.txt. For a definition of what constitutes urban population, see US Census Bureau, 'Urban and rural populations definitions,' http://www. census.gov/geo/reference/docs/ua/urdef.txt.

32 Ellen Hanak, Jay Lund, Ariel Dinar, Brian Gray, Richard Howitt, Jeffrey Mount, Peter Moyle, and Barton 'Buzz' Thompson, 'Myths of California Water – Implications and Reality,' 16 W.- Nw 3, 18 (2010).

33 Press release, Spanish National Statistical Institute (INE), 'Encuesta sobre el suministro y saneamiento del agua Año 2009' (2011), http://www.ine.es/prensa/np659.pdf (Water consumption per capita has been decreasing. The average is higher in water-scarce regions such as Valencia, where the amount is 45.97 per person per day).

34 Agriculture represents 3.4 per cent of the Spanish GDP and slightly less than 2 per cent of California's gross state product (GSP). For Spain, see CIA, 'World Factbook,' https://www. cia.gov/library/publications/the-world-factbook. For California, see Bureau of Economic Analysis, 'GDP by state' (2008), http://www.bea.gov/regional/gsp/ (agriculture's share of GSP amounts to US$27,259 million in current dollars in 2008).

represented between 1.9 per cent and 2.21 per cent and, in Spain, between 2.5 per cent and 4 per cent depending on the year.[35] The agricultural sector uses 80 per cent of the freshwater in California[36] and 75 per cent in Spain.[37] The irrigated land in these regions amounts to 8,097,977.652 acres[38] for California (which represents 8.1 per cent of total land) and to 8,732,044.41 acres in Spain (which represents 7 per cent of total land).[39]

In relation to agricultural production, in the light of the goal the market aims to achieve – efficient water use – more than the mismatch between water use and contribution to GDP, the relevant feature for water markets is the potential for water savings if more efficient agricultural practices are adopted. Usually, the agricultural sector is blamed for its tendency to use water inefficiently by growing low value crops or wasteful irrigation systems, given the subsidized prices it pays for water.[40]

California's agricultural sector has opportunities to reduce its water use without impairing its production. Even though modern systems have already been adopted in different state regions, Cooley *et al.* concluded conservatively that there are still gains in efficiency to be realized: 17 per cent of current water use in California could be saved if certain technologies and management strategies were adopted.[41] All across Europe, Spain included, agricultural water savings are also possible. A case study covered by the report on EU Water Saving Potential examines water saving potential in Guadalquivir Basin in Spain. There, 30 per cent of water could be saved if several cumulative measures were taken

---

35 Spain: OECD, National Accounts; California: US Bureau of Economic Analysis.
36 Center for Irrigation Technology, 'Agricultural Water Use in California: A 2011 Update,' at 3 (2011), http://www.californiawater.org/docs/CIT_AWU_Report_v2.pdf. However, if the percentage is based on dedicated water, which includes environmental uses, then agriculture's share is more in the range of 40 per cent.
37 INE, *Estadísticas e indicadores del agua*, 1 Cifras INE 4 (2008) (2005 data).
38 According to the US Agricultural census, http://www.ers.usda.gov/data-products/state-fact-sheets/state-data.aspx?StateFIPS=06&StateName=California#Pd061eec886304680942d5a603 9ca637d_3_499iT18C0x0.
39 Ministerio de Medio Ambiente, Rural y Marino, 'Encuesta sobre Superficies y Rendimientos de Cultivos' ('Land acreage and Production of crops'), http://www.magrama.gob.es/es/estadistica/temas/estadisticas-agrarias/00ESPANA_tcm7-234252.PDF (2012).
40 'Growing alfalfa in the desert,' http://www.aguanomics.com/2008/12/growing-alfalfa-in-desert.html (22 December 2008). Janet Neuman, 'Beneficial use, waste, and forfeiture: the inefficient search for efficiency in Western water use,' 28 Envt'l L. 919, 940 (1998).
41 Heather Cooley, Juliet Christian-Smith, and Peter Gleick, *Sustaining California Agriculture in an Uncertain Future*, at 52 (Pacific Institute, 2009), http://www.pacinst.org/reports/california_agriculture/final.pdf. The authors analyze three different scenarios – dry, average, and wet years – and three ways to improve efficiency – adopting modern irrigation systems, improving irrigation management, and regulated deficit irrigation. Irrigation management – which includes, for example, improving irrigation scheduling if water is available on demand and not assigned according to an inflexible rotational schedule – provides higher efficiency gains since it does not require important initial investments.

(e.g. change open-channel irrigation techniques to trickle irrigation).[42] This explains why the Spanish central government put forward an Irrigation Plan[43] which aimed to save up to 1.162 hm^3/year and to correct the negative public perception of the agricultural sector.[44]

The explanation of why farmers do not use water efficiently is that they pay very little for it. In California, a farmer may pay less than 2 per cent of what urban users pay for an acr-ft.[45] In Spain, while urban users are charged by volume, farmers are charged according to acreage which makes the comparison difficult, but reinforces the idea of lack of incentives for efficient use.[46] It is politically unfeasible to increase the price for irrigation water and, thus, reduce consumption.

Underlying the idea of water markets is a vision that water will be coming from the agricultural sector because farmers will have incentives to save water and lease it or sell it to growing urban areas, to high value agricultural producers or to agencies or private parties willing to protect the environment. Markets are an alternative to mandated efficiency measures, public subsidies for the adoption of efficient practices, and price increases. The case studies show the different success in achieving the goal of quenching the thirst of high value users with agricultural water savings.

3.3 Dependent variable: market success and market activity

The ideal scenario would be to measure how much markets have contributed to solving shortage problems. The ideal measure of market success would be a combination of no need of mandatory curtailments during drought scenarios, and shift in the distribution of water rights from the low value to the high value sectors, all of which should translate into a decrease in scarcity as measured by the different indexes designed for that purpose, accounting for both supply and demand and their potential mismatch.

However, scarcity is difficult to measure unless the concept of scarcity is reduced to natural phenomena, such as rainfall. The avenue taken here, as well

---

42 See Ecology Institute, 'EU Water Saving Potential. Final Report,' Part 2 – Case Studies, at 11–20 (2007), http://ecologic.eu/download/projekte/900-949/917/917_water_saving_1.pdf (the 5 per cent of savings which would be achieved through a price increase has been discounted).

43 Regulation enacting the National Irrigation Plan, Real Decreto 329/2002, de 5 de abril, por el que se aprueba el Plan Nacional de Regadíos (BOE 101, 2002).

44 For more information, see Ministerio de Agricultura, Pesca y Alimentación, 'Plan de Choque de Regadíos, Objetivo: Ahorro de Agua' ('Crash Irrigation Plan'), http://www.plandechoque-ahorrodeagua.es/pag/esp/040.asp.

45 'Growing alfalfa in the desert,' above note 40.

46 Ministerio de Medio Ambiente, 'Informe Precios y Costes de los Servicios de Agua en España 22–26,' at 173–187 (2007), http://hispagua.cedex.es/sites/default/files/especiales/Tarifas_agua/precios_costes_servicios_%20agua.pdf.

as in empirical studies of water markets, is to understand scarcity not as the dependent, but as one of the independent variables driving market transactions. Instead of scarcity, this book uses some proxies to account for water market success based on water market activity. The measures which could be used to gauge market activity are grouped into three categories, depending on whether they focus on the volume of market activity, the direction of trade which connects with structural scarcity and the conventional wisdom associated with markets, or the impact of markets on water pricing.

3.3.1 Data sources

For California, the Bren School of Environmental Science & Management at the University of California Santa Barbara offers a database on transactions in the western US States, compiling transaction information published by the biweekly magazine, *Water Strategist*. Data on transactions related to water banks is not fully included in the database. For example, the data offered in the literature about the well-known 1991 state water bank does not fit the data offered for it in the database since only three transactions are reported where the bank is the seller.[47] These transactions do not account for the whole amount sold, and, since the bank actually leased the water to subsequently transfer it, the transactions where the bank was the buyer are clearly missing, and these were actually greater than the ones where the bank was a seller, since the bank only managed to sell around half of what it bought. In addition, some agriculture-to-agriculture transactions might not be reported.[48] Thus, secondary literature is also useful because it offers aggregate and complementary figures.

Spanish data is not as widely available. On the one hand, there is no integrated database, public or private, nor a publication reporting transactions. Transactions are not easy to track from primary sources. Private transactions not in the framework of a water bank are supposed to be annotated in Water Registries. However, Water Registries are in a poor state.[49] Not all rights are registered, and not all transactions have been properly registered. Some aggregated data on changes on the rights entries in the registries is available through the reports of each River Basin Authority (RBA), but it is not possible to disentangle

---

47 Apart from lacking the transactions where the water bank is the buyer, the transactions where the bank was a seller seem to amount to the total traded according to other sources. Compare Howitt and Hanak (Richard Howitt and Ellen Hanak, 'Incremental Water Market Development: The California Water Sector 1985–2004,' 30 Can. Water Resources J. 73, 74 (2005)) with the Bren School database. Howitt and Hanak report that 810,713.19 acr-ft were bought and 405,356.59 acr-ft were sold. The database reports sales from the bank of 414,372 acr-ft in 1991 and 50,000 acr-ft in 1992.

48 Email from Zack Donohue, primary contact and manager of the database of US water transfers at the Bren School of Environmental Science and Management (1 May 2013).

49 Libro Blanco del Agua en España, above note 22, at 16.

whether or not those changes in the characteristics of a right are the result of a transaction. The changes reported could be the result from inheritance. Thus, for Spain, after unsuccessful attempts of gathering primary data, the sources used in this project are mainly secondary.

The basic data used is that presented by the Deputy Director of Water Public Domain Integrated Management (Ministry of the Environment), Mr Yagüe Córdova,[50] in Expo Zaragoza 2008, which had water as the main theme. The data he presented was quite comprehensive since it covered all the transactions from the period from 2000 to May 2008 for all the nine interregional RBAs. Before 2001, the mechanisms enacted in 1999 were not used, i.e. no transactions occurred, according to the accompanying documents to the National Hydrological Plan passed in 2001.[51] This might be explained by the succession of wet years. In addition to Mr Yagüe Córdova, other scholars, particularly agrarian engineers, have offered more detailed data on some of the contracts entered into by private parties. These additional articles have allowed the opportunity to cross-check the data, and where possible, to complement it.

Regarding Spanish centros de intercambio de derechos – water exchange centers, which are a type of water bank – some information is available in the official gazette because they have followed the rigid model of public procurement which imposes some limited requirements of transparency. Only the offer and the adjudicatory decisions are published. The level of detail of the latter is highly dependent on the RBA. For example, some offers included particularized information about who the counterparties were, and some did not. Nevertheless, the data presented by Mr Yagüe-Córdova, as well as pieces of news about the water banks, complete the data from official gazettes.

Beyond recording problems, both in California and in Spain, some transfers are not reported. In both jurisdictions, transactions between members of the same organization are often not reported where these members are not individual permit-holders, but receive an allocation from the institution holding the right. In California, for example, some irrigation communities have created exchange programmes which are not reported either. Solano Irrigation District, which does not serve only irrigators, provides an example.[52] Similarly, irrigation communities in Spain acknowledge the existence of trades between their members without any formal recording;[53] these have been happening for

---

50 Jesús Yagüe-Córdova, *Experiencia de los instrumentos de mercado en España*, Expo Zaragoza (2008), http://www.conagua.gob.mx/bancodelagua07/Tema/36JesusYagueCordova.pdf.

51 Mónica Sastre, 'Posibilidades de crear un mercado al amparo de la nueva Ley de Aguas,' 4 Revista del Instituto de Estudios Econ. 293, 294 (2001).

52 A total of 45 irrigators took part in the programme, fallowing a total of approximately 5,000 acres of land, or approximately 10 per cent of the total land historically allocated to grow crops in Solano County. Irrigators were paid US$170 per acr-ft. Doug Malchow, 'A Review of California Water Transfers,' 16 UC Davis Envt'l L. & Pol'y J. 51, 54 (1992).

53 Telephone interview, Juan Valero de Palma, President of FENACORE (Spanish National Association of Irrigation Communities) (14 July 2012).

a long time. They are not even regulated in the irrigation communities' bylaws. Actually, Spanish regulation establishes that such trades are internal acts, not subject to the review of the water agencies. Data on these transactions is not considered because, beyond data-gathering challenges, this book focuses on formal market mechanisms and informal transfers have not solved scarcity challenges.

3.3.2 Proxies for the dependent variable

Market success is measured using the following market activity proxies: number of transactions, volume traded, and from which sector to which sector water is traded.[54]

Using quantity of trades and volume of water traded offers a hint about how active a market is. These measures have also been used to compare trends in contractual forms, and parties to the contract (e.g. agricultural-urban trades or agricultural-environment trades) among different Western states,[55] but these measures are a bit rough. Volume and number of trades could respond not only to market robustness but also to other variables. For example, the number of transactions might be higher in Spain if water rights tend to be granted for smaller volumes. In addition, there might be unaccounted-for external effects, which may damage or benefit other legal users of water[56] and hence more transactions or more water transfer may not imply a greater social benefit. However, given that in California and Spain there are mechanisms to prevent externalities or to compensate for them, market activity does not hide in any of the two jurisdictions effects on third parties.

---

54 Water value and transaction price measures are used in quantitative empirical studies on water. Studies using value normally use a single observation to justify the need for water markets. These studies compare how much an urban user pays for water and how much a farmer pays or they compare the marginal value of water in the semi-conductor industry with the marginal value in alfalfa production. For example in California, an acre-foot used in the semi-conductor industry produces US$980,000 in gross state revenue, while the same quantity to grow alfalfa generates US$60 (Peter Gleick, 'Pending Deal Would Undermine State's Water Solutions,' at B7, *Sacramento Bee*, 25 February 2005). Value data is not readily available. Empirical studies also use the price paid in transactions because if there is a difference in price once transportation costs are discounted between intra-sectoral and inter-sectoral (e.g. agricultural to urban transactions), markets have still work to do. As shown below, price data is particularly incomplete for Spain, and is not helpful in assessing the different entrenchment of water markets in California and Spain.

55 Richard E. Howitt and Kristiana Hansen, 'The Evolving Western Water Markets,' 20 Choice 59, 60 (2005). Brewer *et al.*, *Water Markets in the West*, above note 2. T.C. Brown, 'Trends in water market activity and price in the western United States,' 42 Water Resour. Res. 1 (2006).

56 The potential effects on third parties who do not hold a legal right to use water are not considered externalities from an economic standpoint and should not receive direct compensation, but from a social welfare perspective if these negative effects occur, the transfer may not be socially beneficial. However, potential positive effects may also arise in the areas receiving the water. See Howitt and Hansen, ibid. at 61.

The second group of variables to look at is the nature of the uses of the seller and the buyer because the main idea behind markets is to shift water from those who value it less, normally the agricultural sector, to those who value it more, normally urban areas, but also, lately, the environment.[57] To assess how much water markets have contributed to solving the structural scarcity problem which calls for water to move from rural areas to urban centers, the ideal measure will be the impact on the distribution of rights or at least the consumption of water in each sector, which is an imperfect proxy for the distribution of rights among types of use. There are few anecdotal figures about the percentage of water rights allocated to a given sector. All we know is that agriculture uses most of the water. However, distribution of rights will not capture leases because the titleholder does not change. Consumption, in contrast, would capture both sales and leases, but may be affected by exogenous factors, such as a plague translating into less water consumption in the agricultural sector. Another way to frame this reallocation measure could be the percentage of water used coming from water traded. This measure is to some extent more complete than origin-destination assessment because it gives a sense of how much the market contributes to quenching the thirst of a particular sector. Unfortunately, data on consumption is not available for complete time series in both jurisdictions.

Given the data constraints, this book analyzes data on original and subsequent use of water. Another interesting variable for future analysis is the length of the trades, whether sales or long- or short-term leases. It is useful as an indication of what problem trades might be solving. A short-term lease might be offering relief of a temporary drought crisis, while a long-term lease can offer a more far-reaching structural problem either present or anticipated.

3.4 Timeline

The case studies analyze the first ten years since water markets were introduced or actively pursued. Chapter 4 on California focuses on water trading from 1991 to 2001. The start date of 1991 is not an arbitrary date: in that year, the water bank, which has been a landmark in water policy, was established during a terrible drought, although some market regulations were already in place.[58] Chapter 5 on Spain focuses on the decade after 1999 – i.e. 2000–10 – since,

---

57 Brewer *et al.*, *Water Markets in the West*, above note 2, at 37.
58 Richard Howitt and Ellen Hanak, 'Incremental Water Market Development,' above note 47 ('Although these reforms set the stage, the market did not take off until the next severe drought, beginning in 1987 and lasting until 1994'). See ibid. at 73 ('A series of drought years brought supplies to a low point in 1991. Rapidly formed emergency drought water bank alleviated the short run problem and pointed the way for a structural change in California water allocation and payments').

in December 1999, water regulations were amended in order to ensure that water rights could be transferred more easily, and that, in times of drought, water exchange centers could be established. By choosing the initial stages in both regions, the concerns regarding the fact that trade may grow as a result of experience are mitigated.[59]

However, some potential weaknesses of this approach must be acknowledged. First, California's market is much more active than Spain's, so the learning through time effect might be stronger because trust may increase and agencies may have more experience in reviewing transactions. Second, previous trading history, formal or informal, may have an impact on the subsequent trading activity. Trades occurred before the start date of the project in both jurisdictions, as the case studies note. In any case, prior trade was clearly insufficient to solve the water shortage problems and the misallocation in both jurisdictions as the early 1990s and mid-1990s drought crises for California and Spain, respectively, showed. Lastly, it is important to note that this choice of timeframe leaves intact the possible effect of culture. It might be that one of the two jurisdictions is more predisposed to commerce; conventionally, US culture is supposed to be highly market-oriented. Controlling for this variable is extremely difficult to do, so it has been left out. Moreover, in both jurisdictions, the potential sellers – farmers – are expected to be against the commodification of water.

3.5 Explanatory variables

3.5.1 General analysis

The qualitative study is focused on governmental roles as a – not the – potential explanatory variable for the success of water markets. However, scarcity needs to be factored in since it is a clear candidate for being a market driver. If water is scarce, more transactions are expected to occur and the price is expected to rise. Scarcity is the conventional explanation for market activity. This project does not make the negative case for scarcity – in fact, it includes data on rainfall as a proxy for it – but the affirmative case for governmental roles, which have often been overlooked.

'Governmental roles' is the main variable analyzed in order to explain water market success. If the theoretical analysis holds true empirically, the difference in market activity between California and Spain would be explained by the better fulfillment of governmental roles. In any event, it is useful to describe the portfolio of measures both jurisdictions have taken to deal with water market challenges.

---

59   Richard Howitt and Dave Sunding, 'Water Infrastructure and Water Allocation in California,' in Jerry Siebert (ed), *California Agriculture: Dimensions and Issues*, at 184 (2003), http://giannini.ucop.edu/CalAgBook/Chap7.pdf.

3.5.2 Scarcity

Among the potential explanatory variables, scarcity deserves a separate treatment to explain why it is or is not the driving force of market activity as conventional wisdom suggests. Basic economics says that the price of a scarce good should go up. In water, this is not the case, because water is mostly subsidized. The translation of that economic principle to water markets implies that more trade should occur the scarcer water is and the price in the market for rights to use water will go up. This will incentivize its efficient use and the realization of its opportunity cost.

The relationship between scarcity and trade is not monotonic.[60] If water is abundant, no trade is expected since there is enough water to satisfy all demands. This might be the explanation behind the non-existence of markets in most eastern US States and humid countries. At the other end of the spectrum, if water is too scarce, either there is nothing to trade or, in other terms, marginal values in the agricultural sector are high enough not to motivate trade. The first drops to irrigate crops might be highly valued. Thus, water markets are expected to bloom where water is relatively scarce, i.e. where there are differences in marginal values. This scenario can arise in different situations such as those in which two types of uses have huge disparities in marginal value (e.g. a farmer growing alfalfa and paying a highly subsidized price for water would benefit from selling it to an urban industrial user, an urban water utility, or a farmer growing a perennial crop who values it more) or in which there are two regions which suffer from different relative levels of scarcity.

Scarcity for the purposes of this project is understood to mean availability of water. In fact, this is probably how we often think of water scarcity: as a result of a period of drought. However, scarcity is a richer concept. It is generally defined as the situation where demand exceeds the water resources exploitable under sustainable conditions.[61] The Food and Agriculture Organization considers that 'imbalances between availability and demand, the degradation of groundwater and surface water quality, intersectoral competition, interregional and international conflicts, all contribute to water scarcity.'[62] Underlying this concept, there is a problem for water markets. Supply takes into account regulated resources[63] – i.e. water made available thanks to public infrastructure,

---

60 Katrina M. Wyman, 'From Fur to Fish: Reconsidering the Evolution of Private Property,' 80 N.Y.U.L. Rev. 117, 141 (2005).

61 Communication from the Commission to the Council and the European Parliament addressing the challenge of water scarcity and droughts in the European Union, at 2, COM(2007) 414 final (18 July 2007).

62 FAO water, above note 15.

63 For a definition of regulated water resources, see Arrojo and Naredo, above note 9, at 37. For example, in Spain the construction of dams allowed to increase the exploitation of water resources from 9 per cent (rivers and lakes themselves facilitate their exploitation) to 40 per cent according to L. Berga, 'Dams and Reservoirs in XXth Century Spain,' 3438 Revista de Obras Públicas 37 (2003), http://ropdigital.ciccp.es/pdf/publico/2003/2003_noviembre_3438_04.pdf.

such as storage or desalination – and government may influence it. Government may even create regulatory scarcity by establishing caps on extraction in order to protect the environment which reduce available supply for consumptive uses. Further, governmentally-set prices or educational campaigns, among other factors, affect the demand side of scarcity.

The relationship also works in the opposite direction: scarcity motivates governmental action, particularly harsh drought crises. Demsetz's thesis on the evolution of property rights can be read[64] as suggesting that as scarcity increases and the value of water rights goes up, property rights will be more defined.[65] More defined property rights in water would probably mean more transferable property rights[66] and, thus, more market activity. Given that property rights are a public good, government is providing the intermediate step necessary for water markets to thrive. Additionally, as the discussion of water rights security dimension shows, how government allocates the consequences of scarcity has a large influence on the market depending on how much discretion the public agency deciding on those consequences has.

The potential interactions between the two explanatory variables – government and scarcity – should be less of a problem in a qualitative study because the relationships will be unveiled in a narrative format. Thus, scarcity, in the case studies, would have to be taken into account both as an explanation for the amount of trade and as a driver of governmental action.

As for measures of scarcity, there are several potential indexes which take into account different variables and which have different geographical scope. There are very complex indexes which take into account environmental demands and basic human water needs.[67] None of the indexes is

---

64 Harold Demsetz, 'Toward a Theory of Property Rights,' 57 Am. Econ. Rev. 347 (1967). For an analysis of Demsetz's claims, see Douglas W. Allen, 'The Rhino's Horn: Incomplete Property Rights and the Optimal Value of an Asset,' 31 J. Legal Stud. S 339, S 340 (2002).

65 Hardin proposes, in fact, the definition of property rights as a solution to the tragedy of the commons. Garrett Hardin, 'The Tragedy of the Commons,' 162 Sci. 1243 (1968).

66 This statement must be qualified, however, because the more defined property rights are, the higher transaction costs might be if rights are less fungible. In extreme cases, it could lead to the tragedy of the anti-commons. The term 'anti-commons' was created by Heller (Michael Heller, 'The Tragedy of the Anticommons: Property in the Transition from Marx to Markets,' 111 Harv. L. Rev. 621 (1998)) to describe those situations where the fragmentation of the bundle of rights is such that least to inefficient outcomes because action cannot be taken given the numerous rights to veto. For the application to water, see Stephen N. Bretsen and Peter J. Hill, 'Water markets as a tragedy of the anticommons,' 33 Wm. & Mary Envt'l L. & Pol'y Rev. 723 (2009). The main idea in the paper is that several types of actors may have veto power in the review procedure.

67 For a comprehensive review of Indicators and Indices for decision making in water resources management, see Amber Brown and Marty D. Matlock, *A Review of Water Scarcity Indices and Methodologies*, White Paper n.106, Sustainability Consortium (2011). See also Environmental and Energy Management Research Units, University of Athens, 'Indicators and Indices for decision making in water resources management,' http://environ.chemeng.ntua.gr/WSM/Newsletters/Issue4/Indicators_Appendix.htm.

perfect[68] and data is incomplete and not fully comparable for California and Spain. In order to mitigate the problem of disentangling the abovementioned two-sided relationship between governmental action and scarcity and bypass the data problems, this book takes a rough proxy of scarcity: rainfall data.

3.5.3 Governmental roles: operationalizing the variables

The categories of government action analyzed for these purposes respond to the potential market failures encountered – undersupply of public goods, natural monopoly infrastructures, or externalities arising from water transfers – or enhance water market activity by reducing transaction costs. As Chapter 2 shows, these translate into government having to play a role in defining and enforcing property rights, policing for externalities, ensuring that infrastructure is open to third parties to ship the water transferred, and reducing transaction costs by leveraging the market. For each of these necessary roles, the different actions and the depth with which they have been carried out have to be assessed, in the two jurisdictions. Table 3.2, based on Chapter 2, summarizes the main variables to take into account.

Some caveats are necessary. First, it must be acknowledged that government actions not necessarily targeting water market goals might have an impact on water markets. This might be the case, for example, of the California regulation requiring developers to ensure water supplies for new urban areas and allowing them to count future transfers as part of these. Hence, while undertaking the case studies, these other possibly relevant government actions need to be noted. Second, not all the roles of government necessary for a water market to operate smoothly are directly triggered by water markets since they are also justified for other governmental roles. For example, dams and canals have been built long before the market paradigm entered into the picture; canals transport water to areas where it is scarce, ensuring economic development, but these are also the mains for transfers. Third, some water market policies may have a lagged effect.

3.5.4 A note on interest group pressure as a precursor of governmental action

Potential explanations of why government undertook the roles analyzed may also emerge from the case studies even if it is not the purpose of this project

---

68 For example, a very well-known index for water scarcity is the Falkenmark Water Stress Indicator, which measures the total annual runoff available for human use. Since it is based on individual usage, it captures human-induced scarcity. It has a main shortcoming: it does not take into account seasonal variability, which might be huge and motivate trades in markets. Ibid. Other indexes take into account anthropogenic water demand, which could be problematic since government may influence it. One example is the Water Stress Supply Index.

Table 3.2 Summary of governmental roles

Role	Factors
Definition of property rights	Security: discretion of the agencies affecting the rights Tradability: limits: – tradeoffs with externalities review Role of institutional right holders Definition of instream flow rights/protection of instream flow
Review of externalities	*Ex-ante* v. *Ex-post* Different for short-term and long-term transactions Procedural provisions: length and burden of proof Third party participation/compensation Community externalities treatment
Infrastructure management	Gaps: lack of connections Third party access: – potential for discrimination by the infrastructure owner Authorization procedure to use water infrastructure
Market maker role	Information provision: – water rights registry – transactions Match-maker: water banks Increase in water rights fungibility: – guidelines to calculate the volume tradable Guarantee function

to answer this question. Scarcity has already been mentioned as a type of precursor to governmental roles. Another precursor could be the role of interest groups. Libecap's property rights theory suggests that property rights are provided top-down – i.e. they are provided by government – as the result of interest group competition to strike a satisfactory deal.[69] Thus, under this theory, modification of property rights to establish water markets by public agencies would be explained by pressure by some interest groups.

Accordingly, in this project, interest groups are not analyzed as an explanatory variable, only as part of what explains governmental intervention.[70] Whether certain lobby groups will be more in favor of water markets than others will depend on which group benefits from the status quo, the power to influence the different branches and administrations involved, and the allocation of gains

69 Saul Levmore, 'Two Stories about the Evolution of Property Rights,' 31 J. Legal Stud. S421, S426, S429 (2002). Gary D. Libecap, 'Distributional Issues in Contracting for Property Rights,' 145 J. Inst. & Theoretical Econ. 6, 7 (1989).
70 Carol M. Rose, 'Property and Emerging Environmental Issues – The Optimists vs. the Pessimists,' 1 Wm. & Mary Brigham-Kanner Prop. Rts. Conf. J. 405, 16 (2012).

from the change.[71] Although the analysis is extremely context-dependent, some starting hypotheses about the positions of the three main groups at stake – agriculture, cities, and environmentalists – regarding water markets can be identified. In fact, the seminal idea for water markets was precisely to give incentives to the agricultural sector to sell water to urban areas, allowing the former to make money out of subsidized water to quench the thirst of the latter.

First, the agricultural sector is expected to be reluctant to trade due to certain non-economic, cultural values[72] which reflect the strong ties that the agricultural sector has to its community.[73] According to the general idea of the United States being a more market-oriented culture, we expect the Spanish agricultural sector to be more reluctant. In addition, even though trade had occurred in both jurisdictions before market mechanisms were launched, there may be reluctance to trade using the formal mechanism not for 'cultural' reasons, but for fear of forfeiture if water rights are subject to use-it-or-lose-it kind, or for fear of seeing subsidized prices rise. Although markets could allow farmers to make a profit from water they receive at a subsidized price, farmers tend to be reluctant to favor markets because they fear that government may use it as evidence that they do not need that water.

Second, urban areas could be thought to be in favor of water markets where supply cannot be augmented at a reasonable price, since markets allow them to buy water away from the agricultural industry, which for historical reasons holds the majority of rights. However, urban areas may not be in favor of markets since they may not need to resort to them; if a harsh drought arises, they will not see their water supply curtailed because politicians cannot afford to lose the support of urban areas.

Lastly, environmentalists may prefer to be favored by mandatory regulation, which they may consider fair, given the arguments that either the environment has a value in itself, or that all of us benefit from a cleaner environment. The cost of mandatory regulation may be shouldered either by all taxpayers or by those harming the environment, but not by environmentalists. However, environmentalists may accept markets as a viable strategy to protect the environment by buying water rights in jurisdictions where they are not powerful enough to push for regulation.

---

71 Gary Libecap, *Contracting for Property Rights*, at 21 and 24–25 (1989).

72 See, in general, J.G. Tisdell and J.W. Ward, 'Attitudes toward water markets: an Australian case study,' 16 Soc'y & Nat. Res. 61 (2003).

73 Emerick and Lueck testing the impact of third party effects on the decision to enter a short-term or a long-term transaction in water, find evidence suggesting that farmers prefer short-term agreements when water is traded to outsiders because they care about the pecuniary externalities on their rural communities. Kyle Emerick and Dean Lueck, *Economic Organization and the Lease-Ownership Decision in Water*, at 25 (12 May 2010), unpublished working paper, http://papers.ssrn.com/sol3/papers.cfm?abstract_id=1605523. Tisdell and Ward, ibid. at 66 (farmers are reluctant to treat water as a chattel, but there is increasing acceptance for water trading).

4 California's water markets

4.1 Introduction

California, which has an uneven distribution of water across space[1] and time, is usually regarded as a pioneer in environmental regulation and, also, in water law issues. It was the first US State to recognize that some water rights could be transferred independently of land in early twentieth century.[2] As this chapter illustrates, water markets discussions kicked off in the early 1970s in the scholarly debates as well as in policy discussions at the State and federal levels. Water market legislation was introduced with the aim of increasing efficiency in water use. Such a goal could be in tension with public property over water and the pursuit of public interest.[3]

The period of study selected in this book is 1991–2000, given the relevance of the 1991 drought water bank, highlighted by the scholarship on the topic and the attention paid to water markets in California as a result of it. Despite the Owens Valley stigma,[4] water transactions in California occurred for many years, but the establishment of the water bank is believed to be a turning point where transactions become part of California's water management on a more regular basis. Amendments and transactions occurred before 1991, as

---

1   Meaghan Daly, 'California's Water Bank: A Bank with nothing to lend?' *State of the Planet*, 27 March 2009, http://blogs.ei.columbia.edu/2009/03/27/californias-water-bank-a-bank-with-nothing-to-lend/ (describing California's water natural distribution 75 per cent of the runoff occurs north of Sacramento and 75 per cent of the demand south of it).

2   Jedidiah Brewer, Michael Fleishman, Robert Glennon, Alan Ker, and Gary Libecap, 'Law and the New Institutional Economics: Water Markets and Legal Change in California,' 1987–2005, 26 Wash. U. J. of L. & Pol'y 183, 186 (2008) (citing *Duckworth v Watsonville Water & Light Co.*, 150 Cal. 520, 530–31 (1907); in relation to Cal. Code Regs., tit. 23, §775 (2005)).

3   Aaron Baker, '*Central Delta Water Agency v State Water Resources Control Board*: Exposing Inherent Tensions in the California Water Code with Respect to Water Transfer Markets,' 14 Hastings W-Nw. J. Envt'l L. & Pol'y 1645, 1653 (2008).

4   Marc Reisner, *A Catalog of Obstacles to Water Transfers in California: A Report to the San Joaquin Valley Drainage Program*, at 37 (June 1990) (Owens Valley taints any transaction from agriculture to non-agricultural users).

analyzed below, but again the takeoff is associated with the bank. However, as set out below, water markets cannot thrive without the involvement of government, not only at the outset but also while markets operate. In California, both the State, particularly through the actions of the State Water Resources Control Board (SWRCB), and the federal government, through the United States Bureau of Reclamation (USBR) in relation to the federal projects, embraced markets and fulfilled many of the roles listed in Chapter 2. They did not excel in all of them, but water markets have become part of the toolkit of water management in the Golden State and they help alleviate structural problems as well as prepare for and mitigate the effects of future drought crises and of regulatory scarcity.[5]

This book does not aim to say that the only explanation of market activity is whether or not government has fulfilled the roles identified. Accordingly, the role of natural and regulatory scarcity and of interest groups is also taken into account, even if it is not the aim of this chapter to explain *why* Californian water agencies fulfill certain roles, but *whether* they fulfill them. It is important to note that there is consensus that most interest groups became aligned in the 1990s crisis and there was no opposition to the executive order establishing the water bank. However, this is not a common scenario. In California, transfers, although not uncommon, have been controversial and will remain so.[6] For example, during the period of study the implementation of a well-known, quite controversial transfer started. This is the agreement between the Imperial Irrigation District (IID) and the Metropolitan Water District of Southern California (MWD) that stipulated that the latter would pay the former for conservation measures and the water saved by these methods would be transferred to the MWD. The IID entered into this transaction only after receiving pressure from the SWRCB which threatened to reduce its rights.[7] This transfer between the IID and the MWD was controversial because the IID was not again inclined to accept such a transfer, but it was greatly pressured

---

5 Regulatory scarcity also played a clear role after the period of study when the federal protection of endangered species came into play across the State, not only within the federal projects. Particularly harsh restrictions arise as a result of the Delta problems: the Delta is a hub which requires a certain amount of water and from which water cannot be pumped with even moderate force without catching certain fishes in the pumps. Some of these restrictions were imposed because of court decisions that were highly controversial as a result of the Federal Endangered Species Act, but others were the result of DWR management of the SWP. For more recent experience on using market transactions to make up for reduced supplies, see Shelley Ross Saxer, 'Managing Water Rights Using Fishing Rights as a Model,' 95 Marq. L. Rev. 91, 100–102 (2011).

6 Morris Israel and Jay R. Lund, *Recent California Water Transfers: Emerging Options for Water Management*, at 32, US Army Corps of Engineers (1992).

7 There are several examples of these struggles. First, the SWRCB issued Order 88-20 mandating the IID to Submit Plan and Implementation Schedule for Conservation Measures (30 September 1988). The controversy continued in *Imperial Irrigation Dist. v State Water Res. Control Bd.*, 225 Cal. App. 3d 548, 573 (1990).

by the State legislature and the US Secretary of the Interior, who threatened to reduce the IID's right to Colorado River water.[8] The IID balked at the initial proposal due to its fear of community destruction and the fact that it did not want to share the potential liability for the Salton Sea with the MWD.[9] Those transfers in which pressures by the governing agencies were exercised have been much discussed by authors who think these are not fully real transactions and use them either to deny the possibility of water markets[10] or to highlight the need to actually implement them.[11]

This chapter starts by offering an overview of the water rights and the administrative structure, because these are instrumental to understanding the pro-market legislation presented next and to evaluate how government has fulfilled the different roles set out in section 4.6. Market activity listed in section 4.4 is also instrumental to the latter evaluation, as well as to the role of scarcity, analyzed in Chapter 3, which is another explanatory variable, complementary to the roles played by governmental agencies.

4.2 Overview of water management and water rights in California

4.2.1 Types of water rights

A description of the heterogeneity of Californian water rights is important for understanding which rights were or could have been traded and the procedural requirements associated with those trades.

California has a hybrid regime of water rights: riparianism and prior appropriation. In addition, there are other types of rights such as pueblo rights[12] or federal-reserved water rights,[13] but their relative volume is scant.[14]

---

8 Joseph W. Dellapenna, 'Climate Disruption, the Washington Consensus and Water Law Reform,' 81 Temple L. Rev. 383, 242–425 (2008). Legislation insulated IID (and possibly, the San Diego County Water Authority) from liability for more than US$133 million for impacts to the Salton Sea from the transfer. This was a critical development facilitating the transfer (2002 Cal. Legis. Serv. Ch. 617 (S.B. 482), 2003 Cal. Legis. Serv. Ch. 612 (S.B. 317), and §1013 of the Cal. Water Code). See Brewer *et al.*, above note 2, at 212.

9 David Carle, *Introduction to Water in California*, at 114–115 (2004).

10 See generally, Dellapenna, above note 8.

11 Terry L. Anderson and Pamela Snyder, *Water Markets. Priming the Invisible Pump*, at 104 (1997).

12 Pueblo rights are historical rights recognized under the Treaty of Guadalupe (1888) and held by municipalities. These municipalities have prior rights to surface and groundwater sufficient to meet current and future need of the community. They are similar to reserved rights because both are granted priority and because they are not subject to a use requirement. Pueblo rights are problematic because they can keep expanding. This is still true nowadays under existing California Law. However, as it happens in New Mexico, it is expected that courts in considering contemporary claims of pueblo rights, particularly those which assert dormant rights or those which try to expand affecting other will not blindly uphold those rights but take into account other competing claims. Scott Slater, *California Water Law and*

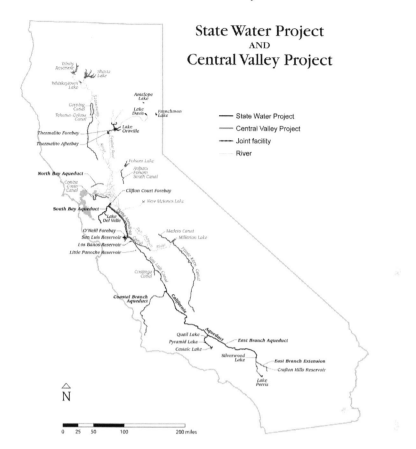

State Water Project
AND
Central Valley Project

—— State Water Project
—— Central Valley Project
---- Joint facility
 River

Trinity Reservoir
Shasta Lake
Whiskeytown Lake
Corning Canal
Antelope Lake
Lake Davis
Frenchman Lake
Tehama-Colusa Canal
Thermalito Forebay
Lake Oroville
Thermalito Afterbay
Folsom Lake
Auburn Folsom South Canal
North Bay Aqueduct
Contra Costa Canal
Clifton Court Forebay
New Melones Lake
South Bay Aqueduct
Lake Del Valle
O'Neill Forebay
San Luis Reservoir
Los Banos Reservoir
Little Panoche Reservoir
Madera Canal
Millerton Lake
Coalinga Canal
San Luis Canal
California Aqueduct
Coastal Branch Aqueduct
Quail Lake
Pyramid Lake
Castaic Lake
East Branch Aqueduct
Silverwood Lake
East Branch Extension
Crafton Hills Reservoir
Lake Perris

△ N

0 25 50   100   200 miles

Figure 4.1 Main water infrastructure projects in California
Source: DWR

Policy, at Ch. 1-5, §5.07 (2015); Amy L. Kelley (ed), 4-37, *Waters and Water Rights*, 3rd edn, at §37.05 (2011).

13   The United States acquires a water right to unappropriated water that vests on the date of the reservation and it is superior to the rights of future appropriators. Slater, ibid., at Ch. 1-15, §15.05. The broad purpose is to protect natural resources for the benefit of future generations, but the specific measure is determined by each particular reservation. Examples of these reservations are National Parks or National Forests. Federal reserved water rights are appurtenant to federal lands. As such the right is not susceptible to transfer for use on non-reserved lands. However, they could be subject to a contract to reduce its use for the benefit of a more junior user down the river. Slater, ibid. at Ch. 1-15, §15.10. A particular type of federal rights are Indian reserved rights, which may be defined by the wording of the specific instrument establishing the Indian reservation and by the previous exercise to meet the subsistence and commercial needs of the tribe. In relation to their potential transfer through markets, 'Indian water rights are property rights appurtenant to the reserved lands. They may not be alienated by conveyance from Indians to non-Indians without the consent of the federal government,' Slater, ibid. at Ch. 1-15, §15.12.

14   SWRCB, *A Guide to Water Transfers*, at 3–4 (1999).

California adopted the riparian doctrine in early times from the east of the United States, a wet area where scarcity was not a problem. Riparian rights are those granted to owners of land adjacent to a stream, allowing them to appropriate the water for reasonable use on their land. In general, riparian rights cannot be traded, precisely because they must be used in the land adjacent to the stream.[15] Riparian rights are senior to appropriative rights. Within the system of riparian rights, water right holders shared the consequences of water shortage equally. Riparian right holders in California are required to file statements of water diversion and use with the SWRCB.[16]

As it happened in other western US States, riparianism soon proved inadequate to satisfy the new needs arising in the west. Mineral extraction required water to be diverted from the stream and used beyond riparian lands. The prior appropriation regime arose from practices adopted by miners to satisfy their needs. Nonetheless, riparian rights were not erased from the picture, but they are the least common form of surface water rights.[17]

Prior appropriation is based on two premises. First, water has to be diverted from the river and put to beneficial use. The principle of beneficial use locks water into historical uses because the uses were beneficial when they were initiated. The criteria to consider what is beneficial and how to update those criteria remain unclear. Second, in times of scarcity, they are satisfied according to the rule 'first in time, first in right.' Seniority matters: in times of drought, more senior appropriative rights would be satisfied and junior ones might not receive anything, or just what is left, no matter the type of use. They are also subjected to the 'use it or lose it' doctrine which requires appropriators to use their rights. If they do not, they will forfeit them to the authorities. The aim of this provision is to avoid the speculative parking of water. Riparian rights are not subjected to the use it or lose it doctrine.

There are two types of appropriative rights in California. First, there are rights that arose from use, without any legal proceeding. This was the case until 1914. Those pre-1914 rights exist by virtue of previous diversion and application to beneficial use. Later, in 1914, a permit system respecting existing ones was introduced for appropriative rights. Pre-1914 rights have priority over all appropriative rights after that date. Holders of pre-1914 water rights are required to file with the SWRCB a document called a Supplemental Statement of Diversion & Use (SSDU). However, such a registration does not validate the right,[18] it serves only to facilitate the SWRCB's calculation of the water used from each stream.

Post-1914 appropriative rights are granted after an administrative procedure, but follow similar requirements as consuetudinary prior appropriation systems

---

15   Slater, above note 12, at Ch. 1-3, § 3.01.
16   §5101 of the Cal. Water Code.
17   Arthur L. Littleworth and Eric L. Garner, *California Water*, at 33–34 (1995).
18   §5106(a) of the Cal. Water Code.

do. These post-1914 rights are defined according to the following variables: source of supply, amount, location of the point of diversion, use, location of the place of use,[19] timing, and point of return flow.[20] Users who want to appropriate water must apply for a permit that grants the right to use a certain volume of water and to build whatever infrastructure is needed for those purposes. Those rights are not exactly analogous to a fee simple ownership of land, but there are certain circumstances in which governmental actions encroaching upon those may still amount to a taking.[21]

Both types of appropriative rights, pre- and post-1914 rights, have been transferable. This chapter analyzes the restrictions on their transferability or the procedures to which they are subject in the context of either the property rights definition or externalities review, since the mechanisms used to ensure the internalization of effects arising from transactions depend upon the nature of the right despite there being no obvious policy reason for such a difference.[22]

Hence, in California we can find several types of surface-water right holders. To this amalgam, yet another layer of complexity needs to be added. Many Californian water users do not hold a right, but rather a contract with a local, regional, State, or federal agency. These public agencies are the right holders of prior appropriation rights and the users hold a right to be supplied with a certain amount of water. Particularly relevant are the contracts between local agencies or individual contractors and one of the big water projects that cross California, either State or federal.

The California State Water Project (SWP) is managed by the California Department of Water Resources (DWR) and the Central Valley Project (CVP) and other smaller federal projects are managed by the USBR, which is the largest supplier in California.[23] Together, the CVP and the SWP provide approximately 30 per cent of the State's surface-water needs. The DWR and the USBR hold post-1914 rights which then they apportion to satisfy their contractual claims. The contracts with the projects do not fully guarantee a specific volume of water. In fact, it must be an extremely wet year for the contractors to receive their full supply. Their contractual rights are in essence

---

19 §1260 of the Cal. Water Code (content of the application). See also the template to apply for a permit at the SWRCB website, http://www.waterboards.ca.gov/waterrights/water_issues/programs/permits/.
20 §1726(b)(2) of the Cal. Water Code (temporary changes related to transfer water).
21 *Casitas Mun. Water Dist. v United States*, 708 F.3d 1340 (Fed. Cir. 2013): the decision does not establish that there is a taking in this case because Casitas Municipal Water District fails to show that it will see the water they put to beneficial use reduced as a result of the restriction imposed by the USBR on the operation of the reservoir project. The reservoir project is owned by the USBR, but operated by Casitas which holds appropriative rights since 1956.
22 Legislative Analyst's Office, The Role of Water Transfers in Meeting California's Water Needs, at 11 (1999).
23 Israel and Lund, above note 6, at 12.

quite similar to appropriative rights, but subject to the oversight of the agency with which they contract. For example, there have been takings questions raised by the imposition by public agencies of regulations affecting those contractual rights.[24]

The SWP provides water supplies for 25 million Californians and 750,000 acres of irrigated farmland.[25] The SWP delivers around 2.3 MAF, but has contracts for 4.1 MAF:[26] its contractors therefore rarely receive their full allocation. From the contracted supply, the majority goes to urban users.[27] The SWP has delivery contracts with 29 agencies in the State. These local agencies which contract with the projects may also hold other types of rights – e.g. pre-1914 or groundwater rights.

The federal projects – CVP, the Colorado River Project, and numerous local projects[28] – provide roughly half of the surface water withdrawn for irrigation.[29] The CVP serves mainly irrigators (15 per cent of its water is for urban and industrial users); 139 landowners and eight water districts.[30] It stores around 17 per cent of State developed water, which amounts to 7 million acr-ft.[31] The CVP was designed to smooth water supply throughout the year, and also moved it south. It is important to highlight that both the post-1914 rights held by the USBR and by the SWP have broadly defined places of use and type of use. However, outside the system, USBR's post-1914 rights are like any other post-1914 water right: they are subject to State regulation. Thus, any contractual right transferred outside the federal system will be under State oversight too since it will imply a change in place of use of the right held by the USBR.

Another project worth mentioning is the Colorado River Project: this delivers to Californians the water they are entitled to according to the Colorado River Compact, i.e. 4.4 million acr-ft. Different districts with different priority rankings share the water allocated. For example, Palo Verde Irrigation District holds the most senior rights. Here it is not the USBR which is the right holder.

---

24 *Tulare Lake Basin v United States*, 49 Fed. Cl. 313 (Fed. Cl. 2001): plaintiffs had suffered a physical taking as a result of the restrictions to protect two species of fish under the Endangered Species Act imposed on their contractual water right.
25 DWR, SWP, http://www.water.ca.gov/swp/.
26 Israel and Lund, above note 6, at 2.
27 Israel and Lund, above note 6, at 15.
28 Israel and Lund, above note 6, at 12.
29 Terry L. Anderson, Brandon Scarborough, and Lawrence R. Watson, *Tapping Water Markets*, at 54 (2012).
30 David Carle, above note 9, at 103.
31 David Carle, above note 9, at 103. Cf. Israel and Lund, above note 6, at 2. According to Israel and Lund, CVP delivers eight MAF.

The framework described until now does not cover groundwater which is in general not subject to a rights system.[32] The only analogous regulation accrues in those basins that have been adjudicated by court decree or managed by local agencies that enact regulations restricting the unfettered extraction and use of the water. The disconnection in regulation between surface and groundwater is problematic since science has long realized that natural interconnection is indisputable. Thus, when analyzing markets, this is a crucial factor since uncontrolled substitutions of surface water for groundwater in order to lease or sell surface water may carry more costs than benefits: both may deplete the same system. In fact, both environmental and community concerns have prompted counties to enact regulations restricting groundwater transfers.[33] Some require those who want to transfer groundwater or use groundwater as a substitute for the surface water they transfer to apply for a permit. In 2002, 22 out of the 58 counties had passed this type of ordinance.[34] These ordinances have been deemed a transaction deterrent: very few users have applied for those permits. Users are afraid of falling under the control of government.[35]

Heterogeneity in water rights does not impair legal fungibility: the holders of any type of right can, in general terms, transfer their right or lease their water to any other party. However, the transactions of different types of right are subject to different requirements, and this may make some rights more attractive than others. Additionally, priority date, which is what determines which rights are going to receive water in times of drought, makes senior water rights more desirable. However, as shown below, there is no data on which type of right is being transferred and, thus, these hypotheses cannot be tested.

---

32 §1221 of the Cal. Water Code. However, 'Water flowing in a known and definite channel under the ground, and thus a subterranean stream, is treated under the surface water rights system in California.(. . .) In addition, some groundwater basins, mostly in southern California, have been adjudicated and many groundwater basins have local groundwater management plans adopted under §§10750 et. seq. (also known as AB 3030 for the Assembly bill that enacted these statues) or other laws,' see SWRCB, above note 14, at 3-1.

33 For a review of the history of counties' control and the arguments sustaining it, see Ellen Hanak and Caitlin Dyckman, 'Counties Wresting Control: Local Responses to California's Statewide Water Market,' 6 U. Denv. Water L. Rev. 490 (2003). Since there is no clear State groundwater regulation, counties using their police powers to protect the area's public welfare have limited exports of groundwater. For a summary of county ordinances up to date, see Ellen Hanak and Elizabeth Stryjewski, *California's Water Market, By the Numbers, Update 2012*, at 16, PPIC (2012) ('These ordinances all restrict direct groundwater exports; most also restrict groundwater substitution transfers, and some aim to restrict groundwater banking with non-local parties').

34 Ellen Hanak and Richard Howitt, 'Incremental Water Market Development: The California Water Sector 1985–2004,' 30 Can. Water Resources J. 73, 78 (2005).

35 Ellen Hanak, *Who Should Be Allowed to Sell Water in California? Third-Party Issues and the Water Market*, at 65–68 and 83–85 (2003).

4.2.2 California's allocation of power over water management

The diversity in water-use rights demonstrates a necessary administrative complexity, even before discussing how markets are organized. In general terms, the responsibility for the allocation and enforcement of rights lies with the SWRCB. The SWRCB's powers have different intensity depending on the type of right they affect.

However, as mentioned in passing, this agency does not manage the two water arteries: the SWP is under the responsibility of another State agency, the DWR, and the CVP is managed by the USBR. Both the DWR and the USBR hold post-1914 water rights subject to the regulation of the SWRCB, but within the projects, the DWR and USBR can dictate the rules. In the federal projects, it is explicitly stated that State regulations are supplemental.[36]

Coordination and co-operation between State and federal authorities has been extremely beneficial. In 1986, the DWR and the USBR entered into a 'Coordinated Operation Agreement' to maintain the Sacramento-San Joaquin River Delta water quality standards.[37] This Agreement seeded ulterior co-operation, such as the establishment of the CALFED Bay-Delta Program in 1994,[38] and eased joint operations during the drought water bank.

However, there are many other bodies with responsibility for water management at a more local level which are likely to be agents in this market. They are the entities holding the rights, while their customers, be they farmers or urban households, contract for their supply with them. Water-providing institutions differ widely in scale and organization;[39] for example, there are water special districts, mutuals, and irrigation districts. The organization bylaws may influence their participation in the market.

In the irrigation sector, there are very different schemes, irrigation districts – a form of public agency – and mutual ditch companies – not-for-profit corporations – being the most common ones.[40] In fact, they are the main suppliers of agriculture in California; there are few farmers who self-supply.

---

36   Richard W. Wahl, *Water Marketing in California: Past Experience, Future Prospects*, at 22, Policy Study No. 162 (1993) (commenting on the following judicial decisions: *California v US* (Supreme Court) and *US v Alpine Land & Reservoir Co.* (US Court of Appeals 9th Circuit)).

37   USBR, 'Coordinated Operations Agreement' (1986), http://www.usbr.gov/mp/cvp/docs/pl_99-546.pdf.

38   CALFED, http://www.calwater.ca.gov/.

39   Israel and Lund, above note 6, at 2. See ibid. at 13: 'The vast majority of the thousands of water suppliers in the state are local. The roughly 1,000 publicly owned water suppliers are formed under more than 40 different water district acts. Another 200 or so suppliers are privately-owned firms whose operations are governed by the State Public Utilities Commission. Another roughly 1,300 suppliers are mutual companies, voluntary non-profit cooperatives supplying cooperative irrigation services' (citations omitted).

40   Mutual irrigation companies are 'typically informally constituted cooperatives of farmers, with no governmental status. Each farmer has a share of the total amount of water available to the company. Water is then transferred by rental or shares to other farmers within the venture' (citations omitted), ibid. at 32.

These irrigation organizations' supply is formed by pre-1914 water rights, post-1914 water rights, contracts with State or federal projects, groundwater aquifers or any combination thereof. Whether farmers who are members of these districts can sell to outside the district users will depend on the internal bylaws of these organizations.

In the urban distribution sector, specialized governance also plays a very important role. Very few urban water suppliers are private, the majorities are utilities operated by the local government, be they general municipal government or specialized water districts. California has, in fact, the highest number of specialized water districts from all the 50 States.[41] Furthermore, the structure is nested: wholesale and retail supplies are intertwined. The MWD, which was an important player in the 1991 drought water bank,[42] is the largest local agency. It performs a role similar to the one played by the USBR in the CVP: it ships water from the sources to the gates of the local agencies. The MWD is the wholesale supplier for 27 sub-regional suppliers and indirectly to 210 local suppliers. The area it serves has a population of around 15 million people.[43] Some scholars consider that this net of contracts between wholesalers and retailers in metropolitan areas constitutes a market,[44] but this is not the type of market on which this book focuses (exchange of water rights).[45]

41 US Census Bureau, 'Census of Governments, Government Organization,' at 1 (2002), http://www.census.gov/prod/ 2003pubs/gc021x1.pdf. California is the State with the highest number of single-purpose special districts managing water supply. To those 113 multi-purpose ones, dealing with both water supply and sewage or natural resources, must be added.
42 Israel and Lund, above note 6, at 6.
43 Israel and Lund, above note 6, at 13. In 2012, 'It is governed by a 37-member board of directors representing 26 member public agencies that purchase some or all of their water from Metropolitan and serve 19 million people across six Southern California counties,' see MWDSC, 'Annual Progress Report to the California State Legislature Achievements in Conservation, Recycling and Groundwater Recharge' (2012), http://www.mwdh2o.com/mwdh2o/pages/yourwater/SB60/SB60_2012.pdf.
44 Israel and Lund, above note 6, at 31.
45 Beyond the period of study, MWD contractors had to use water transactions to make up for the restrictions as a result of the Colorado Water Plan, in which agricultural districts have priority. In fact, an element which must be analyzed in the evolution of Californian water market beyond the period studied is the California's Colorado River Water Use Plan, known as 4.4 Plan. It is important because it shows part of the political economy on the water management scenario. The 4.4 Plan was issued in 2001 despite the fact that a draft version was put forward in the spring of 2000. California was compelled to reduce its consumption from the Colorado to its historical right. California, which shares the lower Colorado Basin with Arizona and Nevada, had been using 5.2 MAF. Its right amounted only to 4.4 MAF, and thus some of the entitlements of California users to the river needed to be curtailed amidst disagreement. From the 4.4 MAF, the first three priorities are given to three agricultural agencies, up to 3.85 MAF. The MWD comes next. If the annual allocation for a year goes over 4.4 MAF, the MWD is granted the priority for this surplus water, followed by the agricultural agencies and other contractors. The likelihood of surplus water or of the other states not consuming their basic allocations is not high. Thus, this shows that the agricultural sector seems to be better insulated from drought risk than urban contractors. Thus, some

In addition, other agencies, State and federal, have responsibilities related to, or affected by, water management. Clear candidates are those bodies responsible for land use, urban planning, or agriculture. However, given their impact on water management and transfers, as shown below, the most important are the environmental ones, on a broad sense, at the State or federal level. These include, among others, the California Department of Fish and Game, the US Environmental Protection Agency, and the US Fish and Wildlife Service. In fact, many transactions will be subject to the requirements of the National Environmental Protection Act or to the California Environmental Quality Act (CEQA) requirements. They must also comply with the California Endangered Species Act or the Federal Endangered Species Act. The protection of endangered species, such as the Delta smelt, has played a major role in California's water policy. Pumping restrictions imposed to preserve the biota in the Delta area have translated into relevant restrictions on water rights,[46] which create what has been labeled as regulatory scarcity because, in the absence of a drought, some users cannot satisfy their water rights.

4.3 Overview of the evolution of water market regulations

This section traces the different waves of amendments at the State and federal levels. Some of the amendments are analyzed in greater depth in the sections describing the roles played by Californian water agencies. As shown below, many amendments were passed after some period of scarcity. The effect of scarcity in the activity of the market cannot be disentangled from these amendments; however, those changes tend to stay after the crisis. In addition, other legislative mandates not covered here may actually make transactions more difficult, particularly those protecting the environment to the detriment of consumptive users of the water.

The 1991 drought water bank has been selected as the starting point of the comparative study. However, markets did not pop up unexpectedly in 1991: the discussion about them had been flowing for more than 20 years, both in academic scholarship of diverse disciplines and in governmental spheres. Most of the early scholarship[47] in the US advocated water markets in general since

buying through the MWD were prompted to resort to the market. The Plan itself, agreed in the early 2000s, assumed transactions as part of the solution. In fact, agreements between the IID and the Palo Verde Irrigation District and the San Diego Water Authority and the MWD are accounted for in the reductions. Colorado River District, http://www.crwcd.org/page_6; San Diego State University, 'Colorado River Plan,' http://www.sci.sdsu.edu/salton/CoRiverBoard4.4plan.html.

46   The Endangered Species Act has been labeled as a driver of regulatory drought, but some authors do not blame the Act, see Ellen Hanak, Jay Lund, Ariel Dinar, Brian Gray, Richard Howitt, Jeffrey Mount, Peter Moyle, and Barton 'Buzz' Thompson, 'Myths of California Water – Implications and Reality,' 16 W.-Nw 3, 22–25 (2010).

47   Economists and legal scholars wrote abundantly on these topics. The legal debate was particularly rich as noted in Barton Thompson, Jr., 'Institutional perspectives on water policy and markets,' 81 Cal. L. Rev. 671, 675 (1993).

they were an innovative tool; politicians were not unaware of the debate. The focus on transfers seems to put an end to the engineering era where the solutions to all water problems seemed to rely on supply augmentation through infrastructure, mainly dams and canals.

The first two policy reports on water markets in the 1970s were put forward at the federal level, despite targeting what was inherently State regulation, by the National Water Commission. The first was commissioned in 1971 and written by Meyers and Posner,[48] and the second was issued in 1973.[49] At the State level, in California, publicly commissioned reports, following the federal example, set the ground for the 1980s amendments, which are mentioned below. Two State reports appeared in 1978 amidst a tough drought: one by the Rand Corporation, commissioned by the State legislature,[50] and the other elaborated by the Governor's Commission to Review California's Water Rights Law.[51] In rough outlines, these reports recommended the amendments necessary to make water rights flexible and to enhance transactions. Some rights in California, as well as in other western US States, were tradable, but the procedure was so cumbersome that it was incredibly difficult to transfer water. State regulation did not respond immediately to these reports, but the federal projects did embrace a form of water markets more quickly. In 1977, the USBR operated a water bank enabled by federal legislation as a response to the drought.[52]

At the State level, small amendments followed in the 1980s, but water markets did not take off until the full involvement of the State government in the 1991 drought water bank.[53] The amendments purportedly aimed to

---

48 Charles J. Meyers and Richard A. Posner, *Toward an improved market in water resources* (1971).

49 National Water Comm'n, *Water Policies for the Future*, at 260–70 (1973).

50 Charles E. Phelps, Nancy Y. Moore, and Morlie Hammer Graubard, *Efficient Water Use in California: Water Rights, Water Districts, and Water Transfers* (1978), http://www.rand.org/pubs/reports/R2386.

51 California Governor's Commission to review Cal. Water Rights Law, *Final Report*, at 62–72 (1978).

52 Wahl, above note 36, at 23–24.

53 Israel and Lund, above note 6, at 66 (these authors, despite acknowledging that there had been transactions before – see ibid. at 67 – already sensed that private transactions would bloom after the bank, 'Overall, the California Drought Water Banks of 1991 and 1992 illustrate the advantages of government involvement in establishing water transfers at the local and regional level. The unique contributions of State involvement were to firmly demonstrate State support for water transfers as part of water resources management, increase the probability of success for individual transfers, lower the transaction costs of transfers, facilitate coordination of transfers with other water movements in the state, and temporarily waive some environmental impact reviews. The experience of the 1991 and 1992 Drought Water Banks will likely encourage the independent pursuit of transfers by individual agencies in the future and serve to establish water transfers as a water management technique even if the State never sponsors another water bank'). For an account on how modest the market was in the 1980s, see Baker, above note 3, at 1651.

enhance transactions, but the market did not flourish simply as a result of legislation. This was, among other reasons, because, given its diverse typology, all rights are not affected by the regulation in the same way. Despite the existence of these laws on paper, unfamiliarity with water markets could explain why they were not working immediately.

In 1980, in part following the recommendations of the mentioned commissions, the California Water Code (Cal. Water Code) was amended to ensure that transferred rights will not be forfeited for non-use or non-reasonable use.[54] The 1982 regulation offered further reassurance for those selling conserved water,[55] further recognizing the need of security for transferability[56] and mandating the agencies to promote transactions.[57] In 1984, a new provision required the consideration of transfers when preparing water plans.[58] Mandates

---

54 Different sections were amended. For our purposes, it is important to highlight §1244 of the Cal. Water Code: Evidence of unreasonable use or diversion: 'The sale, lease, exchange, or transfer of water or water rights, in itself, shall not constitute evidence of waste or unreasonable use, unreasonable method of use, or unreasonable method of diversion and shall not affect any determination of forfeiture applicable to water appropriated pursuant to the Water Commission Act or this code or water appropriated prior to December 19, 1914. This section does not constitute a change in, but is declaratory of, existing law' (Added Stats 1980, Ch. 933, §6).

55 Similarly in 1982, a further amendment adding subsection b to §1010 was enacted in this very same direction allowing explicitly the sale of conserved water: '(b) Water, or the right to the use of water, the use of which has ceased or been reduced as the result of the use of recycled, desalinated, or polluted water as described in subdivision (a), may be sold, leased, exchanged, or otherwise transferred pursuant to any provision of law relating to the transfer of water or water rights, including, but not limited to, provisions of law governing any change in point of diversion, place of use, and purpose of use due to the transfer,' §1010 (b) of the Cal. Water Code.

56 §109 of the Cal. Water Code. Voluntary transfer of water and water rights (the 1980 wording added in italics), '(a) The Legislature hereby finds and declares that the growing water needs of the state require the use of water in an (*a more*) efficient manner and that the efficient use of water requires (*greater*) certainty in the definition of property rights to the use of water and (*greater*) transferability of such rights. It is hereby declared to be the established policy of this state to facilitate (*encourage*) the voluntary transfer of water and water rights where consistent with the public welfare of the place of export and the place of import. (b) The Legislature hereby directs the Department of Water Resources, the State Water Resources Control Board, and all other appropriate state agencies to encourage voluntary transfers of water and water rights, including, but not limited to, providing technical assistance to persons to identify and implement water conservation measures which will make additional water available for transfer.' It also amended §382 allowing water districts to enter into transaction with those outside the agency.

57 For a general mandate, see §109(b) of the Cal. Water Code ('The Legislature hereby directs the Department of Water Resources, the State Water Resources Control Board, and all other appropriate state agencies to encourage voluntary transfers of water and water rights, including, but not limited to, providing technical assistance to persons to identify and implement water conservation measures which will make additional water available for transfer').

58 The mandate to include the potential water transfer opportunities in the water plans was originally in §10632(b) of the Cal. Water Code, but currently the reference is in §10631(d). Wahl, above note 36, at 7.

promoting water transfers in the water legislation are quite broad and may suggest that water markets require the involvement of government.

Nonetheless, not all recommendations from the Governor's Commission were adopted. For example, there was a proposal to license salvaged water that was not passed. It would have granted priority over all the other users to the salvaged water transferred if the transfer did not injure other users or the environment.[59] In addition, not all reforms promoted the ideas of market advocates. For example, in 1982, trials transfers were allowed. These transfers aimed at evaluating the effects of transactions on a trial basis. Although they had been envisioned as a step forward, in 1988 they were repealed.[60]

Some transactions took place before the operation of the 1991 drought water bank, but the activity was at best modest.[61] California's water market lacked drive[62] while other States were more active.[63] Many of California's transfers were operational exchanges, i.e. two parties exchanging water from different sources, mainly for practical reasons. This is the case of the agreement between the Coachella Valley Water District and Desert Water Agency with the MWD. These agencies did not have direct access to the SWP despite holding entitlement to its water: they exchanged these entitlements with the MWD's Colorado River ones.[64] Despite not being transactions where water is exchanged at a monetary price, they show that water changing hands, both in emergency and normal conditions, was not completely unknown to California's regime.

Federal projects did not lag behind. Federal and State governments were walking the same path, but not hand in hand. In fact, as already mentioned, markets were already part of the response to the late 1970s drought when the USBR established a bank. In 1987, the Western Governors' Association[65] compelled the US Department of the Interior to put forward a water-transfer framework. As a result, the Department issued a policy statement in late 1988.[66] In March 1989, the Commissioner of Reclamation issued more detailed

---

59 Caitlin S. Dyckman, 'A Dynastic Disruption: The Use Efficiency and Conservation Legacy of the Governor's Commission to Review California Water Rights Law Recommendations,' 36 McGeorge L. Rev. 175, 176 (2005).

60 Anderson and Snyder, *Priming*, above note 11, at 102.

61 Baker, above note 3, at 1651 ('a modest water transfer market began developing in California during the late 80s. The key word is "modest"' (footnotes omitted)).

62 Hanak and Stryjewski, above note 33, at 19.

63 Israel and Lund, above note 6, at 32. 'MacDonnell (1990) reviews recent transfers of water and water rights in six Southwestern States between 1975 and 1984. This review found almost 6,000 change of water-right applications filed in these states during the period, primarily in Colorado, New Mexico, and Utah.' Citing Lawrence J. MacDonnell, *The Water Transfer Process as a Management Option for Meeting Changing Water Demands*, Vol. I., USGS (1990).

64 Israel and Lund, above note 6, at 12.

65 Western Governors' Association, Water Efficiency: Opportunities for Action, Report of the Water Efficiency Working Group (1987).

66 Wahl, above note 36, at 22.

guidelines.[67] Those regulations allowed transfers within the federal projects in exchange for a monetary payment. Furthermore, these guidelines established that particular transactions, between the subsidized agriculture and urban areas that receive water from the USBR at a higher price, would be taxed by the USBR. This made these transactions less attractive and prevented the agricultural sector from reaping the profits. Nonetheless, it is well accepted that transfers within the CVP are easier than those within the SWP. Intra-project transactions occurred in the aftermath of the reform, but, as the USBR recognized, there was still room for improvement.[68] Intra-project transfers have been very important during the study period as section 4.4 explains.

Despite all these market-oriented steps, some experts did not consider the experience prior to 1991 a change of paradigm: they did not consider it to be a full market.[69] Reluctance to engage in water transfers could still be encountered. This may explain why contemporaneously to the water bank some redundant provisions were enacted emphasizing that transactions will not trigger further reviews of the underlying water rights. More evidence can be found in the fact that, even if it did not express total rejection, the California Farm Bureau Federation, the State's largest farm organization, expressed its fears in relation to water transfers in 1989 because it was concerned with the overall effect on the agricultural sector.[70]

As pointed out above, at the State level, a new wave of reforms took place around 1991, coinciding with the peak of the harsh drought. The main milestone that year was obviously the emergency drought water bank. In February, the DWR announced that its deliveries from the SWP would amount to only 10 per cent of the requests for water.[71] The CVP situation was slightly better, but reductions were still substantial.[72] Another measure, often used to evaluate the seriousness of a water crisis, is reservoir storage: in 1991 it hit levels as low as in 1977, with 54 per cent of storage on average. The situation had not been as harsh since the 1928–34 drought. The forecast was not

67 Wahl, above note 36, at 22.
68 Wahl, above note 36, at 23.
69 Bay Area Economic Forum, *Using Water Better: A Market-Based Approach to California's Water Crisis* (1991).
70 Doug Malchow, 'A Review of California Water Transfers,' 16 UC Davis Envt'l L. & Pol'y J. 51, 55 (1992) (citing G. Argent, 'Water marketing: Driven by low supplies,' *Western Water* (May/June, 1989), 'Bill Dubois, director of natural resources with the CFBF, argues that American farms are needed to feed the American people so that the United States does not become subservient to another country for its food source as it may be for oil. Others believe that farmers who sell their water to transfer to other areas will leave the agricultural area economically and/or environmentally devastated are needed to feed the American people so that the United States does not become subservient to another country for its food source as it may be for oil').
71 DWR, 'The 1991 Drought Water Bank,' at 1 (1992), http://www.water.ca.gov/water transfers/docs/10_1991-water_bank.pdf.
72 Ibid.

encouraging. Governor Wilson signed an Executive Order on 1 February establishing the Drought Action Team, which recommended setting up a water bank in its 15 February report.[73] The water bank was set up in less than 100 days thanks to the quick response of the State government.[74] The situation was so harsh that it did not spur opposition, although water markets are not always favored by all the interest groups.

It can be said that water markets were not part of the water management strategy until the 1991 drought water bank.[75] The water bank affected the number of trades and it is recognized as a milestone, as a catalyst.[76] The 1991 drought water bank bought 810,713.19 acr-ft and sold 405,356.59 acr-ft.[77] The water bank left a mark. The importance of the late 1980s and early 1990s changes, particularly the water bank, can be realized by looking at the increase in the volume committed per year over time. The number of water market transactions was the same as during the 1990s drought or even increased during the wet years after the drought.[78] This trend may also be showing a positive correlation between time and market development, suggesting a type of learning in the administration and especially among private parties, which consequently may feel reassured.[79] However, the numbers suggest that there was not only a mere evolution, but a change of level itself. In 1987 before the later 1980s and the early 1990s droughts, the average committed volume was 186,172 acr-ft. In 1997 and 1998, which were wet years, the average committed volume per year was 4,692,478 acr-ft and 4,521,341 acr-ft, respectively. The changes in 1989 and the water bank seem to have moved the markets to a new level. In fact, California has one of the most active markets in the western US States.[80]

73 Ibid.
74 Ibid. at 19.
75 Richard W. Wahl, 'Market Transfers of Water in California,' 1 W.-Nw. 49, 58 (1994) ('there is little question that if a well functioning review process had been in place and if California had a history of utilizing market transactions to reallocate water, then privately brokered arrangements could have substituted for many of the bank's activities during 1991').
76 Brewer *et al.*, above note 2, at 190. 'The water bank was particularly active during a five-year drought cycle in the late 1980s and early 1990s. It can be seen as a necessary catalyst for a sustainable long-term market, in part because the bank was so successful as revealed in the transfer data described below.'
77 Hanak and Howitt, above note 34, at 74 (report that 810,713.19 acr-ft were bought and 405,356.59 acr-ft round numbers in cubic meters).
78 Richard Howitt and Dave Sunding, 'Water Infrastructure and Water Allocation in California,' in Jerry Siebert (ed), *California Agriculture: Dimensions and Issues*, at 184 (2003), http://giannini.ucop.edu/CalAgBook/Chap7.pdf.
79 Ibid. at 186.
80 Brewer *et al.*, above note 2, at 196. 'Over the 19 year period (1987–2005) in our sample, 493 transfers took place in California, which transferred over 11.3 million acre-feet of water. . . . In comparison, in ten of the other eleven states in the West (excluding Colorado) there were 1047 water transfers totaling about 19.1 million acre-feet. These numbers indicate that California accounts for almost half of the number of transfers and sixty-percent of the amount of water transferred in the West.' Cf. above note 63.

The 1991 regulatory amendments, besides the water bank, more than introducing innovations, reinforced the rules already in place. This suggested that private parties had not internalized the former ones. Part of the reluctance of private parties might have had its origin in the fact that any transfer proposal would trigger detailed scrutiny on their beneficial use. Some new rules were also issued. For example, some amendments were passed enhancing the transferability of post-1914 appropriative rights by regulating short-term leases.[81] This was a provision with no real bite: leases were not used and, thus, this was an unnecessary provision because provisions facilitating short-term transfer were already in place. The lease provision acted more as a reinforcement, an enabler.[82]

Amendments to advance water markets were also abundant after 1991. After the water bank and while the crisis was fading, amendments continued at the State level. For example, in 1993, §382 of the Cal. Water Code, introduced in 1983, was further reformed to state that water districts could sell water which they had for gone using, for example, due to fallowing. Some pro-market regulations were introduced in relation to the projects, both federal and State, also after 1991. In 1992, the Central Valley Project Improvement Act (CVPIA) was enacted. It had multiple purposes, many related to environmental protection, but it also included transfer related regulation.[83] Even though 1993 was a relatively wet year, some authors have categorized 1993 as a drought year – a regulatory drought year because environmental regulations translated into reductions in water rights.[84] However, the CVPIA also ensured that both districts and their individual consumers could trade independently of the project parties, i.e. they could trade outside the project.[85]

In 1999, after the Water Plan update was published which identified marketing as one of the State-wide strategies to go forward,[86] the Water Rights Protection and Expedited Short-Term Water Transfer Act of 1999,[87] sponsored by the trade group Association of California Water Agencies, was passed. The first part of the title is devoted to the security dimension and the second can be seen as both increasing transferability while targeting the

---

81   §§ 1020 of the Cal. Water Code: they allowed the lease of water up to five years, for both pre-1914 and post-1914 rights, but only the 25 per cent of the water that would have been applied, not used, or stored (Deering's California code annotated. Cal Wat Code Div. 2, Pt. 1, Ch. 1.5 Note Added Stats 1991, Ch. 847, §3). For a comment, see Dyckman, above note 59, at 205.

82   §1020 of the Cal. Water Code. Telephone interview Scott Slater, partner at Brownstein Hyatt Farber Schreck, LLP and author of several books on California Water Law (13 May 2013).

83   USBR, Central Valley Project Improvement Act (CVPIA), http://www.usbr.gov/mp/cvpia.

84   Ellen Hanak, *California's Water Market, By the Numbers*, at 11, PPIC (2002).

85   Ibid. at 1. Slater, above note 12, at Ch. 5, §15.31.

86   California DWR, 'The California Water Plan Update Bulletin,' at ES4-8 (1998), http://www.waterplan.water.ca.gov/docs/previous/b160-98/esch4.pdf.

87   SB970, Assem. Bill 28, 1999–2000, Ch. 938, 1999 Cal. Stat.

externalities and streamlining the review procedure to reduce transaction costs for post-1914 rights.[88]

Brewer *et al.* carried out an empirical study of California's water markets. They looked at 21 potential legal factors which could affect water market activity and classified legislative amendments along these factors affecting markets.[89] They found that of the regulatory changes that occurred right before or during the period of study, only the 1989 and 1991 ones – which includes the water bank – were significant. These variables focus on legislative changes and administrative regulations, but they may miss other – maybe more intangible – governmental intervention.[90] In fact, some authors have expressed their scepticism about how much can be achieved by legislative changes in water markets,[91] which suggests that more hands-on governmental action is necessary.

All these changes show that California has made transfers an integral part of its water management, but there was and is still room to improve. The Model Water Transfer Act, elaborated in 1996 by a group of academic experts convened by Brian E. Gray, made this clear.[92] The Model Water Transfer Act, which was the result of a conversation with many stakeholders, proposed, among other things, to expedite the review procedure, to shift the burden of proof, and to include transfers of up to two years' duration under short-term transfers. The Model Transfer Act was not fully embraced by the legislature.[93] Again, in 2002, an Independent Water Transfer workgroup issued a report for the SWRCB on how to improve transfers, given their centrality in the future of the State and the necessity of joint action by numerous agencies and stakeholders.[94]

In any event, as these series of amendments at all levels passed shows the commitment to water markets, particularly in a system such as the one in place in California, where passing legislation is not always so smooth.

---

88 For an overview of the Amendment, see Andrew P. Tauriainen, 'California's Evolving Water Law: The Water Rights Protection and Expedited Short-Term Water Transfer Act of 1999,' 31 McGeorge L. Rev. 411 (2000).

89 Brewer *et al.*, above note 2, at 208. In order to do an econometrics study, they had encapsulated these changes in dummies representing the years where changes have occurred. This means that if there were three changes in one single year, their individual effects are not distinguishable. The years with more changes expanding markets occurred in 1988, 1991, 1993, 1999, and 2003; and most changes limiting water markets occurred in 1988, 1999, and 2001. The dependent variables chosen were number of trades and the volume traded.

90 Brewer *et al.*, above note 2, at 208.

91 Dyckman, above note 59, at 195. Thompson, above note 47, at 706. Norris Hundley, *The Great Thirst: Californians and Water – A History*, at 553 (revised 2001).

92 Brian E. Gray, 'The Shape of Transfers to Come: A Model Water Transfer Act for California,' 4 Hastings W.-Nw. J. Envtl. L. & Pol'y 23 (1996), reprinted in Brian E Gray, 'The Shape of Things to Come: A Model Water Transfer Act for California,' 14 Hastings W-Nw. J. Envt'l L. & Pol'y 623 (2008).

93 Baker, above note 3, at 1658.

94 SWRCB Water Transfer Workgroup, *Water Transfer Issues in California: Final Report to the California SWRCP* (2002), http://calwater.ca.gov/Programs/Water/Transfers/adobe-pdf/Final-Report%20_Water._Transfer_-Group.pdf.

4.4 Market activity from 1991 to 2000

This book uses the data compiled by the Bren School in University of California Santa Barbara which uses the transactions reported by the publication *Water Strategist*.[95] However, the data is far from complete. For example, it does not specify which type of right, pre- or post-1914 water right, is being traded and, thus it cannot be assessed if the market actually values these differently depending on their priority date.

In California, there were 268 trades – sales and leases – from 1991 to 2000, according to the Bren School database. The amount traded was 18,145,103 acr-ft for measures of committed water, i.e. translating into a single year all the water temporarily or permanently transferred during that one year.[96] For example, a lease for 1,000 acr-ft of water signed in 2000 for three years amounts to 2,723.248 acr-ft in the year when the lease is signed.

The most expected reallocation by markets is water rights moving out of the agricultural sector. In the Bren School database, 178 transactions out of 268 had their origin in the agricultural sector in California.[97] The expected recipients are urban areas which have kept growing. From these 178 trades, 59 are agricultural to urban. Another important reallocation is expected to occur between consumptive uses and the environment if flows are to be preserved without resort to command-and-control schemes mandating the curtailment of certain uses. There are 44 with the environment as the new user (40 leases, one sale and three exchanges[98]). It is important to note the existence of intra-sectoral transactions. Agricultural to agricultural are the most common among intra-sectoral transactions. There were 78 operations of this sort in total,[99] which

---

95 Bren School of Environmental Science and Management, University of California Santa Barbara, 'California Water Transfer Records,' http://www.bren.ucsb.edu/news/water_transfers.htm.

96 The database offers different measures: minimum, average, and maximum acre-feet and minimum, average, and maximum committed acre-feet. From them, the average committed variable which accounts for all the water trades was chosen. In the introduction to the database, they state that the committed variable captures 'the fact that long-term leases and sales transfer substantially more water than one-year leases transfer because sales involve the transfer of the right to a certain amount of water annually for perpetuity.' Zack Donohue and Gary Libecap, *Water Transfer Level Data Summary*, at 4 (Bren School).

97 Some transactions reported are not a single transaction but a bundle of transactions. *Water Strategist*, which is the source used for the dataset, aggregates transactions with the same seller, buyer, or single location. Some bundled transaction can be easily spotted because one of the parties is sometimes labeled 'various entities,' but others are more difficult to identify. In any case, bundled transactions will be treated as one.

98 An exchange is a type of contract where water for a specific year will be repaid with water in the future.

99 Despite this majority, California is the western State with relatively more transactions out of agriculture, Brewer *et al.*, above note 2, at 186.

suggests that there are crops of different value. For example, it is expected that those farmers with fruit trees would not risk losing the trees and will buy water from farmers with annual crops, such as cereals, to make sure those trees survive. Given that there are different review procedures for short- and long-term transactions, as shown below, it is interesting to note that the majority of agricultural to agricultural, 65, are leases, which seems to point to the fact that short-term transactions are to solve struggles during particularly dry periods. There are 56 urban to urban transactions. Many reflect urban sprawl[100] because they occur between agents that are geographically quite close.[101]

The overall growth in the market has been enhanced by environmental protection through instream flows purchased by State agencies, such as the USBR as a result of the 1992 CVPIA. In addition to this type of purchase, another type of 'environmental' purchase happened: agricultural users, compelled by environmental regulations which mandated the curtailment of some water rights,[102] ensured their demand will be satisfied by leasing or buying water.[103] Environmental restrictions could have proven an obstacle, instead of a driver of water market activity because uncertainty about when they would be imposed may decrease certainty. The growth of transactions related to the environment continued after the period studied. Environmental restrictions could have caused the market to stagnate which, to an extent, they did because pumping restrictions in the Delta made long-distance trades very difficult. However, local water trades rose, and the market continued to be very active.

In addition to open-market transactions, California established several water banks in times of drought which enabled short-term transactions. The landmark one was the 1991 water bank. It bought around 820,713.19 acr-ft and sold 405,356.59 acr-ft.[104] In total, only 12 agencies bought water – in fact, three agencies bought over 80 per cent[105] – compared to the 348 which sold water. The majority were urban agencies, which suggests that their needs were pressing at that point.[106] There was another water bank established in 1992, based on

---

100 Hanak, above note 35, at 133 (48 per cent of transactions have the agricultural sector as the destination; and 28.27 per cent urban municipal users).

101 For example, in October 1991, there was a transaction between the city of Santa Barbara and Montecito Water District (database of US water transfers at the Bren School of Environmental Science and Management).

102 Hanak, above note 85, at 11.

103 Hanak and Stryjewski, above note 33, at 20.

104 Hanak and Howitt, above note 34, at 74. The figures on volume transferred vary slightly depending on the source of the information. See e.g. Brian E. Gray, 'The Market and the Community: Lessons from California's Drought Water Bank,' 14 Hastings W-NW. J. Envt'l L. & Pol'y 41, 50 (2008) (reports that 821,045 acr-ft were bought and around 400,000 acr-ft were sold).

105 Israel and Lund, above note 6, at 53.

106 Ibid.

the 1991 experience, and it bought 193,000 acr-ft. In 1994, a water bank was established which transferred a huge volume of water (220,000 acr-ft)[107] to few parties, four SWP contractors and eight non-SWP contractors.[108] The latter two banks were mostly agricultural.[109] This pattern suggests that agriculture needed more rain to recover their supplies, particularly groundwater ones, and that their demand is much less elastic.[110] In 1995, the Dry Year Purchasing Program – the name given to the water bank – bought water options, but they were not exercised due to abundant rainfall.[111]

However, if trade within projects (SWP, CVP) is taken into account, even more transactions took place. For a shorter time period, 1995–2001, Hanak and Howitt report up to 1,161 transactions, 668 within projects.[112] Over 5 million acr-ft, which account for more than half of the market, were transferred within projects during the period of study 1991–2000, according to Hanak.[113] CVP contractors are reported to enter into an average of 100 transactions per year.[114]

As for the 1991 drought water bank, secondary literature analyzing critiques of the bank states that the majority of the contracts were the result of fallowing, and, thus, the original use was agricultural.[115] With respect to other purchases, such as groundwater exchanges or stored water, the original use may or may not be agricultural. In the 1992 and 1994 water banks, water bought originated in groundwater and stored water. As for destination, in 1991, the majority of water transferred went to urban users, while in 1992 and 1994, most went to the agricultural sector.[116]

Regarding price – another potential variable that can help to understand how well water markets are working – the California database tries to focus on the value of water. The data manager states that the price reflects, as much as

107 Peggy Clifford, Clay Landry, and Andrea Larsen-Hayden, *Analysis of Water Banks in the Western States Prepared by Washington Department of Ecology*, at 43 (2004), https://fortress.wa.gov/ecy/publications/publications/0411011.pdf.

108 Brent M. Haddad, *Rivers of Gold: Designing Markets to Allocate Water in California*, at 57 (1999).

109 For data for 1993, see Clifford *et al.*, above note 107, at 42. For 1992, see Wahl, above note 36, at 12.

110 Israel and Lund, above note 6, at 9.

111 There were no water banks from 1994 to 2009. For an account of the road to the 2009 banks, see 'California reinstates Drought Bank for 2009,' 9 Global Water Intelligence 14 (2008). For the transfers in the 2009 water bank, see presentation by Bob Niblack, '2009 Drought Water Bank' (2010), https://sunsite.berkeley.edu/WRCA/WRC/pdfs/GW27th Niblack.pdf.

112 Data does not map perfectly given the different time-frame division. Hanak and Howitt, above note 34, at 76.

113 Hanak, above note 85, at 8.

114 Malchow, above note 70, at 53.

115 Malchow, above note 70, at 71. Lloyd S. Dixon, Nancy Y. Moore, and Susan Schechter, *California's Water Bank*, at 5, RAND (1991).

116 Clifford *et al.*, above note 107, at 42.

possible, only the price paid for water,[117] but data on transportation costs is not available, so it is impossible to know whether those costs play a role.[118] The average price of a committed acre foot of water in transactions within the agricultural sector for the period of study (1991–2000) was US$63.82 (st. dev. 95.53), and between agricultural and urban areas it was US$75.51 (st. dev. 94.64).[119] The gap between prices suggests not only that there are different water values, but also that markets still have work to do to close the gap. It is, however, important to control for the seniority of the right transferred. More senior water rights are expected to fare better in the market,[120] but the database does not include information about the dates the rights were acquired.

Table 4.1 Rainfall and transactions

Year	Precipitation (inches)	Precipitation anomaly period: 1991–2000 (st. dev. 6.50)	Number of transactions	Volume transferred (acr-ft)	Volume transferred (committed average acr-ft)
1987	18.69	–3.80	11	98,521	186,672.2
1988	16.11	–6.38	8	170,166	170,166
1989	14.57	–7.92	20	567,926	2,850,467
1990	13.62	–8.89	32	699,382	841,463.4
1991	19.13	–3.38	53	117,128	1,780,737
1992	22.86	–0.35	34	231,578	455,539.2
1993	26.44	–3.93	21	503,027	748,901.1
1994	16.97	–5.54	29	588,868	5,888,868
1995	33.66	11.15	13	572,701	874,742.9
1996	31.09	8.58	9	85,016	1,011,657
1997	19.8	–2.71	22	759,985	4,692,478
1998	35.13	12.62	20	441,560	4,521,341
1999	16.67	–5.84	40	808,258.4	2,531,939
2000	20.86	–1.65	24	543,773	938,900.4
2001	21.91	–0.6	31	707,317	2,414,007
2002	18.14	–4.37	25	633,246	1,253,387

Source: NOAA/Water Transfer Database Bren School.[121]

117 Email from Zack Donohue, primary contact and manager of the database US water transfers at the Bren School of Environmental Science and Management (1 May 2013).

118 Jedidiah Brewer, Robert Glennon, and Gary Libecap, '2006 Presidential Address Water Markets in the West: Prices, Trading, and Contractual Forms,' 46 Econ. Inquiry 91, 92 (2008).

119 There are very few sales compared to leases and data for sales is incomplete. The general idea is that price for sales should be higher than prices for leases since they involve a perpetual claim on water flows. Gary D. Libecap, 'Water Rights and Markets in the U.S. Semiarid West: Efficiency and Equity Issues,' in Daniel H. Cole and Elinor Ostrom (eds), *Property in Land and Other Resources*, at 391 (2013).

120 Brewer *et al.*, above note 118, at 100.

121 NOAA, 'Climate at a glance,' http://www.ncdc.noaa.gov/cag/. Bren School database, above note 95.

In sum, water markets in California were fairly active and fulfill the conventional story that those mechanisms would transfer water from the agricultural sector to urban areas, but they also illustrate that there are opportunities to trade within and across sectors. Table 4.1 summarizes the data available in the Bren School database on the number of transactions and volume traded, and matches it with rainfall per year. It should be noted that in some years when there is less rainfall, transactions do not necessarily increase. Scarcity may have a lagged effect: scarcity may prompt governmental actions that encourage trading some time later or transactions may take time to be negotiated and completed. Further qualitative inquiry into the motives of those entering into transactions at the time may illuminate this point in future research.

4.5 Governmental roles

4.5.1 The uncontested governmental role in water markets: definition of property rights

a. Volume

Volume in prior appropriation water rights is defined according to the amount of water put to beneficial use. That is difficult to quantify. Water rights currently granted by the SWRCB have their volume – the amount they can divert from the river – quantified, but old water rights do not. Subsequently, when it comes to transfer those water rights, it is necessary to figure out how much was historically put to beneficial use. The shortcut has been the volume diverted, but there are neither records nor meters necessarily. Calculating the amount transferable increases transaction costs.

California has established only one regulation of the volume variable regarding water markets. Transactions of post-1914 water rights for less than a year of water otherwise consumed are subject to a less demanding review as shown below. Defining the transferable quantity as the quantity consumed ensures that potentially there are fewer externalities. However, even though in short-term transfers the effects are short lived, given the interdependency of different uses and the reliance of downstream users on upstream users' return flow, the transfer of any type of right – pre- and post-1914 – would have benefited from some direct definition of the volume transferable along the same terms. This is so because, in practice, in over-appropriated scenarios such as California's streams, only the volume consumed can be transferred without harming third parties. Furthermore, if the SWRCB had aimed at reducing transaction costs, it could have offered guidance on how to calculate consumptive use for short-term transfers and beyond.

b. Security

Security can be thought to encapsulate both how the agency deals with natural variability and the discretion it is granted in general.

Prior appropriation has, at least on paper, a clear temporal priority for dealing with natural water variability that leaves little room for discretion. For contractual rights, with the CVP and SWP, the situation is slightly different: their contractor may not receive full allocation if there is low availability of water and the post-1914 water rights of the USBR or the DWR are not fully satisfied.

In the CVP, how wet the winter has been determines what the USBR is going to allocate to the water contractors. For example, in 2011, the initial allocation allocated 75 per cent of their original allowance for municipal and industrial contractors and 30 per cent of their allowance for farmers because it had been a dry winter. This allocation can (and usually does) change in the few months before summer. The 75 per cent/30 per cent distribution is based on the last three full water years when there were no water restrictions, not the full contractual entitlement, since some users may not be fully consuming it. The policy has been to try to set a guaranteed minimum level which would be met every year for municipal and industrial contractors, who pay a higher price for their water. Despite the variability, the scheme is perceived as foreseeable.[122]

The SWP contracts have a provision ensuring a firm yield contract, i.e. the dependable amount that will be delivered in any case. Article 18 (a) establishes the mechanisms to deal with shortages. These mechanisms are known as 'agriculture first,' i.e. agriculture is the first to receive the curtailments. Those curtailments are not to exceed 50 per cent of the firm yield any given year and no more than 100 per cent in seven consecutive years. If there are more long-term, or permanent, shortages, Article 18 (b) establishes that entitlements would be proportionally reduced. The Monterrey Principles in 1993–94, an agreement to modify the SWP contracts, aimed at amending this provision by establishing a pro-rata curtailment, but those Principles were put to rest after several court challenges.[123] Again, here, the scheme is foreseeable, but shields urban contractors, discouraging them, partially, from trying to mitigate the drought effects and not ensuring that water goes to the higher value user, given that type of use is an imperfect proxy for it and tradability is restricted.[124]

II. GENERAL POWERS AND DISCRETION

Leaving aside natural variability, security – defined as the degree to which a water right is expected to be subject to regulations and regulatory discretion – depends on the nature of the right.

---

122 Email from Kurt 'Skip' Born, CEO, Clear Creek C.S.D. (14 March 2012).

123 Leslie Z. Walker, 'Evaluation of Individual Water Transfer Not Considered Improper Piecemealing Under CEQA,' *Abbott and Kindermann Land Use Law Blog* (13 January 2010), http://blog.aklandlaw.com/2010/01/articles/ceqa/evaluation-of-individual-water-transfer-not-considered-improper-piecemealing-under-ceqa/.

124 Slater, above note 12, at Ch. 2-14, § 14.19.

Regarding prior appropriation rights, regulatory power is expected to be stronger over post-1914 permits than over more complete property rights, in this case pre-1914 appropriative rights. The relevance of this dimension is undeniable in terms of the definition of water rights when it comes to transferring them. This is, in fact, clearly stated in the Cal. Water Code which was amended in 1981 and in 1983 to reflect the centrality of defeasibility. After 1981, §109 read:

> The Legislature hereby finds and declares that the growing water needs of the State require the use of water in *a more* efficient manner and that the efficient use of water requires *greater* certainty in the definition of property rights to the use of water and *greater* transferability of such rights.

In 1983, the statement was reinforced by getting rid of 'a more' and 'greater,' thus making the relation between security, transferability and efficiency even more clear-cut.

Rights to use water – riparian, prior appropriation, and permits – are subject to the beneficial use doctrine, and right holders may fear that their use would be considered wasteful if they transfer the water assigned since it would be taken as evidence that they do not need the water. Riparian rights are usually subject to a reasonable use requirement, but, in California, as a result of Article 10, section 2 of its constitution,[125] those riparian, as well as all other water rights in the State, are subject to beneficial use restrictions. Another question which has arisen in California related to security for transferors is forfeiture for non-use regarding prior appropriation rights.

Since 1979, water conserved was not subject to forfeiture according to §1011 of the Cal. Water Code. In 1982, it was made clear that under this section water not used or conserved could be transferred without fear of forfeiture; it is considered that transferred water complies with the beneficial use requirement. However, those provisions were not enough. During the period

---

125   Art. 10, §2 of the Cal. Constitution, 'It is hereby declared that because of the conditions prevailing in this State the general welfare requires that the water resources of the State be put to beneficial use to the fullest extent of which they are capable, and that the waste or unreasonable use or unreasonable method of use of water be prevented, and that the conservation of such waters is to be exercised with a view to the reasonable and beneficial use thereof in the interest of the people and for the public welfare. The right to water or to the use or flow of water in or from any natural stream or water course in this State is and shall be limited to such water as shall be reasonably required for the beneficial use to be served, and such right does not and shall not extend to the waste or unreasonable use or unreasonable method of use or unreasonable method of diversion of water. Riparian rights in a stream or water course attach to, but to no more than so much of the flow thereof as may be required or used consistently with this section, for the purposes for which such lands are, or may be made adaptable, in view of such reasonable and beneficial uses; provided, however, that nothing herein contained shall be construed as depriving any riparian owner of the reasonable use of water of the stream to which the owner's land is riparian under reasonable methods of diversion and use, or as depriving any appropriator of water to which the appropriator is lawfully entitled.'

this book focuses on, the Cal. Water Code was again amended several times to ensure that in the doctrine of beneficial use, conserved water or water unused as a result of fallowing for a transfer was not going to be considered wasteful use or non-use and therefore the rights of the transferor could not be curtailed. In 1991, §484(a) of the Cal. Water Code was introduced, which ensures that the water that the transferor would have used or stored could be transferable without being detrimental to him. Then in 1999, even more provisions trying to increase security were enacted. The 1999 amendments emphasized that neither a transfer nor a proposed transfer could trigger any water rights review, and that the only limitations which could be imposed must be a consequence of the transaction and tied to it.[126] In fact, §1011 of the Cal. Water Code could be seen as redundant, but the 1999 reform also shifted the focus from the transferor to the transferee: so far as the transferee puts the water to beneficial use, it should not negatively affect the transferor's right. If the transferee violates the beneficial use requirement, the water reverts back to the transferor.[127] In sum, water transfers should not imperil the right of the appropriator; here we are not dealing with contractual rights. The fact that so many amendments targeted this issue seems to show that the fear of forfeiture persisted.

An additional problem related to security is the curtailments suffered by right holders as a result of regulations or judicial decisions related to the environment, particularly related to the protection of endangered species,[128] usually during low water availability seasons. This is a concern for transferees since they cannot be sure that the water they buy or lease will actually be available. The Chinook salmon and the Delta smelt have made the headlines: they were listed as endangered, but water for other users was also imperiled as a result.[129] The protection of fish and wildlife through regulation, setting purchases of water by agencies aside, can be approached using measures which may both boost and impair the market. It can impair it because the potential sellers and buyers cannot be sure of the reliability of their entitlement, or it can boost it because users have incentives to resort to the market to ensure their supplies when they know or predict the curtailments.[130] The CVPIA offers an example of foreseeable curtailment of rights to ensure that more water is left in the river going forward which boosts the market.[131] In fact, this explains part of the growth of agriculture as a buyer of water rights.[132]

---

126 §1014 of the Cal. Water Code.
127 §1015 of the Cal. Water Code.
128 Wahl, above note 75, at 65.
129 'Fish Called Imperiled (but Is the Water, Too?),' New York Times, 6 March 1993, http://www.nytimes.com/1993/03/06/us/fish-called-imperiled-but-is-the-water-too.html?gwh=659C2DFC1D6E963A537EE2BB7C412AF0.
130 Wahl, above note 75, at 65.
131 Hanak and Howitt, above note 34, at 76.
132 Wahl, above note 75, at 65. The term has been used profusely, even recently. Hanak *et al.*, above note 46, at 23.

The potential application of the 'public trust' doctrine[133] is also a source of uncertainty which could erode the security of the rights. For example, an agency, as a trustee of the water for the public, may not be able to withdraw as much water as it intended to transfer if the environment is harmed. This is what the Mono Lake decision hints at,[134] but these concerns did not materialize during the study period.

The review of a water transfer to assess its potential effects on third parties is usually analyzed as a way to avoid or compensate for negative externalities, and the amendment of a water transfer to make the process work more smoothly is usually classified as a measure to reduce transaction costs. Relatedly, the procedural regulations could be seen as increasing tradability where the procedure is streamlined to reduce transaction costs and to increase security, since a detailed review procedure should prevent encroachment on other people's rights or to decrease it if the result of the review is unpredictable. In this book, for organizational purposes, these issues are analyzed under externalities.

c. Tradability

Tradability can be defined as whether and to what extent water use rights can exchange hands. As explained in section 4.2.1, Californian water rights offer a very diverse picture. Tradability for each type of right needs to be described in order to understand the different possibilities and trade-offs. It is clear that the heterogeneity of the different types of rights, which implies diversity in the transfer procedures, along with the administrative fragmentation, may hinder markets from fully realizing their potential. However, water rights have proven to be pretty fungible in California; as a general rule, if a right is transferable there are no limits as to to whom it can be transferred, other than the infrastructure available to transfer them to another user, provided the transfer is approved.

I. RIPARIAN

Riparian rights are not tradable generally. Traditionally, they are appurtenant to riparian lands. They are senior to appropriative rights. However, California offers some exceptions. First, from 1989, if they were decreed, they could be traded.[135] Second, riparian rights could be traded in the 1991 drought water

---

133 Legislative Analyst's Office, above note 22, at 12. This doctrine can be seen as a source of uncertainty; but, at the same time, it can also be seen as an opportunity to make the allocation flexible and tailored to every situation. Hanak *et al.*, above note 46, at 51.

134 *National Audubon Society v Superior Court* (Supreme Court of California, 1983, 33 Cal.3d 419).

135 Brewer *et al.*, above note 2, at 210.

bank to be left instream. Third, since the introduction of §1707 (a)1 of the Cal. Water Code in 1999, they can be traded to provide water for instream flow.

II. APPROPRIATIVE PRE-1914 RIGHTS

Pre-1914 appropriative rights are transferable. Transfers of this type of prior appropriation right do not require the approval of the SWRCB, but they are subject to the standard established in §1706 of the Cal. Water Code of no injury to other legal users of water. If injury occurs, the affected party must resort to courts. The amount of water that is transferable is not limited to historically consumed water, but there is a limit: the non-injury rule which ensures that other users would not be injured by the sale or lease of water that had never been used, but that is formally granted by the water right.

However, if the transfer requires the use of State-owned infrastructure, such as the SWP, the transfer would have to undergo a review procedure before the DWR. If the infrastructure needed is federal, the USBR will be the agency responsible. The procedures related to infrastructure use tend to subject rights to a non-injury rule. Transactions of pre-1914 water rights that require the use of that infrastructure are also subject to the non-injury rule by the agency approving the use of infrastructure. Hence, pre-1914 water rights lose part of the advantage they have in terms of lower transaction costs. Their advantage comes because transactions of pre-1914 water rights are not subject to an *ex-ante* review procedure where an agency applies a non-injury standard. Instead, third parties potentially injured by such transactions can bring suit. Third parties rarely bring suit, given how expensive it is to do so. They only do so when the damage is substantial. However, use of infrastructure erodes the advantage because they become somehow subject to *ex-ante* review.

Despite the fact that there do not seem to be real procedural advantages, pre-1914 rights are senior to post-1914 water rights, which is an advantage in times of drought. This would make pre-1914 rights more attractive, and we may expect them to be transferred at a higher price. However, even though pre-1914 water rights are required to file a statement of diversion and use before the SWRCB,[136] those rights were not always fully recorded during the study period, thus, transacting parties could be afraid of buying paper rights. There is no data in the sources used about how much trading of these rights occurred.

III. APPROPRIATIVE RIGHTS GRANTED POST-1914

The SWRCB holds regulatory powers over these rights, and therefore both short-term and long-term transfer requires the approval of the Board. In 1986,

---

136 §5101 of the Cal. Water Code.

the Cal. Water Code was amended to allow transactions for more than seven years. Thus, in the period of study, they were always tradable, either short term or long term.

The quantity tradable is limited for short-term transfers of post-1914 rights (one year maximum): only consumed water can be transferred.[137] 'Consumptively used' water includes 'water which has been consumed through use by evapotranspiration, has percolated underground, or has been otherwise removed from use in the downstream water supply as a result of direct diversion.'[138] This definition gives security to downstream users of the stream and, to some extent, the transferor, since he or she knows how much she can transfer without fearing the results of the review or the claims of other users. This limit does not appear in the regulation of long-term transfers of those very same rights. The difference could be explained by the thoroughness of the review process, which is more expedited for short-term transfers. Externalities in short-term transfers are minimized because there will not be more water taken from the river than was traditionally taken before the transfer, and because if there were negative effects, they would be short-lived.

Short-term transfers are exempted from complying with the CEQA, but not long-term ones. In addition, if State or federal infrastructure is necessary to ship the water, applying for an authorization to do so will mean undergoing a review before the DWR or the USBR.

IV. STATE WATER PROJECT RIGHTS

The 29 local agencies which are contractors of the SWP cannot transfer their rights outside the project. They can transfer within the project if the DWR approves of those transactions after considering the potential effects on other users but, even within the project, State contractors are subject to important restrictions. Logically, they cannot transfer their contractual rights, only their annual allocation.[139] They can only trade on an annual basis using the 'turn-back pools,' a transfer mechanism put forward by the SWP. The price is subject to restrictions and they cannot profit from these transactions. This is so because SWP contractors have to pay their share of fixed costs irrespective of the amount of water they receive – they hardly ever receive the amount their contracts establish – and the price in the turn-back pools does not allow the recovery of all fixed costs.

137 §1725 of the Cal. Water Code (temporary change in the right).
138 §§1745.10 and 1745.11 of the Cal. Water Code.
139 SWRCB, above note 14, at 4-1.

Federal contractual rights are highly transferable both within and outside the project, and transfers of these rights constitute a large share of transactions in California. The majority of contractors enter into short-term transactions to adjust for the changes in delivery.[140] Individual contractors hold interests that can be transferred. This was the policy before 1991,[141] but the CVPIA further specified it. Since the CVPIA was passed, even individual users who are served by one of the federal contractors can transfer their entitlements without the approval of the contractor unless the transfer involves more than 20 per cent of the total allocation of the contractor.[142] Nonetheless, districts do not seem to be open to let their contractors trade.[143]

To understand the powers such transfers are subject to, it is important to differentiate between destinations of transfers. If federal contractual rights go outside the project, then they will be subject to both the USBR review and the SWRCB. They need to be reviewed by the SWRCB because the transferred right will be used outside the place of use that post-1914 water rights held by USBR define. To these, if the SWP infrastructure is used, another review by the DWR will take place. It should be mentioned that, in the 2000s, the SWP and the CVP applied and were awarded a change in their post-1914 permits, enlarging the place of use. The SWRCB granted the SWP and the CVP a temporary joint place of use in their areas south of the Delta, which meant that contractors from the two projects could enter into transactions without applying for authorization before the SWRCB.[144] This joint place of use was achieved through a temporary change on the place of use of permits, exempted from the CEQA requirements because of the drought emergency. This shows

---

140 The water year begins on 1 March and the USBR offers an estimation based on past experience of the amount of water each contractor may receive. This volume may be modified later on as circumstances change. For example, the allocation for the Clear Creek District for 2012 was described as follows by Kurt 'Skip' Born, 'This year the initial allocation allows 75% for M&I and 30% for ag because we have had a dry winter. This allocation can (and usually does) change in the few months before summer gets here. The 75%, 30% is based on the last three full water years when there were no water restrictions.' Email from Kurt 'Skip' Born, above note 122.

141 The US Department of the Interior's 1988 Water Transfer Principles, the USBR's 1989 Criteria Document, and the Mid-Pacific Region's past practices establish that CVP contractors, as well as individual farmers, hold interests in project water that may be transferred to other uses. Moreover, both federal and California law authorize contractors and users of project water to engage in water transfers. Brian E. Gray, Bruce C. Driver, and Richard W. Wahl, 'Transfers of Federal Reclamation Water: a case study of California's San Joaquin Valley,' 21 Envtl. L. 911, 934 (1991).

142 Slater, above note 12, at Ch. 5, § 15.31.

143 Hanak and Howitt, above note 34, at 76. Email from Kurt 'Skip' Born, above note 122.

144 Hanak and Stryjewski, above note 33, at 16.

that there was room to increase tradability of rights during the period of study.[145] So despite the quite impressive market numbers, there were still ways to enhance trades that were not fully explored.

To prevent externalities beforehand, internal CVP transfers are subject to limitations. Historical use is the limit for CVP transfers, but during dry years there might be additional limitations. The CVPIA, enacted in 1992, provides that the water transferred shall not exceed 'the average annual quantity of water under contract actually delivered to the contracting district or agency during the last three years of normal water delivery prior to the date of enactment of this title.'[146] It further limits the amount transferred stating that 'the water subject to any transfer undertaken pursuant to this subsection shall be limited to water that would have been consumptively used or irretrievably lost to beneficial use during the year or years of the transfer.'[147] Another limitation comes in the form of the right of first refusal that entities within the CVP have for transfers outside the CVP area;[148] the period of exercise is 90 days. This could impair transfers[149] to some extent, even though the potential transferor and transferee will be compensated for all the costs incurred. Disincentives arise obviously from the time spent and the opportunity cost of not searching for alternative sources.

Federal rules related to the transfer of water must be also mentioned. As stated in the introduction, the federal government was a pioneer in water markets, but it stepped back in 1991 giving prominence to the Drought Water Bank. However, federal agencies continued to conceive market mechanisms as part of their management tools – the USBR's 'Interim Guidelines for Implementation of Water Transfers under Title XXXIV of PL 102-575,' dated 25 February 1993, and the Final Administrative Proposal on Water Transfers was issued in April 1998.[150] These did not contain any provision specifically allowing the USBR to establish a water bank as it did in 1977, but previous regulations coupled with some of the broad propositions contained in those regulations could have been enough to justify a bank.

---

145   The SWRCB in 2009 stated certain requirements which will ensure that the potential transactions will not injure other users or the environment. It required the parties, among others, to comply with the biological opinions regarding the Delta, subtract from the amount transferred any carriage loss, and imposed the limit of transferrable water on the historical average. The strategy followed in this case could have been pursued well before. Seeking this type of approval in advance could ease transaction when emergencies arise allowing a rapid response. SWRCB, 'Order Approving a Change in the Place of Use of License and Permits of the California DWR and USBR in Response to Drought Conditions' (19 May 2009), http://www.waterboards.ca.gov/waterrights/board_decisions/adopted_orders/orders/200 9/wro2009_0033.pdf.

146   §3405 (a) (1) (A) of the CVPIA.

147   §3405 (a) (1) (I) of the CVPIA.

148   Ibid. at A-5.

149   Brian E. Gray, 'The Modern Era in California Water Law,' 45 Hastings L. J. 249, 289 (1994).

150   SWRCB, above note 14, at 4-2.

One issue covered in Chapter 2 regarding the definition and tradability of property rights is who can transfer water: either the organization holding the right or its long-term members or customers. In 1991, the Assembly Bill 2090 was introduced in the California Legislature.[151] It would have allowed the users of water within water districts to transfer water to potential purchasers without the mediation of the district with a limit on the amount that could be transferred outside the district of 20 per cent. The bill, which, surprisingly, passed in the Assembly,[152] was defeated in the Senate, despite having been watered down. In 1993, a similar bill was introduced,[153] but it did not succeed and the central role of the intermediary institutions remains uncontested, despite the fact that they may not be the best transmission chain. For example, in 1992, §1745 of the Cal. Water Code was added stating that districts can sell not only their surplus water, but also any water saved as a result of contracts entered with those users they supply, or some other water if the users they supply will not be adversely affected without their consent.[154] However, those supplied do not have a right to compel them to enter into such a contract and subsequently sell the water.[155] The regulation remains silent on transactions between users of the same district. Those transactions are believed to have occurred for a long time, but they are not recorded. Farmers from the same district often face the same water challenges, so these transactions may do little to solve the structural scarcity challenges suffered by California. The only place where such a scheme of transferable individual water allowances outside the district materialized was the federal projects. Since 1992, the CVPIA allowed individuals to trade their entitlements, but subject to limited veto authority of the district and the USBR if they are trading more than 20 per cent of the CVP water of the district.[156]

d. Instream purchases: a market booster

Water rights have been purchased to restore instream flows. The role of this type of purchases became particularly important at the end of the study period.

One of the main characteristics of water rights in California is that they must be put to beneficial use. This has been seen as a limit to establish instream flow water rights. Instream uses are not considered among the ones for which a post-1914 permit can be granted. This is not the case in all western US States;

---

151 For an analysis of the bill, see Thompson, above note 47, at 745.
152 'Go With the Flow, Adam Smith Style: Key drought remedy gathers steam,' Los Angeles Times, 8 July 1991, http://articles.latimes.com/1991-07-08/local/me-1271_1_rural-water.
153 Thompson, above note 47, at 745.
154 For water districts, see §35425 of the Cal. Water Code. For irrigation districts, see §22259. For a definition of surplus water, see §383.
155 §1745.09 of the Cal. Water Code.
156 Thompson, above note 47, at 677–678. See also, Slater, above note 12, at Ch. 5, § 15.31.

some allow for public agencies and private parties to hold these types of non-consumptive water rights. Since 1991, existing right holders could transfer water to instream uses (§1707 of the Cal. Water Code). This should allow agents to buy existing consumptive rights, but they do not get a property right in the instream flow and it is unclear how it will be ensured that other transfers do not affect this instream flow.

However, rights were purchased by public agencies. For example, the California Department of Fish and Game bought water at reduced cost from the Yuba County Water Agency in 1991.[157] In addition to intentional purchases, the 1991 drought water bank purchased, as a result of bad planning, much more water than it sold, and therefore the surplus was left in the rivers. During the 1991 drought water bank, another avenue to ensure instream flows through purchases was to buy riparian rights. If riparian land was fallowed and riparian owners did not divert the water, that water, even if it could not be used in other lands, could be left in the flow to ensure certain water quantity and, consequently, quality in the river.[158] In 1992, the water bank pursued environmental goals more directly. In that bank, the Department of Fish and Game had the right to purchase 10 per cent of the first 200,000 acr-ft of water made available for delivery by the bank at the melded rate. The Department could also buy up to 10 per cent of the water made available above 200,000 acr-ft at no cost.[159]

Purchases also took place at the federal level. In the mid-1990s, the CVPIA's Water Acquisition Program, under federal authority, purchased water both for Central Valley wildlife refuges and for instream flow in the San Joaquin River system. The instream flow programme was a multi-year experiment called the Vernalis Adaptive Management Program, and included long-term leases with some irrigation districts.[160] Later, in 2001, the USBR operated a forbearance programme in 2001, which consisted of purchases from CVP contractors in the Sacramento Valley for CVPIA instream flow purchases, CVP contractors south of the Delta, and wildlife refuge supplies.[161] The most renowned programme is probably the environmental water account set up in the framework of the CALFED Bay-Delta Program to restore the Delta, a joint effort of State and federal authorities. It was established in 1999, but purchases did not take place until 2001, i.e. beyond the period of study.

Environmental purchases, thus, started during the study period and are part of the mechanisms to manage water in California, as the 2000s experience shows. However, private parties have not played such a relevant role in purchases

---

157 DWR, above note 71, at 12.
158 Israel and Lund, above note 6, at 6.
159 Wahl, above note 36, at 32.
160 Hanak and Stryjewski, above note 33, at 32.
161 USBR, 'Long-Term Central Valley Project Operations Criteria and Plan CVP-OCAP,' at 2-19 (2004), http://www.usbr.gov/mp/cvo/OCAP/OCAP_6_30_04.pdf.

of water to protect the environment probably because they were discouraged by the fact that there were no property rights over instream flows. Section 1707 of the Cal. Water Code has been used for some environmental purchases within the framework of watershed management programmes; they mostly involve small amounts of water. These acquisitions are made usually as donations, rather than through monetary compensation. There has been discussion about granting tax exemptions for such purchases in order to incentivize them.[162] This issue seems to point to the public good nature of water. If the exemption were to be established, taxpayers would shoulder part of the costs of these transactions. Exemption or not, currently, taxpayers are footing the lion's share of the bill to protect the environment through the numerous public programmes to purchase water, despite some measures which target certain water users through in kind restrictions.

In 1999, §1707 of the Cal. Water Code was amended again allowing buyers of those rights to specify whether the water left in the river could be devoted to meet the federal or State instream flow requirements or whether it was water that should provide additional protection on top of the minimum requirements. This amendment should increase incentives for private parties. However, the scheme still lacks some security regarding the possibility of retracting water from this transaction and putting the water back to another consumptive use.[163] Transferring water to instream uses requires the approval of the SWRCB. The SWRCB, according to the wording in 1999 – previously the provision was rather concise – can impose conditions it considers beneficial for a better satisfaction of the public interest.[164] Such a review should be extremely deferential since fewer externalities are expected to arise if more water flows in the river.

In sum, notwithstanding indirect transfers as a result of restrictions or mandatory curtailments of existing rights from farmers turning to the market to make up for the curtailments, the environment grew as the beneficiary of purchases in the period 1991–2001 as a result of public purchases.[165] Despite the fact that scarcity was less harsh,[166] the market continued its upward trend thanks to the environmental purchases.[167] Nonetheless, a sharper non-consumptive property right could have been more conducive to privately sponsored environmental water transactions.

---

162 Hanak and Stryjewski, above note 33, at 34.
163 See critique by Thomas D. Hicks, attorney at Law, submitted to the California State Assembly Committee on Water, Parks and Wildlife (21 August 2013), http://awpw.assembly.ca.gov/sites/awpw.assembly.ca.gov/files/Hicks,%20Thomas %20to%20CA%20State%20Assembly%20re%20Water%20Bond%208-21-13.pdf.
164 §1707b of the Cal. Water Code.
165 Hanak, above note 85, at 11.
166 Legislative Analyst Office, above note 22, at 2 ('In past years, the average annual supply has generally been sufficient to meet demands').
167 Hanak, above note 85, at 11.

4.5.2 Externalities

Transactions may have effects beyond the parties to those exchanges. As Chapter 2 states, government needs to envision a scheme to ensure that *ex-ante* or *ex-post* those effects are internalized by the parties. The next section analyzes the procedure tackling externalities affecting third parties and the environment. The following section deals with externalities affecting communities which are not right holders.

a. Externalities imposed on other users and the environment

The definition of property rights defines who will have the right to be compensated if another user impinges on his water right, but it can also prevent externalities. This is the case for short-term transfers of post-1914 property rights: the amount of water a user is entitled to transfer is the amount of water historically consumed, which is an amount smaller than the amount users are allowed to divert. This definition indirectly protects other users from increases in consumption. Even though in aggregate the same quantity of water would be flowing, it does not eliminate all effects: the same quantity might not be flowing between the same points since buyer or lessee may take out water from a different point than the seller or lessor. In addition, if the uses are different, the return flow from the buyer or lessor may have different quality properties. Thus, mechanisms of review are needed as a strategy to account for the type of transfer effects just mentioned.

Ex-post mechanisms of review vary depending on the type of right, and target both externalities affecting other users and those imposed on the environment. The first protection is the non-injury rule which covers both pre-1914 and post-1914 appropriative rights. The non-injury rule prevents negative effects such as the ones just described. Potential injuries caused by pre-1914 rights are adjudicated by courts only when those affected file a suit, while transactions of post-1914 rights are subject to review procedures before they can be completed. It is important to remember that the latter include the rights the USBR and the DWR hold. Contractors of the USBR who want to sell outside the project need to undergo not only the USBR's oversight, as explained below, but also the procedure before the SWRCB for the change in the post-1914 water right held by the USBR – of which the contractor receives a certain amount.

For short-term transfers, i.e. for a period of one year or less, the review is carefully regulated in §§1725–1732 of the Cal. Water Code. These provisions regulate any type of change for less than a year of one or several of the rights defining variables (point of diversion, place of use and purpose of use). It is important to note that the one-year limit does not include the potential mitigation measures to be taken before or after, which suggest that third party effects could be addressed if they cannot be avoided, even though no more details are included.

The formal requirements on the petitioner in this review are quite demanding, but so are the services the agency is mandated to offer. The titleholder who wants to change his right to transfer it also has to file a copy of the petition to the California Department of Fish and Game and the supervisors of the county or counties of origin and destination of the water, so that they can participate in the review procedure if they find it suitable. The Board must provide a list of water right holders which could be affected by the change, and the petitioner has to provide written notice to them. Although this might suggest that the burden of proof will fall both on the petitioner defending the transfer as well as other third parties or agencies affected, the Board is mandated to start an investigation of the proposed transfer to ensure that the water involved would otherwise have been consumptively used or stored, and to determine the effects on water quality and instream flows. The timeframe to carry out this review is quite tight. The investigation has to start within ten days of the receipt of the petition, and the Board has, on a normal basis, 35 days after that to render the decision,[168] so the process takes at least 45 days. Extensions are granted in those cases where comments are filed or a hearing is required.

The review procedure was regulated in 1980, amended in 1988, and further revised in 1999. The 1999 reform entailed a modification of the burden of proof along the lines proposed in the Model Water Transfer Act.[169] That reform implied that the standard is preponderance of evidence. The petitioner has to make a prima facie case that the change as a result of the transfer will not result in any injury to any legal user of water, contextualizing it in the potential hydrologic condition which would take place, and which would not unreasonably affect fish, wildlife, or other instream beneficial use. Once the prima facie case is established, the burden of proof is shifted to those who have filed comments, if any. Hearings are not always required, which implies that the process must be quite expedited. This is clearly a more hospitable scheme for transactions, but the reform took place at the end of the study period.

The review procedure for long-term transfers is much less spelled out in the regulation. The standard is almost unaffected: the transaction cannot substantially injure other users or unreasonably affect fish, wildlife, or other instream beneficial uses.[170] This can be conceptualized as a type of embellished

---

168 Thompson, note 47, at 705 suggests that these changes were positive and give some comparative data on the duration of approval procedures in many states, 'any transfer applications take only a month or two to resolve, but the average processing time appears to range from six months to one and one-half years (with controversial transfers occasionally taking up to several years).' His data relies on a 1990 study by Lawrence J. MacDonnell, above note 63. In California, a DWR report from 2005 suggests that for short-term transfers 'action by the State Water Board occurs within 45 to 65 days of the petition receipt.' DWR, *Water Transfers and the Delta Plan – A report to the Delta Stewardship Council,* at 11 (2005).

169 Gray, 'The Shape of Transfers' (1996), above note 92, at 48.

170 §1736 of the Cal. Water Code.

non-injury rule.[171] The changes are slight, but not to be dismissed: the injury here cannot be substantial while in short-term transfers there cannot be any injury. Furthermore, for long-term transfers there is no restriction on which water can be transferred, i.e. consumptive use is not the limit.[172] The explanation for the difference between these two procedures might be the difference in depth of the review procedures and the need to speed up the procedure for short-term transfers. Short-term transfers are aimed to alleviate a pressing contemporary situation and, thus, the review must be swift. The agency cannot spend time assessing whether or not an injury is substantial, none is admissible. In contrast, for long-term transfers, delaying the Board's decision may not make the transaction useless.

In the standards for review of long-term and short-term transfers, California has no specific mention of respecting the instream flow purchases. If less water is flowing as a result of a transaction, even though the instream flow amount bought could still be in the river, less benefit will accrue to the environment. However, both long-term and short-term transfers are subjected to a type of not-unreasonable effect on fish and wildlife standard,[173] and such open-ended standards could be sufficient to ensure that those instream flow purchases are respected. It is expected that the agency will enforce this standard serving the public interest. However, the standard may be considered a source of uncertainty for the parties to the transaction, and may weaken the incentives to purchase water rights to protect the environment.

As shown by the data already presented, transactions within the projects are relevant. The SWRCB is said to have reviewed on average seven transactions over a year and the DWR about 25.[174] Transactions between federal and State project contractors needed, during the period of study, to undergo the review of their respective project agencies, the agencies whose infrastructure they use, and the SWRCB. However, for intra-project transactions, there are differences between federal and State water contractors. The federal projects have certain internal regulations and transactions are subjected to the authority of the USBR. It is important to note that the CVP regulation includes a review project of 90 days regardless of the length of the transaction and that the lack of decision by the USBR implies the approval of the transaction.[175] The USBR charges a fee for reviewing the contract. The practice in the CVP seems to be that the fee will be paid by the lessee.[176] Transactions between federal contractors imply

---

171   Brewer *et al.*, above note 2, at 195.
172   §17351 of the Cal. Water Code.
173   The 'no unreasonable effect' test is not the same as the more common 'no significant impact' test set up under the CEQA. The 'no unreasonable effect' test allows the SWRCB to weigh the effects on fish and wildlife against the benefits of the transfer. SWRCB, above note 14, at 3-9.
174   Legislative Analyst's Office, above note 22, at 8.
175   §3405 (a) (2) (D) of the CVPIA.
176   Email from Kurt 'Skip' Born, above note 122.

that the lessor will receive less water and the lessee will receive more. The USBR will channel the water to one or the other. Since the projects entail human-built infrastructure, it seems that there should not be environmental externalities, but this is not the case. First, the CVP uses water from different sources, and, thus, it matters where the water is pumped from, which may vary depending on the location of the contractor who leases the water. The agency can implement operational changes that avoid those effects. Second, if a contractor uses less water because it fallows the fields, there might be environmental effects such as the destruction of the habitat of certain migrant species. In fact, in the projects, assessing environmental effects is a central goal of the review since the provision of water to other users is not likely to be impaired by the transaction because the agency in charge of the project, be it the DWR or the USBR, is expected to ensure the delivery of the water. While transfers inside the projects are subject to a single review, transfers outside the project would be subject to the review by the project agency, the review by the SWRCB, the review of the DWR if the transfer uses State infrastructure, and they may be required to comply with the CEQA.

The SWP contractual rights internal transactions are subject to review by the DWR, which takes into account environmental impacts since the impact on other rights should not happen because all rights are held by the DWR. Some State contractors, nonetheless, hold other types of rights, such as pre-1914 rights, which may be sold outside the project or within the project. In addition, even though they cannot sell their SWP allocation to outside parties, if their allocation runs short, they may also buy water outside the project. Doing so implies that they will most probably use the SWP infrastructure, which will require undergoing a review before the DWR, as with any other transaction using this infrastructure. The DWR review accounts for environmental and community externalities. Officers at the DWR acknowledge that there is overlap between the SWRCB and the DWR reviews, and that there is deference and reasoning between the DWR and the SWRCB and vice versa.[177]

There are still additional layers of protection for the environment that cuts across the type of rights. An additional layer of protection is the requirement that certain transfers must comply with the requirements set by the CEQA, or the National Environmental Protection Act if the water transferred pertains to the federal projects or uses them. For example, in cases where the agency proposes a discretionary project – and a transfer can be considered to be one – they would have to undergo an Environmental Impact Assessment. The only transfers exempted from the CEQA are short-term ones of post-1914 rights.[178] It must be noted that the standard of review for short-term transfers is 'no unreasonable impact on the environment' while the standard under the CEQA

---

177   Telephone interview with Maureen Sargent, Operations Office, DWR (8 May 2013).
178   §1729 of the Cal. Water Code (it was in force for the whole period of the study).

is 'no significant effect,' which could potentially have different levels of stringency.

However, there are some back doors to escape these requirements. For example, if there is an emergency declared by the governor, and the Secretary for the California Environmental Protection Agency and the Secretary for the California Natural Resources Agency (Natural Resources) find that the proposed transfer falls under the exception established in California Code of Public Resources (§21080, subdivision (b)(4)), that transfer will be exempted from the CEQA. It might be likely that in the event of a drought, transfers will be granted this exception. For example, Governor Brown, in response to the current drought, waived the CEQA requirement for water transactions in an order issued in January 2014.

Lastly, there are still additional measures which seem to target environmental protection. Framed as concerns about the over-exploitation of groundwater, but perhaps also hiding certain worries about community life, two counties, Yolo and Butte, imposed on the buyers of its groundwater the duty to pay 2 per cent for contracts involving groundwater. In Yolo County, the local authority entered into a memorandum of understanding which included the participation of a conservancy district, which reinforces the environmental concern. The proceeds from these were used to update the Yolo County Water Plan, which did also benefit from the data collection around the 1991 drought water bank and which should ensure more sustainability.[179]

In sum, in California, there is an acute need to unify or better coordinate this amalgam of overlapping reviews. The differences in the depth of governmental oversight of the different types of rights fade out given the different layers of review – transaction review and review for the use of infrastructure – and the compliance with the CEQA.

b. Externalities imposed on communities: political necessity

Rural communities fear being impoverished as a result of water transfers which dry up their economies. Although economists do not consider these effects to be externalities, political necessity has dictated the need to establish some type of compensatory relief in certain transfer agreements, where not all the water comes from improvement of the efficiency of irrigation systems. There are several examples that can be highlighted in California.

The MWD commissioned a study which showed that an early 1990s pilot programme caused the loss of about 60 farming or farm-related jobs in the Palo Verde Irrigation District. It also showed that fallowing reduced demand for farm-related services by US$4 million.[180] Accordingly, in the 2004 flexible

---

179 Malchow, above note 70, at 53.
180 'Third-party impacts: The Palo Verde Story,' at 72, Aqueduct Magazine (2006), http://www. mwdh2o.com/aqueduct/ summer_06/article_05_01.html. Israel and Lund, above note 6, at 2.

agreement between the MWD and the Palo Verde Irrigation District which entailed the transfer of 25,000–118,000 acr-ft per year, a US$6 million provision was established to cope with these community effects. A non-profit public corporation was established to manage them.[181] As described next, some of the reviews to which transactions are subject take into account these effects, but it is not clear what the result is. There have been compensatory schemes, but only established ad hoc.

Particularly, fallowing is seen as the most serious threat: fallowing a field implies that less water will percolate into the ground in the area than it used to and that some animal species may suffer from the lack of their traditional habitat, but it also implies that some counties will suffer from a reduction in agricultural production. Water savings from more efficient irrigation should be almost innocuous in terms of community externalities. In California, the definition of transferable water after the 1991 amendments included fallowing as a source of conservation. It did not differentiate between temporary or permanent fallowing. In addition, the 1991 drought water bank allowed transferring water conserved through fallowing the fields. In the framework of the bank, concerns about third party impacts arose. In May 1991, there was an official survey conducted to understand the potential effects on agribusiness, particularly those that transport and store agricultural products.[182] Additional studies about the effects of the fallowing related to the 1991 drought water bank found, beyond the environmental impact, some effects on particular groups, such as agricultural providers, but overall they did not find a significant negative effect.[183] It is important to note that spring rains in 1991 allowed certain farmers who withdrew irrigation, but still planted their crops, such as alfalfa, to harvest almost the same as in a normal year.[184] Most of these empirical studies assessing these social effects do not pay attention to the positive effects on the counties receiving water.[185] Yolo County claimed compensation from the DWR, given the cost that unemployed farm workers laid-off as a result of transactions had on the welfare services of the county (US$129,305 in total for 450 workers laid-off). The DWR, even though it acknowledged the effects, argued that, apart from the lack of legal basis, the DWR had already compensated Yolo County by establishing and funding a groundwater monitoring programme and water planning.[186] Given the critique of the effects of fallowing to sell water to the 1991 drought water bank, even if reported to

181   Hanak, above note 35, at 72–73.
182   DWR, above note 71, at 16.
183   Israel and Lund, above note 6, at 6. Lloyd S. Dixon, Nancy Y. Moore, and Susan W. Schechter, *California's 1991 Drought Water Bank. Economic Impacts in the Selling Regions* (1993).
184   DWR, above note 71, at 7.
185   See the review of those studies in Hanak, above note 35, at 2.
186   Malchow, above note 70, at 56.

be moderate, the 1992 water bank did not allow water originated from fallowing to be sold to the bank.

Several legal provisions have dealt with fallowing in the transfer of post-1914 rights. First, §386 of the Cal. Water Code, added in 1982, stated that the SWRCB, where reviewing a proposed change of a water right petition related to a transfer of surplus water by an agency acting as a water supplier, could deny its approval if the transfer will 'unreasonably affect the overall economy of the area from which the water is being transferred.' Second, §1810, introduced in 1986, allows the public agency owning the infrastructure to deny the use of it if the transfer would unreasonably affect the economy of the community of origin, i.e. the same standard as §386, but it applies across all right holders. However, this provision on community externalities has never barred a transaction.[187] These provisions have two potential flaws. First, they are open-ended and, thus, could be strategically used for goals other than protecting the community of origin; for example, favoring a particular group of constituents. Second, and relatedly, the provisions create uncertainty because there are no criteria to decide on the negative effects on communities. In addition, there is no consideration of the positive effect on communities receiving the water.

Still other provisions are in place. The third provision regarding community externalities hides in §1745.05 of the Cal. Water Code, introduced in 1992, which offers a type of backdoor protection. It requires those suppliers who want to sell water freed as a result of fallowing in excess of 20 per cent of the water supplied[188] to hold a public hearing. This should allow the effects to be transparent and, in any event, would only limit the effects of land fallowing and not of transactions where water has been saved through more efficient use. In addition, the 1999 amendment of the provision protecting against forfeiture those right holders that conserve water, specified that only temporary fallowing and crop rotation are permitted as a source of conserved water.[189] However, this protection would still not be able to prevent serious temporary disruptions to rural areas if water is transferred on a massive scale.[190] Around the same time, other bills tackling fallowing were introduced, but they lacked legislative support.[191]

There have been experiences of compensation ad hoc of community externalities. The well-known, and controversial, agreement between the San

187 Malchow, above note 70, at 81.
188 §1745.05 b of the Cal. Water Code.
189 §1011 (b) of the Cal. Water Code.
190 Tauriainen, above note 87, at 423.
191 Hanak, above note 35, at 83. The legislative history of the two bills introduced by congressman Machado can be found in the following links: 'AB 2027' (1998), http://www.leginfo.ca.gov/pub/97-98/bill/asm/ab_2001-2050/ab_2027_bill_19981130_history.html; 'AB 732' (2000), http://www.leginfo.ca.gov/cgi-bin/postquery?bill_number=ab_732&sess=9900&house=B&author=machado.

Diego County Water Authority and the IID, reached initially in 1998, which combined temporary fallowing with irrigation efficiency improvements, included compensation for the effects on the local economy. It was implemented beyond the period of study, however. The agreement was approved in 2002 by the IID Board of Directors. It contained a clause establishing US$20 million to mitigate third party economic effects,[192] US$10 million paid upfront and the rest later on.[193] A committee of economists appointed by the county supervisors and the purchasing and selling agencies was supposed to administer it;[194] however, the money has apparently not been spent.[195] Similarly, the example of Butte County in 2001 is worth mentioning, despite being also beyond the period of study. There, a fee (5 per cent which amounted to US$3.75 per acr-ft) was established without estimating a fine-tuned model to calculate the specific impacts, given the transaction costs that such a tailoring would have implied. [196] Perhaps this could be the model for short-term or low quantity transactions going forward. More structured ways to deal with community externalities when a considerable percentage of water is transferred outside an area are preferable to the uncertain application of open-ended standards.

4.5.3 Infrastructure: provision and management

Water infrastructure is key for water markets, but its relevance is often downplayed by those who defend water transactions as the silver bullet for California's water scarcity.[197] Water transactions have been presented as an alternative to supply augmentation now that the era of big infrastructure is over, given its financial and environmental costs. However, water needs natural or human-built connections.

a. Provision

This section analyzes, first, whether the current water infrastructure system, which was mainly built prior to the irruption of water markets and with the view of reallocating water to where people settled, is sufficient for market purposes. In other words, whether there is room to convey water transactions between areas with different marginal values for water and whether there is consensus about new infrastructure connections being needed.

---

192   Hanak and Howitt, above note 34, at 78.
193   San Diego Water Authority, 'Historic Water Transfer Agreement Gets Final Approval as QSA Falters,' http://www.sdcwa.org/historic-water-transfer-agreement-gets-final-approval-qsa-falters. Israel and Lund, above note 6, at 2.
194   Hanak and Howitt, above note 34, at 78.
195   Telephone interview with Scott Slater, above note 82.
196   Hanak, above note 35, at 72 and 96.
197   Hanak *et al.*, above note 46, at 28.

Not only is California one of the jurisdictions with more dams, but it also has many water transportation infrastructure projects managed by different agencies, as Figure 4.1 shows. There are six major systems (the SWP, the CVP, a number of Colorado River delivery systems, the Los Angeles Aqueduct, the Tuolumne River/Hetch Hetchy system, and the Mokelumne Aqueduct to the East Bay) and other smaller ones, such as minor reservoirs. They are operated by State, federal, and local agencies. The State and federal systems run from north to south, while some local ones are east to west. State infrastructure is under the control of the DWR, while Federal infrastructure is managed by the USBR. In addition, there are smaller scale projects managed by districts, which serve as more local networks.

As the description above shows, California has an extensive web of water connections. Whether or not they are enough is a debatable question; however, there is no doubt that they have been key for the development of a market. The main problem with the current infrastructure system in California, which has been a constant during the period of study and has become even more problematic since, is the Delta area. In the Delta, the SWP and the CVP meet. Capacity exists. However, the capacity in the Delta is reduced in practice due to environmental restrictions to protect endangered fish species and prevent saltwater intrusion.[198] The Delta complexity prompted the amalgam of agencies to create an operations group in 1994 to ensure the integration of water demands and biological needs, and to help the contractors to navigate the regulatory web. From 1995 on, limitations have been accumulating.[199] In 1995, it was estimated that, on average, the Delta could transfer 350,000 acr-ft/year.[200] Capacity is expected to be larger in wet and extremely dry years, because either local sources are abundant or there is not much water to transfer.

In any case, even with the best management techniques, according to several agents participating in California's water markets, Delta infrastructure is restricting transactions north to south. Not only is capacity not always available but, as shown below, priority is given to the contractors of the infrastructure owner. If the year is quite wet and the SWP can transfer at least 60 per cent of the contracted water, it will not have export capacity to ship the transferred water. Water quality also influences the findings regarding export capacity.[201] On top of these export capacity requirements, carriage water requirements may be applied. This implies that, in practice, there is a type of surcharge for any

---

198   SWRCB, above note 14, at 9-1 (these restrictions are based on: (a) Water Right. Decisions and Orders issued by the SWRCB (Decision 1485 as revised by Orders WR 95-6 and WR 98-9); (b) water quality objectives in the 1995 Water Quality Control Plan for the Sacramento/San Joaquin Delta; (c) the winter run Chinook salmon biological opinion (NMSF, May 1995); and (d) the delta smelt biological opinion (USFWS, March 1995)).
199   SWRCB, above note 14, at 9-1.
200   Ibid.
201   Telephone interview with Maureen Sargent, above note 177.

water carried through the Delta.[202] All these restrictions discourage transactions. In the 2000s, the window for transactions was even more reduced; basically, transferred water could only be shipped during summer months, which is a huge impairment for water transactions.

An additional problem, not unrelated, is the connection east to west, which has been less developed than the ones from the humid north to the dry south. The era of big infrastructure seems to have ended, but the Delta and the less developed connections east to west may need to be addressed, be it through the permanently discussed Peripheral Canal to circumvent the Delta[203] or any type of east to west connection.[204] If those are to be built, it is unlikely that they are going to be undertaken by private parties; they will have to rely on public budgets, particularly given the subsidized price of water that renders the return on such an investment low for private parties. In addition, some infrastructure specifically needed for long-term transactions might be built and funded by the involved agencies, as was proposed for the 50-year agreement between the Cadiz Land Company and the MWD.[205]

The Delta congestion explains, at least partly, why many transfers happen on a smaller scale:[206] more than 20 per cent are within the same county, and around 50 per cent within the same region.[207] Agents involved in water transactions highlight infrastructure as an important obstacle.[208] However, it cannot be assessed how much demand went unsatisfied due to lack of infrastructure. In fact, the position of the stakeholders contrasts with the statement by the DWR in 1999 that it had accommodated most proposed transfers in the years before.[209] The explanation might be that agents were so discouraged that they did not even apply for authorization. Local transactions may or may not have substituted for long-distance ones but, in any event, if the congestion at the Delta was solved, it seems likely that more transactions would take place.

---

202 'California's water wars: Of farms, folks and fish,' *The Economist*, 22 October 2009. Benedykt Dziegielewski, Hari P. Garbharran, and John F. Langowski, Jr., *Lessons Learned from the California Drought (1987–1992): National Study of Water Management During Drought*, US Army Corps of Engineers IWR Report 94-NDS6 (1994). Hanak and Stryjewski, above note 33, at 24.

203 Hanak and Stryjewski, above note 33, at 2 and 12. It compelled the administrations to address the weaknesses in the Delta which cause market frictions.

204 Hanak and Stryjewski, above note 33, at 25 (footnote 39).

205 Legislative Analyst's Office, above note 22, at 5. Ibid. at 6, 'Very few long/term transfers across water basins have taken place. In fact, fewer than a couple of dozen of such transfers have been executed over the last 20 years.'

206 Hanak, above note 85, at 14.

207 Hanak, above note 85, at 17.

208 Telephone interview with Scott Slater, above note 82.

209 Legislative Analyst's Office, above note 22, at 13.

b. Management

This section analyzes whether the infrastructure in place is efficiently managed, i.e. if there are obstacles to using it which may impair the market beyond the lack of effective capacity. Infrastructure refers not only to big channels, but also to the regional distribution net.[210] Both cannot be replicated and are natural monopoly. San Diego, when entering the contract with the IID, could not bypass the wholesaler, the MWD, because it was not feasible, given the time it would take to build the infrastructure and its cost. It would have cost US$3.5 billion and taken 15 years.[211] Hence, San Diego needed to have the water shipped through MWD-owned infrastructure.

The main issue regarding infrastructure management is whether the regime ensures open access to all potential transfers, i.e. whether a transaction between point A and point B can take place even when the parties do not control the infrastructure connecting the two points. This implies that an obligation to allow water to be shipped through the pipes and canals must be imposed on the owners of connecting infrastructure if it is a natural monopoly and replication is not efficient. The duality of certain agencies as right holder/supplier and infrastructure manager could be a problem.[212] This should not be the case for the DWR since its contractors pay their share of the fixed costs to the DWR regardless of the amount of water they receive. However, the situation might be different for others, as the conflict between the MWD and San Diego reviewed below suggests. Strategic behavior favoring the water they supply over water imported from other sources may be expected where the wholesale supplier is also the manager of the infrastructure.

In California, third party access has been granted since 1986. The relevant provisions of the Cal. Water Code are §§1810–1814. They establish that owners of all types of water transportation infrastructure should allow others to ship water up to 70 per cent of their unused capacity. The provisions do not offer much guidance about how unused capacity should be accounted for. If transfers occur during dry seasons, we may expect that the decrease in water availability will imply an increase in unused capacity.[213] The statute confers preference to the contractors of the owner of the infrastructure if there are

---

210   *San Luis Coastal Unified Sch. Dist. v City of Morro Bay*, 81 Cal. App. 4th 1044 (2000) (the court interpreted §1810 as follows: (a) it applied to both wholesale infrastructure as well as local grids; (b) both buyer and seller can request the use of third party infrastructure; and (c) the City could not deny its contractor, the School District, the right to use spare capacity just because the School District was trying to buy cheaper water than the one supplied by the city).

211   'San Diego Buying Water and Its Freedom,' *New York Times*, 6 August 1996.

212   It is considered a problem for the DWR to be the agency managing the information office proposed in the Legislative Analyst's Office report because of its role as a water supply agency so even more as a 'reviewer.' Legislative Analyst's Office, above note 22, at 18.

213   Gray, 'The Shape of Things to Come' (2008), above note 92, at 640.

competing applications to wheel water. This preference plays on top of the preference given to their contractual rights since it is applied to unused capacity. This relates to the natural monopoly nature of infrastructure, suggesting that those contractors may not have alternative ways to receive water, but actors transferring water who are not contractors of the infrastructure owner may not have an alternative way to ship water from upstream to downstream either. A more competitive approach, i.e. less discrimination in favor of the infrastructure owner's clients, but still ensuring the contractual deliveries, would do more to facilitate markets. The provision is too open-ended, and judicial decisions point towards deference to the agency owning the infrastructure, thus, there is the risk of discrimination.[214]

The reasonable rate to be charged for the use of the infrastructure is also controversial. Although the principle of third party access is in place, discrimination can arise not in the review according to the stated standards, but through pricing. Discriminatory pricing could entail the same effects as an outright ban on foreign water being transferred. Section §1811c of the Cal. Water Code tries to address this issue. It establishes the definition of fair compensation as 'the reasonable charges incurred by the owner of the conveyance system, including capital, operation, maintenance, and replacement costs, increased costs from any necessitated purchase of supplemental power, and including reasonable credit for any offsetting benefits for the use of the conveyance system.' Controversies have arisen because even though the provision seems comprehensive, it offers room for disagreement. For example, there is a long-standing conflict between the MWD and the city of San Diego as to how the rates for wheeling should be calculated, and which operational costs of the MWD should be factored in.[215]

In addition, to evaluate the application to use infrastructure, the agency has to consider the economic impact on communities analyzed in the externalities section, injury to other users of the same facilities, and the impact on the environment.[216] These considerations are duplicative as far as effects on the environment are concerned because except for pre-1914 water rights, a public agency must approve the transfer, and in most of the cases transfers will have to comply with environmental regulations such as the CEQA, which require findings on the environmental impact. As a forum for considering community externalities, the approval of the use of infrastructure seems inadequate because it is unclear why the agency managing the infrastructure will be in a better place to assess those effects. In addition, the agency may use the negative effects in the region strategically to deny the use of the infrastructure.

---

214 For a critique, see ibid.
215 For an account of the heated controversy, see 'Water agencies' feud ramps up,' *San Diego Union-Tribune*, 12 March 2012, http://www.utsandiego.com/news/2012/mar/12/sdcwa-vs-metropolitan-feud-escalates-as-rate/.
216 §1810.d of the Cal. Water Code.

In addition, the application for the approval of the transfer and the application for the use of conveyance are separated. The same duality happened during the early 1990s water bank, although both the bank and the SWP were managed by the DWR itself. Again, a more integrated, i.e. single application procedure would be far better than the current system where agencies seem to defer to each other.[217] Documents of the DWR suggest that it defers to the SWRCB when the latter is the agency deciding on the transfer both in terms of effects on other right holders and effects on the environment, but conversations with members of DWR's operations team suggest that deference goes both ways.[218]

Management of water infrastructure also offers room for the protection of the environment and the mitigation of the impact of water distribution on the environment beyond the review. The agencies in charge of the infrastructure could time the deliveries to minimize impact, choosing different avenues to ship the water between two points or substituting sources. Such operations have been the object of water exchanges, i.e. where two users who receive water from different sources exchange their entitlements to receive water from a particular source. The reasons vary: perhaps one user needs higher quality water which is offered by one source rather than the other or because for operational reasons it is easier and saves transportation costs. This type of management operation may also help reduce the effects of water transactions. This is how the projects manage internal transactions, adjusting deliveries to the transfer to minimize impact.[219] The 1991 drought water bank also exemplifies this situation. It had among its goals the protection of the environment. Timing was crucial. For example, some fallowing contracts were modified to allow early flooding to provide habitat for migratory birds.[220] Despite the drought, fish and wildlife were in a better situation than they would have been had the water bank not existed. This was the result not only of the little demand it finally had which resulted in surplus water, but of the appropriate management and timing of water deliveries by the DWR.[221] Hence, even though it is not essential for a water market to exist, public interest dictates that agencies should manage infrastructure in a way that mitigates the effects of transactions.

4.5.4 Market maker

Transaction costs are not the result of a market failure; they are costs related to the operation of water regulation, some of it intended to cure market failures.

217   SWRCB, above note 14, at 9-4.
218   Telephone interview with Maureen Sargent, above note 177.
219   Telephone interview, Craig Trombly, Chief DWR Project Water Management Group (16 April 2013).
220   DWR, above note 71, at 18.
221   DWR, above note 71, at 16.

For example, the review for externalities implies that transactions cannot be straightforwardly completed by private parties, and that certain documents will need to be filed with agencies controlling the effects of the transaction. Hence, some strategies to reduce transaction costs have been analyzed within other sections; for example, legal changes related to the externalities review have an impact on transaction costs since they make the review more or less burdensome.[222] This section analyzes the roles as market maker that California agencies have played, which range from providing information to backing the transactions.

In California, State institutions have played a very important role as market makers and were mandated to do so. The Costa-Isenberg Water Transfer Act of 1986 had several provisions mandating state institutions to fulfill this type of role. Acknowledging how cumbersome the water transfer framework is, §482 of the Cal. Water Code mandates to the SWRCB the preparation of a Water Transfer Guide,[223] which should include a review of the regulations. In the Water Transfer Guide, among other things, there must be a list of agencies which could provide assistance for those willing to enter into transactions and another of regulations. Similarly, §540 of the Cal. Water Code announces, perhaps acknowledging what has always happened in practice, that districts may serve as facilitators for transfers within the district and that they may charge for such services up to the cost of providing them.[224] Hence, the role of agencies as market makers is recognized both in the legislation, as well as in the agency documents.

The establishment of water banks is probably what embodies best the market maker function since it matches buyers and sellers, provides liquidity, and backs up transactions. Transfers do not occur between buyers and sellers but, instead, the bank buys and resells the rights, repacking them if necessary. There have been water bank experiences in California in 1977,[225] 1991, 1992, 1994, 1995, 2001, 2002, 2003, and 2009. Only the first one was managed by the USBR; for all others, the DWR was the managing agency. These banks aimed to facilitate short-term transfers in response to droughts. The 1995 one stands out because it was precautionary and would have consisted in option contracts,[226] which is a strategy to be noted since it allows parties to shield

---

222   Brewer *et al.*, above note 2, at 202–203.
223   In 1999 a draft version of 'A Guide to Water Transfers' was published. See SWRCB, above note 14. It was seminal for the work of the Water Transfer Workgroup issued in 2002, see above note 94.
224   §540 of the Cal. Water Code ('Notwithstanding any other provision of law, a water district, as defined in Section 20200, may serve as an aggregator to facilitate direct transactions within the boundaries of the district in accordance with Chapter 2.3 (commencing with Section 330) of Part 1 of Division 1 of the Public Utilities Code and charge a fee that is equal to the district's cost for providing that service').
225   Wahl, above note 36, at 23–24.
226   Clifford *et al.*, above note 107, at 42.

themselves from future risk, given rainfall uncertainty. However, no trades occurred in 1995.[227] As a consequence, the focus in this chapter is the 1991, 1992, and 1994 ones, the first being the most relevant in terms of volume traded and in overall impact.

One characteristic of Californian water banks is that they are temporary since they are aimed at tackling drought crises. However, there is nothing in the nature of water banks that dictates that they need to be temporary, not even administrative costs. Administrative costs can be shouldered by the private individuals using the bank's services, as is the case in California, where the difference in the buying and selling price precisely accounts for the administrative costs. Temporariness[228] to some extent weakens institutionalization because they are not a routine tool available to users and may delay the response to a drought because banks need some time to be set up. It might be justified if the 1991 drought water bank designers really thought that this was a mechanism necessary to bring Californian water market culture to the threshold from which it can develop on its own. Subsequent history suggests this was not their aim because in 1994 there was another attempt to create a temporary water bank and, beyond the period of study, the Dry Year Water Purchase Program, a water bank, operated again in 2001, 2002, 2003,[229] and 2009.[230] Therefore, it is possible that a more stable structure would have been better and would have favored a quicker reaction; although the speediness with which the 1991 one was established must be recognized: it was set up in just 100 days.[231]

The next section analyzes how California has fulfilled the legislative mandates mentioned using the roles identified in Chapter 2 as a lens.

a. Recording

The need for information in markets is well-known. In water markets, the need is acute, given how fugitive the resource is and the lack of complete registration of the rights. A Water Registry where water rights would be recorded is crucial. Post-1914 rights are recorded because the SWRCB grants them and the application process is public. Contractual rights, both with the DWR and the

---

227 Niblack, above note 108, at 14.
228 For a critique of water banking temporality, see Michael Bazdarich and Christopher Thornberg, *Benefits and costs for California from Water Transfers*, at 144, footnote 7 and associated text, California Policy Options, UCLA School of Public Affairs, UC Los Angeles (2008).
229 Claire D. Tomkins and Thomas A. Weber, 'Option contracting in the California water market,' 37 J. Reg. Econ. 107, 109 (2010).
230 Jim Christie, 'California "water bank" in works amid drought,' *Reuters*, 4 September 2008, http://www.reuters.com/article/2008/09/04/us-economy-california-water-idUSN0457 395520080904.
231 DWR, above note 71, at 19.

USBR, are also recorded. However, this is not the case for riparian and pre-1914 rights. Right holders are required to file an 'Supplemental Statement of Diversion & Use' with the SWRCB. It is important to understand that this filing does not prove the validity or existence of the right.[232] This is particularly problematic for pre-1914 water rights because they are particularly attractive rights, given their seniority to all other rights; however, parties are discouraged from buying them because they cannot be sure what their title is. This filing was required during the study period, but for a long time was considered *de facto* 'optional.' In 2009, California adopted legislation that strengthens its enforcement.[233] The lack of enforcement during the period of study suggests that more could have been done to entrench the market. A unified registry, or at least a database, would have been very useful.

Within this information providing activity, §481 of the Cal. Water Code, as introduced by the Costa-Isenberg Act (1986), requires the Department to prepare a list of entities willing to enter into water transactions and a list of physical facilities available, but this has not been undertaken. Not only is information on prospective trading entities important, but also information on past transactions may be a very helpful guide for those willing to transfer in the market, particularly given the lack of experience and the potential difference in expertise among parties. This information is not only valuable for private parties, but also valuable to design State water policy. However, in California this information is scattered, as the mismatch between the transaction data figures of different scholars shows. There are several private databases on water transactions in California, but they are incomplete, as section 4.4 points out.

The lack of an official publication[234] tracking the evolution of water markets in California has been bemoaned.[235] A full command of data about transactions is difficult to achieve, but public agencies are involved in many transactions either as parties or as reviewers, and, thus, they are the best situated to put it together. The Legislative Analyst's Office in 1999 identified the lack of information on past transactions, as well as on proposed transactions, as a problem.[236] Thus, the performance of water agencies in this role was not satisfactory during the study period. In fact, State water agencies felt compelled to assemble a database. In 2001, the CALFED website posted the 'On-Tap' database of water transfers compiled from various sources which was still full of inaccuracies;[237] in part, most

---

232 §5106(a) of the Cal. Water Code.
233 Stats 2009–2010 7th Ex Sess, Ch. 2, § 6 amending §5107 of the Cal. Water Code.
234 Hanak and Stryjewski, above note 33, at 8.
235 The need for such an instrument is highlighted in the Model Water Transfer Act, see Gray, *The Shape of Things to Come* (2008), above note 92, at 685.
236 Legislative Analyst's Office, above note 22, at 18.
237 CALFED Bay-Delta Program, 'Water Transfers Info Going On-line at "On tap"' (March 2000), http://www.calwater.ca.gov/Admin_Record/F-002578.pdf. CALFED Bay-Delta Program, *On Tap: Water Transfer Information Online* (paper explaining the project), http://www.calwater.ca.gov/Admin_Record/F-002829.pdf.

probably, because local transactions are not easily tracked. 'On-Tap' never took off.

One mandate that California water agencies complied with was the elaboration of a Water Transfer Guide,[238] which was drafted in 1999 and offers guidance to users to navigate the complex web of procedural requirements that any transaction implies.

b. Matching

Water banks are usually described as brokers. Some scholars argue, from a small-government ideological position, that this same role could have been played by private brokers connecting buyers to sellers if a smooth review procedure would have been in place.[239] In fact, the 1991 drought water bank did compete with private brokers. Apparently, some private brokers participated in bank transactions, but there is no reliable data to assess their real contribution[240] and it is not possible to project what they could have achieved if the bank was not in place. Nonetheless, it is possible that the fact water banks' institutionalized process offers the backing of a public agency, the DWR,[241] may ensure private parties of the reliability of the supply.

Nonetheless, private water brokers, compared to the bank, could offer more tailored transactions, while the bank[242] fixed several extremes; for example, the buying and selling price. However, fixing those extremes is positive because it reduces transaction costs.[243] Among other things, fixing prices avoids negotiations that would otherwise delay the rapid response the bank surely provided to the harsh situation faced. The 1991 drought water bank bought water at US$125 per acr-ft and sold it at US$175, which included the costs of contract and monitoring, and the outflow requirements to move water throughout the Delta. This price did not include full conveyance costs; the buyer was responsible for the costs from the Harvey O. Banks Delta Pumping Plant.[244] Obviously, all transactions were mutually beneficial by nature, but not all potential surplus was realized given the fixed prize. Some farmers could have been willing to sell water at a higher rate and some sellers may be willing to pay as much. The bank's price neither took into account the source where water came from nor other relevant variables.[245] The 1992 water bank did not

238   SWRCB, above note 14.
239   Wahl, above note 36, at 16.
240   Wahl, above note 36, at 16.
241   Lawrence MacDonnell, 'Water Banks: Untangling the Gordian Knot of Western Water,' 41 Rocky Mtn. MN. L. Inst. 22 (1995).
242   Wahl, above note 36, at 17.
243   Israel and Lund, above note 6, at 38.
244   Clifford *et al.*, above note 107, at 42.
245   Israel and Lund, above note 6, at 4.

formally fix prices, instead, it implemented a system of pools, which end up establishing homogenous prices.[246]

On top of fixing some extremes in the contracts, the water bank in 1991 put together a model contract for buying water from the bank put together by a committee of stakeholders[247] as a way to reduce transaction costs. Not all circumstances could be incorporated into the contract, but the model was useful to many. In 1992, the DWR also developed a series of standardized contracts, including option contracts. The portfolio of contracts allows, therefore, a certain tailoring for the different transactions.[248]

The central role of the agencies overseeing water banks may explain why third parties have little opportunity to participate in the process and protest those transactions, compared to the possibilities in the review procedures for open-market transactions. This has been criticized,[249] but the heightened oversight of the DWR may justify preventing third parties from protesting transactions because the agency is expected to fulfill the public interest and ensure that other users or the environment are not harmed, without increasing transaction costs.

In addition to State water banks, there were similar banking arrangements in the SWP, the turn-back pools already mentioned, which imply a matchmaking role by the DWR,[250] but the terms of such a match are not favorable to transactions.[251] Similar bank structures have been implemented at a more local level, such as the 1991 Solano County water bank, to facilitate local transfers. These banks operate at a smaller scale, but their success, coupled with the evidence that transactions tend to be local, shows that, even in the absence of both complex infrastructure systems and wide climatic variations, there is room to make current allocation more efficient. In addition, this smaller scale experience should result in fewer community externalities and, likely, fewer environmental ones,[252] and be wrapped in a stronger sense of solidarity or community.[253] Therefore, these local experiences should be encouraged.

---

246 Ibid. at 58.
247 DWR, above note 71, at 1.
248 Israel and Lund, above note 6, at 63.
249 Ibid. at 7. In fact, regulations granting more participation were found to reduce the number of trades. Brewer *et al.*, above note 2, at 210–211.
250 DWR, 'Notice to State Water Contractors in re Turn Back Pool for 1999,' see http://www. water.ca.gov/swpao/ docs/notices/99-01.pdf.
251 The price is lower than the price SWP contractors paid for their water; thus, this is only a mechanism to mitigate the losses for the water not being used. Hanak, above note 85, at 13, footnote 7.
252 Israel and Lund, above note 6, at 14.
253 Relatedly, Kyle Emerick and Dean Lueck, *Economic Organization and the Lease-Ownership Decision in Water*, at 25 (12 May 2010), Working Paper, http://papers.ssrn.com/sol3/ papers.cfm?abstract_id=1605523 (analyzing contract length they find that, in areas where agriculture is the main activity, the contracts are not so long reflecting a concern by farmers about pecuniary externalities).

c. Fungibility

Standardizing the volume transferable would decrease transaction costs across all types of transactions. The only regulation of the volume transferable relates to short-term water transactions of post-1914 water rights. For those, at least, there should be official tables to calculate consumption in cases of crop substitution or fallowing. This could have saved time to enter into certain short-term transactions where only the volume consumed can be transferred. The Model Transfer Act (1996) included proposals to adopt such guidelines[254] and the Legislative Analyst's Office suggested that standardization to analyze third party impacts is necessary.[255] Another source of transaction costs is the diversity of procedures parties have to follow.[256] As it has been pointed out, coordination of those would be a great advancement.

Governmental agencies fare better in increasing fungibility in the water banks than in open market purchases. Water banks provide both liquidity and guarantee since the agency managing them, in most cases, buys the water, repackages it according to the seller's needs, and resells it. It is important to understand that besides what private parties or private brokers could do, in water banks, the agencies which are in charge of the bank and the infrastructure have the potential to pool the water and deliver it using the most sensible time, source, or route.[257] In fact, the DWR was chosen to take care of the bank because it oversees and manages the SWP,[258] and thus it can minimize some external effects on other parties, which can be seen as a way to make rights more fungible. Not all opportunities offered by the integration of the two functions, broker and infrastructure manager, in the DWR, were exploited in the banks. Despite the fact that, in the water banks, most water was delivered through SWP facilities, parties needed to enter into conveyance contracts, separately from the water purchase one.[259] This seems dysfunctional because the agency running the water bank is the same agency in charge of the management of the SWP.[260] The conveyance rate depended upon whether or

---

254   For any analysis, see Gray, *The Shape of Things* (2008), above note 92, at 675 (differentiates between transfers where the use of water was discontinued and transfers where water comes from improvements in irrigation efficiency. Tables apply only to the first given the complex matrix arising from water savings which should combine, at least, previous irrigation system, type of crop, and type of improvement implemented. The rationale behind this difference is that it is very difficult to calculate the amount of water savings with every single improvement).

255   Legislative Analyst's Office, above note 23.

256   The complexity of the review system is perfectly illustrated by the Water Transfer Decision Tree in SWRCB, above note 14.

257   DWR, above note 71, at 9–10 (patterns of supply and demand did not match each other. Supply was accumulated during the irrigation season, but demand was satisfied also later by storing the water).

258   Telephone interview with Maureen Sargent, above note 177.

259   Israel and Lund, above note 6, at 5 and 8.

260   DWR, above note 71, at 1.

not the parties were contractors of the SWP. If they were not, in addition to the energy costs of pumping water, they had to contribute to the general operation and maintenance costs. It also included a charge for the share of costs to offset fish losses resulting from pumping at the Delta.[261] Monetizing the potential externalities in a tax or surcharge is a positive measure because it may avoid subjecting the transaction to open-ended standards, which generate more transaction costs. Not all costs were tied to the quantity of water transferred, disadvantaging small transactions of non-SWP contractors. A further restriction which may impair transactions related to infrastructure was the requirement that water transferred must not conflict with normal SWP deliveries, and receives a lower priority.

Large infrastructure projects offer the same advantage as the DWR did for the water bank: the agency manages the infrastructure and approves the transactions between project contractors. Within the projects, rights are pretty liquid as the amount of trade within the CVP shows: USBR water rights have been defined over large places of use and the CVP contractors can transfer among themselves without being reviewed by State agencies. Contractors can sell their water and the USBR will supply to the buyer its allowance plus the amount bought from another contractor. However, some USBR rights do not have a wide place of use and not all areas have been consolidated and, thus, transfers between contractors of these different areas will require the approval of the SWRCB. There is, thus, still room to improve.

Contractual rights in the SWP are also liquid, given how broadly place of use for post-1914 DWR rights are defined, but its internal regulations prevent those transactions, as already mentioned. The joint area created between the SWP and the CVP after the period of study illustrates that California could still do better regarding the fungibility of water rights.[262] Similar areas where externalities are not expected to be huge should be identified in order to streamline the review in those cases.

A critique of the water bank as a non-pure form of market is based on the requirements imposed on those buying water from the bank which a private broker is unlikely to adopt and which somehow made water rights less fungible. The conditions imposed responded to both efficiency and non-economic

261 Israel and Lund, above note 6, at 54.
262 Such a change is subject to a review by the SWRCB. The review is, however, different from the transfer reviews. In the application for change, the petitioner has also to show that it has provided notice to the Fish and Game Department, but the review by the SWRCB does not seem to require it to take into account the effects on fish or wildlife, 'Before permission to make such a change is granted the petitioner shall establish, to the satisfaction of the board, and it shall find, that the change will not operate to the injury of any legal user of the water involved.' However, SWRCB, interpreting the rule contextually, takes the effects on wildlife into account. 'SWRCB 2009-0033,' at 6 (2009), http://www.waterboards.ca.gov/water rights/board_decisions/adopted_orders/orders/2009/wro2009_0033.pdf (citing SWRCB Order 95-9).

considerations. Buyers had to demonstrate that they were using current available water supplies in the most efficient way, implementing appropriate conservation practices.[263] Markets are supposed to encourage efficient use on both sides, buyers and sellers, because water will be properly priced and, thus, buyers would implement conservation measures if it was cheaper to do so, and sellers would be encouraged to save if saving water was cheaper than the price they would get in the market. However, California's rules imposed conservation requirements, which meant that buyers had to implement water saving measures even if they were more expensive than actually buying water before entering into transactions, thus making rights less transferable by reducing the pool of buyers.

d. Guaranteeing

The government's umbrella has been essential, as the data shows. Open market purchases have never been the key factor in California's water markets. From 1991 to 2000, they constitute only 8.06 per cent of the total volume of transfers.[264] In addition, from 1991 to 2001, direct governmental purchases accounted for 27.29 per cent of the volume transferred in the market.[265] Further in the water banks, the DWR buys and sells the water, it does not act as a mere clearinghouse. The buyer can rely on the guarantee that buying from the DWR provides. Furthermore, given how intricate and uncertain infrastructure management has proven to be, the fact that the DWR manages part of it may contribute to parties having greater confidence in the positive outcome of the transaction. The presence of an administrative agency helps to increase the trust in the market and reduces the fears that, by entering into transactions, water rights may be reduced because an agency will perceive the contract as evidence that a farmer does not need as much water.

The guarantee function is somehow heightened for some users. In the 1991 drought water bank, there were rules to prioritize between different buyers according to how serious the effects of the shortage are for them. Demands arising from emergency situations related to health and safety are satisfied first, then critical needs such as those of urban users receiving less than 75 per cent normal supply or farmers growing permanent crops.[266] However, these priorities did not need to be applied since there was less demand for water than water purchased and, thus, the DWR ensured more water flowing and carryover storage.[267]

263   Ibid.
264   Author's calculation from Ellen Hanak and Elizabeth Stryjewski, 'California's Water Market, By the Numbers, Update, Technical Appendix' (2012), http://www.ppic.org/content/pubs/other/1112EHR_appendix.pdf.
265   Ibid.
266   Ibid. at 5.
267   Hanak and Howitt, above note 34, at 73.

4.6 Conclusions

California's water policy embodies the idea of water markets as a piece of the management puzzle. As Gray put it:

> it has been the policy of the state to prefer negotiated, rather than compulsory, reallocations from lesser to higher valued uses. At the same time, however, the State Water Resources Control Board and the courts have recognized that resort to the compulsory process may be required either to induce negotiated transfers or, in extreme cases, to accomplish reallocation through the adjustment of water rights.[268]

However, the areas of mandatory administration and of market transactions should be more clearly delineated because, otherwise, disincentives could abound.

Water regulations related to transfers have been amended several times. These changes show the will to make water markets work. However, legislative reforms alone have not brought change. Government has been necessary to set the stage for a robust, though far from perfect, water market in California, and it still needs to play significant roles once the market has been established. The different roles played by government are summarized next, emphasizing the roles that have enhanced the market and the main critiques, even though it is not possible to assess how many transactions have been enhanced (or deterred) by each of these positive (or imperfect) features.

4.6.1 Definition of property rights

Property rights in California are very heterogeneous, which leads to many different procedures and degrees of regulation. The different depth of regulation responds to the different nature of the rights involved and translates into different review procedures. There are no restrictions in relation to who can trade water with whom, except riparian rights which can only be transferred to instream flows. According to the written law, entering into a water transaction does not trigger further oversight of the right being transferred, i.e. transferring rights will not result in a review of the right that could reduce the amount on the basis that the previous use was wasteful. There have been several amendments mitigating the fears of private parties about whether entering into transactions will affect their initial right.

Among the different types of rights there are no non-consumptive rights to the instream flow. In relation to instream flows, the strength of the strategy followed by California agencies is the mix of market and regulation. Public agencies have often bought water to ensure that the Chinook salmon can

---

268 Gray, above note 149, at 261–262.

properly breed, but they also imposed restrictions on existing rights to protect the Delta smelt. These protections have been despised by many because they are thought to amount to a taking if we conceive of water rights as a property right akin to land. Some claim these have eroded the security of water rights, particularly when they are not quantified upfront. However, some of the right holders affected by those restrictions have resorted to markets to secure their supply, which has counteracted the reduction of transactions. In addition, §1707 of the Cal. Water Code opened the door to private parties who want to provide water for the environment by buying water rights, but it does not formally give them property rights over that water.

4.6.2 Externalities

California has a scheme of transaction reviews[269] that should prevent any externality from being imposed on other right holders or the environment. However, the multiplicity of review procedures may increase transaction costs unnecessarily. Even though there have been changes to try to streamline the procedure, there is substantial overlap between the different reviews the parties may need to undergo, and the fairly open-ended standards of review have different stringency levels. For example, a post-1914 water right leased from someone who increases her irrigation efficiency to a user within the SWP for three years will have to undergo a review before the SWRCB, prepare the assessment required by the CEQA, and another review to use the SWP infrastructure before the DWR. There are synergies between these reviews, and formal coordination[270] or, even, integration, is in the interest of transaction cost minimization.

In addition, review procedures still partly rely on a type of scheme where other users potentially affected could protest a transaction and agencies other than the water agencies can participate. The Model Water Transfer Act, which was not implemented, suggested another potential solution for short-term transactions outside the water bank: a lighter review procedure coupled with a tax or deposit which would be part of a fund.[271] Right holders who would suffer harm from those transactions could apply to the fund for compensation, the amount of which would already be set according to certain parameters. This is similar to what happened in the water bank experiences where third parties did not get a chance to protest because the DWR was expected to safeguard the effects on other users and the environment. Part of those taxes could also be allocated to environmental conservation.

---

269 SWRCB, above note 14, at 2-3 (decision tree).
270 Legislative Analyst's Office, above note 22, at 14.
271 Brian E. Gray, Richard E. Howitt, Lawrence J. MacDonnell, Barton H. Thompson, and Henry J. Vaux, Jr., 'A Model Water Transfer Act for California: A Proposed Statute,' 4 Hastings W.-N.W. J. Env. L. & Pol'y 3, 15 (1996).

However, short-term transfers constitute the majority of transfers in California, which suggests that their review procedure with third party participation was not too big of a problem, but it also suggests that a more streamlined review procedure translated into more transactions. However, as repeatedly stated in this chapter, many transfers occur within the projects where rights are more fungible.

Externalities affecting communities have been addressed in California mostly on a case-by-case basis. There are sparing mentions of community externalities in the regulation. The mention in the framework of conveyance use seems to open the door to abuse of discretion by the agency owning the facilities and maybe supplying the water to the area where the seller acts. It is advisable to make these operations transparent. Butte County implemented a temporary relief programme funded through a tax on the water sold. Be they real externalities or not, granting some type of remedy for the communities ensures a smoother market environment, rather than a conflict-ridden one. A more structured solution, which has been proposed in the past,[272] would improve the response to these externalities.

4.6.3 Infrastructure

Regarding infrastructure, California has a pretty sturdy net of water connections. The SWP at the west side and the CVP at the east side are the arteries connecting the humid north with the arid south, for both urban areas and agricultural valleys. However, the connection between these two arteries occurs at the San Joaquin Delta, which is a critical habitat for many species. Agencies have done a great deal of operational management, but it is not enough. Rights depending on the delta conveyance have been, and need to be, curtailed. The rules to decide on curtailment are complex. The problems at the Delta explain partly the fact that the majority of transactions are regional because the Delta imposes restrictions on transactions which need to ship water through that hub. The need for further connections is an eternal discussion. The peripheral canal has been on the agenda for years. It would undoubtedly benefit transactions and decrease the burden on agents receiving water to the Delta, but its environmental impact may be too huge.

It cannot be known whether more transactions would have occurred if more infrastructure would have been present, but agencies could have done a better job in managing existing infrastructure beyond the Delta hub. California opened up spare capacity in water infrastructure to the use of third parties. However, common carrier-like regulation relies on standards which offer opportunities to infrastructure owners for blocking transactions. These owners may want to discriminate against third parties who compete with them in water

---

272 Hanak and Howitt, above note 37, at 78.

provision. Despite the duty to convey water if there is spare capacity, the discrimination against the water not owned by the manager of the transportation facilities can arise because the standards to decide on conveyance use, reasonable rate, or impacts on the local economy are far from clear.

4.6.4 Market maker

The role of government as a market maker reducing transaction costs in California has been by far the most distinctive one. Given the heterogeneity of rights and review procedures, administrative agencies have been mandated to play informational and matchmaking roles. Although agencies provide guidance, a complete registration of rights, a database of past transactions, and a water transfer guide were lacking during the period of study, and the first two still are.

The role of market maker in California is perfectly embodied by the water banks, which must be praised for their role as lever of water markets in California; i.e. they – particularly the 1991 one – helped the internalization of a formal market culture. Informal trades had been happening for centuries between neighboring parties, but they were reluctant to enter into transactions which would trigger the review of the public agencies. The presence of a publicly sponsored bank may enhance transactions more than private brokers, which may find their niche in advanced stages of the market. Water banks have this effect because they buy and resell the rights, serving both guarantee and fungibility functions. Buyers believe that water is going to be delivered because they are buying it from a governmental agency. Maybe efficiency is not fully realized, given the fixed contract terms in the water banks, but these reduce transaction costs.

Agencies are quite open to market solutions in California.[273] What seems clear is that water markets, despite the ideological bias in the literature, have not been a divisive issue and, thus, have been accepted by those who manage water as one of the tools in their toolkits in California. Even though water market regulation in California has been criticized, Israel and Lund consider that the mechanisms in place have offered great flexibility in practice, greater than anticipated.[274] However, there is always room for improvement and innovation in water markers,[275] but California has institutionalized water markets. Acute water shortages prompt private and public agents to explore all the open avenues; in California, market ones have been pursued where available. Certainly, improvements and innovations in water markets will come, perhaps as a response to a new water crisis, as the different market regulations have during the period of study.

273   Wahl, above note 36, at 1, 4.
274   Israel and Lund, above note 6, at 1.
275   Hanak and Stryjewski, above note 33, at 8.

5   Spain's water markets[1]

5.1 Introduction

Spain, whose water regulation can be traced back to Roman Law principles,[2] introduced market mechanisms to alleviate the structural or temporary mismatch between supply and demand in December 1999. Hence, the focus of this case study on Spanish water markets is the decade after the 1999 amendment, i.e. 2000–09, inclusive.

These market-tools coexist with the pre-existing administrative scheme, born of the Water Act of 1879 and entrenched by the 1985 Water Act (hereinafter, WA). The WA assumed an even purer administrative system than the 1879 Act, despite its recognition of some historical private property rights. From an organizational viewpoint, it confirmed river basins as the management units, which had been the norm in Spain since the early twentieth century.

Water markets had been succinctly advocated by scholars before being discussed in the political arena. The first appearance in official discussions was when the 'Irrigation Improvement Plan' was being drafted in 1996 by the Socialist party's government.[3] There, the discussion was whether intra-agricultural transactions should be one of the strategies adopted to enhance irrigation efficiency. Markets did not make it to the final document.

Water market ideas reappeared during the first term of the conservative Partido Popular (People's Party) government 1996–2000, when Benigno Blanco, a lawyer,[4] was the Secretary of State of Waters.[5] He put forward the

---

1   An extended version of the case study on Spanish water markets was published by the author in 'Missing Water Markets: A Cautionary Tale of Governmental Failure,' 21 NYU Envt'l L.J. 157 (2015).
2   See Dante A. Caponera, *Principles of Water Law and Administration*, at 47 (2007).
3   'El PSOE aprobó un mercado "libre" en 1996' ('The Spanish socialist Party approved a "free" market in 1996'), at 86, ABC, 3 May 1999.
4   It is important to understand who the people behind this proposal were. Benigno Blanco was a 38-year-old lawyer who worked before for Iberdrola, an electric company. This made him suspect of favoring the hydroelectric companies. Jointly with him, the team was composed of two civil engineers, one who had been the representative on behalf of Iberdrola in the Jucar River Basin Authority and another who was the designer of the Tajo-Segura transfer

draft of a bill reforming the WA early in the term, but it was not passed until 1999. Even if these water market ideas were based on some academic debates, the People's Party added an ideological gloss to the bill. More flexible concessions were seen as reducing government involvement. In fact, the changes in water regulation and its push towards markets were understood as part of the overall liberalization agenda[6] of that government which included privatization of public services such as power, gas, telephone, and postal services, which were national monopolies. However, compared to other commodities, water has always been more local, non-State wide; there was no national monopoly to dismantle after its privatization. Perhaps recognizing water's special nature, those proposing the bill amending the WA were softer on the liberalization rhetoric than they were in other market reforms in the legislative debate, which often referred to the experiences in California.[7] Opponents – mostly farmers and environmentalists – criticized the commodification of water because water was public property.

The regime based on concessions – permits – allocated by administrative agencies did not seem to be providing the correct incentives for efficient water use. Hence, water markets were portrayed as a vehicle of efficiency, solving the structural problems due to historical water allocation and the impossibility of easily increasing the supply. The proposal was also motivated by the mid-1990s' drought crisis which awakened the need for reforms, as the 1999 amendment of the WA's preamble shows.[8] Scarcity and drought were precursors for

and a hydrogeology professor highly critical of the Socialist Party Water Policy. See 'El Gobierno ultima una reforma legal que abre el camino a la compraventa del agua' ('Government is about to introduce a bill which allows for water sales'), *El País*, 26 January 1997.

5   He reports to the Minister of the Environment on water management issues.

6   Editorial 'Las dos Españas' ('Two Spains'), *El País*, 1 February 1999 ('even those extreme liberals (libertarians) who inspired this idea [of water markets] do not think that water markets can be the solution').

7   See Comisión de Medio Ambiente, Session No. 38 (1999) (Diario de Sesiones del Congreso de los Diputados 1999, 723). See also Antonio Embid Irujo, *Asignación del agua y gestión de la escasez en España: los mercados dederechos de aguas* (*Water allocation and scarcity management in Spain: water rights markets*) (2008).

8   L. 1999/46 (BOE 1999, 298), preamble, 'En este sentido, la experiencia de la intensísima sequía, padecida por nuestro país en los primeros años de la década final de este siglo, impone la búsqueda de soluciones alternativas, que, con independencia de la mejor reasignación de los recursos disponibles, a través de mecanismos de planificación, permitan, de un lado, incrementar la producción de agua mediante la utilización de nuevas tecnologías, otorgando rango legal al régimen jurídico de los procedimientos de desalación o de reutilización, de otro, potenciar la eficiencia en el empleo del agua para lo que es necesario la requerida flexibilización del actual régimen concesional a través de la introducción del nuevo contrato de cesión de derechos al uso del agua, que permitirá optimizar socialmente los usos de un recurso tan escaso' ('In this sense, the experience of the intense drought suffered by our country in the early years of the final decade of this century, calls for the search of new alternative solutions, which, regardless of the best reallocation of available resources through

governmental action. The Popular Party used the crisis to introduce this reform which, for them, was also an ideological battle. The drought was instrumental in achieving a consensus among high ranking civil servants working at the water agencies that something needed to be done. The support of public officials working on water management for years was indispensable for success.

Drought was a precursor, but there was a time lag. The drought period happened from 1990 to 1995, but it was not until 1999 that a comprehensive reform of Spanish Water Law took place. The political process may have caused this delay. In fact, this later reform can be considered an achievement, because usually such a deal is hard to strike during wet years: once water scarcity loses saliency, it generally drops out of the agenda.[9] However, the mid-1990s' crisis left such scars that memories were not easily forgotten. Ideology kept it high on the agenda. In 1999, amendments to the WA introducing markets were passed and in 2001, the Consolidated Water Act (hereinafter, CWA) was enacted,[10] incorporating the 1999 changes and giving coherence to the existing rules. Exchanges could occur since the regulation contained in the 1999 amendment was enough, but in 2003 the administrative regulations implementing the CWA were passed.[11]

The next drought episode, in mid-2000, prompted government to activate some of the 1999 mechanisms. However, as shown below, market reallocation did not constitute a great share of the solution to the drought challenges.

Since water market mechanisms are a piece in the overall administrative puzzle, an understanding of the water management scheme is needed to identify the role envisioned for water markets in Spain as well as to assess whether their goals have been achieved. Section 5.2 describes that water management scheme. A particular aspect of this administrative scheme is explored further in section 5.3: types of water rights and tradability of those prior to the 1999 amendment of the WA. Section 5.4 explains the water market regulations and their evolution, putting an emphasis on the political discussion around those regulations. Section 5.5 lists the data on transactions available coupled with scarcity. This section is necessary to establish the relative success of water markets in both jurisdictions studied in this book, California and Spain.

---

planning mechanisms. These new solutions should, on the one hand, increase water production using new technologies, granting legal status to legal procedures desalination or reuse, and, on the other, enhance efficiency in water use given the flexibility needed under the current concession regime through the introduction of the new contract for the transfer of rights to use water, which will optimize socially uses of such scarce resource').

9   'Presente y futuro(s) del agua potable' ('Present and future of drinking water'), *El País*, 14 March 2013 (José María Perez is cited saying 'Es cuando está lloviendo cuando toca hablar del agua' ('It is when it is raining that we should talk about water')).

10   Consolidated Water Act (CWA) (BOE 2001, 176).

11   In 2003, the rules implementing the Act were enacted. RD 606/2003 (Decree modifying the Decree approving the Regulations of the Water Public Domain, which implements the Water Act) (BOE 2003, 135). The latter, hereinafter RDPH.

Lastly, section 5.6 examines whether and to what extent the different government roles listed in Chapter 3 as necessary for a water market to flourish have been fulfilled in the Spanish case. Through the analysis of these roles, the changes in water market regulation throughout the period of study are noted and put into context with the data on drought periods and on transactions.

5.2 Spain's allocation of power over water management

Water management is under the power of the central government when the river basin is shared by different autonomous communities, which are the political decentralized units or regions. If water is within the territory of only one region, the autonomous community has power to manage the resource although the main regulatory framework is set by the central government.[12] There are more than a dozen River Basin Authorities (Organismos de Cuenca, hereinafter RBAs)[13] which manage a basin or a group of basins belonging to the same hydrological district. Figure 5.1, portraying canals and other transfer infrastructure, shows the different basins. Some of the basins are grouped together since they are considered part of a single hydrological district. There are eight inter-regional RBAs (Norte, Duero, Ebro, Guadalquivir, Guadiana, Júcar, Segura, and Tajo)[14] and six regional RBAs administering basins which are within the boundaries of a single autonomous community (Andalucia, Balearic Islands, Basque Country, Canary Islands, Catalonia, and Galicia). There has been some fluidity regarding the configuration of basins: some basins have been re-defined as intra-regional areas which before were considered inter-regional. Even though the term 'basin' should be a hydrological concept, it has been politically twisted. This has been the case, for example, of Andalucia which extended its claims to an inter-regional river, the Guadalquivir, only to be reversed later in court.[15]

As mentioned in Chapter 3, central government regulation sets the framework for water management for all of the basins, both intra-regional and

---

12 Art. 149.22 of the Spanish Constitution (BOE 1978, 311).
13 Art. 22 of the CWA. The European Water Framework Directive also adopted a basin level approach for water management. Arts 3 and 13 establish river basins districts as the units for management plans without imposing a specific administrative structure for them.
14 Only Ebro's CH was implementing an online register. This operation is subsidized by the Ministry of the Environment through 'Programa Alberca,' http://www.mma.es/portal/secciones/aguas_continent_zonas_asoc/uso_dph/alberca.htm. It gives funds to update the Water Registries and progressively computerize them. The update of the registries is very important because it increases the certainty of the rights traded and, hence, may increase the number of transactions entered into.
15 David Sampedro Sánchez and Leandro del Moral Ituarte, 'Tres décadas de política de aguas en Andalucía. Análisis de procesos y perspectiva territorial' ('Three decades of water policy in Andalucia. Analysis of procedures and territorial perspective'), 53 Cuadernos Geográficos 1 (2014).

inter-regional. The Spanish Constitution gives central government the power to establish the basic regulations regarding administrative agencies, the public property regime, and certain water law principles that the autonomous communities' water institutions and the RBAs have to respect.[16] These principles include issues such as the nature of water as public property or participation of the water users in the management. In fact, it has been disputed whether the market regulations run against this nature. However, the Constitutional Court in 2011 declared that the market provisions did not amount to a privatization and that public agencies retained the control.[17]

The RBAs managing inter-regional basins – i.e. basins covering more than one Spanish autonomous community – are the Confederaciones Hidrográficas (hereinafter, CHs). Co-operation between different jurisdictions and layers of government is essential because basins are an additional institutional level superimposed on the general institutional structure. The composition of their board ensures the participation of a broad range of agents whose interests are at stake. Participants range from users to the different layers of government affected. Users – both urban and agricultural – must represent at least one-third of the members of some RBAs' boards, inter- or intra-regional.[18] In CHs, the central government has the most representatives in the different decision-making boards.[19] Who controls these organs is a relevant point because they are the ones approving private contracts transferring water rights,[20] determining the procedures to approve transactions, and deciding whether to establish exchange centers, which also require central government's approval. Despite their diverse composition, there are often claims of capture by some interests to the detriment of others.

A key component of water management in Spain is planning. Plans are not merely guidelines, they are binding. There is a National Hydrologic Plan (NHP), complemented by specific plans regarding each of the water basins. Water planning at the basin scale makes ecological sense and it is mandated by the European Water Framework Directive. The approval of the NHP by central

---

16 Arts 14 and 18 of the CWA.

17 Sentencia 149/2011 (BOE 2011, 258).

18 Autonomous communities have flexibility to shape the structure of the agency, and some have created an independent organ instead of following the CH model. For instance, see Agencia Andaluza del Agua (Water Agency of Andalucía), which is an independent agency, http://www.juntadeandalucia.es/agenciadelagua/. See also Agència Catalana de l'Aigua (Catalan Water Agency), which has been incorporated as a private, but publicly owned corporation, http://acanet.gencat.cat/redireccionament/web_es.htm.

19 Art. 27 of the CWA (central government has five representatives on the Board – *Junta de Gobierno* – and appoints its President – see Art. 29 of the CWA – while users will have one-third of the seats at most, and autonomous communities and provinces will have a number of seats according to their population and territory covered by the basin). See also Arts 31, 32, and 35–36bis of the CWA for the other committees; in some of them apart from the representatives of the central government, the RBA itself is represented.

20 Art. 18.1.b of the CWA.

government has always been conflict-ridden. Being a highly controversial issue, political reasons sometimes prevail to the detriment of technical requirements. The NHP was envisaged by the WA,[21] but it was not approved until 16 years later in 2001 when it was proposed by the People's Party Government of President José María Aznar (in office from 1996 to 2004).[22] The most contentious and ambitious issue in the 2001 NHP was the mandated transfer from the Ebro River to the south east Mediterranean area, an area undergoing huge urban development as part of the housing boom at the time.[23] Opponents claim that the water transferred would have decreased the flow of the river and endangered the Delta. The NHP was regarded as serving particular interests from the Mediterranean coast.[24] It was supposed to quench the current and future thirst of urban developers and tourism on Valencia's and Murcia's coasts. In fact, some argued that the NHP transfer, coupled with the 1999 market reform, would unleash rampant speculation. This fear was not completely justified because water rights have to be put to use and, thus, buyers must already be right holders. The Ebro transfer infrastructure was envisioned to transfer water from the Upper Ebro River, not reducing existing rights. However, the apportionment rules in times of drought were unclear, and farmers downstream feared that they would not receive water during harsh times.[25] Funding from the European Union was necessary to complete the transfer project. Concerns were raised to the EU institutions about the environmental impact. The European Parliament echoed those environmental concerns in a general resolution in February 2002.[26] However, the EU institutions did not need to formally decide on the legality of the NHP because the transfer was abolished in 2004[27] and the Plan was substantially amended in 2005[28] after the 2004 election brought a change in the central government: President José Luis Rodríguez-Zapatero, a member of the Socialist Party (in office from 2004 to 2011), was elected. The Ebro transfer was one of the most

---

21 Art. 38.2 of the WA.

22 L. No. 2001/10 (NHP Act) (BOE 2001, 161).

23 Santiago Navarro and David Cerdan, 'Especulación urbanística y caracoles para Aznar' ('Urban development speculation and snails for Aznar'), *El País*, 20 October 2002.

24 Interview to Pedro Arrojo in *El País*, 11 January 2004 (he suggests that there are many hidden interests behind the NHP, 'Hay grandes negocios en la teastienda del Plan hidrológico').

25 Ibid.

26 P5_TA(2002)0081 European Parliament resolution on the sustainable development strategy for the Barcelona Summit (DOCE C293-E84, 2002) (point 12: no explicit mention to the Spanish NHP but it states that the Parliament 'Is deeply concerned about the precedent set by proposals for the development of unsustainable water management schemes across Europe, and calls on the Commission for these reasons not to provide any EU funding for these water transfer projects'). For a comment on the impact in the Spanish NHP, see 'Plan Hidrológico Nactional: el informe que reforzó la Enmienda 10' ('NHP: the report which reinforced its amendment for the 10th time'), *El País*, 20 October 2002.

27 RDL 2004/2 (Decree-Act abolishing the Ebro Transfer) (BOE 2004, 148).

28 L. No. 2005/11 (BOE 2005, 149).

controversial issues during the electoral campaign. President Zapatero fulfilled his electoral promise: the mandatory Ebro transfer was abandoned in his amendment of the NHP.

Even without an NHP, some River Basin Plans were enacted in the 1985–2001 period.[29] These are the key tools of water policy according to the European Water Framework Directive.[30] Their provisions range[31] from the definition of environmental protection areas or pollution levels to the abstract allocation of water through the definition of priority and compatibility of users, definition of instream flows, and the economic analysis of water use.[32] River Basin Plans are elaborated by RBAs, but the central government approves them if they are inter-regional.[33] It is important to emphasize that they establish the ranking of uses, which has an effect on new permits granted and on water markets, as shown below.[34] These plans are updated only periodically and, thus, the guidance they can offer as to what is to be the best management of water is limited.

However, River Basin Plans were not the key documents to manage droughts. Drought responses were ruled by emergency decrees.[35] Drought Preparedness Plans have been in place only since 2007[36] and there was not a serious drought before the end of the study period to test whether the RBAs or the governments will deviate from them and use their emergency powers to overrule them, frustrating expectations.

Apart from the levels of government already mentioned, it is important to highlight other institutions with an important role in water. First, it is important to emphasize that urban water distribution is the responsibility of the local governments.[37] Thus, local governments may decide to self-supply or outsource to a private company. Urban water suppliers are expected to be buyers in the market, but they may also be sellers. Second, irrigation communities are formed by farmers and supply water to the farmers of a certain area. Irrigation communities have a very important role because often they are the ones holding the right and supplying water to some individual farmers. We expect them to

---

29 See 3rd transitory provision in L. 2001/10, above note 22.

30 Art. 13 of the European Water Framework Directive.

31 For a list of the issues those cover, see Art. 72-90 of D. 927/1988 (Decree regulating Water Administration and Planning, implementing the Water Act) (BOE 1988, 209).

32 Art. 42 of the CWA. See also Art. 72-90 of D. 927/1988 (Decree regulating Water Administration and Planning, implementing the Water Act) (BOE 1988, 209).

33 Art. 40.5 of the CWA.

34 Art. 60.1 of the CWA.

35 List of the 23 decrees (18 of the central government; four autonomic; one local) enacted to cope with the drought from 2005 to 2009, http://www.magrama.gob.es/es/agua/legislacion/Medidas_Legislativas_tcm7-197416.pdf.

36 Inter-regional drought plans were approved by the central government: Orden MAM/698/2007 (Order approving the special plans for alert and drought scenarios in interregional basins) (BOE 2007, 71).

37 Art. 25.2(l) of the CWA.

be sellers. Apart from being potential participants in the market and the transmission chain between end users and the market, irrigation communities can also be a forum for an internal market between their members. However, those internal transactions are not the focus of this book since they are not transferring permits to use water but the allocations by the irrigation community, and there is no data available to track them.

5.3 Water rights in Spain: administrative concessions

5.3.1 General overview of the property rights over water

As already stated, the Spanish water regime is a public property one.[38] All hydro resources are public property, and are thus under the dominion of the State as established in Article 1.2 of the WA,[39] according to Article 132.2 of the Spanish Constitution.[40]

Water is allocated to individual users mainly through administrative permits called 'concesiones.'[41] These are the rights this chapter primarily focuses on since they are the object of the market regulations. There are some other types of rights: historical private property rights and some quasi-concessional rights in certain irrigable areas recognized as 'areas of public initiative.'

5.3.2 Concessions for water use

a. General description

Concesiones are required for both surface water and groundwater. These administrative permits[42] give their recipients the right to use water. The RBAs grant these permits on a discretionary basis, taking into account water

---

38   Under the 1879 Water Act, private property over water, though exceptional, existed as it did in other civil law countries following the French model. See Caponera, above note 1, at 69. See also Gaspar Ariño, *Leyes de Aguas y Política Hidráulica en España* (1999) (Chapter 1 offers an overview of the development of water regulation in Spain).

39   As the WA preamble stated, 'Surface continental water, removable groundwater, which both form the hydrologic cycle, are a unitary resource subordinated to the public interest part of the State public property as hydrologic public domain.'

40   'Assets under the State's public property shall be those established by law and shall, in any case, include the foreshore beaches, territorial waters and the natural resources of the exclusive economic zone and the continental shelf,' see Art. 131.2 of the Spanish Constitution, above note 12.

41   Art. 59 of the CWA. However, there are exceptions to this rule since some private use permits are statutorily granted. Basically, Art. 54 of the CWA establishes that without being granted a concession, an owner of a piece of land can scoop rainfall water, can use water held back on it, and can exploit up to 7,000 m³ from a spring or a well.

42   Permits and concessions will be indistinctively used in reference to the form rights to use water take in Spain.

availability[43] and the type of use it will be devoted to, since the issuance of permits has to respect the ranking of uses established in the River Basin Plan.[44] If there is a pool of competing applicants, the applicant proposing the highest ranked and most efficient use of water will be preferred.[45]

The procedure for permit application is quite cumbersome and may include the participation of users who might be potentially affected, autonomous communities, and irrigation communities.[46] Furthermore, the application is open to competition.[47] In other words, there is a public notice and other applicants can compete for that same water with no clear advantages for the first applicant, except the fact of being the first mover and perhaps having gathered more information about the availability of water and the potential impacts. However, usually there are not many applicants and, thus, the efficiency of the water use is not evaluated on relative terms.

Permits are granted to individual users, companies supplying urban areas, irrigators' communities,[48] or corporations that will supply irrigation water to farmers.[49] Communities of users can also be formed by individuals who hold their own water rights.[50] This could be the case for groundwater users who have to constitute a community if their groundwater basin is over-drafted or at risk of being so. In some extreme cases, unitization is mandated in those groundwater basins.[51]

These permits are defined according to different variables: term, maximum volume of flow, time of use if it is discontinuous, equivalent average volume of flow, and location. If the permit is for irrigation, the permit will also establish the acreage to be irrigated, the location, maximum flow to be derived per acre per year, and the maximum flow per month.[52] Any change to be introduced

---

43 Art. 59.4 of the CWA.
44 Art. 60.3 of the CWA.
45 Art. 79.2 of the CWA.
46 Arts 109–110 of the RDPH.
47 Art. 105 of the RDPH.
48 Art. 61.5 of the CWA. See also Arts 81–92 of the CWA for the structure and powers of the community of users (for irrigation purposes, these are called 'Comunidades de regantes,' which are formed by farmers from a certain area. They self-regulate, but their organic-charters and regulations must be approved by the basins' administration. Nevertheless, Art. 81 of the CWA imposes hurdles to the Administration's review since if it wants to change what has been drafted by the irrigation community, a ruling from the 'Consejo de Estado' – an advisory board from the central government – is required. Generally, these communities are privately formed but the Basin Administration might impose their establishment. 'Comunidades de Regantes,' where votes are commonly granted according to the stretch of land owned, are responsible for the allocation of water among the different members. To solve disputes, some of these institutions have a traditional jury composed of users; custom is recognized as a source of law for these matters).
49 Art. 62 of the CWA.
50 Art. 81 of the CWA.
51 Art. 56 of the CWA.
52 Art. 102 of the RDPH.

to these variables requires approval by the issuing institution, the RBA organization.[53]

Water rights for irrigation are granted in relation to the land they will serve: the permit holder has to be the owner or lessee of the land that will be irrigated.[54] The exception to this is the collective permit for irrigators' communities and the permit for companies supplying water to individual farmers; but even with those, the recipients have to demonstrate their connection to the lands.[55] It is common for farmers to receive water from an irrigation community or district. So, both institutional actors and individual farmers holding rights could enter the market. Potentially, those farmers holding just a share could also enter the market if such an entitlement were to be made tradable. In any case, this link to the land does not prevent water to be leased to another agricultural land or to urban use.

Water for urban users is generally provided through a system of distribution with two phases: a company, either publicly or privately owned, holds the permit and brings water to the cities, and another agency or company, again either public or private, distributes it to end users. Sometimes, these phases are vertically integrated. As stated, urban supply is under the power of the municipality which chooses the system of management of the water supply system: private, public, mixed, etc. For example, the two big Spanish metropolitan areas are dominated by two companies, Agbar – private – in Barcelona and Canal de Isabel II – public – in Madrid. Agbar, part of the Suez-Lyonnais water empire, holds its own water rights, buys water from wholesalers and distributes it to end consumers.[56] Agbar also supplies to more than 20 municipalities near Barcelona. There is no competition in the supply at the household level. Again, urban suppliers are the ones expected to participate in the market, not the individual households.

As already noted, every permit is restricted to a certain use. The use stated has a lot of implications for water management since its position in the ranking will determine the result if there are competing applications which are not compatible.[57] Each river basin can set up its own rankings in its plans, but if it does not, central water regulation establishes a default one. In any case, mandatorily, the highest rank is granted to household uses, even if these household uses include watering gardens. Rankings have effects on market transactions, as described below. This ranking does not matter for the sharing of the consequences of low availability of water during drought seasons. In other words, the ranking of uses is not equivalent to the temporal priority on a prior appropriation system. However, in practice, in drought decrees and

---

53   Art. 62 of the CWA.
54   Art. 61.4 of the CWA.
55   Arts 61.5 and 62.1 of the CWA.
56   See section 1.4.1.
57   Art. 60.1 of the CWA.

in Drought Preparedness Plans – enacted after the period of study – by each river basin, household/urban uses have taken priority and they would hardly ever suffer cuts.

Relatedly, it is important to emphasize that the permit's grant does not entitle the grantee to the volume there allocated. The actual volume received will depend on water availability at a given time.[58] In addition, at any time, the public property nature of water implies that the administrative agencies have important powers over its use.[59] For example, a CH may impose on a water user the substitution of the water it normally uses for water of another source or type, even under conditions which may or may not amount to an emergency.[60] For example, during the 2008 drought, the Catalan Water Agency considered an exchange of water used by irrigators from the Llobregat River for reused water.

Another variable mentioned is length. These permits' maximum length is 75 years from the time of the application,[61] although this maximum can be modified by the specific hydrologic plan for a specific river basin or by regional water regulations. For instance, in Catalonia's internal basins it is 50 years,[62] and in Andalusia (south of Spain), since 2010, it is 20 years.[63] Each permit has its own start and end date, they are not particularly clustered around a specific date, but the issue date does not grant priority.

The fact that permits are temporary is not enough to ensure that water adapts to new needs by changing hands because they have long-term limits. Only when the permit's term expires can the administration either free the water by not renewing it and wait for new needs to pop up, or renew the concession, opening a competitive process for alternative applicants with perhaps a higher-ranked use. In any case, the efficiency analysis has a reduced scope and only takes into consideration the incumbent use and that of those who may bid. It is inherently difficult for particular decisions to account for the overall interdependency of uses inherent in water. This is the case for both first time applications and renewals. Even though renewal could be an avenue to free the water or put it

---

58   Art. 59.2 of the CWA.
59   Art. 61.3 of the CWA.
60   Art. 59.6 of the CWA.
61   The Canary Islands, which do not share any water resource with other parts of Spain, present some peculiarities. Its system is mainly managed by their regional government according to their Water Act (L. 1990/12, B.O. Canarias 1990, 94). According to the 3rd transitional provision of this Act, previous private rights are grandfathered and can operate as they used to even if water is public domain according to the national WA. Trade of water rights is clearly stated in Art. 112 of Canary Water Act but notice of every transaction has to be provided to the water administration.
62   ACA, 'Pla hidrològic de les conques internes de Catalunya' ('Water Plan for the internal basins of Catalonia') (1999), http://aca-web.gencat.cat/aca/appmanager/aca/aca?_nfpb= true&_pageLabel=P1204554461208200513322.
63   Art. 45.4 of Ley de Aguas de Andalucía (Andalucia's Water Act) (BOJA 2010, 155).

to a better use, there is a certain automatism in the review of concessions.[64] In general, it must be said that those holding the title have important advantages if they want to renew the permit once it expires. Even though in the abstract, time limits seem to be the defining difference between a private and a public property system, in practice there seems to be an approximation between these two systems.

In order to ensure efficiency, apart from granting the rights in the first place on a case-by-case basis following the broad guidelines set forth in the water plans and the renewal control, both of which could be used to push users to be efficient in their water use by granting a volume lower than they requested, the administration can take several decisions regarding permits to maximize efficient use. First, public agencies could incentivize technologies that would reduce water consumption. It can do so through subsidies or increasing the prices paid by irrigators not holding water rights, but receiving water from a supplier or irrigation community. The RBAs have a second set of mechanisms which could be used as direct avenues to shift current distribution: revision of the permit if the same use could be satisfied with a lower volume, mandatory reallocation during drought, or expropriation of current permits to allocate them to higher-value uses.[65] These review mechanisms have never been used, despite being the most direct way to tackle wasteful uses and free water.

The shortcomings of administrative control are illustrated by the Spanish water regime. The Spanish water management system had tools to increase efficiency, but they would never be enough because they can only be used on a case-by-case basis and at specific points in time, and agencies fell short of making the most of them. Hence, there is margin for voluntary reallocation via markets to aid in the achievement of efficiency.

b. Tradability of permits prior to the 1999 amendment

Prior to the amendment, tradability of permits was succinctly addressed in the WA.[66] Users could enter into transactions, but it was not a mechanism envisioned with the purpose of shifting the allocation of water. According to the WA, any transfer had to be communicated to the RBA,[67] which could bar the transaction *ex-post*.

However, transfers usually implied changes in the permit; for example, change in place of diversion, place of use or changes in river flow as a result of return flow.[68] These changes required authorization from the CH or a

---

64   José Antonio De la Orden Gómez, Amelia Pérez Zabaleta, and Juan Antonio López Geta (eds), *El análisis económico en la Directiva Marco del Agua: Incidencias e implicaciones para España* (2006).
65   Art. 58 (drought scenario) and Art. 60.2 of the CWA.
66   Except in the water regime of the Canary Islands, see above note 61.
67   Art. 61 of the WA.
68   Arts 151.2 and 151.3 of the RDPH.

regional equivalent.[69] Only a change of just the permit holder would not have triggered this authorization procedure. Hence, a transfer would require in the majority of cases a prior authorization because of the changes implied on the permit characteristics, although the transfer itself only needs to be communicated. The type of exchanges relevant to this book, i.e. transfers of permits to satisfy uses with a different marginal value, required authorization through the long and demanding permit modification review procedure.[70]

In this scheme, which is still in place today, and was the only way to modify permits and transfer them prior to the 1999 reform, the period for review can take up to 18 months.[71] After those 18 months, if a decision has not been made, the silence is understood to mean that the modification is not allowed. The review proceedings offer instances which could possibly be analyzed as tragedies of the anti-commons:[72] they allow different instances of public participation and require reports from different governmental agencies. It is important to note that the 1999 amendment does not cover all potential trading situations, as shown below. For those not covered, this scheme still applies. For example, the 1999 lease of permits provision requires both parties to be users. If someone who does not already hold a right wants to buy water, this pre-1999 procedure is triggered.

It is surprising that the Spanish literature, from economics, to engineering and law, dealing with water markets, has paid little attention to this mechanism. The focus has been on the 1999 amendment probably because the pre-1999 change in water rights procedure was so demanding that it made trading too costly. There were exceptions: some scholars do believe that there was a formal market prior to the amendment.[73] Some advocates of water markets used this previous procedure as a shield to say that the 1999 amendment was not such a break with the former legal tradition, but just an incremental improvement, even with an experimental shade to it.[74] In fact, Benigno Blanco portrayed it as an incremental improvement.[75]

Very few examples of transactions following this cumbersome procedure before and after 1999 appear in the literature because data about them is not

---

69   Art. 62 of the WA.
70   Art. 62 of the WA.
71   Art. 116 of the RDPH.
72   Michael Heller, 'The Tragedy of the Anticommons: Property in the Transition from Marx to Markets,' 111 Harv. L. Rev. 621 (1998). For the application to water, see Stephen N. Bretsen and Peter J. Hill, 'Water markets as a tragedy of the anticommons,' 33 Wm. & Mary Envt'l L. & Pol'y Rev. 723 (2009).
73   José Luis Moreu Ballonga, 'Una explicación jurídica sobre el Mercado del agua' ('A legal explanation of the Water Market'), *El País*, 31 May 1999.
74   Interview Benigno Blanco, *El País*, 5 August 1996, 'No me sirve el Plan hidrológico de Borrell' ('Borrell's Plan does not suit me').
75   Ibid. The Constitutional Court has recognized that the leases do not strip water from its public property nature. STC 149/2011 (BOE 2011, 258).

complete. A few RBAs offer some figures in their annual reports about changes in permits,[76] but the potential sales cannot be disentangled from other changes in the permit, such as inheritance. There are, nonetheless, some well-known pre-1999 trades, particularly those by Emasesa, the company supplying Sevilla, the capital of Andalusia. This southern city suffered accutely during the 1990s drought; there were even serious daily curtailments for household uses. Emasesa bought water from the nearby irrigation community of El Viar, which was portrayed as exceptional even if it was not totally uncommon as the company had to resort to this strategy several times.[77] However, it was criticized because urban supply is granted pre-eminence and it seemed against the public interest to opt for a market mechanism.[78] Later, even when urban areas resort to the market, the price has been distorted by subsidies.[79]

Apart from these mechanisms, other trades existed in Spain. First, trades among members of the same irrigation community were and are a common practice. Ostrom studied the auctions held by traditional irrigators' communities in the Valencia region.[80] In fact, intra-community trades are still possible after the 1999 reform and are not subject to administrative review because they are considered to be internal acts of the irrigation community.[81] Individual farmers who contract their supply with the irrigation community do not have a right to sell the water supplied via the permit lease mechanism introduced in 1999.

Second, water markets existed in the Canary Islands.[82] Water rights in the Canary Islands are groundwater ones and there is a type of water pool. Multiple

---

76 CH Duero, 'Memoria' ('Report'), at 97 (2007), http://www.chduero.es/Inicio/Publicaciones/tabid/159/Default.aspx.

77 Javier Calatrava Leyva, 'Mercados y bancos de agua en España. Legislación y experiencias recientes,' Agricultura Familiar en España 2006, at 99 (2006), http://www.upa.es/anuario_2006/pag_099-105_calatrava.pdf. Antonio M. Rico Amorós, 'Sequías y Abastecimiento de Agua en España,' 37 Boletín official de la AGE 137, 168 (2004), http://www.boletinage.com/37/07-SEQUIAS.pdf.

78 Ibid.

79 In 2006, the central government exempted the Mancomunidad de los Canales del Taibilla, a public company supplying water to municipalities in the south-east of Spain which entered into transactions following the 1999 amendment, from certain water tariffs to compensate for the economic effort it had made by leasing rights to cope with the crisis. RDL 2006/9 (Decree-Act Adopting Urgent Measures to Lessen the Effects of the Drought on the Population and Water-Intensive Agricultural Sectors in Certain Watersheds (BOE 2006, 222)).

80 Elinor Ostrom, *Governing the Commons*, at 79 (1992) (The irrigation community in the Tibi Dam in Alicante (Spain) made available important information – such as water storage, water delivered in the previous rotation, or price and quantities of water sold in the previous rotation – to the farmers prior to the auction to facilitate their choices). See also Comisión de Medio Ambiente, Session No. 38 (1999), above note 6, at 20260.

81 Art. 343.5 of the RDPH.

82 See Ariño, above note 38, at 197. See also Comisión de Medio Ambiente, Session No. 38 (1999), above note 6, at 20661, 20663.

companies hold the extraction permits and others transport the water to the final customers. Third, black markets for water have always existed despite the improvements in policing and metering, and they may remain active.[83]

However, the focus of this book is how to make formal water market mechanisms work well thanks to governmental action. Regarding formal transactions, before 1999, water trading existed, but was supposedly only marginal. Regulation was not aimed at promoting transactions. The review mechanism for changes in the permits, a necessary step in the majority of transactions, was extremely cumbersome and not much different from an application for a new permit; it did not allow for a flexible response in times of crisis. There were other administrative mechanisms to purportedly guarantee that water would flow from low value to high value users, as already explained, but those were not effective either.

Neither the centralized mechanisms, nor the potential transactions undergoing this cumbersome procedure, nor informal trading helped much to cope with the effects of the 1990s' crisis. Rivers were dry; people in certain areas could not shower at any time they wished.[84] It made it obvious that there was a mismatch between where the majority of water was allocated, and where there was a shortage, but water was highly valued. The crisis was managed through harsh curtailments and emergency measures, but the situation was so severe that reforms needed to be undertaken. They were not taken immediately, however, and when they were, they seemed partially motivated by a general right wing reform agenda in 1999.

5.3.3 *Private property rights*

Apart from the administrative permits for water use, in Spain, there are still some private property rights.[85] These are residual rights, deriving from historic regulation, but they have been maintained by the WA and its amendments. The aim has been to homogenize all rights under the administrative permit system by giving incentives to the private right holders to exchange them for concessions, which are time-limited and offer the protection provided by the

---

83 'El Gobierno reconoce que hay un mercado negro del agua en algunas regiones' ('The executive recognizes that there is a black market for water in some regions'), *El País*, 29 November 1996. 'El fiscal denuncia un "mercado negro" del agua en Murcia' ('The public attorney claims that there is a "black market" for water in Murcia'), *El País*, 2 February 2004. Greenpeace, 'El negocio del agua en la cuenca del Segura' ('The water business in the Segura basin') (2007) http://www.greenpeace.org/espana/Global/espana/report/other/el-negocio-del-agua-en-la-cuen.pdf. Fundación Nueva Cultura del Agua, *Aguas Limpias, Manos limpias, Corrupción e Irregularidades en la Gestión del Agua en España* (Clean water and clean hands, corruption and irregularities in Spain) (2004).
84 'La transición en la política del agua en España' ('Transition in Spanish Water Policy'), *El País*, 22 March 1999.
85 Transitional provisions 1–4 of the CWA.

inscription in the Water Registry and the RBA.[86] Homogenization would ensure that planning covers as many water uses as possible, because otherwise planning cannot fully achieve its sustainability and efficiency goals. These historical rights are property rights, but they are not absolute: they are subject to certain restrictions, for example the timing or type of use. However, they are less subject to administrative powers than permit rights are. For example, transactions over those rights are subject to general contract rules.

The WA claimed that the rights would not be harmed by the transformation into permits,[87] but users want to remain shielded from the regulatory powers of the administration. They even fear the mere registration in the Water Registry. Hence, few of these types of rights have opted to take the form of a permit. However, in accordance with homogenization goals, the WA establishes that if a right holder wants to change any of the definitional characteristics of his or her private property rights, the right becomes a concession.[88] A similar effect is envisioned if a right holder enters into permit leases, the mechanism authorized after 1999.

Although it is beyond the period of study, it is worth mentioning an even more straightforward attempt at homogenization: the issuing of an emergency decree from May 2012,[89] wherein the central government authorized an exchange center in the Upper Guadiana Basin. Private rights would be bought by the public agency and the agency would sell time-limited permits.[90] The buyer would buy a permit, instead of a private right, with all the characteristics associated, such as stronger administrative oversight, and would receive less water in order to preventively mitigate some potential externalities.

Stronger property rights are expected to do better in the market because they offer more security and, thus, they might be traded more often than permits or be traded for a higher price. However, these old, stronger property rights may not even be entering the market in Spain for fear of falling into administrative oversight as a consequence of participating in the transaction.

5.3.4 Irrigation rights in irrigation areas of public initiative

These types of rights are not recognized by water regulation, but by agricultural regulation from the early twentieth century. These rights are a strange category: they are administrative rights, such as concessions, but the oversight of the

---

86   Art. 80.3 of the CWA.
87   Spanish Central Government Cabinet, Report accompanying the 1985 WA (on file with the author).
88   3rd Temporary Provision (transitional) of the CWA.
89   RDL 2012/17 (Decree-Act establishing urgent measures on environmental issues) (BOE 2012, 108).
90   Ibid. at Art 7.

administration is more intense, given the investment of public funds that these areas have received as a way to promote economic development by government. These quasi-concessional rights generally cannot be leased or transferred, but their lease was authorized from 2006 to 2009 by emergency drought decrees.[91] These rights could be considered somewhat similar to the rights of contractors of the USBR.

5.4 Evolution of water market regulations, prompted by scarcity

5.4.1 Content of the amendment

The 1999 Water Act amendment would not have reached enough support if it were not for the mid-1990s drought crisis which was widely suffered in Spain, making the need to find a solution to the blatant scarcity problems very tangible. In the face of water scarcity, the consensus seemed to be that new water permits were not the solution because water supply could not keep growing via infrastructure projects. One way to mitigate the problem was to reallocate water from current low value users to those who value it more. However, the concession system was very inflexible, and changes to current uses, motivated by transfers or not, were extremely cumbersome. Market tools offered a good way to shift current allocation and adapt it to changing times. The idea was to increase the tradability of water use rights mainly to respond to droughts, but also to the ossification of uses as a result of the system of concessions with extended length. The two market mechanisms introduced were a lease of permits contract between private parties and a mechanism similar to water banks called exchange centers (centro de intercambio de derechos). The lease seemed to be aimed, despite the time limit, at mitigating structural scarcity, while water banks were, according to Spanish regulation, a mechanism for alleviating the effects of a drought. These mechanisms are analyzed below in relation to the different governmental roles. The 1999 amendment included also other strategies to ensure that new demands could be met, given the scarce resources, such as setting a regulatory framework for desalination of water and metering household consumption in order to charge tariffs according to volume

---

91 Emergency decrees for the inter-regional basins were adopted in 2005: RD 2005/1419 (D. Adopting exceptional administrative measures to manage water resources and correct the effects of the droughts in the Guadiana, Guadalquivir, and Ebro basins) (BOE 2005, 301). RD 2005/1265 (D. Adopting exceptional administrative measures to manage water resources and correct the effects of the droughts in the Júcar, Segura, and Tajo basins) (BOE 2005, 256). These decrees were prorogued by RDL 2006/9 (BOE 2006, 222); RDL 2007/9, de 5 de octubre (BOE 2007, 270); and RDL 2008/8, de 4 de octubre (BOE 2008, 258); RD 2008/233, de 15 de febrero (BOE 2008, 88). So, the measures adopted in the fall of 2005 were in effect for over three years.

consumed, thereby disincentivizing misuse.[92] This pricing amendment is in line with the European Water Framework Directive enacted by the European Union which establishes the principle of full cost recovery.[93]

5.4.2 Political debate on the amendment

To better understand the introduction, design, and implementation of water markets, some description of the political debate surrounding them is needed since it shaped their development.

The discourse about water markets was deliberately toned down by its proponents, the People's Party. Interestingly enough, these mechanisms were not labeled as 'market' in governmental and congressional documents by the pro-market right-wing party in power at that time. Those who opposed these market mechanisms used 'market' as a stigmatizing word.[94] When it was used by its defenders, however, it was with many disclaimers or caveats. For example, the People's Party 1996 Electoral Program used 'controlled market.'[95] Even though the liberalization programme was the center of the People's Party's electoral platform, this scant usage of the term 'markets' by its proponents suggest how special water is. The People's Party wanted to make this reform more palatable for both the opposition and the electorate.

---

92   The preamble of L. 1999/46 summarizes the purposes as follows, 'However, the practical application of 1985 WA has encountered several practical problems in the management of water at national level, which have to be solved taking into account the future. It lacked effective instruments to face the new demands in relation to the mentioned resource, in both quantity – since its consumption has increased exponentially – and in quality. There is a clear need to deepen and to perfect the existing mechanisms of protection in the 1985 WA. In the same vein, the experience of the very intense drought, suffered in our country in the first years of the last decade of this century imposes the research of alternative solutions, which with independence of the best reallocation of the disposable resources through mechanisms of planning, allow, on the one hand, to increase the production of water through the utilization of new technologies – giving legal status to the regulation of desalination and reuse of water – and, on the other hand, promote the efficiency in the use of the water which requires relaxing the current concessional regime through the introduction of the new lease contract of the use of the water, which will optimize socially the uses of a scarce resource. Finally, policies of saving the mentioned resource will be introduced, either establishing the general duty to measure the consumption of water through standardized systems or administratively fixing administrative reference consumption levels for irrigated lands.'

93   Spain is not complying with such principle more than a decade later. José A. Gómez-Limón and Julia Martin-Ortega, 'Agua, economía y territorio: nuevos enfoques de la Directiva Marco del Agua para la gestión del recurso,' 29 Estudios de Economía Aplicada 65, 78 (2011). See also Enrique Cabrera, *Water pricing in Spain: A case study*, Working Paper Fundación Botín (2012).

94   Comisión de Medio Ambiente, Session No. 38 (1999), above note 6, at 820260.

95   Popular Party, *Con la nueva mayoría* (With the new majority), Electoral Program, at 174 (1996), http://www.pp.es/file_upload/recursos/pdf/20090915093224_127951152.pdf.

In statements put forward at the time of the reform, Mr Blanco, the Water Secretary, maintained that he was not introducing a market,[96] only making the concession regime flexible,[97] as an experiment. In fact, even the word used to denote transfer was 'ceder,' which is less harsh and common than sell or lease and does not necessarily require the payment of a price in Spanish. In fact, some stakeholders, such as the president of an organization called Foro del Agua and former president of the Canal Isabel II, argued that 'ceder' was a euphemism.[98] The treatment received in the news also illustrates this point.

While Mr Blanco was publicly denying that it was a market, the left-wing, world-renowned newspaper *El País* headline announcing that the bill was to be debated in the Spanish Parliament said it all: 'The Cabinet is going to approve the free water market.'[99] As Chapter 2 argues, a water market is never a free one, and the Spanish case, as explored below, is far from the ideal of a free market.

The majority of opposition parties voted against the 1999 reform of the WA,[100] focusing their critiques on the lease contract which, according to them,[101] weakened the control of the administration over water, a public resource, despite the administrative review. In fact, these provisions were challenged before the Constitutional Court. The Court in 2011 declared that the water market regulations were not against the constitutional regulation of public property.[102] Water banks were more acceptable for those opposing the reform, even for agricultural unions, because they understood the role of the

---

96 'Ni se modifica el régimen económico, ni se privatiza la gestión del agua' ('There is neither a change in the economic regime nor a privatization of water') ABC, 25 May 1995 ('Por ello, [Benigno Blanco] asegura que no se crearán mercados del agua, ya que los usos los sigue decidiendo el Estado a través de las concesiones, garantizando que, según las necesidades y la disponibilidad de los recursos, se produzcan reasignaciones de agua dentro del titulo concesional sin perjucio para el medio ambiente.' ('[Benigno Blanco] states that water markets are not being established since the uses will still be decided by government when awarding the concessions, taking into account the availability of resources and needs, will ensure that water reallocations will occur without environmental damage').

97 Interview Benigno Blanco, *El País*, above note 74. See also 'El Mercado del Agua queda bajo control con un precio máximo de 60 pesetas por metro cúbico' ('The water market will be under control with a maximum price of 60 pesetas per cubic meter'), at 44, ABC, 3 May 1999 (the article states that Benigno Blanco suggests that the introduction of water markets was an experiment and, as such, government may either eliminate it or strengthen it eliminating some of the cautionary provisions which could be obstacles).

98 'El Consejo de Ministros aprobará esta semana el mercado libre del agua' ('Congress will pass this week a bill establishing a free market on water'), *El País*, 27 April 1999.

99 Ibid.

100 'Oposición y sindicatos agrarios recelan del libre mercado del agua' ('Opposition and agricultural unions are reluctant to accept water markets'), *El País*, 17 August 2000.

101 'La nueva Ley de Aguas da vía libre a la compraventa de derechos entre particulares' ('New Water Act will enable the free Exchange of water rights between private users'), *El País*, 26 November 1999.

102 STC 149/2011, above note 75.

administration to be more central in those. The main opposition party, the Socialist Party, despite its quite head-on opposition to water markets,[103] favored water banks, which it did not consider to be markets.

Farmers did not welcome the 1999 amendment either. Consider the intervention of Mr Moraleda Quílez, the representative of the Association of Small Farmers (Asociación de Pequeños Agricultores), during the Congressional Environment Committee hearings regarding the 1999 amendment. He opposed the proposed amendment and emphasized that, prior to this amendment, reallocation was occurring and, hence, instead of introducing market mechanisms, it would have been better to reinforce the framework of the practices already in place. He feared that opening the doors to formal markets would entail a rise in prices paid by irrigators to their suppliers.[104] It is important to note that irrigators have always received subsidized water, and that they have managed to carve exceptions into the full cost recovery principle which should guide water pricing according to European regulation. Thus, they feared that they would be out of business if there were an increase in the price of water, which they considered unfair, as a result of water market transactions. Only big companies, either agricultural[105] or hydroelectric, were purportedly going to benefit. Every time an important water law bill has been discussed, even those not dealing with market reallocation, farmers' associations have always criticized markets. For example, these critiques were repeated in relation to the 2001 NHP,[106] which was seen as serving the same big corporate interests as the 1999 water markets amendment and as part of the overall liberalization strategy of the People's Party.[107]

In addition, a high profile environmental organization devoted to water management policy, called Nueva Cultura del Agua (New Water Culture), which would be generally considered close to Socialist Party lines despite its claims that it is apolitical,[108] has mildly favored markets.[109] Nueva Cultura del

---

103   They did not consider water banks markets, see 'El PSOE planteará hoy al Gobierno su rechazo a los mercados de agua' ('PSOE will state his opposition to water markets to the executive'), *El País*, 15 March 1999.

104   See Comisión de Medio Ambiente, above note 6, at 20261.

105   'Los expertos anteponen la gestión racional del agua en cuencas deficitarias a los trasvases' ('Experts favor efficient water management to mandated transfers'), *El País*, 6 October 2010.

106   Interview to Pedro Arrojo in *El País*, above note 24.

107   Interview Jose Manuel Delgado, Technical Cabinet, small farmers' unión Unión de Pequeños Agricultores y Ganaderos (UPA), Madrid (3 July 2012).

108   Interview to Pedro Arrojo in *El País*, above note 24.

109   Fundación Nueva Cultura del Agua, 'Manifesto,' http://www.unizar.es/fnca/index3.php?id=1&pag=16&fund=04. Hearing Pedro Arrojo at Comisión de Medio Ambiente, Session No. 38 (1999), note 6, at 20653. Pedro Arrojo defended water markets, but he thought that some other measures should be taken before them, like the actual revision of the concessions, limiting the amount of water to be used under current permits, which seems to resonate towards a cap and trade idea.

Agua praises water banks, and emphasizes the role of the administration in markets.[110]

Given the comparative approach adopted in this book, the references to the Californian experience in the political debate on the bill to amend the WA in 1999 must be highlighted. These references also serve the purpose of understanding the misguided ideological opposition. The Californian experience was treated strategically by the opposing parties in Spain. The Socialist Party defended water banks based on the Californian experience, but explicitly opposed markets.[111] In contrast, Mr Blanco regarded California as a successful experience, but his reform went beyond water banks, which many opponents seemed to consider the only transfer mechanism available in California.[112] In fact, it seems that there was quite a deeply rooted understanding of California as only using water banks. In the left-wing *El País* newspaper, a piece on the water reform finishes by stating:

> The water market was an initiative of the State of California. It worked only during a period of drought and allowed the purchase of water from farmers to meet urban water needs. However, the decrease in agricultural production activities caused losses in all the related economic sectors, such as the agricultural and fertilizer industry.[113]

This statement equates water market with the 1991 water bank since the only temporary market structures were the banks. This statement acknowledges that the 1991 Californian experience was a water market, but emphasizes the

110 Ibid. at 20655 ('Todo ello mediante bancos de agua en forma de mercados intervenidos y gestionados por la Administración. Segundo, acotar tales experiencias de bancos de sequía a marcos de cuenca durante un primer plazo experimental de diez años o algo así – no me hagan caso del tiempo – con el fin – ténganlo en cuenta – de asentar procesos y criterios de racionalización y redistribución de concesiones, bien vía administrativa – lo que he dicho antes –, bien vía estos otros, recomposiciones en momentos de sequía, que nos lleven a tener una experiencia práctica, más estable antes de dar pasos más arriesgados en las zonas deficitarias'). ('All this through water banks, markets operated and managed by the Administration. Second, limit banks to a basin region during the first experimental period of ten years or something like that with the aim to establish processes and criteria to use water efficiently and reallocate permits, and redeployment of concessions, administrative fine, what I said before, either administratively or via these other rearrangements in times of drought, in order to gain practical experience before taking risky steps in deficit areas').

111 'El PSOE planteará hoy al Gobierno su rechazo a los mercados de agua,' *El País*, above note 103.

112 'El Mercado del Agua queda bajo control con un precio máximo de 60 pesetas por metro cúbico,' ABC, above note 97 ('Hay experimentos de mercados de agua que han funcionado muy mal en el mundo, como en Chile, y otros que han dado juego, como en California' ('there are water market experiences which have not worked well, like the Chilean, while other did, like California')).

113 'El Gobierno ultima una reforma legal que abre el camino a la compraventa del agua,' *El País*, above note 4.

purported negative effects. In the debates in the Congressional Environment Committee, Professor Arrojo, one of the main representatives of New Water Culture and an economist who wrote a book comparing water management in California and Spain,[114] emphasized that precisely what was key in California was administrative control.[115] Arrojo's hearing aimed to suggest that water markets in Spain were going beyond the schemes introduced in California, despite the fact that Spanish markets were relatively timid, and even though it was claimed that they were an upside down reform,[116] as shown below.

It is important to highlight that the discussion on water markets, despite making it to the headlines, did not resonate with the public as much as other water management questions have done, such as large transfer projects.

5.4.3 Evolution of water market regulation

Apart from the 1999 amendment and the CWA of 2001, the next landmark was the approval by the central government in 2003 of the regulations implementing the 1999 amendments and giving coherence to the regulations subordinate to the WA.[117] But these 2003 regulations only specified further what was included in the amendments. Lawyers involved in water transactions do not consider that those regulations made any difference.

Related to the political debate, it is important to note that once the Socialist Party regained power in 2004, it never repealed these market tool provisions; this fact signals either that water markets were not as ideological and controversial as they had seemed, or that they were just non-operational. The Socialist Party had always been in favor of water exchange centers and they implemented the provisions related to them once in power. In fact, exchange centers, i.e. water banks, were one of the tools proposed to substitute the Ebro transfer by the Socialist Party during the discussion of the highly controversial NHP in the 2000s and during the 2004 political campaign, in which the Socialist Party ran on an anti-Ebro transfer platform.[118]

In 2004, the Socialist government authorized in 2004 water exchange centers for several basins.[119] As shown below, the RBAs could not establish them without such authorization. Additionally, in 2006, an emergency decree,

114 Pedro Arrojo and Jose Manuel Naredo, *La gestión del agua en España y California*, at 37 (1997).
115 Hearing Pedro Arrojo, above note 109.
116 'El Gobierno ultima una reforma legal que abre el camino a la compraventa del agua,' *El País*, above note 4 (the article uses the expression of folding a sock upside down).
117 See above note 11.
118 'El decreto para paralizar el trasvase del Ebro estará listo en un mes' ('The Decree stopping the Ebro transfer will be ready in a month'), Diario de Leon, 30 April 2004.
119 Acuerdo del Consejo de Ministros (15 October 2004) (authorizing the establishment of centros de intercambio de derechos).

triggered by the beginning of a harsh drought, authorized CHs and regional equivalents to launch public offers to lease or even buy rights for environmental purposes.[120] These purchases were made in the framework of water exchange centers. This decree had a sunset provision, but it was extended several times and was in effect until 2009. The same 2006 decree authorized the titleholders of the irrigation rights in public interest irrigation areas to enter into contracts.

5.5 Transaction figures: were water markets in Spain active?

In order to be able to ascertain whether water markets have been more successful in California than in Spain, and to try to trace the causes of such success, data on the activity level of water markets – which is an imperfect proxy, but is chosen given the scarcity of data – is presented next. As shown below, the level of market activity in Spain was low, except for the water exchange centers, which end up being similar to environmental water accounts because the majority of the water they leased or purchased was devoted to environmental protection. Chapter 6 compares the market figures of California and Spain.

5.5.1 Data shortcomings

Spanish data is not widely available, there is no integrated database, public or private, nor a publication reporting transactions, and transactions are not easy to track from primary sources. Private transactions not in the framework of an exchange center are supposed to be annotated in Water Registries. However, Water Registries are in a poor state. Not all rights are registered, and not all transactions have been properly registered, as some public servants working there have acknowledged. Some aggregated data on changes in the Registries' entries is available through the reports of each RBA, but it is not possible to disentangle whether or not those changes in the characteristics of a right are the result of a transaction or an inheritance. For Spain, the sources used are mainly, but not only, secondary literature.

The basic data used is that presented by the Deputy Director of Integrated Management of Water Public Domain (reporting to the Ministry of the Environment), Mr Yagüe-Córdova,[121] in the Universal Exhibition Expo Zaragoza 2008, which had water as the main theme. The data he presented was quite comprehensive since it covered all the transactions from 2000 to May 2008 for all the inter-regional River Basin Administrations. Before 2001, the mechanisms enacted in 1999 were not used, according to the accompanying

---

120   3rd additional provision RDL 2006/9, above note 79.
121   Jesús Yagüe-Córdova, 'Experiencia de los instrumentos de mercado en España,' Expo Zaragoza 2008, http://www.zaragoza.es/contenidos/medioambiente/cajaAzul/37S12-P1-JesusYagueCordovaACC.pdf.

documents to the NHP passed in 2001,[122] i.e. no transactions occurred. This might be explained by the succession of wet years. In addition to Mr Yagüe-Córdova, other scholars, particularly agrarian engineers, have offered more detailed data on some of the contracts entered into by private parties. These additional articles have allowed data to be cross-checked.

Regarding Spanish centros de intercambio de derechos – water exchange centers, which are water banks – some information is available in the official gazette since they have followed the tight model of public procurement which imposes certain requirements of transparency. Only the offer and the adjudicatory decisions are published, however. The level of detail of the latter is highly dependent on the CH; for example, some offer particularized information about who the particular counterparties are, and some do not. Nevertheless, the data presented by Mr Yagüe-Córdova, as well as pieces of news about the water banks, complete the data from official gazettes.

5.5.2 Not so active water markets and the mediated role of scarcity

The data for Spain is more scattered and incomplete than California's. The number of private transactions – which must be leases since sales are not permitted and permits are time-limited – is more than 38 intra-basin transactions and 25 inter-basin ones from 2000 to 2009,[123] not including water exchange center transactions. They amounted to 25,294.252 acr-ft.

Regarding transactions in water exchange centers, i.e. water banks, in Spain the focus is on how much water they bought, since very few sales from the bank occurred. Instead, many water banks purchases have been devoted to environmental protection.

First, the Guadiana River Basin Administration, from 2006 to 2008, entered into 204 transactions. In 2009, the number of transactions skyrocketed to 223, giving a total of 427. In volume, 23,561.76 acr-ft were bought.[124] Second, for the Jucar River Basin, there have been four public offers of acquisition in the framework of a public exchange center. Data on purchases has only been published for two of them, and the number of transactions is not reported, only the amount spent. Data on the volume bought in the first one is available through secondary sources: 46,048.509 acr-ft,[125] which amounted to €5.3 million. On the second one, the amount spent was higher: €9 million,

122   Mónica Sastre, 'Posibilidades de crear un mercado al amparo de la nueva Ley de Aguas,' 4 Revista del Instituto de Estudios Econ. 293, 294 (2001).

123   Calatrava Leyva, above note 77, at 103.

124   Rosa Requena, 'Centro de intercambios en el alto Guadiana' ('Exchange Center in Alto Guadiana'), at 8 (2011), http://www.ceigram.upm.es/sfs/otros/ceigram/Contenidos%20Investigaci%C3%B3n/contenido%20seminarios%20cientificos/CENTROS%20DE%20INTERCAMBIO%20MADRID_27062011.ppt. (In practice, from these, only 11,015.31 acr-ft were actually transferable, because the volume bought was calculated according to paper-rights.)

125   Yagüe-Córdova, above note 121, at 10.

from which, even though there is no official data, we can infer that a higher quantity was likely transferred, given that the type and location of the rights purchased were very similar.

As for the Segura Basin, the third basin where public offers of acquisition were enacted and trades took place, data on the adjudication of the two public tenders is not available in the official gazette. However, from secondary sources, some figures are available for the first tender. Forty-one transactions occurred, which amounted to a total of 2,352.068 acr-ft.[126]

Regarding volume, adding all the available data for transactions in Spain, which includes the water bank transactions, the volume traded amounted to 296,521.785 acr-ft. As for the number of transactions in Spain, they amounted to 531 during the period of study (2000–2009).

Data on annual transactions is less complete for Spain, so it is not possible to plot transactions against rainfall data. Table 5.1 summarizes the transaction information and Table 5.2 summarizes the rainfall data. The latter shows that while the beginning of the study period was wet, there were drought episodes in the later part to the 2000s decade. The wet years after the 1999 amendment may explain the lack of trading until 2001. Spain indeed had more transactions from the mid-2000s on, but it is difficult to disentangle whether this was due to the low availability alone or the enabling function performed by government regulation in responding to the crisis, such as setting up water banks or allowing the use of inter-basin infrastructure.

Table 5.1 Transactions in Spain 2000–2009

Type of transaction	Year	Number of transactions	Volume in acr-ft
Private transactions	2000–09	63 (38 intra-basin; 25 inter-basin)[1]	25,294.3
Guadiana water bank	2006–08	204	No data available
	2009	223	No data available
	Total	427	23,561.7[2]
Júcar water bank[3]	2006	No data available	46,048.5
Segura water bank	2007	41	2,352.0[4]
	2008	No data available	No data available

Source: Adapted from Casado Pérez, 2015.[127]

Notes
1 Calatrava Leyva, above note 77, at 103 (reporting transactions between irrigators and urban users in the Guadiana Region, but without offering further details).
2 Requena, above note 124.
3 The publication by Yagüe-Córdova mentions other offers of acquisition by the CH Jucar, but no further information has been found. Yagüe-Córdova, above note 121, at 10.
4 Yagüe-Córdova, above note 121, at 11.

126 Yagüe-Córdova, above note 121, at 10.
127 Vanessa Casado Pérez, 'Missing Water Markets: A Cautionary Tale of Governmental Failure,' 21 NYU Envt'l L.J. 157 (2015).

Table 5.2 Precipitation (inches)

Spain	Average annual precipitation (measured in October) (Anomaly around the years of study: 26.20 inches)	January–December (base period: 1940–2009; St. dev. 4.22) (Deviation from the historical average (anomaly))
1995	31.47	5.27
1996	30.15	3.95
1997	28.6	2.4
1998	19.99	−6.21
1999	22.19	−4.01
2000	30.99	4.79
2001	23.5	−2.7
2002	28.8	2.6
2003	29.11	2.91
2004	17.24	−8.96
2005	24.41	−1.79
2006	27.7	1.5
2007	23.41	−2.79
2008	23.76	−2.44
2009	33.15	6.95

Source: Compiled by the author from data from the Agricultural Ministry.[128]

Spanish data is even more scattered in relation to origin and destination than in relation to volume and number of transactions, but some figures can be highlighted. For private contracts – i.e. permit leases – there is no data about who is the seller in the transaction in any of them.[129] Those analyzed in more depth by scholars all have their origin in the agricultural sector.[130] This idea of agriculture being the source of the water rights is reinforced by the drought emergency decrees of the central government, which allowed the quasi-concessional rights of the irrigation areas of public initiative to be sold. As for water banks, even though it is not explicitly stated, all transactions between the seller and the bank use acreage cultivated as a unit of measure, therefore, sellers were invariably farmers.

As for the destination, i.e. whether the water is devoted to urban, environmental, or agricultural uses, the data for Spanish private transactions is not complete. Some of them, usually the most commented on by scholars, have an urban supplier as the buyer.[131] Water bought in Spanish *centros de intercambio de derechos* has been applied mostly to restore rivers.

128 http://servicios2.marm.es/sia/indicadores/ind/ficha.jsp?cod_indicador=01&factor=det.
129 Yagüe-Córdova, above note 121.
130 Yagüe-Córdova, above note 121, at 5.
131 See Calatrava Leyva, above note 77, at 102–103.

Secondary literature on Spanish markets offers certain aggregated data on price. The data is insufficient to reach any conclusion. However, some data points illustrate certain market predictions. First, in the Segura Basin, prices increased with scarcity.[132] Second, inter-basin transactions where an urban distribution company (Mancomunidad de los Canales del Taibilla) is the buyer are identified as the most expensive.[133] Urban users are supposed to value water more than low-value agriculture. Third, water in the market behaves like the majority of goods: the more you buy, the cheaper it is. In the Taugus Basin, the first acr-ft were more expensive than the rest, which contrasts with how household water is normally priced. In order to discourage consumption, many urban suppliers use block tariffs which increase in price the more water you consume, penalizing those who consume water beyond the amount required for basic needs.

In sum, data on water transactions is scattered. More transactions occurring in the mid-2000s when Spain was experiencing a drought, but the majority of the activity occurred in the water exchange centers where water did not change hands, but was bought by public agencies to purportedly assign to environmental protection. To establish those banks, an authorization by the central government was required, which implies that the effects of scarcity were mediated by governmental action.

5.6 Governmental roles

5.6.1 The uncontested governmental role in water markets: definition of property rights, a public good

Having already covered in broad terms what the changes were, this section addresses the two variables identified as key in the definition of property rights in relation to markets, security and tradability in Spain after the amendments of 1999. It also analyzes the possibility of protecting instream flows through the definition of property rights.

a. Volume

The amount of water traded is limited to the amount used on average by the lessor in the last five years, not the formal amount granted in the permit. The amount granted in the permit is likely to be higher because it reflects the amount

---

132 Calatrava Leyva, above note 77, at 102. Under normal conditions prices ranged from US$159.12/acr-ft to US$636.48/acr-ft (average US$238.68/acr-ft) and under extreme scarcity prices were not only higher, but also more variable: US$238.68 to US$954.71 (average US$556.92).

133 Ricardo Segura Graíño, *Evaluación de la Implementación de los Mercados de Agua en España*, Working Paper, Expo Zaragoza (2008).

diverted, which is higher than the amount consumed; part of the water diverted goes back to the river via return flow. The average consumption is a limit which ensures there will be fewer externalities since it ensures, at least, that there will be no increase in consumption, so the same water will be left in the river. It is a positive feature that the consumed volume is averaged over a period of five years, as a shorter period would discourage savings – in the last period before leasing their permit, lessors would have incentives to increase their consumption. How to calculate this consumption and whether the regulator could make it easier to do so are covered in the market maker function because it is not a necessary element of the definition of property rights, but a way to reduce transaction costs.

In relation to the volume consumed, there is a problem common to other jurisdictions: the fear of disclosing too much information about current consumption and triggering a permit's review. The permit could be reviewed if the object of the permit could be achieved with less water if it was used efficiently.[134] The 1999 market provisions protect against total forfeiture,[135] not the revision power mentioned above. However, Andalusia's – a southern Spain region – Water Act allows for partial forfeiture, while specifically protecting against partial forfeiture for those who save water by implementing a more efficient system[136] in order to, perhaps, sell it at a later date. This administrative power of reduce or forfeit water rights is usually granted to agencies to strike a balance between the need to grant individual users rights to use the water and the public property of overall water resources, which requires the prevention of unproductive speculation and hoarding. Market regulations should completely shield potential sellers or lessors from its application, but building trust in the protection itself may take time. What market provisions do not seem to protect against is the RBAs' power to reduce water permits if the same purpose could be fulfilled with less water,[137] which selling part of the water could be understood to show. In any case, this latter procedure has not been used by the administration, so it should not be such a source of fear, but the reluctance to trade seems to suggest that this concern is still in place.

b. Security

Security is a dimension inherently related to tradability because its absence may impair tradability in practice. Beyond natural variability, security is affected by all those limits imposed onto the decision-making capacity of the title-holder

---

134   Art. 65.2 of the CWA. This even more demanding than the forfeiture because it is a type of partial forfeiture which seems less likely to occur in a prior appropriation system.
135   Art. 69.2 of the CWA.
136   Art. 45.5 of Andalucia's Water Act, above note 63.
137   Art. 66.2 of the CWA.

which are not fully triggered by objective, foreseeable factors, and often involve some discretion of the administrative agencies.

I. NATURAL VARIABILITY

Setting aside the discretion of the agencies, water management requires a system to allocate the consequences of low water availability. RBAs can reduce the amount of water granted to permit holders due to unavailability of the resource,[138] given that the amount is not guaranteed.[139]

Over-exploitation of the resource or severe droughts expand the powers of the water administrations. Since late in the first decade of the twenty-first century, the emergency powers have been more regulated because Drought Preparedness Plans have been put forward. Those plans allocate the consequences of low water availability, but they still grant plenty of discretion to the administration. In any case, during much of the period of study, the first decade of the 2000s, the response to droughts was not heavily based on these powers, but piece-meal, and channelled through ad hoc emergency regulations, which undermines even more the security of the permits.[140] Those regulations have usually favored urban users. Not only does this discretion increase the uncertainty and make uncertain the supply of potential sellers, but also the shielding of urban areas by the emergency regulations may reduce the incentives of those urban areas to resort to the market to protect them from low water availability because urban areas expect to be bailed out.

II. DISCRETION BEYOND MARKETS

Beyond the enhanced powers during drought periods which erode security, there are other RBA powers that have a huge impact on whether and how water users plan ahead and interact in the market. For example, users may not be sure whether their own supply or that of a potential seller is reliable, due not only to the natural variability of the resource, but also to the agency's decisions.

Apart from the fact that the volume of the water permit is not guaranteed, the first power that RBAs enjoy even in normal conditions is the possibility of reducing the volume granted in the permit if they consider that the user could achieve the same goals with less water, used efficiently.[141] The provision was less invasive when the WA[142] was enacted. Then, revision was only allowed where there had been changes in the conditions under which the concession

---

138   Arts 55 and 58 of the CWA.
139   Arts 50–55 of the CWA.
140   See above note 91, and see section 1.3 for a description of emergency measures adopted in Catalonia.
141   Art. 65.2 of the CWA. This provision was introduced by L. 1996/9 (BOE 1996, 15).
142   Then Art. 63 of the WA.

was granted. In 1995, when the mid-1990s drought crisis was in its beginnings, the WA was amended by an emergency decree introducing the possibility of revising the concessions if the same use could be achieved with a lower volume granted both in normal conditions and during droughts.[143] Thus, the first move to cope with the 1990s crisis, and since then, with scarcity in general, could prove detrimental to the market, because it increases the powers of the administration. Despite the later assurances that leasing water in the market should not be a trigger for a revision, the existence of this unilateral revision power may increase the reluctance to trade in the market. However, it must be noted that, in Spain, this power has seldom been used. If it were used, it could be more powerful than reasonable use or beneficial use doctrines in riparian and prior appropriation US States.

Second, an additional step which the RBA could take, and which may erode security, is the forfeiture of the permit if it has not been used for three years. The wording of the forfeiture provision seems to suggest that the permit must not have been used at all. Partial non-use should not trigger it.

A third administrative prerogative, already analyzed, which undermines security, is the renewal of permits or, in other words, their time limits. It may trigger changes in the permit if the administration considers that the same use could be achieved with a lower volume when going up for renewal, and this may reduce security. Renewal is quite similar to applying anew.[144]

Fourth, during emergencies, expropriation of a water concession by a public agency paying compensation is eased regarding water permits since they can be expropriated in favor of another use which ranks higher in the priority of uses established in the River Basin Plan. This is a coercive 'sale' since the RBA encourages the parties to decide on the price. If they cannot agree, the RBA will set it.

There is still a fifth instance where security plays a role in the definition of property rights. It deals with the volume that can be traded after the 1999 amendment. The volume is limited to the amount effectively used by the lessor, but subject to corrections due to extreme hydrologic circumstances, with respect to instream flows, or, where instream flows have not been defined, based on the 'proper use' of water. Such standards involve discretion and, if they are not properly implemented, users could fear arbitrariness.

Security is thus related to administrative prerogatives such as expropriation or the mechanisms of revision, some of which are actually imperfect alternatives to markets since they centralize the cure for inefficient allocation. However, the shortages experienced in Spain show that these administrative powers are ineffective at actually achieving an efficient response and making the allocation

---

143 RDL 6/1995 (Decree Act adopting extraordinary, exceptional and urgent measures in relation to water supply in response to the drought) (BOE 1995, 174).
144 Arts 140–142 of the RDPH.

flexible. The emergency decrees dealing with the crises and the general powers, exercised or not, weaken the decision-making capacity of the water right holders and their incentives to trade. For example, a farmer may be reluctant to sell water due to the fear that it will be understood that he has a right to more water than he needs and consequence. Hence, if these powers are seldom used, or if their use is not achieving the intended goals, it might be questioned whether it would not be better to reduce many of these powers in order to enhance markets by making water rights more certain.

III. DISCRETION IN MARKETS

Agencies have many discretionary powers in markets when it comes to the authorization of the transfers. The review procedure is analyzed under externalities, but there is a provision that stands out. The volume to be transferred may be reduced not only to protect other existing users, but according to the amount set in the Water Plans for uses of its nature.[145] This seems to suggest that the volume to be transferred could be lowered even if it did not harm other users if the seller was using more water than the typical user in similar conditions. This provision generates uncertainty and clearly disincentivizes potential water conservation. For example, if a farmer is using flood irrigation and shifts to sprinklers, he may not be able to sell the water saved with the change, if the Water Plan measures the volume of users of its type according to sprinklers.

IV. ENVIRONMENTAL INSTREAM FLOWS

Instream flow protection could be an obstacle for water markets if it is not done in a way which does not create uncertainty for those trading water. Spain has opted for a strategy dominated by quantification of environmental instream flows as a result of European regulation.[146] RBAs decide on the specific instream flow volumes in their Plans. Flows are volumetrically configured, apart from the water quality regulation. During droughts the instream flow regime is allowed to be relaxed.[147] This is the case in some River Basin Drought Preparedness Plans, while in others, instream flows are a priority just below domestic uses.[148] The way instream flows have been implemented tries to be as respectful as possible of already allocated rights, given the risk of having to

---

145 Art. 345.1.b of the RDPH.
146 European Water Framework Directive.
147 If there is a long period of drought the instream flow requirement could be relaxed. See Art. 8.4 of RD 907/2007 (Decree regulating Water Planning) (BOE 2007, 162) – current regulation of water planning.
148 For a review and critique, see Rafael Sánchez Navarro and Julia Martínez Fernández, *Los caudales ambientales: Diagnóstico y perspectivas*, at 23, Working Paper fundación Nueva Cultura del Agua, http://www.unizar.es/fnca/varios/panel/12.pdf.

pay compensation to those who see their rights reduced.[149] Critiques abound regarding the definition of instream flows because, in many cases, they have been found as not scientifically sound.[150] These instream flow volumes are binding in cases of modification or new permits. This implies that the sale of a permit will have to comply with instream flows. Quantification offers more security than the protection of river-flows through open-ended standards, so the Spanish strategy may be positive in the long run for water markets. However, quantification is far from complete, and one of the reasons for the delay is how contentious this issue is.

b. Tradability

I. RESTRICTIONS

The possibility of leasing or selling the right to use water to someone else is essential for a market and, thus, has been the target of the different amendments to the WA. In general, the 1999 amendment tried to lower the barriers, mostly legal, for permits to exchange hands. It defined which permits could be traded and the review mechanisms. The analysis focuses mostly on the regulations for permits to be leased, more than on the exchange center where the RBA may work as a broker and, thus, pertains more to the market maker function.

Since the passing of Act 1999/46, permits can be leased,[151] which was not clearly possible before this new regulation. In the previous scheme, permits could be transferred, which would imply that concessions could also have been leased, but it might not have been feasible to do so since applying for modification of the permit title took up to 18 months. Eighteen months might be too onerous a time cost, particularly because users need to undergo the review at the beginning and at the end of the lease, given that the review is triggered by every change in the water right.

The 1999 lease contract presents constraining requirements. It is important to note that some of the requirements, though limiting the potential transactions, could be a way of increasing tradability if they translate into a less demanding review proceeding. If some externalities do not even arise because certain transactions are not allowed, there is less need for scrutiny.

The first of the requirements is that the lease only operates between a seller and a buyer who would employ the water for a use ranked equally or higher.[152] This ranking of uses requirement can be waived during drought times.

---

149 Art. 26 of the NHP approved by L. 2001/10, above note 22.
150 See Sánchez Navarro and Martínez Fernández, above note 148.
151 Art. 67 of the CWA.
152 Ibid.

The default ranking is set in Article 59 of the CWA, but the River Basin Plans can modify it, except for the highest rank being household uses.[153] The default ranking is as follows: domestic users and small industry connected to the municipal water net; agriculture; hydroelectric or other electric power producers; industry; fish farms; recreation; and navigation.

Even though ranking purportedly expresses the public interest, it is a very rough proxy for marginal value. Take, for example, industrial users, a beverage producing company may have a very different marginal value for water than a plastic producer, but none of these industrial users can lease from a farmer because industry is ranked lower.[154] Ranking seems to be more a proxy of the social, not only economic, valuation of water, probably lagging behind the times, and of the relative abstract inelasticity of demand of the different uses, which assumes that domestic consumers and farmers cannot do without water. The rationale seems to be that by only allowing transfers within the same type of use or higher, the public interest will be preserved or even improved. Nonetheless, rank should not be a huge obstacle to achieving the reallocation goal between the agricultural sector and the cities, which is the prototypical transaction that water market proponents had in mind. However, it may prevent some useful transactions if some industrial users, such as new power plants, would like to buy water from the agricultural sector.

Another issue embodied in the rankings requirement is prevention of externalities, but there is no mention of this in the debates on this regulation. The idea would be that uses which harm the environment less should not be allowed to sell to uses which harm the environment more. However, industrial uses can sell to farmers, but there is no guarantee that farmers pollute less than certain industries because runoff includes pesticides and can be very harmful for the environment.

A second limit is the length of the permits or, in other words, the time-limited nature of the lease contract. The 1999 amendment allows for leases, not sales. Sales would undergo the procedure of change in permit which existed, and still does, prior to the 1999 amendment. The 1999 lease is, thus, time limited. There is no specific amount of time set for the lease but, at maximum, the limit is the expiry date of the permit, which could be decades away.

---

153 For example, in the River Basin Plan of the Segura River Basin, industry takes precedence over electric power production. Art. 14 of the CH Segura River Water Plan, Normative Section, http://www.chsegura.es/export/descargas/planificacionydma/plandecuenca/contenido_normativo/docsdescarga/NORMATIV.pdf. Another example of a plan that has changed, slightly, the order is the Miño-Sil River Basin Plan where section 2.1.3.1. establishes the following precedence: (a) domestic; (b) farming not irrigation; (c) industry with low water consumption; (d) irrigation; (e) industrial uses; (f) electric energy uses. CH Miño Sil Plan, Normative Section, http://www.chminosil.es/chms/documentos/file/planificacion/plan_demarcacion_vigente/01_Normas.pdf.

154 'El Mercado del Agua queda bajo control con un precio máximo de 60 pesetas por metro cúbico,' ABC, above note 97.

Third, both the buyer and the seller have to be permit holders. There are exceptions: as briefly pointed out already when describing the types of rights present in the Spanish water regime, those historical property rights that have been recorded and transformed into concessions can also be transferred,[155] and from 2006 to 2009 irrigation rights from areas of public initiative could also be leased.[156] Transactions of those quasi-concessional rights was particularly relevant in the exchanges between the Tajo and Segura basins since many of the leases in that area involved those types of rights in 2006.[157]

On the buyer's side, this limit on who can trade poses a problem for new users because they want to buy water in already fully allocated streams or avoid the time-consuming permit application. This implies that all new users must apply for a permit. Without it they cannot count on transactions to quench their thirst. This is a stark difference from the California 'show me the water' laws – SB 610 and SB 221 – which require developers to ensure long-term water supplies and to consider potential water transfers as one of the tools to ensure them.

A fourth limit is that non-consumptive uses cannot be transferred to consumptive ones. This did not appear in the early drafts, but in order to gain more support, government decided to introduce this restriction to respond to those who feared that the hydropower companies would control the market.[158]

There is a potential fifth limit. The maximum price for leases could be fixed by governmental regulation.[159] In fact, before the 1999 amendment was passed, government leaked the information that, after careful analysis, the maximum price would be 60 pesetas (less than US$0.5), but no official regulation was enacted.[160] Most probably, government wanted to reassure those who feared that the price of water would skyrocket as a result of the market speculation,[161] making it too expensive for farmers. This regulation has never been implemented.

Lastly, there is a sixth limit, the preferential acquisition right by the RBA. During the period granted to the RBA to review the transaction, it can take

---

155 Art. 343.4 of the RDPH.

156 RDL 2005/15, above note 91.

157 Email from Professor Antonio Embid Irujo, expert in Spanish Water Law (27 April 2013). Abel La Calle suggests that the leases did not happen because the rule authorized them but because the lessor and lessees asked government to change the rule. Email from Professor Abel La Calle, expert in Spanish Water Law (30 April 2013).

158 'La nueva Ley de Aguas da vía libre a la compraventa de derechos entre particulares,' *El País*, above note 101. For a critical account of the Chilean experience where hydropower companies accumulated many water rights, see Carl J. Bauer, *Siren Song: Chilean Water Law as a Model for International Reform* (2004).

159 Art. 69.3 of the CWA (instead of price, the word used is 'compensation').

160 'El Mercado del Agua queda bajo control con un precio máximo de 60 pesetas por metro cúbico,' ABC, above note 97.

161 In fact, the price was defended by the Ministry of the Environment and Benigno Blanco on those terms. See ibid.

over the contract since it has legally granted priority to get the water, in order to leave it instream.[162] This, which could be considered another limit to tradability, is a provision introduced to purportedly preserve the public interest over a resource which is public property. The preferential right of the RBA to take over the permit may deter private actors from entering into negotiations since once they apply to have their transaction cleared, they might be told that they cannot buy the right because the reviewing body will buy the water under the same conditions. The costs other than the price, such as costs incurred in negotiation, are not mentioned as part of the compensation the RBA would have to pay.[163] Nonetheless, the preferential right has never been exercised and the literature has never paid attention to it, nor do the actors involved seem to be worried about it. So, it might be inactive in practice, but its chilling effect could still be present.

The transferability of permits following this lease procedure is also defined by the review procedure that transactions go through in order to be authorized, since the costs it imposes may be anticipated by those considering whether to enter into transactions, and may impair their will to do so. The suitability of the Spanish review scheme is analyzed next, taking into account whether some of the limits imposed *ex-ante* on who can enter into a transaction or what can be traded translate into a more lenient review procedure.

The tradability is slightly more expanded if, instead of a trade between private parties, the trade occurs through a water bank. While private parties without the brokerage of the administration cannot enter into 'sales' unless they go through the pre-1999 procedure, water banks can either enter into sales or into leases. The text of the 1999 amendment to the WA, the CWA, and its linked regulations only mention sales, but it seems clear that leases are also implicitly allowed. The subjective limit also appears in water exchange centers: only holders of permits or those with private rights inscribed in the Water Registry can participate. However, in the Andalusian Water Act, enacted in 2010 and applicable only to internal basins of Andalusia, even non-right holders can be buyers in the potential regional water bank, which sells water bought from private parties as well as recovered as a result of revision of concessions.[164] This suggests that there is room for improvement in the general Spanish regulation.

II. ENVIRONMENTAL WATER RIGHTS: A MISSED OPPORTUNITY?

There are no permits for environmental uses. Instream flows are considered a restriction on uses.[165] Environmental uses are not generally included in the

---

162 Art. 68.3 of the CWA.
163 Art. 349 of the RDPH.
164 Art. 46 of Andalucia's Water Act, above note 63.
165 Art. 59.7 of the CWA.

general rankings of uses.[166] Nonetheless, in order to make a clear statement of the central relevance of environmental protection, some River Basin Plans classify instream flows as uses, but without a permit attached.[167] This means that someone cannot lease a permit and use it for environmental purposes. The fact that environmental uses are not specifically recognized prevents private parties from applying for a permit or from entering the market to buy and self-provide this public good which is highly valued by their members. Furthermore, buying a permit, not using the water and leaving the water in the river could be considered equivalent to not using it and the right could be forfeited.

Other non-consumptive uses – such as hydropower generation or fishing – do not offer avenues to use them instrumentally to protect the environment, i.e. even if someone were to buy existing water rights and assign them to non-consumptive uses and leaving water instream, there is no guarantee that such water will be reserved for such purposes. Recreational or navigational uses are part of the ranking of uses. However, they are not subject to a permit to use the water.[168] Navigational uses and quays are subject to a communication requirement, i.e. they do not require an explicit authorization, but the communication ensures that whoever is undertaking the activity can be held responsible for the damage. Hydroelectric uses require a permit, but despite the fact that they are non-consumptive, as with the other instream uses mentioned, they are not particularly compatible with environmental protection since they need to alter natural water flow, among other actions. It is important to note that hydroelectric uses are ranked quite low in the ranking of uses. In fact, the default ranking set by the CWA ranks hydropower higher than other industrial users.[169] In fact, the undue influence of the powerful electric companies in water management has always been a source of concern in water regulation.[170]

In sum, a permit for environmental uses cannot be obtained, either directly or indirectly. This also implies that those who want to protect the environment cannot buy permits in the market because they are not users in the first place.

Nonetheless, government can acquire rights on behalf of the environment. First, RBAs have a preferential right, which they have never exercised, to lease the right object of the contract between two parties applying for its authorization.[171] Thus, there is no clear barrier for them not to retire those permits from use. Second, direct public purchases have occurred. When the

---

166 Art. 60 of the CWA.
167 Art. 6 of the CH Segura River Water Plan, Normative Section (BOE 1999, 207), http://www.boe.es/boe/dias/1999/08/30/pdfs/A31958-31994.pdf.
168 Art. 50.1 of the CWA.
169 Art. 69.2 of the CWA.
170 See above note 4.
171 Art. 68.3 of the CWA.

1999 approval was being discussed, the government[172] saw the use of sales as a mechanism to recover water (which, again, is to some extent public property) for the environment. In economic and political terms, it was cheaper than expropriation or mandatory reductions imposed on third party rights, but the 1999 regulation did not expressly authorize that. There were no institutions similar to environmental water accounts, and water exchange centers were regulated as clearinghouses/brokers. Even so, environmental purchases were allowed by a 2006 central government decree through the water exchange centers.[173] Using these, Guadiana, Segura, and Jucar RBAs have bought water rights in order to improve the quality of the aquatic ecosystem, particularly of aquifers' overdraft. In practice, then, only public agencies were entitled to purchase water for solely environmental purposes, and in Spain there were no NGOs willing to fight the battle to get environmental uses recognized.

5.6.2 Externalities: apparently not a major concern

Externalities have been the primary focus of the US literature and regulation on the topic of water markets. It is quite striking how little attention the externalities review procedures have received in the Spanish literature and regulation, given that in water shortage scenarios, any water transfer is going to cause effects on other users.

Neither the CWA nor the regulations which implement it offer detailed information about how externalities are to be accounted for in the review of permit leases,[174] and the procedure is not described in detail. There are no public records on the applications, review documents, or decisions,[175] the focus of this section is on what the written law was, with some references to the perceptions of water law practitioners.

The authorization to lease a permit could be denied if the formal requirements and the procedural steps are not fulfilled or if, in the review, the transaction is found to adversely affect the basin, the rights of others, environmental flows, or the state or preservation of aquatic ecosystems.[176] The wording of these standards is quite open-ended, which may increase uncertainty, thereby impairing transactions.

Regarding the environmental effects of a transaction, the lease contract authorization could be denied not only if it affects instream flows,[177] but also

---

172 'El PSOE aprobó un mercado "libre" en 1996,' ABC, above note 3.
173 3rd additional provision RDL 2006/9, above note 79.
174 Arts 346–348 of the RDPH; Art. 68 of the CWA.
175 Art. 348 of the RDPH refers to the reasons listed in Art. 68.3 of the CWA without further elaborating on them.
176 Art. 68.3 of the CWA.
177 Art. 68.3 of the CWA.

if it negatively affects the aquatic ecosystem.[178] In theory, according to the CWA, instream flows should be set taking into account ecological criteria.[179] Respecting instream flows should reduce the problem of environmental externalities, particularly given that, in addition, the tradable volume is already restricted to historical use. However, potential effects on water quality may not be captured by instream flow regulations or by the historical consumption limit. These open-ended standards protecting the environment could be restricted to those cases where the type of use changes, making the review less demanding and more certain to those who do not change uses; such as an agricultural to agricultural transaction, where once instream flows have been respected, there should not be huge changes in water quality.

Procedural regulation has a great impact on transaction costs. The RBA has one month to reject a contract between users of the same irrigation organization or two months if they are not of the same irrigation organization. The difference in the procedure's length very likely takes into account the externalities differential that might arise, given the scope of the different markets. The written contract has to be submitted within 15 days of the agreement for its approval. In the requirements to which the contract's content is subject, there is no mention of any document assessing the impact on other users or the environment. The only requirement is a report by the health authority in leases where the lessee will be supplying water for domestic users. In other words, in the review procedure, the burden of proof is not allocated,[180] and so it seems to lie with the administration. Actual practice indicates that the parties do not supply information to the administration beyond their application and contract unless it is requested. Lawyers working on water transactions confirm that they do not present any other documentation.

This idea of the agency being the trustee of the public interest seems also to be reflected in the fact that the procedure does not allow for the participation of third parties. Despite the lack of participation, one may hypothesize that parties could bargain *ex-ante* and the transaction may include them, but this would be the case in a world free of transaction costs. However, the regulation assumes that the RBA reviewing the transaction does not have incentives to favor the parties to it over other interests, and that it will be guided by the public interest. In addition, it makes the potential compensation of negative effects impossible. Instead of compensating other affected users for the negative effects, parties to the transaction may need also to enter into transactions with those affected because the RBA cannot approve a transaction harming other users. Hence, the solution seems to be a more complex transaction. However, in 2011, the Constitutional Court, deciding on a challenge to the water market

---

178   Art. 68.3 of the CWA.
179   Art. 42.1 of the CWA.
180   Art. 344 of the RDPH.

regulations, said that the lack of participation of third parties was a gap that could be filled with the general principles of administrative law which will always favor the participation of those potentially affected.[181] By allowing third parties' participation, the administration may save on information costs, since those affected will provide it, but it is still the case that the procedure does not allow for compensation of third party effects instead of barring the transaction altogether if there are third party effects.

Even though private parties do not have a clear avenue to participate, public agencies do. In leases regarding irrigation permits, the Agricultural Department of the central government, the autonomous communities involved and the irrigation communities all have a say.[182] They must issue a report within ten days of the date they receive a contract involving an irrigation right. This requirement clearly causes a delay and may increase uncertainty about the criteria underlying the review even if the reports are mandatory but not binding. This regime seems closer to an anti-commons.[183] The participation of those other bodies does not seem to contribute much if the review focuses on external effects on other water users or the environment. It is not clear what information or concerns these entities could raise that would be relevant to the findings the RBA needs; the administration should have the type of information provided in those reports for its planning functions. The participation of these other public agencies increases the uncertainty surrounding the authorization, and may delay or impair transactions that are beneficial from a water management perspective.

The burden placed on the administration is even more striking, given that there are no fees for the review procedure. Instead, it is funded by the RBA's general funds. This has not been questioned. The reason might be that there are so few transactions that they do not represent a substantial share of the workload at the RBA or, perhaps, that leases are supposed to work for the overall social interest and, thus, their review costs should be shouldered by all taxpayers. It will save information costs for the agency if the parties would have to bring evidence about the potential effects on other users.

While in California it is often argued that the review must be eased, in Spain, lawyers do not seem particularly troubled by this review.[184] In fact, one of the arguments made to challenge the 1999 amendment and the 2001 CWA by the Autonomous Community of Aragon was that the administration did not have thorough control in this review. The Constitutional Court considered the

---

181 STC 149/2011, above note 75.
182 Art. 346.3 of the RDPH.
183 See above note 72.
184 Interviews with Jordi Codina, Miquel Corredor, and Oriol Camacho, Water Lawyers at Codina Advocats in Prat del Llobregat (2 July and 28 August 2012). Interview with Mónica Sastre, attorney at Ariño Villar, Madrid, Spain (27 July 2012).

two-month period was enough for the administration to reach a meaningful decision.[185]

There is no provision related to the review procedure in the centros de intercambio de derechos (water banks). There seems to be an assumption that, given the requirements that the RBA establishes for those who wish to participate, there is no need to undergo a review procedure. Instead, the high barriers to entry in the bidding process ensure fungibility between the rights; and, further, RBAs are expected to be truly involved in the process. The public offers issued by the CH or the RBA must establish: the maximum volume that can be leased, which type of users can participate, the maximum and minimum prices, contract length, the criteria to be used to decide which rights will be leased or bought, and the procedural deadlines. However, current regulation only establishes the rules which have to guide the offer of acquisition, but not the selection of the buyers, which will obviously have an effect on the potential externalities. Given that the RBA generally controls the infrastructure, it is assumed that it will either ensure that no effects happen, set the buyer's price at a level which accounts for the compensation of externalities, or not accept certain bids. In the Jucar Basin,[186] externalities, affecting the environment or third parties, were planned for since the amount sold by the water bank was lower than the volume bought in order to contribute to the recovery and maintenance of the river. Given that most of the water rights have been reallocated to the environment, not to other users, leaving more water in the river, no negative effects are to be expected. However, in the Guadiana Basin, there have been serious claims of fraud. Some users kept using the water they were required to transfer to the bank.[187]

So far, the analysis has focused on externalities affecting other water users or the environment, but externalities imposed on communities need to be considered. Given the lack of major reallocations in Spain, the need to discuss the externalities affecting communities as a result of market transactions has not been a big issue, despite the fact that it was one of the major concerns in the legislative debate. At that time, many representatives of the farmers claimed that water markets would dry up traditional, small farming and benefit corporate agricultural interests, or other enterprises.[188] Community externalities appeared in the 2001 NHP, which discussed the major reallocation from the Ebro to the Mediterranean area. The communities along the river, and particularly at the Delta, argued against the transfer on the basis of environmental and community impact. The arguments about economic effects were blurred with

---

185   STC 149/2011, above note 75.

186   Yagüe-Córdova, above note 121, at 10.

187   'An expensive groundwater governance,' http://www.aguanomics.com/2013/01/an-expensive-groundwater-governance.html (22 January 2013).

188   Hearing of Mr De las Heras, General Secretary of the Agricultural and Cattle Breeders Union in Comisión de Medio Ambiente, Session No. 38 (1999), above note 6, at 20670.

a feeling of entitlement to the water flowing as part of the landscape of the territory without further qualifications, and a sense of opposition between the rural areas and the growth of urban ones, which were the potential water recipients. It is important to remember that this was a mandated transfer, but this reaction may suggest that similar attitudes may arise if market reallocations occur that are unwanted by those in the community not participating in the transactions. Spanish regulation does not offer any avenue to deal with them.

In sum, the review for externalities does not seem to be an obstacle in practice, but it may well be if transactions peak. The procedure formally set up could be improved by specifying the informational duties of the parties to the transaction and, also, the participation of potential users affected, instead of certain public agencies which could make the transaction review an instance of the tragedy of the anti-commons. There is room for improvement, particularly because there is little detail in the regulation about how this procedure is to be conducted. Furthermore, the limits on the tradability of rights are quite stringent in Spain, but it cannot be assessed whether they have translated into a more mechanical, less demanding, review procedure.

5.6.3 Infrastructure: provision and management

a. Existing connections: never exempt from controversy

As the map shows, Spain has quite a few infrastructure connections, but none straight from the humid north to the dry south, unlike California, which does have such a connection. The existing connections were not built with the market in mind, they were just part of the command-and-control strategy to provide water for all at a subsidized price and to regulate its distribution; the idea was to transfer surplus water. However, in many of the rivers where water originates, more permits have been granted, and it is not clear that real surplus still exists. In any event, even during the drought crisis, there were larger water reserves in the areas of origin,[189] and hence, if allowed, there is room for transactions, as shown below.

Among these connecting infrastructures, the most important one is the Tajo-Jucar-Segura aqueduct, which was designed to solve the structural deficit of the Segura Basin, the only basin which has a demand higher than its supply under normal conditions.[190] This connection has the capacity to transfer more water than it can sustainably do, but although it transfers less water than it was

---

189 Rafael Méndez, 'Las diez claves para entender la guerra del agua' ('10 key issues to understand the Water Wars'), *El País*, 16 April 2008.

190 Ministerio de Medio Ambiente, *Libro Blanco del Agua en España* (*White Book on Water in Spain*), at 602–605 (2000), http://hercules.cedex.es/Informes/Planificacion/2000-Libro_Blanco_del_Agua_en_Espana/Cap5.pdf.

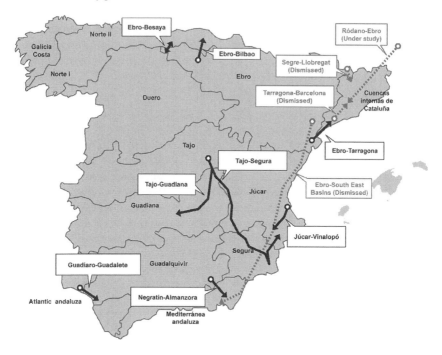

Figure 5.1 River basins and infrastructure for water transfers

Source: Figure 1 in Andrés Molina and Joaquín Melgarejo, 'Water policy in Spain: seeking a balance between transfers, desalination and wastewater reuse,' 32, 5 International Journal of Water Resources Development 781–798 (2016), http://www.tandfonline.com/doi/full/10.1080/07900627. 2015.1077103.

originally intended to, it is still a necessary piece of infrastructure.[191] However, the fraudulent mismanagement in the Segura Basin[192] raises the question of whether water savings and more efficient management could reduce the water needs and whether, if the full cost of water were internalized, less water would be consumed.

Other examples of connections include the Negratín Alzamora, which connects the Guadalquivir Basin with the south, and the interconnection between the two main internal Catalan rivers (Ter and Llobregat). The most recent one built,[193] beyond the period of study, was the connection between the Jucar River and the Vinapoló in the Valencia region, which had been

---

191 Interview with Pedro Arrojo in *El País*, above note 24 ('La nueva cultura del agua no es ni de derechas ni de izquierdas' ('The New Water Culture is not right wing or left wing')).
192 Greenpeace, 'El negocio del agua en la cuenca del Segura,' above note 83.
193 Rafael Méndez, 'Las diez claves para entender la guerra del agua,' *El País*, above note 189 (acknowledging that government is mandating transfers but not using the word transfer).

discussed for many decades, to quench the thirst of the farmers in the Vinapoló area. This transfer has been envisioned, again, as a mandated transfer of water surpluses existing in the river, not as a channel for water transactions of existing rights. It opened in September 2012, and it remains controversial since there is some contestation over whether there are surpluses.

In general, there is a sense that connections must be improved to ensure reliability in water provision. New connections could be built to achieve the ideal pool envisioned by the novelist and engineer behind some of the big hydraulic projects in Spain, Juan Benet, who firmly believed that the water system in Spain should replicate the electric one in terms of network.[194] Some new connections, such as the Ebro one established by the NHP, which may have made the Spanish water system closer to this ideal description, have been proposed, as the next section explains.

b. Provision

As shown below, infrastructure has been used for market transactions. It is not easy to determine whether there is a need for new infrastructure and which form it should take. When crises have arisen, infrastructure has been front page news. Usually water-scarce regions, with urban development outpacing water provision, hope that a transfer will take place. This was particularly the case in the sprawling tourist areas of the south-east. Infrastructure might be needed, not for mandated transfers, given how doubtful it is that there is water surplus, but to ensure that efficient transactions can occur; with this aim in mind, some infrastructural connections would be extremely beneficial since there are areas such as the Ebro River where water is relatively more abundant than in others. New infrastructure does not necessarily need to be as colossal as the SWP in California; a relatively small system of pipes might be sufficient. In fact, during the 2008 crisis where a connection from Tarragona to Barcelona for a mandated, non-market, transfer of water from the Ebro was discussed, one option was a removable connection through a pipe.[195]

Historically, big infrastructure was a public monopoly of the central government and an expression of national pride – as is the case with gigantic dams – and it is still subject to its control. They are considered 'public works of general interest,'[196] and only government can undertake them. This definition

---

194 Julio Llamazares, 'El sueño de Juan Benet' ('Juan Benet's dream'), *El País*, 27 January 2009 (reviewing the ideas of the engineer for the Spanish water system).

195 For an account on the opposition of the irrigators to the market framing of the catchment, see Observatori de Projectes i debats territorials a Catalunya, 'Transvasament del Consorci d'Aigües de Tarragona a l'Àrea Metropolitana de Barcelona' ('Transfer from the Tarragona Water Consortium to Barcelona') (2008), http://territori.scot.cat/cat/viewer.php? IDN=174.

196 Art. 124 of the CWA.

suggests their public good characteristics, although infrastructure to transport water is a natural monopoly. Infrastructure is excludable, thus refuting its definition as public good. However, these works might not be politically excludable. That means that a connection, which may be either a channel or a pipe connecting one basin in the humid north with one basin in the dry south-east will mandatorily be part of procurement by either the central government or the RBA if there is a specific compact delegating power to it.[197] However, even if it is a public agency which operates the infrastructure, it could engage in discriminatory practices. Opposition to connecting infrastructure is one of the problems government encounters in attempting to provide infrastructure, as the Ebro case illustrates. However, less salient mandated transfers have taken place contemporaneously, such as the one from the Ebro to the city of Santander, in the northern basins.[198]

New public infrastructure could be more palatable[199] if it were made clear that the aim was not to mandate transfers, but to allow voluntary reallocations, on a more or less temporary basis. Users in the areas of origin could decide whether or not to sell water, and should not fear that a mandated reduction of the river flow due to a transfer would harm their rights. If necessary to overcome public opposition in the areas of origin, compensation schemes could be envisioned.

Given current regulation, private initiative would have more of a role in the smaller scale infrastructure, for which authorization is still needed.[200] Irrigators' communities can be granted a permit to build and manage the infrastructure by themselves without competitive bidding.[201] Usually, irrigations manage infrastructure because there is no reason to have independent connection for each single irrigation in an area to the stream. If any private party wants to build infrastructure specifically to carry out a transaction at the same time, it has to apply separately for a special building permit and the procedure to grant it might be competitive.

---

197   Art. 125 of the CWA.
198   'Santander recibe por primera vez agua del Ebro con el trasvase reversible a Cantabria,' *Heraldo*, 31 August 2010. http://www.heraldo.es/noticias/aragon/santander_recibe_por_primera_vez_agua_del_ebro_con_trasvase_reversible_cantabria.html.
199   Some Ebro irrigators, in early stages of the discussion, defended market transactions instead of direct water transfers. See 'Ramón-Llin no descarta la compra de agua como alternativa al trasvase' ('Ramón-Llin, then Minister of Agriculture, considered transfers as an alternative to the transfer'), *El País*, 19 December 1998. Afterwards, in 2008, during the Catalan water crisis, they changed their minds. For an account on the opposition, see Observatori de Projectes i debats territorials a Catalunya, above note 195.
200   Art. 70 of the CWA.
201   Art. 125 of the CWA.

c. Management

Regarding provision of infrastructure, it is indisputable that a more connected market offers more opportunities for transactions, and setting aside the question about whether there are enough connections, which is highly contingent and about which there is not much evidence aside from the debates around mandated transfers, the analysis must focus on whether current regulation impairs the full use of the existing infrastructure. In Spanish regulation, before analyzing the risk of monopolization intrinsic in the natural monopoly, there is another obstacle: an authorization from the central government is required to use infrastructure connecting two different basins.

Permit leases are supposed to take place between parties in the same river basin unless there is an express authorization to use infrastructure by the central government. Inter-basin transfers were authorized in 2005 by Real Decreto-Ley 2005/15, given the extreme drought suffered in Spain during the summer of 2005, the harshest since the 1940s.[202] In particular, the use of two infrastructure connections in the south-east of Spain was allowed: the Aqueduct Tajo-Segura and the Connection Negratín-Alzamora. This Real Decreto-Ley included a sunset provision, which dictated that it would expire on 30 November 2006, but it was extended several times and ended up expiring on 30 November 2009.

The key role of infrastructure in the success of water markets is made clear by looking at the data: 2006 was the year with the most transactions, more than the period of 2000–05 combined. The main reason was that the use of these inter-basin connections was allowed. It is true that 2006 was a drought year, but so were 2004 and 2005, and transactions did not flourish. In fact, 2004 and 2005 were much drier years than 2006. Alternatively, it may be said that there is a lag in the effects[203] of the lack of precipitation and, additionally, parties need time to reach an agreement.

Nonetheless, the fact that the majority of transactions were between the areas connected by infrastructure – mainly Tajo Segura and Negratín Alzamora – cannot be denied. The situation was so harsh that the government, in order to promote transactions, waived transportation fees for the use of the Tajo-Segura infrastructure. This resulted in a rebate of between €0.9/m³ and €0.11/m³.[204] This suggests that governmental action and scarcity are clearly complementary. The use of the infrastructure was allowed at more or less the

---

202 Francisco Martínez Gil, 'Las sequías en España, un fenómeno frecuente,' at 2, Expo Zaragoza, 2008, http://www.unizar.es/fnca/duero/docu/cz1.pdf.

203 Ministerio de Medio Ambiente, 'La gestión de la sequía de los años 2004 a 2007' ('Management of the Drought of 2004–2007'), at 30 (2008), http://www.magrama. gob.es/es/agua/temas/observatorio-nacional-de-la-sequia/SequiaPub2004-2007_tcm7-197604.pdf.

204 Calatrava Leyva, above note 77, at 104.

outset of the crisis, no counterfactual is available, and thus it cannot be known whether other transactions without infrastructure, i.e. more local ones, would have occurred. Given that transactions will be reviewed, it would be better to establish a blank authorization for the use of inter-basin infrastructure.

Large infrastructure is owned by government, but smaller ones can be owned by private parties,[205] such as the irrigation communities. These irrigation communities are precisely mechanisms to pool resources in order to buy connections to the watercourses.[206] All these infrastructures are natural monopolies, and parties willing to enter into transactions may be barred by the public or private agents who own the infrastructure.

Regarding the problem of exclusion, it is important to distinguish precisely whether a public entity or a private one manages the infrastructure. When the infrastructure is owned by the RBA approving the transaction, the application to use the pipes, canals, and mains is independent from the application for the review of the lease contract. This seems quite an unnecessary duplication of proceedings since it is often the same administrative body, the RBA, which would authorize both, and provided there is spare capacity, there should not be a need for many other findings. Interestingly enough, even the periods to decide the authorization of the contract and of the use of infrastructure are different, the one for the use of infrastructure being longer (four months). However, if the administration does not decide on time, the use of infrastructure is considered to be authorized. The general consensus among those lawyers who deal with lease contracts is that the authorization for the use of intra-basin infrastructure is less of a hurdle than the use of inter-basin infrastructure.[207] In some cases, this may become a political question, and some externalities might be disregarded to serve particular interests.

When infrastructure is private, regulation establishes that for the use of infrastructure for a lease of permits, the owner of the infrastructure and the parties to a transaction need to agree. There is no imposition of any common carrier duties.[208] The regulation does not rule out direct denial of permission to use or other practices such as discriminatory rates. For example, Agbar, the company supplying Barcelona, receives water from Aigües Ter Llobregat (ATLL), a public company (at that time) that is in charge of wholesale infrastructure shipping water from rivers to cities' gates. Agbar should not be captive to ATLL: if Agbar decides to buy water from a third party, ATLL should not be entitled to discriminate against external water if there is capacity. When ATLL was managed by the Catalan government or was a publicly owned company, it was expected that ATLL would protect the public interest and not discriminate, but the same may not be true now that it is in the process of

---

205   CH Duero, Executive Summary Water Plan Proposal 9 (2008) (on file with the author).
206   Art. 125 of the CWA.
207   Interview with Mónica Sastre, above note 184.
208   Art. 70 of the CWA.

being privatized. A private ATLL may charge excessive rates or simply deny the use of its infrastructure, if this transaction would be detrimental to its own business, rendering the transaction impossible.

5.6.4 Market maker role

Transaction costs underlie all regulations, and reduction of these costs was one of the major motivations for the very birth of the market tools in Spain. Spain's administrative water allocation system prior to the 1999 amendment was too rigid to correct the outdated distribution of water rights which allocated the majority of water to the agricultural sector. Transaction costs are not market failures, but if they are too high, they simply prevent market transactions. That was almost the situation prior to 1999, with the cumbersome administrative procedures which potential permit transfers had to undergo. The mechanisms to change any of the definitional characteristics of a permit were too demanding to allow for a more decentralized solution. In 1999, the idea was to ease the requirements without changing the paradigm of water as public property.

Many of the roles identified in Chapter 2 as potential transaction cost-reduction strategies or market maker roles have been adopted, such as assuming broker functions, at least on paper. However, they have not been bold enough, particularly when it comes to their implementation. The roles analyzed next are: recording and information, guaranteeing rights and transactions, increasing fungibility, and the match maker role through the water exchange centers.

a. Recording and providing information

According to the written law, transactions must be recorded in the basin's Water Registry.[209] In the case of trade of permits for agricultural use, the origin of the unused water must be registered, i.e. the fields let fallow or where water will be more efficiently used are specified in the Registry's entry.[210] The shortcomings of the Water Registries are well known: the recording of trades is, like the recording of concessions, more a desideratum than a reality,[211] as evidenced by the lack of transaction data detailed earlier. In addition, meters are not common and, thus, monitoring of actual use is not easy. In addition,

---

209 Art. 68.4 of the CWA.
210 Art. 67.1 of the CWA. Art. 67.2 of the CWA authorizes the Ministry of the Environment to exceptionally and temporarily allow transactions that do not observe the rank of uses.
211 For example, the public official in charge of the Segura River Basin's Water Registry in a telephone conversation confirmed that not all trades are recorded (April 2011). For an official claim that Water Registries in Spain lack reliability, see Environmental Ministry, *Libro Blanco del Agua en España, Documento de Síntesis (White Book on Water in Spain, Executive Summary)*, at 15–17 (4 December 1998), http://www.magrama.gob.es/es/ag ua/temas/ planificacion-hidrologica/sintesis_tcm7-28955.pdf.

the CWA establishes the setting up of a central database for all rights in Spanish basins which has never been implemented.[212] There have not been any private initiatives to record the transactions.

b. Guaranteeing

Water Registries in Spain claim to protect water rights by recording them, but they are not reliable.[213] Beyond Registries, government can offer a stronger guarantee in water exchange centers: RBAs act as brokers and also back up the transactions, since they actually buy and sell the water. There might even be a type of securitization if different rights bought are pooled together. The transfer of water rights to the authority could help improve buyers' confidence because there would be some type of governmental guarantee that the contract will be fulfilled. This seems well-tailored to the early stages of a water market where buyers may not be as experienced and can figure out less perfectly how to shield themselves from risk in a contract. But those advantages have not been realized.

c. Fungibility

The definition of water property rights shows that tradability is restricted and, thus, water rights become less fungible, since, for example, a water right devoted to agricultural use cannot be sold to an industrial user. Another issue covered under the definition of property rights is that the amount tradable is defined according to historical use. This can be considered a part of the definition of property rights, but it is not essential for a market to exist. It also, and mainly, reduces externalities which should ease transactions. However, the regulator could have gone further and reduced transaction costs by capitalizing on information which should already be under the control of the administration.

Calculation of the volume historically consumed is not easy, and parties may need to spend resources in doing so to know how much they can transfer. Meters are not common. In fact, permit leases require them to be installed, which makes evident that they are not in place.[214] However, meters do not help to measure past consumption, and given how difficult it might be to calculate certain features such as leakages and return flows, sellers and buyers may be uncertain about how much they can transfer. Calculating it on a case-by-case basis would be expensive for private parties. Government could have offered a model to calculate past consumption. River Basin Plans define

---

212   Art. 197 of the RDPH.
213   According to the Socialist Party, 80 per cent of the permits were not registered in 1999, see 'El PSOE planteará hoy al Gobierno su rechazo a los mercados de agua,' *El País*, above note 103.
214   Art. 347.1 of the RDPH.

reference values of water used depending on the type of crop,[215] and these could serve as a basis for the calculation of consumptive use. Nowadays, the regulation establishes that the reference volume in the River Basin Plans can be used to correct the volume the parties can transfer. This suggests that the reference volume is used more as a threat than a tool to save transaction costs.[216] Reference values are approximations, but the lack of complete exactitude is a price to pay for the decrease in transaction costs. Parties could decide to run their own calculations, but that would be expensive. In addition, it could be established that if the parties use the reference values provided by the agencies to calculate the volume transferable, approval of the transaction would be automatic, even if that implies ignoring certain small effects of those transfers.

d. Match maker: water exchange centers

The clearest instance where public agencies could take up the role of match maker is through water exchange centers (centros de intercambio de derechos). According to the CWA, RBAs work as a middleman in these centers. There has been no competition by private parties. The only private brokers were in the Canary Islands, which have a different water regime consisting of a groundwater pool. As already stated, water banks are usually more readily accepted than private contracts over water rights. They were included in the Socialist Party alternative to the NHP of 2001[217] and even UPA, the union of small farmers, favored them.[218]

Water exchange centers – the name given to water banks in Spain – are not permanent: RBAs are allowed to set up water exchange centers in the exceptional circumstances of overdrafting of aquifers, severe droughts, and those cases where the uses should be limited to guaranteeing a rational exploitation of the resource.[219] They last only until the crisis is over. These structures were inspired by California's experience in 1991, but the scope of water banks in Spain is smaller; it is not the whole country, but a basin. It would be similar

---

215 Art. 345.1.b of the RDPH. Reference values are not exempt from controversy, see 'Feragua advierte que las dotaciones propuestas por la administración andaluza arruinaran los cultivos más competitivos' ('Feragua, a union of farmers, claims that the values set in the Andalucia's regulation will make the most competitives crops go bankrupt'), http://www.feragua. com/FERAGUA-ADVIERTE-QUE-LAS-DOTACIONES-PROPUESTAS-POR-LA-ADMINISTRACION-ANDALUZA-ARRUINARAN-LOS-CULTIVOS-MAS-COMPETIT IVOS_a1178.html (claiming that the reference values set by Andalucia's water plans are not high enough to ensure the viability of many highly profitable crops).

216 Art. 345.1.b of the RDPH.

217 'El Plan Hidrológico del PSOE anula el Mercado del agua aprobado en 1999' ('PSOE's National Hydrologic Plan voids the Water market established in 1999'), *El País*, 8 March 2001.

218 Interview Jose Manuel Delgado, above note 107.

219 Art. 71 of the CWA. The exceptional situations are described in Arts 55, 56, and 58 of the CWA.

to the water banks organized by local organizations in the United States if it were not for the centralization effect: authorization by the central government cabinet is required before the CH establishes them. Such an authorization can be quite broad, such as the one in 2004 authorizing the establishment of centros de intercambio de derechos in the Guadiana, Segura, and Jucar Basins.[220] This authorization was given in October 2004, a rainy month, ahead of the drought to come.

This prior authorization can entail a delay in any reaction to a drought unless the authorization is granted in advance, as was the case in 2004. The time taken to overcome these bureaucratic hurdles may be precious time wasted in other cases. The nested nature and the lack of permanency slow down the reaction to a crisis. For example, in the Segura Basin, it took more than two years from the announcement to the actual implementation of the center.[221] Currently, in the Drought Plans passed since 2007, several CHs include the exchange centers as a measure triggered by certain drought scenarios.[222] However, as stated, they cannot be automatically triggered, and this ends up being only aspirational: it is required that the central government gives them the green light beforehand.

Water exchange centers are very similar to public procurement regulations,[223] which impose several formal requirements to ensure that the process is competitive and prevent corruption. Private parties have to adapt to the requirements of the tender. This complicates transactions and may reduce the pool of potential sellers. These procurement-like requirements do not seem to target the needs of water management since they slow down the process and, in general, water market transactions involve the buying, leasing, or reselling of small water rights and, thus, the risk of favorable treatment of some contractors should not be large. These constraints also curtail the flexibility of the administration since the time period between the publication of the offer, the receipt of the tenders, and the resolution is quite long. It is also unclear how then they will reallocate acquired rights. For example, in the Jucar Basin, an offer was published in the *Official Gazette* in December 2006 and the decision about which rights were to be leased was published in July 2007.[224] Water banks are expected to be closer to spot markets; Spanish centros de

---

220 Acuerdo del Consejo de Ministros (Cabinet Decision) (15 October 2004) (authorized the establishment of centros de intercambio de derechos in the Guadiana, Segura, and Jucar Basins).

221 Calatrava Leyva, above note 77, at 103.

222 For example, 'Executive Report Drought Preparedness Plan Tajo River Basin,' at 97 (2007) (it even mentions that more water leases might be expected), http://www.chtajo.es/DemarcaTajo/SequiasyAvenidas/Documents/Memoria.pdf.

223 Art. 355 of the RDPH.

224 Announcement (BOE 2007, 165). There was an extension to present more offers of rights to be acquired.

intercambio de derechos are far from being so. Parties may not want such a slow process, even if they could benefit from the guarantee.

On paper, centros de intercambio de derechos are devoted to shifting water from low value users to high value ones, serving the broker function mentioned, i.e. matching buyers and sellers. However, in 2006, an emergency decree authorized CHs and regional equivalents to launch public offers to lease or even buy rights for environmental purposes.[225] Almost all centers actually set up have been devoted to buying water for the environment. In Guadiana, the bank performed a type of indirect broker role, but not based on market criteria. Guadiana launched six public offers to acquire water from 2008 to 2012 within the Plan to recover the Upper Guadiana basin under the framework of a water exchange center. These banks were supposed to assign the acquired water, mostly groundwater, either to the environment or to the Autonomous Community of Castilla-La Mancha (the regional government). The latter would re-assign it to farmers who fulfilled certain social criteria. Social criteria tried to favor certain kinds of farms, such as those run by young farmers. In practice, the rights bought were devoted to regularizing certain illegal water users who did not have a permit, but were using illegal wells.[226] This is an example of how politics trump a market's operation. In addition, there was a severe enforcement problem. Many of the rights sold had not been used in previous years, i.e. they were 'paper rights,' according to the NGO WWF Aena. Further, some others continued to be used after they were sold. The NGO reached these conclusions after using satellite data. The CH Guadiana could have done the same to prevent this blatant enforcement problem.[227]

Exchange centers could exist in the purely regional basins. Catalonia and the Balearic Islands announced exchange centers in their internal basins, but they never took off. These cases illustrate also how, despite the availability of the structure, politics may prevent the success of water exchange centers. In Catalonia, drought decrees enabled banks,[228] but the political will never materialized to bring them about. In the Balearic Islands, they were set up by a left-wing coalition government – including a 'green' party – which reinforces what is described in the introduction, i.e. that water banks are more palatable to left-wing parties than other types of market mechanisms. The Balearic bank was created to respond to the risk of over-exploitation of groundwater. At the

225   RDL 2006/9 (BOE 2006, 222), above note 79.
226   WWF AENA, 'El fiasco del agua en el alto Guadiana' ('Water fraud in Alto Guadiana'), http://www.wwf.es/?22540/WWF-denuncia-la-compra-pblica-de-agua-fantasma—en-el-Alto-Guadiana-por-66-millones-de-euros. See also, 'An expensive groundwater governance,' above note 187.
227   WWF AENA, ibid.
228   3rd Additional Provision Decree 84/2007, de 3 d'abril, d'adopció de mesures excepcionals i d'emergència en relació amb la utilització dels recursos hídrics (Catalan Decree adopting exceptional and emergency measures in relation to the use of water resources) (DOGC 4860, 4.12.2007).

same time, some existing rights were curtailed, and it was expected that those users whose rights had been reduced would resort to the market to make up for the water they were no longer receiving. No exchange occurred.[229]

5.7 Conclusions

Water market mechanisms were introduced in 1999 in Spain as a reaction to the mid-1990s' drought. The ruling People's Party had an agenda focused on economic liberalization, and water markets were regarded by many opponents as a part of that wider agenda. Market mechanisms were expected to help make the system more flexible than the traditional, constrained, administrative permit system, and better able to cope with droughts and solve the structural scarcity problems. The liberalization agenda helps explain why in Spain, as in many other areas, water markets have been attacked with the same critiques as any privatization and liberalization proposal, even though in this case only existing rights were tradable and the administrative oversight established is extensive, as this chapter explains.

Trading happened, but only in a very limited manner. Some trades occurred during the mid-2000s drought, but, in general terms, markets have not achieved their full potential. Water market regulation establishes many of the governmental roles identified as necessary in Chapter 2, but the regulation was not designed to really enhance water markets. Further, government has not made the most out of the avenues, albeit imperfect, opened by the 1999 amendment. Water markets have yet to play a part in routine water management in Spain.

The main findings regarding each of the roles are summarized next.

5.7.1 Definition of property rights

The definition of property rights is a prerequisite for water markets and it must provide security and ensure tradability. Transferability of concessions was timidly expanded, but the security dimension of the water rights was not strengthened enough.

The apportionment of water in times of drought did not respond to rules set in advance, which makes right holders doubt the reliability of the rights. In addition, drought emergencies have bailed out many water users, mainly urban ones, and thus, they do not feel the need to resort to markets to shield them from the risk of low water availability. In Spain, natural uncertainty is compounded by uncertainty created by regulatory powers. Powers such as the

---

229   Decree 2003/50 (BO Balearic Islands 2003, 76) (establishing the center of water use rights exchange); D. 2005/58, derogatory provision (BO Balearic Islands 2005, 85) (acknowledging the lack of trade and, hence, abolishing the water bank).

revision of permits, expropriation in times of drought, forfeiture, and so on were theoretically held by the RBAs, even before market mechanisms were introduced, to ensure that water is efficiently used by those who value it the most. However, those powers have been seldom used, thus signaling the lack of political will to really enhance efficiency. That lack of implementation of those powers was also used as evidence against markets because those command-and-control mechanisms were remedies for the supposed problems market mechanisms were aimed at solving – structural scarcity and droughts – and they had gone unused.[230] Those powers erode security of water rights and may discourage participation in water markets because right holders may fear that selling water in the market may trigger those powers, and buyers may be reluctant to buy those concessional rights which may be reduced at a certain point by the agencies. Transactions could replace these powers in promoting water use efficiency. Accordingly, if those powers are inactive, they should be abolished because they are not used and they may be deterring market transactions.

Turning now to tradability, the assessment of government performance is not very positive either. Transferability was expanded, but cautiously. In Spain, water permits can be leased in a private contract and leased or sold in a water bank, which only operates in times of drought. However, they can only be leased or acquired by other current users, which may be useful for solving existing problems, but proves unhelpful for responding to new needs. In addition, tradability is subject to further limitations. For instance, permits can only be leased by other titleholders employing the water for a use ranked equally or higher than the ranking of the lessor. Regulation should give leeway to the parties to decide their counterparties instead of making assumptions about which is the most valuable use beforehand. If water transactions respond to the model envisioned by market proponents of transferring water from farmers to urban dwellers, however, the ranking should not be a problem.

Tradability restrictions would have been acceptable if they were coupled with a more lenient review procedure, as should have been the case if the real purpose of those tradability restrictions was to reduce externalities. However, the procedure to review for externalities does not seem streamlined enough.

The environment is one of the potential recipients of water bought on the markets theoretically, but in Spain there are no permits for environmental use, i.e. private parties cannot apply for a concession and devote the water to protect the environment. Concessional rights to instream flows could have made the market more active and rivers less endangered. RBAs, with the authorization of the central government, have circumvented the lack of property rights over instream flow by buying rights through the water exchange centers and letting

---

230 See Hearing of Mr Moraleda Quiles, General Secretary of the Unión de Pequeños Agricultores (Small Farmers' Union) Comisión de Medio Ambiente, above note 6, at 20623.

the water in the river. A positive feature regarding security is that environmental instream flows are defined, or expected to be defined in the future, and quantification of them makes water right holders less subject to the whims of the administrative agencies because users know what amount they need to respect.

5.7.2 Externalities

Administrative procedures for assessing externalities only take place in relation to permit leases. There is no mention of externalities review in water exchange centers regulation. In fact, those water exchange centers have almost always not worked as water banks, but as public purchase programmes for the environment, and fewer externalities, if any, should arise from more water flowing in the river. In addition, RBAs, when establishing water banks, fix some of the characteristics of the rights which can be sold to the bank and, thus, some externalities might be prevented.

Under the permits' lease, restrictions on which rights can be traded and to whom might serve the same purpose as the requirements in water banks. However, as the analysis of the review procedure for leases shows, it has not clearly translated into a streamlined procedure. In fact, the procedure should be even less cumbersome because the volume tradable is defined as the average amount used in the last five years by the lessor, and parties know they need to respect instream flow requirements.

The short period of time for review (two months) as well as the default rule stating that a lack of decision implies the transaction is approved are advantageous features for promoting transactions, which improve the situation compared to the pre-1999 transactions scheme, which had a length of 18 months. However, the criteria for denying authorization are quite broad, and there do not seem to be guidelines that could curtail administrative discretion. Those standards include the protection of the environment even though instream flows are supposed to be defined.

It is hard to assess how cumbersome the review procedure is because many extremes are left undefined. The information requirements for the parties to a transaction are not established, and the entire burden seems to be placed on the administration. The RBA is the steward of the rights of third parties, which are not expressly allowed to participate by the regulation. However, general administrative rules may be applicable, which should ensure that those affected can participate. Even though third parties are not included, there is the possibility of an anti-commons effect because other public agencies, such as the Department of Agriculture, are required to report on the transaction. The participation of the regional agencies or other departments does not add any value to the review because the review focuses on the effects on other users and on the water resources in the basin. The information required to assess these effects is in the hands of other users or the agency approving the transactions, not in the hands of these other agencies with different interests. The RBA is in a better position to assess those issues. There is little information as to how the review procedure to ensure that transactions do not cause externalities on third parties and the environment has worked in practice, but the regulations on paper with their open-ended standards seem to leave private parties at the mercy of water agencies. There is so little information that it may well be the case that if those agencies are committed to enhance transactions, the review procedure will be a mere formality, which could be not protective enough of other users and the environment.

5.7.3 Infrastructure provision and management

Regarding infrastructure, the Spanish water basins are fairly well connected. This is not to say that there are not areas still lacking infrastructure, but assessing whether it is beneficial to build infrastructure is difficult. The Ebro connection to the urban areas on the east Mediterranean coast, which, if undertaken, would be built by the central government according to current regulation, seems to be a gap which needs to be filled, but which is unlikely to be, given the political controversies that arose in 2001 around the NHP which left open wounds. Political objections to any infrastructure might be softened if the result of water transactions would be water transferred and not mandatory reallocations.

Several shortcomings in the regulation of the use of infrastructure by third parties transferring water must be noted. Regarding infrastructure owned by private parties, the regulation only establishes that its use should be agreed between the parties, without imposing a common carrier duty or regulating rates. Such a scheme is prone to monopolistic abuses by the infrastructure owner. Where infrastructure is public, the parties to the water transactions have to undergo two separate, duplicate applications, one for the authorization of the lease and another for the authorization of the use of the infrastructure, which unnecessarily increases transaction costs, since both procedures may ultimately be decided by the RBA if it is the manager of the infrastructure. Furthermore, in some cases, where public infrastructure managers are also water suppliers, those agents may discriminate against third parties willing to ship water.

5.7.4 Market maker

On paper, law has granted RBAs the powers to excel at this function. Unfortunately, their practices have failed to do so.

According to written law, Spain should have recorded all rights and all transactions, but Water Registries are in a poor state. This reduces the ability of private parties to rely on each other's rights when entering into transactions, or to locate potential willing sellers or buyers based on past records.

In order to prevent externalities, the volume transferable is defined according to the amount consumed on average during the previous five years. This is a difficult calculation for parties to a transaction. Government could have reduced transaction costs by providing guidelines or a model to calculate it. River Basin Plans include reference values for water use by different crops, which government can use in order to revise water rights, but it could also use them to make the calculation easier for private parties. Furthermore, they could ease the transaction review if those values are used by private parties.

Water banks, known in Spain as centros de intercambio de derechos, are temporary, can only be established during emergencies, require a series of approvals by the nested levels of government, and must fulfill the constraining requirements of the formal offer, similar to the requirements in public procurement, even though these requirements are of no service for low-stakes water contracts. They were envisioned as match makers, but they have not even been fully implemented as clearing houses, but mostly as mechanisms to buy water to devote this water to environmental protection. Both from regulation and from implementation standpoints, water banks present a lost opportunity: they could have helped to mitigate crises and to kick off water markets as an everyday water management tool.

In sum, the limited version of markets attempted in Spain is too constrained to succeed. Markets were never portrayed in Spain as the ultimate solution to water scarcity, but they were expected to at least contribute to a better allocation of water and to be useful as a management tool for water crises. Unfortunately, more than a decade after their introduction, they have achieved very little in these regards.

Administrative intervention in the market is both too little and too intense at the same time. Too little if it is considered that the enabling roles such as management of infrastructure and reduction of transaction costs are not performed to a satisfactory extent; and too intense regarding, for example, the definition of water rights, their tradability or water exchange centers.

It is worthwhile to sketch some of the political issues operating backstage as potential drivers of governmental inaction. Beyond the failure of government to effectively play the abovementioned roles, a further problem is that some regulations do not convey appropriate incentives to participants in the market. Markets may not be favored by any interest group. Urban users are shielded from drought curtailments, while the agricultural sector receives cheap water the rest of the time, even if it is curtailed during harsh times.

The rules setting forth that domestic users are at the top of the rank for the assigning of new permits and giving them priority in times of drought discourage the participation of the potential buyers, urban suppliers. Even setting aside that priority, it seems widely known in urban areas that the political costs of cutting water for households during certain hours of the day are undesirable, and urban suppliers – the purportedly potential buyers – do not have incentives to resort to the market to satisfy their current or future needs. Nor do they have incentives to do so for new urban developments, since the market does not provide water rights to satisfy future demands.

The opposition of farmers to water markets is problematic because they are the group envisioned as the seller. Many of the arguments raised by agricultural organizations were cloaked as concerns related to the public property over water, and the importance of protecting the public interest, but they most probably hide concerns about keeping subsidized water for the agricultural sector. This worry makes no real sense, given that markets are voluntary mechanisms and if farmers did not want to enter into transactions, they did not need to. Of course, even if this strategy could make sense collectively, individual farmers, who are titleholders, may decide to sell their water, opening the path for water prices to rise. This same idea about keeping water cheap and protect farmers could be behind the provision that allows government to fix a maximum price in water leases, even though RBAs have never implemented it. Farmers' ideological opposition waters down the incentives of the RBAs to enhance them, because the agricultural sector is a powerful constituency, usually favored except during low water availability periods. However, even then, they are sometimes compensated *ex-post* with public subsidies for the effects of a drought.[231]

Hence, beyond ideology, it is not clear that government was catering to any of these interests by enhancing water markets. Perhaps, initially, the idea was to favor certain corporate interests, such as the hydropower sector and the construction sector, which were developing certain areas. However, in the end, water market mechanisms were watered down in order to ease the concerns of the opposition and some of the lobby groups. Even though the mechanisms in the final bill were less ambitious than the initial proposals, the Members of Parliament of the opposing political parties did not vote in favor. When the main opposing political party, the Socialist Party, regained power in 2004, it did not repeal the market mechanisms, perhaps because they were not working in practice. The Socialist Party had defended water banks and, coherently, authorized water banks to deal with the 2006–08 water crisis. However, water banks regulation was too constraining and water banks mostly did not work as brokers, missing an opportunity to make private parties at ease with markets.

The regulation, even if far from perfect, is still in place, and perhaps another drought will provide the necessary impetus to fully use water markets, increase their expected benefits and build a proper coalition in their favor.

---

231 For example, flower farmers have received loans so that they can distribute drought-related losses over several years, and then subsequently received subsidies to cover these already favorable loans. See Ordre AAR/433/2010 (DOGC 2010, 5713) (awarding subsidies to flower and ornamental plant farms to mitigate the borrowing costs of loans after the 2008 droughts).

6 Comparison between water markets in California and in Spain

6.1 Introduction

This chapter compares water markets in California and Spain with the ultimate goal of assessing whether Californian water markets have been more active than Spanish ones because California has better fulfilled the governmental roles discussed in Chapter 2. The conclusions offered here illustrate the main theoretical finding, namely, that water markets require public agencies to fulfill certain roles, justified under economic theories of regulation, to work successfully. These roles relate to defining property rights, reviewing for externalities, providing access to natural monopoly infrastructure, and reducing transaction costs. Independently, the two case studies offer lessons for other jurisdictions about which water market regulations work and which do not.

The research question mentioned in the previous paragraph implies: (a) that California and Spain are comparable; and (b) that water markets have been more active in California than in Spain. As to the comparability, Chapter 3 demonstrates that comparing these two jurisdictions is meaningful, since California and Spain share relevant characteristics such as climate, agricultural water use or urban population growth. The comparison is admittedly imperfect; this is not a natural experiment where all but one explanatory variable can be held constant. Nonetheless, existing differences are unlikely to drive the observed differences in water market activity.

As to the activity of water markets in both jurisdictions, section 6.2 establishes that trading in both regions differs significantly. Californian water markets were more active from 1991 to 2000 than Spanish ones from 2000 to 2009, confirming the underlying assumption of the first part of research question. Section 6.3 studies the performance of agencies in both jurisdictions by comparing how well they fulfill the relevant governmental roles identified in Chapter 2. Section 6.3 argues that California's agencies have fared much better in this regard than their Spanish counterparts. Section 6.4 interprets the findings and concludes that different levels of market activity can be traced back to the degree to which governmental roles have been fulfilled in each jurisdiction. This comparison necessarily builds on Chapters 4 and 5, which trace the evolution of water markets and the role played by government in California and Spain, respectively. They are instrumental to the comparison undertaken here to assess which actions boosted water markets. The focus of the analysis is on the actions undertaken by government, not what lies behind them. Thus, even though the case studies point towards potential political economy explanations, the conclusions are best regarded as a starting point for further research.

6.2 Dependent variable: water market activity

As Chapter 3 makes clear, activity level is, for good reasons, a proxy frequently used in the literature. The hypothesis is that the more activity there is, the more successful a market is, and the more it should be fulfilling its goals, provided there are not uncompensated externalities. Comparing the volume traded in California and in Spain is not an easy enterprise due to incompleteness and comparability challenges of the data from both jurisdictions.[1] Nonetheless, California's overwhelming lead cannot be denied. Adding all the reported intra-basin, inter-basin, and water bank transactions, the volume traded from 2000 to 2009 (inclusive) in Spain amounted to 296,521.785 acr-ft. The equivalent figure for California from 1991 to 2000 (also inclusive) is, reportedly, more than ten times that volume.

The number of transactions presents a less acute difference, but still a relevant one. Adding open-market transactions and water bank transactions, Spanish reported transactions amounted to 531 and Californian ones to 619. The figure for California would be even higher if intra-project transfers – transfers within the state or federal infrastructure projects – were included, since these transfers may amount to more than 100 per year. The numbers are even more striking when analyzed in the light of the scarcity of data. Spain suffered a serious drought in the mid-2000s, and scarcity should prompt more transactions. There were more trades during the drought, mostly in water banks established by government as a response to the water crisis, but the increase in trading was not enough to match California.

The data (or lack of data) regarding other variables may call for caution when interpreting these figures to explain the driving force behind the better performance of market tools in California. For instance, total water consumption is higher in California, and no data could be obtained for the average volume per permit. While there is no point in denying that these other variables may have some relevance, they are insufficient to explain the huge gap in the volume and number of transactions. It is undeniable that California from 1991 to 2000 had more active water markets than Spain from 2000 to 2009.

Regarding the use by the seller and the use by the buyer of the water transferred, both jurisdictions seem to confirm the idea that low-value users in

---

1 See Section 4 of Chapter 4 on California's water market activity, and section 5 of Chapter 5 on Spain's water market figures.

the agricultural sector are those that will sell the water. The main aim stated by market proponents is for transactions to help alleviate the structural scarcity problem; i.e. thanks to the market, the limited supply of water will be put to use by those who value it the most and, thus, there will be fewer economic losses as a result of drought crises, and a more efficient use of water. The underlying assumption is that the agricultural sector has more water allocated to it for historical reasons, but it does not always value water as highly as do modern urban areas, or even the environment. Farmers are expected to let their fields fallow, shift to less water-intensive crops, or to improve the efficiency of their irrigation systems.

The data on California shows overwhelmingly that the origin of the vast majority of transactions is the agricultural sector, and that the majority of the volume transferred is transferred between the agricultural sector and urban areas. However, the number of intra-sectoral transactions within the agricultural sector is higher than trades between the agricultural sector and the urban areas. This is not surprising, given that agriculture is the larger user. The agriculture to agriculture transaction figures show that there are differences in marginal values between different agricultural sectors: those growing more valuable crops benefit from transactions. For example, those whose fruit trees require irrigation might be interested in buying water during drought times, if their rights cannot be fulfilled because of the low availability and the date of appropriation.

Data for Spain regarding origin and destination of trade is not complete, but the available data seems to confirm the hypotheses regarding where water should be coming from: farmers. In the 2000s, water exchange centers bought water from farmers. The destination was mostly environmental, a type of transaction allowed since 2006. Overall, the only exception was the Guadiana River, which reallocated water based on public policy goals other than protection of the environment. The data for permit leases is anecdotal, but it suggests that water originates from agricultural areas and that at least in certain cases it moves towards urban areas.

Lastly, results arising from the set of variables related to the price paid in transactions are not conclusive. Chapter 5 shows that Spanish data is clearly insufficient to reach any conclusion on the robustness of water markets based on price gaps and, consequently, a comparison of price gaps in Californian and Spanish water markets would be useless.

In sum, notwithstanding data limitations, there is sufficient empirical basis to claim that water markets were more active in California than in Spain for the periods considered. Data on number of transactions and, particularly, the volume transferred, clearly points to this conclusion. Whether the observed differences in water market activity are related to the different performance of the governments in both jurisdictions is the subject matter of section 6.3.

6.3 Fulfillment of governmental roles: comparison and critique

6.3.1 Definition of property rights

California and Spain face challenges as a result of a heterogeneous portfolio of water rights, but these are less acute in Spain, since historical property rights are not abundant and permits are commonly used to allocate water rights. This is expected to impair transactions if, for example, right holders of different types of rights cannot trade with each other, or if the procedures for transferring each type of right are very different, making it difficult for potential participants in the market to access and process the information needed to decide whether to enter into a transaction. This section compares how these two jurisdictions fare in the dimensions of security and tradability.

Focusing on the two most comparable set of rights, the post-1914 California appropriative rights and the Spanish administrative permits granted by the RBAs, California has fared better in terms of security. Both types of rights are subject to administrative control, but there is a significant difference between these two types of rights that could affect market performance. Spanish permits are subject to a time limit, albeit a long one, up to 85 years. Users in Spain may be reluctant to buy time-limited permits. However, they could just pay less for them. Unfortunately, there is not enough price data to assess whether this is true. In any event, California was characterized in the early years by short-term transactions, so a time limit should not necessarily discourage transactions in Spain, because time-limited water rights could also be leased for short periods.

The first issue that greatly affects security and the incentives of private parties to resort to the market is how the effects of low water availability are apportioned. In California, in broad terms, the lack of water is shared according to the order of appropriation, the exception being how the projects decide how much water they deliver to their contractors. However, regarding the SWP and the CVP rights, there is foreseeability, and users can plan accordingly because they announce their allocation at specific times. In Spain, this is not the case. RBAs retained significant discretion regarding how water was to be allocated during droughts. Until 2007, emergency decrees were used to respond to those crises, which implies that the rules were enacted on a case-by-case basis and users could not plan ahead. In addition, urban users seem to be shielded from the low availability of water by emergency decrees, since it is politically costly to curtail urban water users. In 2007–08, Drought Preparedness Plans were enacted, but their effect on transactions cannot be analyzed; there has not been a harsh drought since their enactment falling within the period of study. Even if some of these plans still shield urban users from the restrictions required to cope with low water availability, other types of users may have more security as to whether or not they will receive water and use market transactions to respond to it. The decisions by Spanish governmental authorities in times of emergency erode the security of the rights, so private parties may be unsure whether or not the water right they are buying will end up being fulfilled. In addition, those bailed out, urban areas, do not have an incentive to plan for future droughts by buying water.

In both California and Spain, rights are subject to administrative powers which may grind down the security of water rights. Both jurisdictions, for instance, have use-it-or-lose-it provisions and rules against misuse. These provisions were part of an administratively centered system where the administration needs a mechanism in order to achieve dynamic efficiency. In the case of California, those provisions, now administered by the SWRCB, were inherited from prior appropriation common law rules. Those transferring water may fear triggering those provisions as a result of the transfer, since this may be interpreted as not needing the water being transferred, particularly where the water transferred comes from adopting a different irrigation system which uses water more efficiently. Thus the forfeiture provisions or rules against misuse would deter transactions and even be counterproductive to the goal of conserving water. California has done a great deal to mitigate the fear of forfeiture, by taking incremental steps towards reassuring lessors that their rights will not be diminished as a result of the lease; transferring water is not be considered evidence of waste or of previous misuse. In Spain, when provisions enhancing the tradability of rights were enacted in 1999, it was expressly stated that no total forfeiture is to be expected as a result of water transactions. A more reassuring statement was needed. California, in fact, needed to enact several provisions reassuring right holders in this regard. However, it is unclear what exactly right holders should and should not fear, since Spanish water authorities have never applied the forfeiture provisions or revised a permit merely because the same use could be achieved with less water.

While in California there are almost no restrictions on who can trade with whom, there are plenty such limitations in Spain. Only water right holders can trade with each other, and only if the seller was using the water for a type of use ranked equally or higher in the River Basin Plan. A new user in California could apply for a permit or buy any right on the market, as illustrated by recent legislation requiring new urban developments to certify that they have enough supply for the next few years and allowing transfers to be part of the plan for supply. In Spain, users do not have such a choice. The only exceptions to this scheme in California are the SWP contractual rights, which can only, and with restrictions, be traded among SWP contractors, and riparian rights, which can only be transferred for environmental uses.

The role of instream flow rights could also explain part of the different outcome in market activity. In the period under consideration, Californian water markets kept up a high volume of trade once the drought crisis was over, roughly 1994 and after. This is in part thanks to purchases directly or indirectly related to the environment. Both public agencies and private parties were allowed to 'buy' water rights for this purpose, including riparian rights which could not be traded under any other circumstances, and leave them to flow in the stream. This does not amount to a property right over instream flow, since California does not have non-consumptive rights for environmental use as such.

It is a way to increase instream flow without reducing rights, and boosting the market by transferring water and reinforcing the security of existing rights because they will not be curtailed to protect the environment. Environmental protection, particularly the protection of endangered species, also contributed to water markets indirectly, because those who saw their water rights reduced to comply with endangered species protection regulations bought water to make up for the reduction. In Spain, instream flows are protected by defining the minimum instream flow, which all users have to respect. Once enacted, the regime will give certainty to users and should not deter transactions once they are established. In addition, if markets worked, those mandatory instream flows could have a similar effect that endangered species protection had in California: prompting users to buy water that they need but do no longer receive because their rights are reduced.

In Spain, where there are no fully-fledged non-consumptive environmental water rights, environmental purchases by the RBAs amount to a large share of the water market activity. From 2006 to 2009, water exchange centers – Spanish water banks – could purchase water to protect the environment, and several RBAs established water exchange centers to mitigate environmental damage as a result of the drought at the time. Those purchases may have prevented unpopular curtailments of existing rights. In fact, environmental purchases are the main activity undertaken by the water exchange centers, at least formally. The at-least-formally caveat is needed here because at least one of the water exchange centers has been singled out for twisting its own goals, by purchasing water not to protect over-exploited aquifers but to grandfather illegal wells giving those surface water rights.

Instream flow purchases have represented a good share of the market in both jurisdictions, both of which have room to improve the regulation of those transactions.

All this suggests that neither California nor Spain had fully undertaken all the actions required to define water rights in a way conducive to more market transactions. This is probably the result of, on the one hand, the intricacies and variability of water as a resource and, on the other hand, the obstacles posed by existing regulations designed with an administrative system of water management in mind. As to the latter, this is not to say that regulations are not necessary to some extent: after all water markets are part of the administrative management of water and they seldom work perfectly. However, the scope of such regulations needs to be narrowly defined for the market not to be negatively affected or, if regulations are inactive, they should be repealed.

Take, for instance, regulations in California and Spain granting an administrative agency powers to review the rights previously granted by that same agency, provided they are misused. In a perfect market where water is priced according to its real value, the user will not misuse water because it will realize the full opportunity cost of doing so, and, thus, the administrative review of the underlying right will cease to be necessary. However, given that water markets are far from perfect, it may be worthwhile to keep the review provisions. The challenge for lawmakers is to phrase those provisions without eroding certainty for markets. Another instance where both jurisdictions could do better is the definition of instream property rights.

However, in California, diverse property rights are more secure and more tradable. For example, in Spain, the subjective and use-related restrictions to trade have not meant an expedited administrative review. In California, those restrictions do not exist and the rules of curtailment are known at the outset, not established by a series of emergency decrees and do not necessarily shield a particular use as is the case in Spain. Right holders in California may know when to resort to the market and they know they may not be bailed out.

6.3.2 Enforcement of property rights or externalities

Transactions alter water flow and that may affect other users or the environment. For transactions to fulfill their goal of efficient water management, externalities must be internalized. Thus, beyond the definition of property rights, government must protect rights of other users and the environment, normally through a review procedure; but a review procedure adds transactions costs. Transaction costs may have a negative impact on water transfers and, consequently, on the performance of water markets. Not surprisingly, amendment in the review procedures for changes on property rights have been introduced in both Spain and California with the ultimate goal of enhancing water markets.

The review procedure for transferring water rights is heavily dependent on the attitude towards a change in titleholder and towards how much control the administrative agency should have. If water markets are to play a role in water management, a balance must be met between increasing transfers of water rights and reducing the externalities arising therefrom. Both jurisdictions are far from achieving a perfect balance.

In Spain, before 1999, the only procedure to transfer water rights was to introduce a change in the original permit. Hence, it did not make much difference in terms of review procedure whether one chose to modify a characteristic of the right itself or to temporarily transfer such right to another user. It goes without saying that under such a system transaction costs abounded, making a negotiation impracticable. In California, the situation was not much different until a number of successive amendments were introduced in the 1980s to increase the tradability by streamlining the procedure for post-1914 appropriative rights.

In 1999, Spain introduced the lease of permits. Instead of the previously cumbersome review procedure, after the amendment leases between right holders would undergo a shorter review procedure, which can take up to two months. If the administration does not decide, the transfer is approved by default. Duration of the review procedure can be a proxy for the transaction costs involved, particularly opportunity costs and, actually, a longer duration is a transaction cost itself. Both agencies fare similarly because the review procedure in California takes, at a minimum, 45 days.

California has a complex web of review procedures. The procedure and the agency responsible depend, among other things, on the type of right, the length of the transaction, and the infrastructure used. California water agencies have invested resources in helping users to navigate the complex web of reviews.

In contrast in Spain, there is not much information about how the RBAs have operationalized the review procedure. For example, while in California, the documents that the parties need to file with the agency are detailed in the governing statutory provisions, in Spain there is almost no mention of this in the relevant statutory sources. What is mentioned in the Spanish legislation is the participation of non-water agencies and regional governments. Such participation may lead to a tragedy of the anti-commons situation and open the door to interests beyond the goals pursued by water markets. For example, it is unclear what information the regional government can bring to the table that is not already included in the River Basin Plans or that private parties could not bring themselves. The effects on agricultural production do not have a role to play in the Spanish review because community externalities are not tackled by the regulation. One of the fears expressed by those opposing water markets when those were debated in Spain was the fact that externalities will occur. A proper review could have enhanced the acceptance of water markets and make those part of routine water management.

The standards of review in both jurisdictions are similar. In California, for post-1914 appropriative rights, which constitute the majority of rights in California, it is the result of a number of amendments and can be fairly summarized as hinging on: (a) a *non-injury to other right holders* standard for short-term transfers; (b) a *no substantial injury to other right holders* standard for long-term transactions; and (iii) a *no substantial effect on the environment* standard for all sorts of transactions. Thus, California does differentiate according to the length of the transaction. Short-term transactions are subject to more restrictions *ex-ante* because only previously consumed water can be transferred, but they are subject to a less demanding review. Pre-1914 water rights must also comply with the non-injury rule but, in their case, it is enforced by the court system. Spain also has a non-injury rule. However, while its wording is no different, the participation of agencies with different goals seems to suggest that issues beyond the effects on the amount and quality of water available for the environment or for other users could enter into the picture.

Spanish RBAs could have the same level of control as California if they were to actually implement the review procedures and control mechanisms already in force, but the procedure has not been routinized, and nor has expertise been built up. Perhaps if the number of transactions in Spain goes up, Spanish RBAs will gain both expertise and the impetus necessary to operationalize the procedure. Furthermore, while restrictions in water rights' tradability for short-term transfers in California have translated in an easier ex-ante review, restrictions in Spain have not.

On a different note, compensating community externalities may be a deterrent for water transactions. It raises concerns to ask water buyers or sellers to pay for community externalities while other business reallocate without facing these types of hurdles, even if the reallocation has negative implications for a community in terms of jobs, taxes, and so on. Both in California and Spain, large transfers between areas have produced major conflicts, such as the Owens Valley in California and the defeated Ebro transfer in Spain. In California, perhaps due to having learned from the 1991 drought water bank experience, there are several examples where important reallocations of water have come with allocation of funds to compensate for those effects in the selling regions. In addition, and also in California, effects on the economy of the regions where water originates are taken into account when evaluating whether to grant access to infrastructure for shipping water. Despite the fact that taking into account those externalities entails more obstacles for water transfer, those mechanisms may be a way in which to increase support for markets, so not all the effects are negative. In Spain, only the farmers' associations mentioned the negative community externalities in debates regarding water legislation and in the discussions of using market tools to tackle water crises. Community externalities have never been directly addressed or discussed publicly in relation to a particular market transfer in Spain, though they may have been discussed behind closed doors. Perhaps community externalities are the rationale behind the participation of certain central or regional agencies in the review procedure. As California does with the infrastructure review, if those externalities are to be taken into account, it should be stated in the regulation, and an established procedure might be the best option. California does a better job, but still a more structured procedure to deal with community externalities in all cases, not only in those transactions where third party infrastructure is used, could be better.

In sum, in California, transfers and their review seem to have become routinized, while in Spain they clearly have not. Conversations by the author with private attorneys and government officials in both jurisdictions confirm this. California has a fully-fledged framework for dealing with externalities, and therefore it is difficult for any externality to go unnoticed. Review procedures may be considered complex and cumbersome to navigate, features that may, at first sight, seem negative for market enhancement purposes. However, it should be noted that this procedure gives security to all the other users. It may make the idea of water markets more palatable, given that the oversight of the administrations is thorough, and environmental and social considerations are taken into account. While there are claims in California asking for measures to streamline the review procedures, in Spain, lawyers specializing in water issues do not see these procedures as a threat. This might be either because the procedures do not ensure enough oversight, as those opposed to water markets argue when advocating for more governmental control, or because the tradability of rights is so restricted that only transactions that do not have external effects are allowed in the first place. Be that as it may, written law in Spain offers the opportunity to develop a system as well-established as the one in California.

6.3.3 Infrastructure management

Water infrastructure is key for water market transactions. The uneven distribution of water across the year partially explains the profusion of dams in both jurisdictions, usually provided by the central government. Particularly relevant for water markets are interconnections that allow water to be shipped across the territory, because water is not variable only across the year but also across the territory. The relevance of infrastructure can be shown by looking at the Spanish figures. The central government allowed the use of inter-basin infrastructure from 2006 to 2009 during the drought. During that period, 25 open-market inter-basin transactions occurred, compared to 38 open-market – i.e. outside water banks – intra-basin ones completed in the ten years of the study period.

Both jurisdictions have a complex net of water infrastructure, being more prominent in California where two arteries, the SWP and the CVP, connect the dry south with the humid north. There are some connections in Spain, particularly to the Mediterranean area, and some others have been incessantly debated, such as the Ebro one to Barcelona and Valencia. In this vein, California also has its long-discussed project: the Peripheral Canal at the Delta which would solve the problems at the Delta. Congestion at the Delta, particularly beyond the study period, decreases the security of water rights because some may be reduced to protect the Delta and its species and reduces the tradability of rights between the northern (and wetter) part of the state and the southern (and drier part of the state).

The regime to use existing connections is far from optimal, but yet again the California one scores higher. As to infrastructure management, the ideal regime for water markets would be a framework allowing non-discriminatory third-party access. California's regulation ensures, on paper, third party access to any human-built infrastructure at a reasonable rate for up to 70 per cent of unused capacity. However, parties need to apply for the use of infrastructure owned by a third party, usually a public agency, and the agency managing it can deny access if there could be negative externalities to other users, the environment or local economies in the areas of origin. These standards could be subject to tinkering, i.e. they could be manipulated to suit the agencies' own interests. Particularly when agencies themselves are participants in the market as suppliers, the open-ended standards may be twisted in favor of the agencies' interests. Additionally, how to establish compensation at a reasonable rate has been subject to heated controversy. There is an ongoing dispute between the MWD and the San Diego Water Authority on the use of the MWD infrastructure to ship water from the IID to San Diego, because the city disagrees on what costs should be charged to those using the infrastructure to ship water. Furthermore, there are separate application procedures for the approval of a transaction and the use of third party infrastructure to carry the water transferred. This was the case even during the water bank operating in the early 1990s where the DWR was the agency managing both the bank and the infrastructure. There are overlaps between these reviews, often carried by different entities, so coordination should be improved to reduce transaction costs and not duplicate procedures.

In Spain, the situation is more problematic. Even setting aside the central government authorization for the use of inter-basin infrastructure, there is nothing close to common carrier duty. Instead, if the infrastructure is private, parties need to negotiate with the owner of the infrastructure and there are not even published guidelines for acceptable reasons to deny the shipment of third-party water. Therefore, owners could outright deny the use with a hidden discriminatory aim. In addition, even when the owner is the RBA and the RBA must authorize the transfer, the use of infrastructure is subject to a separate application procedure than the transfer itself.

Both jurisdictions missed the opportunity to reduce transaction costs in the regulation of infrastructure management. California could define more precisely how to calculate unused capacity or which costs can be part of the calculation of a reasonable rate, and Spain could establish a real system of third party access to natural monopoly infrastructure. In addition, both could unify the procedures authorizing the transaction and the use of infrastructure.

6.3.4 Market maker

Among the specific tasks for governments to perform as market makers – i.e. to reduce transaction costs – are to register rights and to record transactions, which can also be seen as part of the role of enforcing property rights. Both jurisdictions show deficiencies in fulfilling these roles. In California, water rights have not been fully registered. Post-1914 water rights are granted by the SWRCB, so there should be public records for them. Although there is a mandate for pre-1914 rights to be registered, this mandate has not been enforced until recently. However, even if recorded, the registration of water rights does not attest the validity of the rights according to §5101 of the Cal. Water Code, which implies that the guarantor function does not play a role. Such a scheme contrasts with land registries, which in many countries provide not only information, but a sort of guaranty since what is recorded in land registries is considered conclusive evidence. Nonetheless, it might be that there is an implicit public sanction in any public registry, because the public agency is sponsoring it and people rely on the information as though the agency guaranteed it.

In California, there is no mandate to record the transactions. There have been private brokers collecting the information, but those in a better position to get information are public agencies, since in almost all transactions they must be involved in one way or another. Hence, it would be cheaper for them to undertake this endeavor and they would benefit from it, since they would be able to plan water use across the territory with better information. There was no public initiative to offer a full record of transactions during the 1991–2000 period, and the databases prepared by researchers, although helpful, are flawed and somewhat inconsistent, given the scattered nature of the information. However, there was an attempt in the 2000s to create a website – 'On-Tap' – to create a database of transactions. California agencies, however, have been mandated since 1986 to facilitate transactions by providing guidance on the market procedures and identifying potential parties willing to enter into transactions. In 1999, the SWRCB fulfilled the first part of the mandate while it still has to do so with the second.

In Spain, mandates exist to register all rights (both private property and, more importantly, permits), and to record transactions. However, the state of the RBA's water registries, where rights and transactions should be recorded, is improper to say the least. This, of course, constitutes a problem for water market development and water policy in general. Even transactions within a water exchange center are not always fully transparent, despite the fact that they are subject to public procurement regulation: there is no mandate to publish all records of those transactions. The shortcomings of the registries are a lost opportunity because in Spain, water registries are supposed to guarantee that what is recorded on them is true. California data gathered by private parties, brokers or researchers, might be scattered, but in Spain it is almost non-existent.

Another crucial feature in reducing transaction costs to enhance water markets relates to the fungibility of rights. Spain established that only the average consumption of the last five years can be transferred. By restricting the amount transferable, Spain has lessened the possibilities that there will be negative externalities and this should have translated into a less demanding review procedure. This is what has happened in California, where short-term transfers of previously consumed water are subject to a shorter review.

Both jurisdictions could have provided guidance on how to calculate past consumption because agencies have information and knowledge about it, and it would have saved time and expenses to private parties and ease the review.

Also notably for California, a good share of transactions has occurred within the projects, particularly the CVP, because rights within the projects are highly fungible. Water rights are usually defined according to many different characteristics, for example, type of use, volume, and place of use. These characteristics are important to cope with the natural variability of the resource and the interdependency between users. CVP and SWP rights are fungible because the USBR and the DWR have broadly defined uses and places of use that cover, in most cases, all the territory they serve. Hence, their contractors could transfer their rights within the project without external review by the SWRCB. The DWR, however, restricts the potential exchanges of SWP rights between its contractors with external parties and among themselves, either directly or by preventing them from profiting from the sale. This is not the case for transfers within the CVP and they actually abound, amounting to more than 100 per year. Since such transfers occur within the Project, the only approval is, generally, that of the USBR, which has been favorable to those exchanges. In Spain, there is no clear counterpart to the USBR. Perhaps the RBAs could have done more to improve markets in their territories.

Water banks – called water exchange centers in Spain – are the structures which best embody the market maker function. They reduce transaction costs by performing the matching function as with any clearing house, but they also buy and sell rights in both jurisdictions, offering security to market participants and making rights more fungible by repacking them. Spanish water banks have not actually played these roles at the same level as the Californian ones have, despite the fact that the model of Californian water banks had been praised in Spain over and over again. In Spain, trading between private parties through a water bank never actually happened during the study period. The exchange centers have never resold directly to private parties; they have mostly allocated the water to the environment or reallocated it to users according to some social criteria. One key potential disadvantage of the Spanish system is that transactions are subject to regulations similar to those of public procurement, which reduces the flexibility of the contracting process. At least for low-stakes transactions – e.g. leasing small quantities of water – such constraints are not worth imposing. Water banks could have increased the trust on water markets. Spain lost that opportunity. Conversely, in California's water banks of the 1990s, the roles of matching, guaranteeing and making rights fungible were pretty well performed. The banks bought water rights, repackaged them and sold them. In addition, they reduced private costs by offering model contracts. The banks were not flawless, but each iteration learned from the mistakes of the previous one. Water banks may have been key to the institutionalization of water markets as a piece of water management.

Governments in California have outdone their Spanish counterparts as market makers. Spanish regulations aim high and expect government to play all the roles identified under the label 'market maker' – record rights, record transactions, make rights fungible by defining the amount tradable, match private users, and guarantee transactions in the framework of a water bank – but it has done a poor job in implementing most of them.

6.4 Concluding remarks

Water markets are tools advocated and implemented to deal with structural water scarcity and periodic droughts. Structural water scarcity is the result of a combination of dwindling supplies, the costliness of increasing water supply and competition between growing demands. The agricultural sector has always been – and still is – the main water consumer, but urban areas need increasing amounts of water to quench the thirst caused by population growth and changes in habits. In parallel, river ecosystems have also suffered from lower water availability. The rise of environmental concerns and, subsequently, protections has translated into a potential new type of water demand: environmental instream flow.

The administrative systems intended to cope with such a mismatch have proven insufficient or unresponsive. Water market mechanisms have been adopted to fill that gap by voluntarily reallocating the water from low value users to higher value users which do not receive enough water. Urban areas are expected to be those higher value users willing to pay a higher price for the water. Market mechanisms should also replace, to the extent possible, emergency measures designed to cope with drought crises, on the assumption that short-term transactions in water rights may solve the current mismatch between the rules governing allocation of water and the actual differences in value among different type of users, and thus may provide a shield for users against the risk of not receiving water.

Water markets have been proposed since the 1970s, and the debate has often been framed as though those markets were an alternative to the existing system, which is usually portrayed as a system managed by administrative agencies captured by interest groups. These proponents of water markets portray them as systems where government is out of the picture, despite assuming that property rights will be defined and enforced by government. At the other end of the spectrum, some scholars oppose markets because they believe water should not be commodified. According to these scholars, the public good nature of water requires that it be administered by public agencies. Meanwhile, a narrower policy-oriented literature stands in the middle, but focuses on practical aspects of how market tools are, or should be, implemented.

Both extremes of the debate are misguided. One of the aims of this book is to bridge the debate between the two sides by: (a) theoretically identifying the roles that government has to play in water markets for them to succeed according to economic theories of regulation; and (b) empirically testing whether different market activity can be linked to different degrees of fulfillment of previously identified government roles.

The roles – identified in Chapter 2 – are the definition of property rights, establishing a procedure to account for externalities, managing infrastructure ensuring third party access, and enabling the market by reducing transaction costs. The first role, definition of property rights, is based on the public good nature of the definition of property rights, and includes expanding tradability where possible, providing security that the right is not going to be subject to the discretionary powers of the administration as a result of entering into transactions, and, relatedly, establishing clear rules on how water is to be apportioned under low availability conditions.

As a corollary to the definition of property rights, government should establish a procedure to protect other users and the environment from externalities and its effects, without unnecessarily burdening those who want to transfer rights.

Regarding infrastructure, beyond the regulation of whether government or private parties should provide it, government is supposed to establish third party access to infrastructure, thus ensuring, on the one hand, that the infrastructure owner receives an appropriate rate of return on its investment and, on the other hand, that the possibility for the owner to exploit its natural monopoly power is reduced.

Lastly, to fulfill the role of market maker reducing transaction costs, government should: (a) register the rights to ensure third parties that they can rely on them and record transactions to facilitate information gathering to private parties; (b) make rights as fungible as possible; (c) act as a broker – particularly where rights are small; and, where appropriate, (d) guarantee the transactions.

Even in the framework of water markets, some other roles might be undertaken by those public agencies in order to fulfill goals other than efficiency, the underlying paradigm in markets. These other roles, such as compensating community externalities, justified on the basis of equity concerns, may help markets to entrench themselves, by mitigating the concerns of those opposed to the commodification of water.

In the empirical part of the book, the comparison of water market development in 1991–2000 in California and 2000–09 in Spain suggests that those governmental roles matter. Water markets were more active in California than in Spain, even though Spain suffered from lower water availability. Chapters 4 and 5 show how the different performance of the roles identified in the theoretical part correlate with the volume of market activity. California's legislature and agencies could do a better job than they currently do, but they are performing better than their Spanish counterparts when it comes to water markets.

California and Spain seem to illustrate different approaches to water markets, which can be perceived in the written law and in the attitudes towards markets. In California, water markets are not considered an exception, even if they represent a small share of the total amount of water used in the state. Water markets are regarded as a tool to deal with structural scarcity and drought on a regular basis. They are even included in the River Basin Plans. The opposite is true in Spain. Water markets are regarded as exceptional and remain highly exceptional, even though scarcity was harsher during the study period than it was in California. For example, in the mid-2000s, the Spanish government authorized the establishment of water banks and, in 2006, amidst a harsh drought, allowed RBAs to buy water to preserve instream flows. Water banks were never used as a match making institution, only as a marketplace where RBAs could buy water for the environment. The reasoning for that may well be that RBAs wanted to avoid curtailing existing consumptive rights for political reasons. Private transactions did not contribute much to mitigate the effects of the drought. Urban suppliers did not have an incentive to resort to markets. Emergency measures ensured urban supply and, where needed, government bought them water to avoid the political cost of household curtailments.

In any event, both California and Spain have room to improve their water market frameworks. The late 1980s and early 1990s crisis in California and the mid-1990s drought in Spain prompted the enactment of market regulations; perhaps future droughts will bring improvements to the existing framework.

Even though this book does not attempt to fully explain *why* the different roles have or have not been undertaken in both jurisdictions, but *whether* they have, some hypotheses stem from the case studies: the lack of market culture and explanations grounded in political economy. Several interest groups do not seem to fully embrace markets. The agricultural sector seems to be willing to foot the bill during drought in exchange for subsidized water; urban areas are electorally powerful; administrative officials fear losing their decision-making power to the markets; and environmentalists may prefer to protect the environment using taxpayer money than their own. Further research may illuminate how these attitudes were overcome in certain jurisdictions where agencies fulfilled the required roles.

In conclusion, this book portrays water markets as tools available to public agencies for water management, but not as the only tools in the toolkit. Markets operate to transfer rights to use water initially allocated by government when allocation becomes inefficient. Hence, water market reallocation does not need to amount to a huge percentage of the water used, but it is a very important amount for the purpose of mitigating current misallocation and the effects of low water availability during droughts. This book shows that if a specific jurisdiction wants to implement market tools, government needs to play certain roles. This book may also pave the way for designing a much-needed framework for analyzing the management of other natural resources and environmental markets more generally.

Index